MINISTRY AND MEANING

Preface

———— ✦ ————

Twenty years ago I ventured into the relatively uncharted area of Catholic health care when I began research on the history of the Alexian Brothers, a nursing order that founded institutions for the mentally ill in Germany and the Low Countries, nursing homes in England and Ireland, and general hospitals in the United States. To narrate their history from their origins as medieval lay mendicants dedicated to burying the victims of plagues to their contemporary nursing ministry was a stimulating experience, one that has allowed me to explore this book's landscape of health-care ministry with a modicum of confidence. Hence, I am grateful to Brother Felix Bettendorf, a former superior general, Brother Roy Godwin, archivist, and several Alexians in each of the provinces for their encouragement, direction, and hospitality.

As chair of the history department at St. Louis University, John Bannon, S.J., introduced me to the Alexian Brothers. Over the years John Tracy Ellis, Colman Barry, O.S.B., James Hennesey, S.J., and Robert Trisco have referred me to orders and associations in search of a historian, including the sponsor of this work, the Catholic Health Association (CHA). I will be forever grateful to each of these historians for their regard for my work as well as their inspiration. Many thanks to Michael McCauley, Patricia Carlyle, Sherry Schilling, and Robert Stephens of the CHA, and John E. Curley, Jr., president of the association; because of their professionalism, assistance, and openness to the complexities of historical writing my relationship with the association is grounded in civility and mutual respect.

In the research and composition of this history my personal and professional contexts have been significantly affected by the assistance of many historians, archivists, and health-care professionals. Many thanks to my friend Joseph P. Chinnici, O.F.M., for breaking open the text and helping me to frame particular salient themes imbedded in the narrative. I am grateful to other historian friends, Joseph M. White, Thomas Spalding, C.F.X., James Hennesey, S.J., Karen Kennelly, C.S.J., who made several corrections and suggestions related to accuracy and rhetorical coherence of the text. Justus George Lawler, friend, mentor, and an encyclopedic resource person has been a faithful critic of my work over these twenty years. His easeful articulation of the myriad matrices of religion, history, and culture has had an imprint upon my intellect, spirit, and historical work. Thanks, George!

Martin E. Marty, the premier scholar of American religious history and editor of *Church History* and *Second Opinion: A Journal of Health, Faith and Ethics,* has had a significant influence on my perspective. Of course I am most appreciative for his foreword to this work.

Some years before completing the manuscript I submitted a portion of the work in progress to CLEO, an ad hoc association of historians in the Baltimore-Washington area interested in American Catholicism. I am grateful to the following devotees of the muse of history: R. Emmett Curran, S.J., John Farina, John Ciani, S.J., Dolores Liptak, R.S.M., Elizabeth McKeown, Timothy Meagher, Paul Robichaud, C.S.P., and Jon Wakelyn. For nearly ten years CLEO has been a source of encouragement, friendship, and stimulating discussion. I have also benefited from the manuscript of George C. Stewart's recently published work, *Marvels of Charity: History of American Sisters and Nuns.* Congratulations, George!

Many thanks to several colleagues at the Catholic University of America who have graciously provided assistance. Ms. Nellie Brown, librarian of the Nursing School, developed an excellent historical collection that was quite helpful in the contextualization of the work. The library holdings included several masters and doctoral dissertations directed by Sister Olivia Gowan, O.S.B., the school's first dean. One of her successors as dean, Sister Rosemary Donnelly, S.C., now the administrative vice president of the university, has been a valuable source of historical information. Dr. Anthony Zito, Sister Ann Crowley, John W. Shepherd, Lynn Conway, and Brother David Richardson, O.S.C., of the university archives were always ready to assist me. The rare book librarian, Ms. Carolyn Lee, guided me through the Catholic Americana section with interest and concern. Colleagues in the church history department, Robert Eno, Jacques Gres-Geyer, Nelson Minnich, and Robert Trisco manifested interest in my progress and seemed to instinctively understand the vagaries entailed in the life of a long-distance researcher. Thanks also to the department's administrative assistant, Ms. Gloria Wilkerson, for her occasional work at the computer.

Research visits to many archives of religious communities and dioceses yielded an abundance of material. I am grateful to Margaret Susan Thompson for her recommendations of valuable archives among communities of women religious with a tradition of hospital ministry. It is with a deep sense of admiration and gratitude that I acknowledge the many archivists for their assistance, ranging from unearthing that special letter, photo, or book to photocopying and mailing material: Sisters Elaine Wheeler, D.C., Aloysia Duggan, D.C., Daniel Hannefin, D.C., of the Northeastern, Eastern, and Central provinces of the Daughters of Charity respectively; Sister Mary Rose McPhee, D.C., administrator of the Daughters' Hotel Dieu Hospital in New Orleans; Sister Bernadette Kirn of the Wheaton Franciscans; Sister Mary Lou Stueber of the Franciscan Sisters of Mary in St. Louis; Sisters Charline Sullivan, C.S.J., and Mary Kraft, C.S.J. of the St. Louis and St. Paul provinces of the Sisters of St. Joseph of Carondolet; Sister Rita Bergamini, S.P., and Ms. Loretta Zwolak-Greene of the Sisters of Providence archives in Seattle; Sister Mary Campion, C.S.C., of the Sisters of Holy Cross archives at St. Mary's of Notre Dame; Sisters Petronella Gaul, R.S.M., and Marilyn Gouailhardou, R.S.M., of the Burlingame Sisters of Mercy; the late Sister Elizabeth Jean DeMuth, R.S.M., of the Sisters of Mercy in St. Louis; Anella Martin, R.S.M., of Mercy Medical Center in Baltimore; Linda Leslie Mobley of the archives of St. Joseph's Hospital in Atlanta; Sister Felicitas Powers, R.S.M., was a valuable consultant for the health care of the Sisters of Mercy; Sister Helen Jacobsen, S.F., of the archives at St. Joseph's Hospital of Baltimore. I am indebted to Peter Hogan, S.S.J., of the Josephite archives in Baltimore for his support and direction in research of African-American history. I also wish to thank Michael Grace, S.J., of the archives of Loyola University in Chicago; Paul Robichaud, C.S.P., and Patricia Pyne of the Paulist Fathers archives in Washington, D.C.; and Nancy Merz and William B. Faherty, S.J., of the archives of the Missouri Province of the Society of Jesus; Rev. Paul Thomas of the Archdiocese of Baltimore; Dr. Jeffrey Burns of the Archdiocese of San Francisco; and Ron Patkus of the Archdiocese of Boston. Thanks also to Helen Ciernick and Geoffrey Gay, graduate students at the Catholic University, for their research assistance.

Seven years after the publication of the history of the Sulpicians in the United States I still have an office in the Sulpician archives. Thanks to

Gerald Brown, S.S., the provincial, to William J. Lee, S.S., the former secretary of the province, and particularly to my close associate and loyal proofreader, the archivist, John Bowen, S.S. Hence, I work in an atmosphere characterized by hospitality and friendship.

Today, as a non-computer-literate writer I could be designated as a "cultural lag." However, to have discovered a seasoned computer expert who can read my handwriting and is such a delightful person meant that this manuscript reached print with expertise, refinement, and grace. I am very grateful to Denise McCord for her many gifts.

While I was researching and writing this work, our three children, Jane, Christopher, and Kathryn Ann, graduated from college. The pursuit of their mature lives did not preclude manifesting their traditional interest and concern for the progress of this work. More significantly they are engaged in developing their life interests with enthusiasm, sophistication, and a sense of irony. With love and pride I acknowledge these old friends.

My first book was dedicated to Helen, with a quote from an e.e. cummings poem: "and life is not a paragraph and death, i think is no parenthesis." Though I am still experiencing her "inner sight," these lyrics from a favorite song aptly convey my feelings for Helen: "Love you are love far better than a metaphor could ever, ever be"!

Foreword

MARTIN E. MARTY

You can drive past churches, clubhouses, seminaries, and hospitals a thousand times without wondering how they came to be, who put them there and why, how they survived, and what any of that has to do with the present and the future.

You can, that is, until someone like historian Christopher J. Kauffman takes you touring in one or another of his books. In previous volumes he has opened a window on the past of the Knights of Columbus and then the door on Catholic seminary education in America. Now he pushes the sliding curtains back so that the whole vista of Catholic hospitals and other health-care institutions can be surveyed as never before.

"Institutional history," some critics snort when they dismiss people who probe the records and then write about the buildings and places where the works of charity, education, or mercy occur. In favor these days is "social history," which does a marvelous task of bringing to light the ordinary lives of ordinary people—for example, the extraordinary nuns who pioneered in Catholic hospitals. Not as popular, but certainly honored by elites, is "intellectual history," which isolates ideas from the bodies and the groups of people who hold them. Also in vogue is "cultural history," which studies the symbols and artifacts of people. But "institutional history"?

Admittedly, it can be dull. Who outside a particular institution—or inside it, for that matter—cares how the profit-and-loss statement of a particular hospital reads for the year 1888, or any year after the statute of limitations runs out, for that matter? Who needs the names of the board of trustees in 1931 if one can get by not knowing any from 1995? Those are good questions, easily answered with "nobody," and "nobody," in the case of *bad* institutional history.

Christopher Kauffman, however, is known for writing good institutional history, and this book will add to his reputation. It is good because it addresses the curiosities evoked by other sorts of histories. This work is nearly as much a social as it is a religious history. In such, the historian is mindful of the institutions that provided a *social* setting under a religious impulse. Thus, without seminaries there are no locales where the lives of seminarians can be studied; without hospitals, where does the work of hospital-people go on? And people who built and staffed hospitals had to be alert to the ideas about medicine, faith, and philanthropy current in their times: so *intellectual* history has a home in institutions, too. The cross on the hospital room wall, the existence of a chapel, the very presence of the building awakens the curiosity of the *cultural* historian in a time called secular and often seen as postreligious.

Kauffman, by setting and seeing the institutions he studies in their changing contexts, provides a handle on the age he studies, and describes the dynamisms by which institutional leadership interacts with other forces, in order to survive and serve.

Such interaction is urgent in the late twentieth century. Some of this results from declines: decline in the number of people in the religious orders that built the hospitals. Decline in the dependence of hospitals on the contributions of the faithful and the loyalty of Catholics to Catholic institutions. "Back then" many of these places had to be built for ethnic and religious groups that were ill-served or not served by existing health-care agencies. New governmental and economic patterns now have changed all that, and most people today go to the hospital of their choice or, better, the hospital of their managed care agency's choice, be it Catholic or not.

One can write such a history as this also in terms of increase: increase in medical sophistication; the pluralism of peoples who make up staffs and patient rosters; the involvement of government and outside agencies; the percentage of the population served; the intellectual and emotional and spiritual energy that it takes leadership to bring together the worlds of faith and research and healing in a technological age. So Kauffman writes no "decline and fall of" sort of history, but history full of ambiguity, disappointment, achievement, and hope.

For some years I have put some historian energies into studying the history of health care, inspired by the investment of a church-related institution to the pluralist culture. The Lutheran General Health System asked me to help found the Park Ridge Center for the Study of Health, Faith, and Ethics. Our scholars have tried to make sense and often have made sense of moral, ethical, and medical issues in a changing world. Lutheran? Our books deal with Hinduism, Mormonism, and Orthodoxy, etc. Lutheran? The staff of the Lutheran health institutions may be Jewish and Muslim, secular—and even Christian and most even Lutheran, but the particular faith tradition there is a minority lineage. And our Center staff is headed by a Catholic, with Lutherans being a small minority.

Aware of all this, and talking in executive offices of high-tech Lutheran General hospital, webbed as it is into complex governmental and insurance networks, I heard the CEO say that daily he passed a grainy old enlarged photograph of some Norwegian-American Lutheran Deaconesses posed stiffly in front of the abandoned grandparent Deaconess Hospital. He said, "I ask myself every day, would those women, our founders, understand and affirm what we are doing today?" He had to know that their understanding would be partial, because no one now alive begins to understand the complexities of a modern institution. Their affirmation would have to be qualified, because the kind of "Yes-person" who would approve everything that went on amid the ambiguities and contradictions of a modern hospital would be useless.

Overall, however, we assessed, yes, they would approve. The garb, the architecture, and the character of the photograph reminded us that we could not go back to the old ancestral hospital and the ways of its staff— and would not want to. But one can measure later mission in the light of the *intention* of the founders, "to whom you cannot go back," as Pope John XXIII used to tell heads of reform-bound religious orders.

As Kauffman moves from the chapters illustrated with shots of archaic garb, obsolete architecture, and primitive photography to the modern scene, some readers may and must feel that the story is getting out of hand. Thus, chapter eight on "national structures and hospital standardization" tells of some imposed rubber stamping that threatened the marvelously idiosyncratic Catholic agencies. How find roots there? And at the end, there is "Health-Care Reforms," some of them, as Kauffman says, envisioned on such a grand scale that they might threaten the specialnesses and descriptnesses of every health-care agency that would be a bit different. It is possible, after all, to forget or obliterate a tradition so radically that one cannot retrieve anything on which to build today or from which base to project tomorrow.

If such amnesia is to afflict the modern Catholic health-care institution, and if such obliteration is to occur, it is at least valuable to have a sense of what had been there, what was being lost. If one *wants* to lose, which means reject it all, there are good reasons to ask with what to replace it. Kauffman does not try to answer questions about the future, but he enlarges the repertory of options for those who will have to do so. Meanwhile, he has provided an informative and engaging story for people who stand outside this particular history, but as bystanders find themselves somehow involved. The issues of health and faith are too urgent in our time of change for many to remain disengaged or uninvolved. Nothing attracts more than a good story, so let this one do its attracting as I now stand aside and give a tug to those Kauffmanian curtains that open on the window to a world.

Exploring the Boundaries

HEALTH CARE in the United States originated in the early phase of development of the private or voluntary hospital. The latter gradually eclipsed the almshouse and city poorhouse, caretaker facilities for the chronically and mentally ill, aged prostitutes, alcoholics, vagrants, and the homeless. Though there were priests, sisters, brothers, and lay people ministering to the sick in their private homes throughout the nineteenth and into the twentieth century, this study focuses primarily on the public places where religious communities responded to the physically and mentally ill, in peace and war, in times of pestilence and economic crisis, in urban centers, rural towns, and on the expanding frontiers. They nursed in ethnic Catholic enclaves and in Protestant areas of the South and West, and in hospitals maintained by physicians, cities, counties, states, mining companies, railroads, and by their own orders. While the parish, school, and diocese have a public presence only the hospital is inherently a public place; here Catholics ministered to the physical, mental, emotional, and spiritual needs of people representing the entire spectrum of religious and secular traditions. Because the nurses in these public places were committed to the vowed life as sisters (we will discuss only one order of brothers), their prayer life and nursing ministry developed in an atmosphere of interdependence. Their rule of life may have separated private and public roles, but in fact they brought their ministry to prayer in chapel and their prayer life was frequently embodied in ministry. Theirs was an activist missionary spirituality that tended to be based on a positive appreciation of human experience rather than on its denial.

In a republican climate, infused with the principles of religious liberty, of separation of church and state, and of religious pluralism, there was and still is a tendency to draw clear boundaries along denominational lines, particularly among minority religious and ethnic groups intent upon preserving their creed, code, and cult in a religiously competitive setting. Though Catholic hospitals may have been founded within such boundaries, their inherently public character fostered an accommodation to religious pluralism.

Such spatial delineations have elicited metaphors among scholars of religion and culture. Karl Jaspers uses the boundary or limit situation to distinguish that existential area where one experiences the "ultimate limit or horizon to his or her existence."[1] Victor Turner has elaborated on the liminal, as a place where the sacred is disclosed at pilgrimages, shrines, and during initiation rites.[2] Sociologist Peter Berger popularized the metaphor of sacred canopy while another sociologist, Robert Wuthnow, focuses on symbolic boundaries.[3] The religious historian Martin E. Marty, perhaps *the* scholar of public theology and religious behavior, entitled chapters in one of his works in terms of cocoons and canopies as he explored the interaction of public and private mentalities.[4] However, Marty warns against thinking of religion in spatial terms of public and private spheres, particularly within the contemporary "modes of experience," such as in the patients' world of the hospital where "Religion is interwoven with concepts of care, cure, well-being and the like."[5]

Each of these spatial metaphors helps to elucidate portions of this work. Central to the theme of this book is that Catholic nurses and chaplains brought prayer, ritual, and symbol to those suffering on the limits of existence; in this sense both the sick and their care givers dwelt in an environment conducive to perceiving the ultimate horizon as a religious experience. In the paternalistic traditional nineteenth-century hospital, with its emphasis on caring rather than curing, the ministry of sisters was manifested in a personalist context, while in the modern technological hospital the concern is to struggle against the dehumanization of patients by fostering a countercultural appreciation of religious boundaries. In either context the most commonly accepted understanding of the religious meaning of health care derives from gospel imperatives to minister to the suffering, including those experiencing illness. Catholic tradition is abundant with references to sisters' and brothers' dedication to see Christ in the sick poor and to assume the role of the *alter Christus* in responding to the sick and dying. As Vincent de Paul said to the early Daughters of Charity: "When you leave your prayers for the bedside of a patient, you are leaving God for God. Looking after the sick is praying."[6]

This religious meaning permeated Catholic health care and influenced the dynamic of denominational interaction within the pluralist setting of the Catholic hospital.

Professors Charles E. Rosenberg and Rosemary Stevens elaborate on the structural ambiguity and contradictions of the private hospitals that were administered by boards of trustees and physicians dedicated to the *public* welfare but were dependent upon *private* paying patients, thus developing policies of *exclusion* on grounds of class (the undeserving poor), race (African Americans), and ailment (the chronically and mentally ill).[7] These private hospitals also tended to reflect social trends such as nativism and anti-Catholicism, not always manifested toward the innocent patients but usually toward their "papist" superstitious pastors presumably engaged in antirepublican conspiracies. The private/public ambiguity also characterized Catholic hospitals along similar lines, but with some exceptions. Catholic hospitals tended to have little or no endowment and were therefore more dependent on private patients. Although they accepted the indigent, many of the latter had their care paid for by the guardians of the poor-law fund, and only a few beds were designated for black patients in inferior wards. However, the charitable imperative derived from the religious calling of sisters tended to be a countervailing factor to purely economic aspects of policy. In contrast to the religious competition in the urban areas of the East, Catholic benevolence tended to be less defensive and more publicly oriented in the Midwest and far West, where it was not unusual that the Catholic facility was the only hospital.

According to David O'Brien's models of public Catholicism, Catholic hospitals tended to be "republican," a style that sought accommodation through enlightenment, mutual respect, and civility. However, because the sisters were religiously motivated care givers, the public Catholicism of the hospital was also evangelical, fostering conversion experiences in both Catholics and Protestants.[8] Since many areas of the country experienced a shortage of priests, sisters became unofficial chaplains, primary religious witnesses, who "heard" confessions, prayed with the critically ill and dying, and presented "homilies" to their patients.

Catholic historians have been particularly concerned with illuminating episcopal and intellectual leadership in the church's encounter with a Protestant dominated society. Implicit in this work is the Catholic hospital's quotidian experience with religious pluralism. Though there was no critical reflection on the legitimacy of conflicting religious beliefs, public policy articulated by some Catholic hospitals did recognize the primacy of conscience so basic to the vitality of religious diversity.[9] Religious pluralism and the evangelical drive for conversion appear to be complementary; in a condition of religious liberty the sources of faith seem to require continuous illuminations, awakenings, and conversions, not only for the parish congregations or for the community of hospital patients but also for the ministers and the religious care givers. Perhaps implicit in prayerful invocations for deathbed conversions was a prayer for one's own conversion experience. While pluralism tended to inhibit strategies of overt convert making, respect for conscience proffered positive anthropology, congenial to an incarnational spirituality and the accessibility of grace.[10] Catholic physicians, nurses, and patients were nurtured on narratives of the intervention of saints, on the role of novenas, on pilgrimages to sacred places and within settings replete with material culture, that is, statues, medals, holy water, and pictures. Hence, the atmosphere of a Catholic hospital was imbued with an affective devotionalism that seems to represent symbolic boundaries of group identity. This devotionalism conveys a community of religious meaning for those Catholics relegated to the extreme limits of society. From the vantage point of the immigrant community, besieged by anti-Catholicism and nativism, this popular religiosity provided a secure refuge and simultaneously a means of accommodation to American pluralism. The religious culture of hospitals established by German, Italian, and Polish communities was often a lavish display of colorful statues and holy pictures of patron saints from the "old country." In such ethnic enclaves an immigrant style of public Catholicism, with its clearly defined symbolic boundaries, characterized nineteenth- and twentieth-century hospitals. Though these hospitals were strongly rooted in European traditions, their public character, which became increasingly modernized, represented a strong tendency toward Americanization. In many areas where Catholics formed a small minority, such as portions of the South and West, there was a tendency to privatize the faith; in these areas symbolic boundaries of devotionalism and its material culture were present but more in the private places of the sisters' residences than in the public spaces of their hospitals.

Within patriarchal society, Elizabeth Johnson notes, "women are projected as the 'other,' the repository for qualities that men cannot integrate into their self-image, and therefore the antithesis over against which they define themselves." Perhaps many of these women-religious chaplains internalized the language of their otherness. However, their continuous encounters as religious witnesses to persons in the crisis limits of severe

illness and death may have awakened in them a horizon beyond patriarchal definitions which validated their experiences as women. Certainly
as hospital administrators these women religious were role models for
women in authority, while on the frontier sister-nurses were primarily
proactive not reactive, in their responses to the sick in a society yet to be
fully institutionalized.[11]

Margaret Susan Thompson, a historian of women religious in the
United States, illustrates the significance of sisters in the horizon beyond
patriarchy, a perception that was often illuminated in conflict. Thompson notes that in Catholic schools, orphanages, and hospitals, "nuns
enjoyed tremendous authority and autonomy from men—more, perhaps, prior to the present day, than virtually all of their female counterparts."[12] Though this work is not intended as a contribution to gender
studies, I have relied on Johnson, Thompson, and others to expand my
understanding of women's experiences, past and present.

Part one of this work opens with a chapter on European traditions and
illustrates its principal concerns: the religious understanding of illness
and the self-understanding and religious motivation of the nursing ministry within various social and political contexts. The next five chapters
show how this ministry was profoundly affected by its public roles in
American life, with particular focus on the nursing experiences of
women religious founded in the United States, for example, Elizabeth
Seton's Sisters of Charity. Each chapter has its own organizing principle,
but they are all unified by the twofold purpose of the entire book: to
sketch in broad strokes the historical development of Catholic hospitals
and to explore and analyze the religious dimensions of the Catholic nursing experience. In this premodern period, permeated by social paternalism and traditionally eclectic medical care, Catholic sisters brought
order, cleanliness, and compassion to the hospital, characteristics frequently associated with domestic virtues.

In chapters two, four, and six the emphasis is on the evolution of
Catholic nursing, from its origins in Maryland through its first institutional phase in a "defensive" Catholic benevolence and culminating in an
expansive adaptation on the westward frontiers. Chapters three and five
focus the nursing experience on epidemics and war, while all of part one
intertwines the religious and public spheres of general hospitals, mental
hospitals, and almshouses. During this period nursing was frequently
expressed as a religious calling to heroic service, articulated according
to the prevailing ethos of domesticity.

Among the general public there was a structural ambivalence toward sisters; impassioned anti-Catholic portrayals of women held prisoner in convents vied with emotional tributes to their selflessness in times of crisis. The sisters' heroic ministry in epidemics and war tended to dispel biases, but stereotypes persisted on the fringes, and periodically gained popular currency. Among Catholics familiar with the religious life, particularly bishops and superiors of communities, heroic ministry was perceived in terms of "purity of intention," the foundational virtue that identified selfless service for the glory and love of God. Urged to respond with Christlike compassion and to see Jesus in their patients, sisters and brothers absorbed the ideals of the religious life but—as mentioned earlier—their public ministry was also a significant source of their spirituality. Hence, the ecclesiology implicit in American Catholic health-care experience reflects the missionary-church dynamic: care givers and patients dwelling in the limit-situation of illness and forming a provisional community of faith.

Rosemary Stevens's understanding of the pluralistic, nonsystematic character of twentieth-century health care may be applied to the Catholic experience of diversity: ethnicity, regional variations, periodization, differing types of hospitals and pluralistic charisms.[13] There is a tendency among Catholics as well as those who view the church from the outside to perceive authority in terms of a pyramidal structure with decisions affecting public policy made by Rome, episcopal councils, or particular bishops. Though there were medical-moral decisions that reflect this authority structure, and though there have been bishops who maintained tight control over their institutions, most hospitals were *de facto* self-governing institutions. Hence, flexible governmental patterns, forged by the interaction of particular communities and hospitals, characterized the American Catholic experience. As will be noted in the introduction to part two, the modernization of medicine parallels the modernization of ecclesiastical structures and the proliferation of Catholic professional societies, such as the Catholic Hospital Association and the organizations of Catholic physicians and nurses.

Part two treats the interaction of Catholic tradition and modern health care. It opens with a chapter on the convergence of the religious and hospital subcultures, particularly focusing on the pull of tradition amid the initial changes in the life of the modern hospital. Chapter eight, "National Structures and Hospital Standardization," represents a synthesis of medical progress and Catholic faith. "Illness and Popular Devotion," chapter nine, traces the history of devotionalism and of material culture relating to miraculous cures, and concludes with an explanation of devotion to Jesus the Divine Physician. Chapter ten discusses the separatist reaction to modern culture, with particular emphasis on the ideal Catholic hospital, physician, and nurse.

Part three begins with a chapter on the demands of realism: the need for social justice in the health apostolate; the meager Catholic concern with the needs of African Americans; the drive for professionalism in the Sister Formation Conference; the meanings of Vatican II; and Medicare and Medicaid. Chapter twelve summarizes the significance of such major trends as the post-Vatican II world and the continuous renewal of women and men religious, the rise of lay leadership, the religious congregations' sponsorship of health care; the evolution from chaplaincy to pastoral care; the problems of mission effectiveness; the dilemmas of medical ethics. The epilogue deals with health-care reform and contemporary issues of mission and identity.

The artist/scientist roles of the historian, popularized by the work of H. Stuart Hughes, have influenced the methodology of this work.[14] With materials gathered from the archives of religious communities and dioceses, and secondary literature on several topics, and governed by the canons of historical criticism, I have composed sketches of hospital ministry that provide sufficient detail to give shape to general contours. Each of the scenes is framed by a particular topic, trend, or pattern of the Catholic presence in health care. Most were sketched with an economy of detail, but those of the frontier and of the convergence of religious and medical cultures required considerable attention to numerous areas to illustrate the ethnic and regional diversity, to portray the interaction of tradition and modernity, and to establish the historical record.

My assumption is that there are several ways to portray the past, none of which can re-present the story with complete accuracy or objectivity. Though one should struggle against bias, the subjective experiences of the historian will inevitably impinge on the way she or he frames the past. Since I have had no experience as a religious care giver I have developed a hermeneutical bridge spanning the gap between present experience and past reality based on analogy. Boundaries, limit-situations, the liminal disclosures of the sacred, which help elucidate this history of Catholic health care, are understood within the experience of "mystery" or the field of the "thou"— experience that I hope allows me to grasp the religious meanings of the Catholic health phenomenon. The drive for historical accuracy is motivated by the spirit of historical skepticism. The fact that this work is the first comprehensive religious history of Catholic health care engendered a cautious approach, one that has inhibited excessive license in rendering the past. Without an alternative model and with a superabundance of material, it seemed appropriate to draw a broad mural depicting historical scenes of the Catholic health-care ministry. Defining the perspective are representations of ecclesial, ethnic, social, gender, and medical trends and patterns; hence, the overall picture is as much unified by contexts as by themes. The public and diverse character of American hospital life generated a religious openness among Catholic care givers that allowed them to adapt to the pluralism and voluntarism of society, and in the process they mediated Catholicism with distinction and creativity.

or theologian may refer to as superstition or magic. According to Henry Sigerist, the Christian faith transformed society's care of the sick, and represented a "revolutionary and decisive change." Because Christianity was proclaimed as "the religion of healing, as the joyful Gospel of the Redeemer and of Redemption" it urged the faithful to respond to the poor, the sick, and the alienated to whom was promised healing in spirit and body. "The sacred position of the sick man . . . became the preferential position which has been his ever since."[4]

The Incarnation magnified the Jewish belief that humanity is made in the image and likeness of God—underscoring the call to respond to the poor, the sick, and the homeless. The Greeks and Romans responded with "civic philanthropy" rather than charity based on love. Christian emphasis on the inherent dignity of human life contrasted with the Greco-Roman belief that linked human dignity "to citizenship status, or virtue...." The incarnational foundation of Christianity was manifested in a moral code that condemned "abortion, infanticide, the exposure of children, euthanasia (either as homicide or suicide) and the gladiatorial games."[5] With the legalization of Christianity imperial decrees as well as church councils refined the code and its implementation.

Christianity's healing ministry was principally mediated in the tradition of anointing the sick, based on Mark's reference to apostolic times when "they cast out many demons, and anointed with oil many that were sick and healed them" (Mark 6:13). James's reference to anointing was even more explicit: "Is any among you sick? Let him call for the elders of the church, and let them pray over him anointing him with oil in the name of the Lord; and the prayer of faith will save the sick man, and the Lord will raise him up; and if he has committed sins, he will be forgiven."[6] Because James was prescribing the official prayer of the community this would not be considered charismatic healing associated with particular gifts of individual persons. Rooted in the Hebrew culture, which, unlike the Greek, did not separate body and soul, the foundation of anointing was inherently holistic affecting personal, physical healing. Recognized as a sacrament by Pope Innocent I (d. 417) that could be administered by unordained as well as by ordained ministers, anointing as a liturgical rite appears in the ninth century. Because James linked forgiveness of sins and healing of the sick, penance and anointing were perceived as one rite with the consequence that the laity were excluded from anointing. Because penance required severe acts of contrition, such as abstaining from sexual intercourse for life, people tended to delay penance until close to death; hence, they became the last rites, that is, extreme unction and viaticum. Recent sacramental theology has removed unction from "extreme" and placed it in the rite of anointing the sick, which blends several prayers imbedded in tradition and which is appropriate in situations of illness and of dying.[7]

During the late Middle Ages the church's ministers to the sick tended toward venality. Bernard Poschmann, a scholar of the development of penance and anointing, lists several reasons for the corruption: "Laziness and indifference often kept priests from visiting the sick and the faithful from troubling about the sacrament. Matters were made worse by the custom, which soon developed, of remunerating the priest for his services and what was at first a free will offering became in a very short time a considerable burden for the poorer people."[8] An anonymous writer of the day stated that because "unction required many priests and twelve candles, only a man worth two cows could afford the sacrament."[9] As will be discussed later in this chapter, medieval nursing communities filled this void with religious witness of the healing presence of Jesus in the lives of the sick poor in late medieval society.

In the early Christian communities the sick were cared for in their homes by deacons and deaconesses. In Paul's letters there is a reference to Phoebe as not only the first deaconess but also the first visiting nurse. In Rome, Paula taught nursing and Fabiola opened the first Roman "hospital." These noble women were responding to the sick poor on the fringes of society. After Christianity achieved legal status, institutions for the sick, the stranger, and the homeless were established. The most notable early hospital was founded by Basil the Great as early as 372 in Caesarea in his diocese of Cappadocia. In the West, Benedictine monasteries included infirmaries. Monks were acquainted with the works of the Greek physicians, copied and translated into Latin their manuscripts, and in their gardens planted herbs used as medicines for the restoration of many illnesses. Gradually hospitals evolved at Benedictine monasteries, and as they expanded into northern Europe in the Middle Ages they spread a rudimentary knowledge of Hippocrates and Galen.[10]

Women religious were in the forefront of medieval nursing care. There were instances when nuns and monks nursed in the same institution, caring for those of their own sex. The Knights Hospitalers of St. John (Knights of Malta), a military nursing order, was established during the Crusades in the eleventh century while the Knights of St. Lazarus, founded in the twelfth century, cared for victims of leprosy, a general term that included a variety of infections. Several women's communities were attached to these orders, but it was the Sisters of the Holy Ghost, originally a lay society, who founded the city hospital in Rome in 1204. Named after the order, the Holy Ghost hospital set the pattern for the development of nearly one thousand city hospitals throughout Europe. The community of sisters who founded the Hôtel Dieu de Paris and later adopted the Rule of St. Augustine is the oldest extant order dedicated specifically to nursing. These Augustinian nuns were committed, in addition to poverty, chastity and obedience, to a fourth vow, the care of the sick poor.[11]

In the fourteenth and fifteenth centuries, artists depicted the seven corporal works of mercy in portraits of heroic women, such as St. Elizabeth of Hungary, caring for the sick, and of nursing sisters in a hospital situation. Natalie Boynel Kampen, a scholar of art and society who has focused on nursing in painting and sculpture, explores the common features of scenes of nursing sisters:

> They nurse patients who are most often men lying in bed; they work in a distinctive location that does not look like a house; they wear distinctive costumes; their activities are domestic and religious rather then specifically medical; and, most important, they are never subordinated to patients or doctors.[12]

Rather than view these renderings as the growth of professional nursing, Kampen emphasizes the "Christian theological vision of the hospital." She refers to the French "Hôtels Dieu, or God's hospice/hostel/home" and concludes that the sisters within this context were "God's brides, who cared for His family under His fatherly supervision. Christianity created a synthesis from the nurse as kin and the nurse as a public worker; the nursing sister brought this about because she was a holy woman and a servant of Christ." Hence, the nursing sister was understood within "the bounds of tradition and propriety."[13]

One school of "women healers" traced the history of sisterhoods of nursing, of notable women writers on medicine, such as Hildegard of Bingen, and concluded with a remarkable document penned by Pierre Dubois.[14] In his letter to Edward I of England and Philip the Fair of France, *De recuperatione Terrae Sanctae*, Dubois suggested that these two monarchs "let maidens be instructed in medicine and surgery . . . so that when desirable they may be given in matrimony to the higher princes, the clergy and other wealthier men of the East, whom they would convert to the Roman Catholic faith."[15] Indeed he envisioned these western European medical missionaries "networking" among the women of the Orient through the medium of medical training, thereby gaining a foothold for the faith in the homes of pagan oriental families.[16] Such a farsighted proposal was doomed to be shelved in the archives because allowing lay women such independent roles would have entailed a revolution in gender relations that western societies have only recently experienced. Women religious attached to hospitals were permitted independence only within the boundaries of their ministry, which frequently included monastic enclosures separated from the active life of society. Some forty years after Dubois's letter, Europe experienced the ravage of the Bubonic Plague, the profoundly disastrous Black Death that reduced the population by over twenty million.

II

In 1334 the Aachen city council registered a gift of alms to the Brot-Beghards living on the *Scharportzgrave,* which is today *Alexianergraben,* where the Alexian Brothers maintain a mental hospital.[17] As lay mendicants who begged "Brot durch Gott" the anonymous founders of the modern Alexian Brothers were participants in that heterogeneous movement of lay piety characterized by its dedication to the *Vita Apostolica.*[18] The early Alexian family included other Brot-Beghards in Cologne (1306)[19] and Lollards or Matemannen in Antwerp (1345).[20] Though the Alexian founders predate 1348, the height of the catastrophic Black Death, their passage through the recurring waves of plague established their specific identity as ministers to victims of pestilence. Later called Alexian Brothers after their major patron, St. Alexius (of many legends), the Brothers devolved from the genus Brot-Beghard, Lollard, and Matemannen to species Cellite or Brothers of the Cells, as a result of their expanding self-identity as a family of mendicants who nursed and buried plague victims.

The etymology of the terms "Beghard," "Lollard," and "Matemannen" suggests certain themes that provide a glimpse of the history of the early Brothers. "Beghard" may have been derived from the German word *begga,* "to pray" or "to beg,"[21] or may have originated as a common pejorative for all those suspect groups who were associated with the Albigensian persuasion, with *Bigen* as the common root.[22] The *Oxford English Dictionary* states that the word "Lollard . . . was originally applied c. 1300 to the members of the Cellite or Alexian fraternity. . . . Usually it was taken to connote great pretensions to piety and humility, combined with views more or less heretical."[23] Dietrich von Kurze, a recent scholar of the continental Lollards, concludes that the term was derived from the Dutch words *lollen, lullen,* "to mumble" or "stammer." It is thought that these unlettered burial brothers stammered through the Latin funeral liturgy. Von Kurze does note that the term "Lollard" was applied to the Cellite family in the Low Countries to whom he refers as "Municipal Lollards."[24] A few chroniclers cite the Lollards and Matemannen as poor or humble folk who united to take care of the sick and bury the dead.[25] Each of these meanings is reflected in the early history of the brothers. The original Alexians were lay-mendicant, nonliterate, burial brothers, who may have stammered through the funeral dirge. Though they were associated with heterodoxy, they survived many encounters with diocesan and papal inquisitors because of their crucial social service to the towns inundated with waves of plague. The pejorative character of the term "Lollard" led the brothers to gradually adopt the name "Cellites" or Brothers of the Cells in the late fourteenth century.[26] In Worms they were called Seelbrüder [sic], "soul brothers";[27] in Aachen Zielbrüder, which could have derived from the Dutch word meaning "soul brothers."[28] Mendicancy and ministry to the dying are the most characteristic connotations of all these names.[29]

Among the many groups committed to voluntary poverty and burial service to the plague victims, only the Cellites survived the late medieval period with these characteristics as their hallmark. Before the Black Death there were houses in Cologne, Aachen, Liège, Antwerp, Louvain, and Tirlemont. In the latter half of the century they settled in Ghent, Bruges, Brussels, Hasselt, and Diest. Their expansion was concurrent with the epidemics of 1357-62, 1370-76, and 1380-83. By 1472, when they were officially recognized as a religious order, there were thirty-six Cellite houses. The Black Death appears to have acted as a catalyst in expanding the familial consciousness of these burial brotherhoods that spontaneously emerged in the early fourteenth century.[30] Pope Eugene IV described the Cellite ministry: "They take poor and wretched persons into their own places for the sake of hospitality, and take care of them in their illness; during the time of pestilence they bury the bodies of the faithful who have died with ecclesiastical burial."[31]

Of all the Cellite communities the Antwerp brothers appear to have been most absorbed into the town welfare system. According to a contract between the town and the community, only the Cellites were to bury plague victims and were to be paid twice the amount charged for a normal burial. If plague victims were buried by someone other than the brothers, they were still entitled to their fee. Lastly, the Cellites were instructed to "always have a rather good number of Brothers in order to serve the community easily, in times of pestilence as well as during all other contagious sicknesses whatever they are and however they may come, without fraud or guile."[32] In 1628 after a five-year period of plague, Pater Jan van der Linden, the brother superior of the Antwerp Cellites, appealed to the city council for financial aid that had been promised the community during the epidemic. He reminded the council that five brothers and four novices had died in service to plague victims. He also stated that the mayor of Thienen had offered him one thousand guilders a year for the "care of the infected sick."[33] Though there is no record of the council's immediate response, on July 27, 1632, it appointed Brother Jan *pestmaster* of Antwerp and the next month granted the brothers a two-thousand guilder subsidy.[34]

By the seventeenth century the Cellites were ministering to a variety of social outcasts. Since 1556, a Cologne brother would stay with a convicted criminal on the eve of his execution and before the executioner lowered the ax, the brother would place a picture of the crucified Jesus before the face of the criminal for him to kiss.[35] As early as 1592 the Nijmegen Brothers were known for their care of mentally ill men at the *Dolhuis*, "madhouse."[36] Though few of the other Alexian houses became large confinement institutions before the nineteenth century, by the seventeenth century most of them had become hospices for the mentally ill.

In 1634 Etienne Binet described the Alexian death-poverty way of life:

> They [the Cellites] offer their services to those afflicted with the plague, and to all those who are seized by infectious diseases. Day by day, they are exposed to the danger of falling victims to the same diseases themselves; thus standing on the edge of their grave every day. To live amongst the dead, without fearing death, which otherwise strikes terror into people, is really a valiant calling, which could have extorted admiration even from a Caesar or an Alexander. These servants of God bury the dead and pay them the last tribute of respect being filled with the true divine compassion and leaving nothing undone to console the sick and to assist the dying. . . . The Alexian Brothers are so secluded and surrounded by the dead, by coffins and pest-stricken that the remembrance of their merits also seems to be buried and forgotten with the dead. But the day will once come which will bring to light the value of these noble-minded and glorified warriors of Christ, who have waged the battle against death, against the plague and against the most incurable diseases.[37]

The Alexian Brothers represent one of many male and female groups along the path of the *Vita Apostolica*. Most medieval hospitals did not survive economic and social dislocations. War and plague of the late Middle Ages and the Reformation added to the instability of the times. Two male nursing communities were founded in the sixteenth century:

the Camillians, priests and brothers founded in Italy by Camillus de Lellis, and the brothers founded by St. John of God in Spain. Identified with large institutions and associated with saintly founders these orders, like the Alexians, are still active today. The anonymity of the original Cellites and their identification with the mentally ill exiles from society set them apart from these sixteenth-century communities. However, by the sixteenth century, particularly in France, nursing became feminized and opened to women of the lower classes.

III

The Counter Reformation in France, during the first half of the seventeenth century, witnessed what one historian called "a fantastic conventual invasion."[38] Jean Delumeau and others have placed this dramatic rise in new orders and revitalization of old religious communities within the general rechristianization of society.[39] For example, by 1631, some seventeen years after Pierre de Bérulle founded the Oratory in France, there were seventy-one houses. The Lazarists (later known as Vincentians), founded by St. Vincent de Paul in the mid-1630s, numbered forty houses in 1660. Among the older orders of women the Carmelites and Ursulines experienced even greater growth than the men's communities, while such new communities as the Order of the Visitation of Our Lady and the Daughters of Charity expanded at a rapid rate. When the Visitandines were founded by St. Francis de Sales and St. Jane de Chantal they were committed to visiting the sick, but because the archbishop of Lyons would not tolerate an uncloistered community of nursing women, they took up teaching.[40]

The Daughters of Charity, founded by St. Vincent de Paul and St. Louise de Marillac in 1633, were committed to serving the poor, the sick, and children, particularly those who were abandoned. Because St. Vincent had learned from the Visitandine experience, he did not place the Daughters' canonical status in the realm of a religious order; rather, they were founded as the "Confraternity of the Servants of Our Poor," who by 1660 had sixty houses.[41]

The Visitandines and the Daughters were manifestations of the Counter Reformation "burst of feminine energy," a sort of "anarchy of religious activism"[42]—phrases in which Elizabeth Rapley captures the spirit of the devôtes, who were "deeply religious women, very often unmarried, and with time and energy to devote themselves to the exercise of piety. Their 'rush' into the religious life during these critical years was a phenomenon in itself, which preceded the existence of convents in which to live, or even suitable jobs to perform."[43]

Much of this activism met severe resistance in the first half of the century, such as the Visitandines had experienced. However, "a second 'rush' of women into religiously inspired activities took place," and ultimately they "broke down the opposition; a massive complex of charitable institutions began to rise, built upon their support, protection and training." The suppression of active orders made it quite evident that they could not by canon law dwell in the religious life; so they lived the active life in "*uncloistered* congregations" and their members were all named *filles seculières*, "nuns in all but name."[44] This religious/secular dichotomy had been allowed among some men's religious groups, such as the Alexian Brothers, but had been prohibited for women. The *filles seculières* were permitted this new status because of the deep need for nurses, teachers, and catechists. Rapley concludes that women were not playing passive roles by merely filling social or religious needs. "The religious energy came first and the need to channel that energy into meaningful action came second. Then came the need for institutions within which the women could be protected and maintained while they carried out their new activities, in other words communities. At this state, the involvement of Catholic society, as provider and support, became imperative."[45]

Through his influence among church and civic dignitaries Vincent de Paul guaranteed that the Daughters of Charity would be an uncloistered congregation. Drawn from the peasant class, accustomed to the difficult work of their calling and the social milieu of the poor, the Daughters were to wear the garb of the simple people, "a plain dull gray habit" with no veil. From their origins until the present, they take only annual vows. According to Delumeau, Vincent said "half jokingly and half seriously," "Their monastery, the house of the sick, for a cell a hired room, for a chapel the parish church, for a cloister the streets of the city, or the wards of the hospital, for a grill, the fear of God, for a veil, holy modesty."[46]

The Catholic Reformation in seventeenth-century France was manifested in a widespread proliferation of charitable works for the poor, including hospitals, home-relief institutions, and schools. Confraternities of the laity flourished; St. Vincent de Paul founded the "Confraternity of the Ladies of Charity" at Chatillon-les-Dombres in the Lyonnais in 1617. Over the next two decades such confraternities spread rapidly throughout France.[47] In the development of new public policy for hospitals, the Company of the Blessed Sacrament, "a clandestine organization of religious activists from the highest reaches of the social elite," had an enormous impact.[48] Concerned with both the religious and social condition of the poor, the Company supported the construction of a new type of facility, the *Hôpital Général*, which became both a workhouse for the poor and a hospital for the confinement of the sick and all those on the fringes of society—beggars, vagrants, prostitutes, the aged, abandoned children, and the infirm. It was identified as the *renfermement des pauvres*, "the general confinement of the poor." The undeserving poor were subjected to a "draconian regime of short, sharp shocks" while the deserving poor were given secure hospitality. The Company of the Holy Sacrament played a role in the foundation of the first Hôpital Général in Paris in 1656–57. By 1700 a network of such hospitals developed with the common character of poor houses rather than of shelters for the sick. The Hôtel-Dieu, however, housed the sick poor, many of whom had curable diseases.[49]

The Daughters of Charity, who began their ministry under the Confraternity of the Ladies of Charity, whose husbands had reacted against their wives' work in poor neighborhoods, gradually gained independent status. Louise de Marillac, who since 1625 was widowed and under Vincent's spiritual direction, had committed herself to serving the poor. It was she who suggested hiring servant women to assist the Ladies of Charity. Louise took these lower-class women into her home and became their spiritual director and mentor in the work of the charities. Thus in 1633 the Daughters of Charity were established. In a short time they spread to the countryside; in 1638, they were assigned to the household of the niece of Cardinal Richelieu in Tourain, where they attended the sick and educated the daughters of the poor. They worked with Vincent's Lazarists in their pastoral care of injured soldiers and were soon managing hospitals where the Lazarists were in mission. Louise and Vincent encouraged the autonomy of the Daughters and preserved their "active" status outside the enclosure; before he died, Vincent placed them under the authority of the Lazarists. Not only did the motherhouse in Paris provide spiritual formation but the adjacent area became a training ground for their vocation as servants of the poor.[50]

The daily life of the Daughters of Charity in a Hôpital Général or a Hôtel Dieu, or in visiting the homes of the poor, was replete with severe physical and moral challenges. As Vincent remarked, it was "impossible to persevere for long in this very distressing vocation, and to overcome our natural repugnance for it, if one does not have a great store of virtue." Colin Jones describes the horrible conditions of seventeenth-century France:

[F]amine, plague, contagious disease and wars both foreign and domestic punctuated the lives of the laboring poor at a hectic tempo. Even at the best of times, moreover, the homes of the poor were the perennial locus of dirt and disease, fetidity and fevers, while the stench of the hospital made even the able-bodied retch. There were psychological deprivations too which worsened the lot of the Daughters of Charity. No sister was allowed to serve in her native region for example; to belong entirely to God, Saint Vincent reasoned, you must be estranged from your native-land. . . . A certain kind of mental fortitude and physical toughness were thus the *sine qua non* of Daughters of Charity.[51]

Marguerite Naseau, who became known as the first Daughter of Charity, died in 1633 as a result of an illness while she was nursing a plague victim. By the time of Vincent's death in 1660 there were forty houses, including a foundation in Poland. They had control of the hospital in Angers; they were nursing soldiers on the battlefield and galley slaves in the port towns; they cared for foundlings, the aged, and the insane, and were teaching the poor children in several schools.

The spirituality of the Daughters was immersed in ministry, as Vincent stated, "the poorest and the most abandoned are our Lords and Masters."[52] (The Alexian Brothers were participants in a lay movement, the *Vita Apostolica,* and they were viewed as *pauperes Christi.* By serving the poor of Christ, the Daughters of Charity were radically identifying with the *alter Christus* in those they served.) Colin Jones describes this commitment with a blend of eloquence and realism. "Every poor man at the gate was to be for the sisters an epiphany; every foundling or orphan cared for, the Christ-child incarnate; every sick man immobilized in his bed the human representation of the crucifixion." When nursing the sick in a critical time, the bell for prayer was to be ignored, a symbol of the identity of spirituality with ministry which was a reversal of the traditional priority of prayer over work. Of course prayer was evoked in the "work." Though the Daughters engaged in preparing herbal medicines in their own apothecary and though they performed minor surgical procedures, their priority was to administer spiritual balm to the sick. Their rule stated that they must attend to the sick

spiritually, by instructing the sick of the things necessary for salvation, in insuring that they make a general confession of their past lives, so that by this those who die leave this world in good estate and those who get well resolve never more to offend God.[53]

The growth of the Daughters reflected the expansion of charitable institutions in the seventeenth century. By 1699 there were 163 institutions identified with this burgeoning community, which, by episcopal permission in 1655 and papal decree in 1668, was authorized to "live in the world" rather than in the canonical enclosure decreed by the Council of Trent. By the time the Daughters united with St. Elizabeth Seton's Sisters of Charity of Emmitsburg, Maryland, in 1850, Louise and Vincent's sisters were located in several nations throughout the world.

IV

While the Alexian Brothers had no founder and the Daughters had two founders apart from their community, an Irish woman, Catherine McAuley (1778-1841), was the founder and the first Sister of Mercy. Orphaned as a young girl, Catherine lived with her physician uncle; after the latter's death she was adopted at age fifteen by a Protestant couple, the Callaghans, who had known her uncle. Raised in an upper middle-class Dublin family, Catherine became a devout young woman well known for her commitment to serving the poor, particularly visiting the homes of the sick and impoverished. Upon the death of Mr. Callaghan in 1822, Catherine inherited £25,000, comparable to well over one million dollars today. Soon she rented a house next to "the Poor School" as a kind of store where she exhibited the needlework and crafts from her classes. As her charity became more regularized she saw the need for a permanent home that would be suitable for teaching and boarding young poor girls as well as for accommodations for a few women called to share her commitment of fostering economic and social independence among the girls, bringing food and clothing to the poor, and visiting the sick in the lanes of urban poverty. A house on Baggot Street, built and furnished with her inheritance, was officially opened on September 24, 1827; because it was the feast of Our Lady of Mercy the house was designated by Archbishop Daniel Murray of Dublin as the House of Mercy. At this point Catherine had no intention of instituting a religious community. She turned over the remainder of her inheritance to the archbishop. After two years the nascent community numbered ten women. The Baggot Street house was somewhat controversial because of its "competition" with the Irish Sisters of Charity, founded by Mary Ailenhood; the archbishop, therefore, asked Catherine either to drop the quasi-religious character and become a secular organization or become a canonical community of women religious. Reluctantly Catherine embarked on the latter course and, with two other women from her community, entered a formation program at the Presentation convent in

Dublin. Drawn to the Presentation community because the founder had also been committed to serving the sick poor, Mother Catherine McAuley, Sister Elizabeth Harley, and Sister Anne Doyle professed simple vows on December 12, 1831; thus the Sisters of Mercy were founded.[54]

The rule and constitution of the new community were based on the rule of St. Augustine that had been adopted by many congregations. However, Catherine added two chapters dealing with the two particular apostolates of the institute: "the visitation of the sick" and "the protection of women."[55] The chapter on serving the sick is marked by references to scripture and the lives of the saints. It begins:

> Mercy—the principal path marked out by Jesus Christ for those who desire to follow him—has, in all ages of the Church, excited the faithful in a particular manner to instruct and comfort the sick and dying poor—as in them they regarded the person of our Divine Master. . . .[56]

Catherine McAuley's instructions for visiting the sick are rich in detail. The sisters should begin with a visit to the chapel "to offer their Divine Master their action they are about to perform, and to ask from Him the grace necessary to promote his glory, and the salvation of souls."[57] The sisters were instructed to approach the sick "with great tenderness; and when there is no immediate danger of death, it will be well *first*, to relieve distress, and to endeavor . . . to promote cleanliness, ease and comfort of the sick person; since we are always better disposed to receive advice and instruction from those who show compassion."[58] Because the principal motivation is "the good of souls," Mother McAuley urges the sisters to be concerned particularly with those patients "who have been long negligent of their religious duties, and in whom coldness and indifference predominate." To such persons the sisters were instructed to "arouse them by speaking of the dreadful judgements of God towards impenitent sinners, and by warning them, that if we do not seek His mercy and forgiveness in the way He has appointed we must be miserable for eternity." To underscore the pastoral ministry of the Sisters of Mercy, Catherine urged these visitors of the sick "to pray in an audible voice, and in a most earnest impressive manner that God may look with compassion on His poor creatures and bring them to repentance. . . ." Pastoral care of the sick also included catechesis: "The sisters shall question them on the principal mysteries of our Holy Faith, and, if necessary, instruct them therein."[59]

When the sisters encountered a dying patient ("recovering is hopeless") they were to proceed with "great caution" and notify the patient gradually "assuring him of the peace and joy he will feel when entirely resigned to the will of God." If this deathbed dialogue included concern for disposal of the property of the patient, the sisters were to "avoid taking part in it, confining themselves to general matters." However, they could suggest to the patient that he or she talk with a "suitable person deserving of his confidence."[60]

The Sisters of Mercy were, therefore, remarkably autonomous women, free from the domestic ideals associated with the heroic women's calling to mother and nurture the sick. Indeed, the ideal sister-"pastoral-minister" appears as comparable to the deaconess of the early church free to pursue a religious witness without a physician or priest present to control the physical or spiritual care of the patient. Because the original rule details the responsibilities of the sisters, one is struck by the absence of any directive to provide for sacramental ministry to the dying. Perhaps it was understood that priests would not be accessible in a precipitous crisis. In later constitutions there are more detailed instructions on the physical care that reveal the development of the sisters' role as nurses, but the guide for pastoral care is essentially unchanged and remains the principal focus. Of course, in the hospital setting the physician's control becomes evident, and there were chaplains to complement the sister's ministry. Even in the hospital the nursing sister and later the lay nurses under their supervision will assume responsibility for the spirituality of the patient. Though the sisters visited the hospitals in Ireland and England, the first of the Mercy hospitals opened in Pittsburgh on January 1, 1847.

In 1854, the year that the sisters assumed responsibility for one of Dublin's hospitals, the old Charity Infirmary in Jervis Street, five Sisters of Mercy left the English house to nurse the wounded soldiers in the Crimean War. According to one historian, they departed before Florence Nightingale was commissioned by the British War Ministry to head the nursing staff. Another fifteen Sisters of Mercy in Dublin, who responded to the call for nurses, departed for the Crimea in December of 1854. Throughout the war the sisters received many commendations from doctors and military leaders, but there were severe conflicts with Nightingale because she suspected them of placing religious responsibilities to Catholic patients above their nursing duties. The sisters were also subjected to an anti-Catholic animus that envisaged them as "proselytizers" rather than as nurses. Because of a conflict with Nightingale, Mother Francis Bridgeman, superior of the sisters, left for Ireland just as the war ended. According to Mother Francis's diary, Nightingale took notes as the Sisters of Mercy explained the nursing practices of the sisters. In a letter after the end of the war Florence Nightingale apologized to Sister M. Clare, superior of the English house. "I will ask you to forgive me for everything and anything I may have done which could have given you pain, remembering only that I have always felt that it has given me more pain to reign over you than you to serve. You were far above me in fitness for the General Superintendency, both in worldly talent of administration, and far more in spiritual qualifications which God values in a superior."[61]

The hospital experience in the Crimean War, which included the death of two sisters, was of historical significance in the self-understanding of the young community of Catherine McAuley. Though their nursing care was on center stage in the war effort, Florence Nightingale played the leading public role while the Mercy sisters were an almost invisible supporting cast until later in the century when historians revealed their extensive contributions in the Crimean War.

The European experience of the Alexian Brothers, Daughters of Charity, and Sisters of Mercy represent diverse religious responses to the poor, sick, and dying. There were women religious, such as the Bon Secours Sisters (founded in Paris in 1824) who also nursed the sick in their homes. Though their patients included the poor, they were responding to the sick of all classes rather than the poor alone. The Bon Secours Sisters came to the United States in 1881 and eventually opened hospitals.[62]

In the context of the tripartite etiology of illness as sin, demons, and nature that were referred to in the opening of this chapter, sin and nature dominate the concerns of the three principal religious communities upon whom we have focused. Since the Daughters were apothecaries and apprentice-like surgeons who dealt with physicians on almost a daily basis, the role of medical treatment of natural illness permeated their hospitals by the late eighteenth century. The Sisters of Mercy were to provide the rudiments of nursing care, and the Alexians were usually caretakers of the mentally ill outsiders. All three communities were primarily religious care givers; theirs was a pastoral care in the traditional sense of a call to respond to the *alter Christus* in the poor and diseased with prayer and preparation for a "happy death." By the time these communities arrived in the United States, there were five communities of women religious founded in the young republic who reflected the traditional world's call, but one that was mediated by Americans in structures suitable to the young republic.

CHAPTER TWO

The Maryland Experience
1634–1850

THIS CHAPTER OPENS in colonial Maryland where the priests of the Society of Jesus responded to the sick and injured among the native Americans. As the center of Catholic life and as the locus of the first nursing experience of the Sisters of Charity, Maryland plays a foundational role in the history of Catholic health care. The chapter concludes with a lengthy exploration of two nursing manuals composed by Sisters of Charity which reveal several historical developments: a concern for the holistic environment of the hospital; a nurturing attitude toward the sick characteristic of domesticity of a later period; a blend of nursing and pastoral care; and a sensitivity toward religious pluralism. One of these nursing manuals, composed by a sister with vast experience in care for the mentally ill, provides us with one of the few glimpses of specialized Catholic hospitals.

I

The distinctive character of the religious ethos of the United States had a significant impact on Catholic health care. Voluntary hospitals, sponsored by religious denominations and medical colleges, developed alongside state and city institutions. The Spanish and French colonial governments united crown and altar and supported Catholic hospitals. Santo Domingo was the site of the first Spanish hospital in 1503. The oldest existing hospital was founded in 1524 by Cortez in Mexico City, the *Hospital de Jesus*. The French established the *Hôtel Dieu de Precieux Sang* in Quebec in 1639. It was Spanish Florida that gave birth to the first hospital in what is now the United States.

In the late Middle Ages Canon Law prohibited the priest from practicing medicine because clergymen were not allowed to shed blood. The practice of medicine, it was argued, would inhibit pastoral responsibilities; and because medical practice was frequently ineffective, the priest-physician may have engendered anticlericalism. However, priests persisted to practice even after the Council of Trent reenforced the prohibition.[1] This was the case in remote regions, particularly in the mission lands. In 1641, *Propaganda Fidei*, the Roman congregation responsible for the missions, permitted priests to practice medicine "as a means of aiding the conversion of unbelievers." However, they were to be "truly learned in the profession," were prohibited from surgery, were to be uncompensated, and were to practice only when the mission was without a qualified physician.[2]

The superior of the tiny Jesuit community in colonial Maryland, Andrew White, lived with the Piscataway Indians in Kittamaquidi. In the summer of 1639 White responded to the tribe's leader, Tayac, whom he referred to as "King." The annual report of 1640 to the Jesuit Provincial includes this description:

> Shortly after Father White's arrival, the Tayac was in danger of death from a severe disease; and when forty conjurers had in vain tried every remedy, the Father, by permission of the sick man, administered medicine, that is, a certain powder of known efficacy mixed with holy water, and the next day, with the assistance of the boy whom he had with him, opened one of his veins for blood letting. After this, the sick man began daily to grow better, and soon was completely cured. Having recuperated, he resolved to be initiated in the Christian rites as soon as possible; not only himself, but his wife also and his two daughters; for as yet he had no male offspring. Father White is now diligently engaged in their instruction; nor do they idly receive the heavenly doctrine, for by the grace poured upon them, they have long since discovered the errors of their former life. The king has exchanged the skins, with which he was heretofore clothed, for a garment made in our fashion; he makes also a little effort to learn our language. Having put away his concubines, he lives content with one wife, that he may the more freely (as he says) have leisure to pray to God. . . .
>
> Not long ago, when he held a council of the tribe, in a crowded assembly of the chiefs and people, with Father White and some of the English present, he publicly attested that it was his advice, together with that of his wife and children, that they should forsake their native superstition and give themselves to Christ; for there was no other true god but that of the Christians, nor could men in any other way save their immortal souls. . . .
> For the greatest hope is that, when the family of the king is baptized, the conversion of the whole empire will speedily take place.[3]

On another occasion Andrew White responded to an injured Piscataway whom he perceived as near death. "When he saw the danger was imminent, he briefly ran over the principal articles of faith . . . heard his confession, recited the gospel . . . for the sick and the litany to the Blessed Virgin, and told him to commend himself to her most holy intercession and to call unceasingly upon the sacred name of Jesus." After White applied the relic of the cross to the "patient's" wounds he instructed his friends that when the dying man passes to place the body in the chapel. Several hours later the injured Piscataway had been cured and revealed the healed wounds to White. "All who were in the boat with the Father, after they confirmed his claim, broke forth in praise of God and thanksgiving."[4]

Andrew White's experience in Maryland was roughly contemporary with the nascent foundation of the Daughters of Charity, the administrations of Pater Jan van der Linden in Antwerp (the Alexian *pestmaster*), and the foundation of the first hospital in Quebec. Throughout seventeenth-century Europe and its colonies in the new world, popular devotions to particular saints, pilgrimages to shrines, and veneration of relics imposed a religious boundary separating Catholicism from Protestantism. The Council of Trent (1541–65) reaffirmed traditional belief through its refutation of Protestant doctrines and passed reform decrees aimed at eliminating widespread financial and administrative abuses relating to shrines and relics, and contributing to the venality of the clergy and the pagan tendencies of the laity. The Council underscored the sacramentality of belief and practice and the importance of good works in contrast to Protestantism's credal foundation, that is, faith, fidelity to scripture, and the gratuity of divine favor unaffected by good works. The new theology also excluded popular devotions to saints, sacred places and relics, as well as the separate life of women and men religious.[5]

Robert Bellarmine, a major figure of the Catholic Reformation, wrote on the role of illness and pain in the drama of redemption, while popular religious belief sought miraculous cures in a variety of cults, many of which originated in the Middle Ages. To maintain their health Italian women had quotations from scripture on their bodies; in seventeenth-century Naples there were eleven statues of Mary associated with miracles.[6] Marvin O'Connell explains succinctly what he perceives as the persistence of superstition within the Catholic community:

> The survival of so much superstition among the masses of tridentine Catholics appears, at first glance, to have confirmed the strictures of Protestant polemics upon the intrinsically idolatrous character of Catholicism. The truth, however, is considerably more complicated. Certainly the

melding into bizarre combinations of crude rural nostrums with pagan ritual and Christian symbol (or vice versa) was commonplace, no less in
Catholic Europe than in the Mission lands, and it persists to this day. The
fact is that tridentine Catholicism, imbued with the principle of immanence, was peculiarly vulnerable to popular cults that involved distorted
sacramental acts. The difference between the institutional church—which
recommended veneration of relics, blessings for animals, and rogation-day
processions to seek divine aid for the bounty of the seasons, to say nothing
of the formal ritual grounded in oil and bread—and a populace that
invoked age-old rites and incantations, more or less Christianized, to ward
off evil was a difference of *degree*, not of a kind. The parish priest, fresh
from a tridentine seminary, might disapprove of what he conceived to be
the excesses of his people in, say, mixing herbal potions with prayers to the
Virgin or seeking cures from a wandering seer with talismans pinned to his
hat. But the sin lay in exaggeration, overindulgence, and extravagance, not
in the use of physical things for sacred purposes. Neither the priest nor his
hierarchical superiors were prepared to deny the reality of an interven-
tionist God who sanctified the Christian people through ritual observance,
who, within the confines of the village church, worked the physical miracle
of changing bread into Christ's body every morning. And, in any case, how
far removed was the average parish priest, despite his time in the seminary,
from the tribal instincts of the people from whom he had been taken and
to whom he had now returned?[7]

Protestantism may have banished the popular cults that bordered on
the realm of magic and the occult, but it had no replacement for the
people's need for hope and consolation. The repudiation of belief in
demons and the evil eye led to the belief that there is one explanation for
illness, divine providence. As Keith Thomas has explored in his work on
the decline of magic, it was the development of Protestant religious
thought and not medical science that eclipsed the belief in magical cures.
Despite the putatively progressive character of Protestantism it led to
exaggerated emphases on illness as the consequence of moral transgres-
sion. Folk superstitions also lingered in the Protestant community.[8] Jon
Butler's *Awash in a Sea of Faith* documents widespread use of amulets
and other magical practices among the several American religious
denominations in the mid-eighteenth century; almanacs with their astro-
logical renderings were best-sellers in Protestant American life.[9]

When catastrophic epidemics scourged the port cities of the United
States, Protestant mayors, discerning the hand of God in the sickness,
would call for a day of repentance. When the yellow fever struck Baltimore in the summer of 1800 John Carroll, the first bishop in the United
States, issued a pastoral letter to the Catholic congregation of Baltimore.

Though he referred to Divine Providence as allowing the epidemic he did not call for a collective penance to assuage guilt and alter the will of God, but rather he stated that "It is an awful warning to remind us all of that uncertainty of our continuance in this life, and the necessity of being prepared for the coming of the Lord."[10] However, the principal purpose of the pastoral was to encourage all Catholics to be reconciled with God while they were healthy because the ravages of the fever had been responsible for the death of eight priests since 1793; six others were "reduced to the point of death so that their recovery appears rather a miracle of God's fatherly beneficence than the effect of natural causes. . . . It is not possible for religion to bear, in its present state in our country, a continuation of such heavy losses. The number of Clergymen is so reduced, that many congregations are deprived of all spiritual assistance." Priests must pastorally respond to the sick, but they also must urge the well to "withdraw themselves from the most dangerous scenes of infection" and, since there may not be a priest available if they would become inflicted with the disease, they should immediately prepare for death.

Characteristic of his enlightened Catholicism, Bishop Carroll implied humanity's relatively easy access to grace when he said that the people's pastor "will remain and be ready to give his ministry to all of you, who will recur to it, and will strengthen in the grace and love of God, and best dispositions to stand before his awful tribunal by admitting you here to the tribunal of reconciliation, and feeding you with heavenly manna as a sacred viaticum to support you in passage from life to death."

Carroll did specify, however, that a priest must "be governed by the rules of Christian prudence in preserving himself for the benefit of others. . . . After this public notice, your pastor is instructed to visit only those in their sickness, who have not had opportunities of recurring to him before." Carroll asked his people to repent and trust themselves to God's "adorable mercy" rather than to be the "cause of depriving" the community of the "benefits of a Catholic ministry."[11]

Bishop Carroll's diocese included the entire nation in 1800. His designated coadjutor bishop, Leonard Neale, was told to stay away from Baltimore during the epidemic. Hence, his consecration had been delayed. Without an ordained successor, Bishop Carroll was warned "by the universal voice of all my Brethren in the Priesthood," that it would be "criminal" for him to risk "sharing in all your dangers and anxieties." Indeed he wrote this pastoral letter from the "city of Washington."[12]

In 1800 there were two parish communities in the Baltimore area, St. Peter's pro-Cathedral situated a block south of the present Basilica of the

Assumption of the Blessed Virgin Mary; the other was attached to St. Patrick's community in Fells Point, a separate town in 1800. Founded in 1792, the year after over one thousand refugees from Santo Domingo arrived at this port town, the Fells Point parish was the principal focus of Carroll's pastoral letter. Father Antoine Garnier, a French Sulpician from St. Mary's Seminary, was the first pastor. In 1795 John Floyd, a convert who studied at St. Sulpice before he and three others formed the first seminary class in the United States, became pastor. During the epidemic of 1797 John Floyd became infected with the disease after administering the sacraments to a yellow-fever victim.[13] Four days later the twenty-nine-year-old priest died at the home of John Carroll.

During a yellow-fever epidemic of 1804 Father Floyd's successor, Michael Cuddy, died of the disease that he contracted during his pastoral care of his parishioners.[14] By this time St. Patrick's parish had grown considerably; in 1807 a new church was dedicated, built under the supervision of John Francis Moranville, a Holy Ghost missionary who fled French Guiana because political conditions had inflamed anticlerical sentiment and because he had retracted his oath to support the Constitution of the Clergy during the French Revolution. He ultimately took up residence in Baltimore, associated with the Sulpicians, and taught at a private school in the city. The fifth pastor of the parish, Moranville lasted for nearly twenty years. However, like his two predecessors he experienced a yellow-fever epidemic (1819–21), the worst to hit the seaport, and Fells Point was its principal area of attack.[15]

In an article on Moranville in the *Religious Cabinet* of 1842, the first Catholic periodical published in Baltimore, the author recalled that "the young and vigorous, as well as the aged and infirm, were alike victims of the fatal malady. Business was in most measure suspended; most of those whose means enabled them to remove from the infected district . . . sought refuge in the country. . . . The poor and the sick were almost the only inhabitants. . . ." During normal times, Moranville regularly visited the sick immediately after breakfast. According to Bernard U. Campbell, the author of this "Memoir of the Reverend John Francis Moranville," Protestant ministers had deserted the area while Moranville was "for a time the only clergyman in the district. . . . Not content with the performance of his spiritual functions, Mr. ["Father" was a term that gained popularity in the latter half of the nineteenth century] Moranville administered temporal relief. . . ." He provided food, medicine and even paid nurses to care for the afflicted. During the two years of the epidemic, Moranville was struck twice with the fever and never fully recovered. He died in 1824 while visiting his home in France. The parish community at St. Patrick's draped the church in black, "and the people clad in mourning lamented the death of a most tender father." The trustees of the parish wrote to Simon Bruté, a Sulpician priest and later bishop of Vincennes, who was in France, and they communicated the news of their pastor's death. They told him of the Protestants' general high regard for Moranville: "They speak of him in the most unqualified terms of approbation and admire those heroic virtues which he so long practiced among them. . . ."[16]

During the epidemics Baltimore established temporary hospitals for the victims. The permanent facility was actually a poorhouse or an almshouse that cared for the homeless, prostitutes, alcoholics, incurably and chronically ill, both physically and mentally, and the sick poor, both the infirm and the acutely ill. The caretaking character of nursing allowed the city board to assign several patients there (inmate is a more appropriate designation), some of whom became full-time staff after their recovery. Except for the availability of Bibles and occasional visits from Protestant clergymen, the religious needs of the inmates were generally ignored.[17] Charles E. Rosenberg writes: "the internal logic of the almshouse allied it more closely to the hospice of the Middle Ages than to the twentieth-century hospital. Few who entered the almshouse did so voluntarily; it was the last resort for the city's most helpless and deprived."[18]

The origins of voluntary hospitals reflect social and medical concerns. There was a need to care for the "deserving poor," to separate them from the immoral dredges of society in the almshouses and to provide care for paying patients, many of whom were sailors whose fees were paid by what we would refer to as third-party providers, the managers of a fund based on monthly premiums. There was also a need for improved medical education; dispensaries and out-patient facilities were less than adequate. A parallel to this almshouse system developed: private, voluntary hospitals that could provide for attending physicians instructing resident staff and for their own continuing clinical education.[19]

In October of 1823 physicians at the University of Maryland opened an infirmary in Baltimore that was staffed by five Sisters of Charity. The Ursuline sisters had been at Charity hospital, a state facility in New Orleans, and the fifty-four St. Joseph Sisters of La Flèche had been associated with the first hospital in Montreal since 1659, but these were almshouses. The Baltimore Infirmary, a fifty-bed institution, was the first university hospital managed and staffed by the first Catholic community of women religious established in the United States.[20] Elizabeth Seton founded the Sisters of Charity in 1809 in Baltimore but soon moved to Emmitsburg, Maryland, and adopted the rule of the Daughters of Charity. The American rule states, "The end which our Sisters of Charity of St. Joseph proposed to themselves was to honor our Lord Jesus Christ as the source and model of all charity, by rendering Him every temporal and spiritual service in their power, in the persons of the poor, the sick, prisoners and others."[21] The articles of incorporation in Maryland stipulated the legal purpose is for "works of piety, charity, and usefulness, and especially for the care of the sick, the aged, infirm and necessitous persons, and the education of young females."[22] Since Mother Seton died in 1821 she did not witness the sisters' first encounter with health care. However, the desperately sick poor were not in the Baltimore Infirmary but in the poorhouse or almshouse. Neither were their patients from the middle and upper classes who could afford to be treated in their homes. In any event the sisters represented a new dimension in American health care, an explicitly Catholic culture in a pluralistic society. Because of its flexibility and the directive that the sisters consider the areas of poverty as their enclosure, the constitution adapted from the rule of the Daughters of Charity was particularly suited to American conditions. The decision to enter nursing was influenced by the traditions of the Daughters of Charity in France and by the fact that Elizabeth Seton's father and brother were highly regarded physicians.

By the time they arrived to assume duties in the Baltimore Infirmary, the Sisters of Charity had established schools in Emmitsburg and Baltimore and orphan asylums in Philadelphia and New York; the Baltimore school had an asylum as well. The devastating impact of epidemics, particularly of the cholera scourge, greatly exacerbated the need for orphanages.

Mariann Patterson, recently widowed wife of Robert Patterson, a notable Baltimorean whose sister married Jerome Bonaparte, was the liaison between the university physicians and the Sisters of Charity. One of the three Caton sisters, granddaughters of Charles Carroll of Carrollton, Catholic signer of the Declaration of Independence and one of the wealthiest landowners in the young republic, Mariann corresponded with Jean DuBois, the priest-founder of Mt. St. Mary's College and superior general of the Sisters of Charity. In response to Mrs. Patterson's letter DuBois related the "joy" the sisters felt and that "they accept most willingly the offer Dr. Patterson [sic, the physician's name is Granville Sharp Pattison] makes to them of taking the management of his infirmary." The superior general indicated that the medical staff could rely on "the sisters' exertions, their economy, their human attentions to the sick [nursing was a human not a professional responsibility], their cleanliness in every part of the house." In return the sisters must have "full confidence in their management" and be "at liberty to follow the rules of their [religious] institution." He also expressed concern for the need to establish rules to assure "modest deportment in language and behavior which in Catholic countries is never departed from but may easily be forgotten here where they know nothing of the dignity and purity of those Religious women who with so much charity stoop to the meanest offices of servants."[23]

In a later letter to Mrs. Patterson, DuBois summarizes the religious character of the sisters' role in the infirmary: "Spiritual comfort will consist in instructing the grown people and children who are well . . . preparing for death those who are sick, laying them out when dead, and providing the means of a decent burial. . . ." These comforts would be adapted to conditions; "very intelligent [sisters] must be appointed" to the infirmary, stated DuBois.[24]

When the infirmary opened near the corner of Lombard and Greene Streets, the site of today's University of Maryland medical center, there were fifty beds located in four wards, and only acutely ill patients were admitted. There were five Sisters of Charity, including a superior, assigned to the infirmary; four more arrived within a year. The superior had responsibility for the keys, symbolic of the regulation of the visiting hours as well as the time limit for the resident staff's evenings out, that is, 10 P.M. Within the first year a conflict between the sisters and interns led DuBois to urge Dr. Pattison to discontinue the intern program. He said that as superior general, he had placed the time of locking the doors at 10 P.M.; he doubted that the interns would still be satisfied. According to DuBois the source of the conflict "is the spirit of independence which prevails among our American youths, they have little idea of the momentary slavery which they must submit to in order to become skilled in their profession—they want to unite the pleasures of life with the serious studies of the medical art." He assured Dr. Pattison that the sisters could "do everything the young men have to do—dressing wounds, bleeding, administering medicines etc. . . . In Europe our Sisters have no young students to do that."[25]

This situation led to a list of regulations approved by the board of trustees. The 10 P.M. curfew was to be observed by all residents of the infirmary and the sisters were responsible for the "care, management and ordering of the interior concerns and labors of the Infirmary," and they were accountable to the board of trustees. Each sister was assured of room, board, free medical care, and twenty-one dollars every six months; the board respected the governance of the community in Emmitsburg and the significance of the rule in the life of the sisters. They were also charged with patient admissions and dismissals, visitation hours, inventory of furniture, and the property of patients. There was a stipulation that all patients should be equally treated.[26]

In 1823 the Sisters of Charity had no experience in nursing other than whatever domestic practices they had learned from their mothers. However, located in the archives of the Midwestern Province of the Daughters of Charity is a pocket-size "reference work" divided into two parts. The first part, dated 1796, was composed by a priest and addressed [in French] to the Daughters of Charity and other religious hospitals. On pages 15 and 16 the author notes: "The above instruction was written in the time of the French Revolution when the priests of France could not exercise their functions, much of this duty devolved on the Sisters of Charity, such as instructing the poor sick, etc. etc."[27]

The anonymous author urged the sisters to respect the bodies and the souls of the sick poor, who, because they were generally so "ignorant of the first and most important truths of our holy religion," must be led to "conversion." "You should try to win their confidence, in order to dispose them the better to listen to the words of salvation; and to gain their souls to God when the favorable moment offers itself for you to undertake this important work . . . viz. to instruct them; to press them gently and prudently towards their conversion; lastly to help them die well." In his summary of their religious calling to nurse the sick poor, Jean DuBois, a refugee of the French Revolution, mentioned such instruction. Because the paucity of priests in the United States was a severe problem throughout the nineteenth century, these instructions were routine pastoral concerns of sister and later brother nurses. They became, in fact, chaplains whose prayer witness at bedside was mediated in the pluralist public setting of the hospital.

While in part I the priest emphasized the catechesis for the sick poor, part II, entitled "Instructions for the Care of the Sick by M. X.," includes a section on nursing; but the larger portion is devoted to pastoral care. The author is, according to Sister Daniel Hannefin, Mother Mary Xavier Clark, superior general from 1839–45. Mother Clark came to the United States from Santo Domingo during the slave rebellion. She was married at the age of seventeen to a Captain Clark, but shortly after the birth of a son her husband died, followed by the death of their son less than a year later. Through the intervention of two priests she joined Elizabeth Seton's tiny community. Like the founder, she was a widow committed to the activist religious life. Elizabeth Seton appointed her novice mistress, and in 1821 she was elected assistant to the founder shortly before she died.[28] Her manual of instructions was signed in 1841. She may have had several copies made for distribution to those on nursing mission. She returned to formation work of sisters in 1845.

No doubt Mother Clark's "Instruction for the Care of the Sick" was at least orally presented to the young aspirants to serve the sick poor. Her introduction set forth the principles as a spiritual compass: "our charity must be extended to all. All are the redeemed souls of our savior." Though patient care had to be proportioned to the needs of the sick, the sister should not confine her compassion for "this or that one" patient. "To act in such a manner would indeed be a sin and a great breach of our engagements with God, for whose sake we have promised to serve the poor sick. . . . Let us be wise, dear sisters, and like the good and faithful servant of the Gospel, mind what we are about. . . . For God alone we must toil and spend our lives; we must wait on the sick to please God and not to follow our miserable self-love, which makes us go through labours, to please creatures and draw a little breath of praise to gratify our foolish self-love. Oh! this is real misery, and might indeed be called insanity." This "purity of intention" was so integral to the religious vocation because to serve the sick poor could easily entail discriminating for intentions contrary to the calling. For example, in Mother Clark's admonition to distribute medicines and food with precision and care and without discriminating against the unworthy patients she warned the sisters "not to depend upon" secular nurses or other employees "to give remedies and nourishment. Such persons love money more than conscience and have always their favorites; they would without scruple, give the best of everything to those they like and neglect others."[29] Selfish intentions were in opposition to the purity of intention so central to their calling as religious.

The section on preparing and distributing medicines was detailed, as it was the only nursing instruction prior to assignment to an infirmary or almshouse. The guiding principle was to establish a routine. "Order promotes peace of conscience and makes us happy; but disorder generally creates unhappiness, troubles the conscience, offends God, and grieves those around us." The practical consequence of order was that the sisters' manifold duties will be fulfilled with economy and graciousness.

The instructions included a section on mixing drugs properly and purchasing medicines that were the "best and never get indifferent things because they are cheap; nor even when given free of cost." The nursing sister should also "foresee the wants of her poor sick and never wait till her patient asks for a drink, or to be changed, or to have the bed and pillows fixed, etc. She sees all that without being asked. . . . There are some patients who are afraid to give trouble, or sometimes think it more perfect or agreeable to God not to ask for what they need . . . of what a relief is not a cooling drink? Oh! give it, and wait not till it is asked." Mother Clark urged the sisters to remember the thirst of Jesus on the cross. "Oh! then go with a holy faith and joy; cool the parched lips and burning thirst of that poor sick patient and see our Jesus smiling on you,—hear his words 'I was thirsty and you gave me to drink.'"[30]

The sister was instructed never to "speak in a loud tone of voice to her poor sick. A few words said in a mild firm tone (when the case requires it) will do a great deal more good than many rude, loud, quick words." Gentleness ought to accompany all the actions of a sister: "hurried, bois-terous movements, noise with chair, beds, basins and dishes in the apart-ments of the sick is very annoying and frets the poor patients, creates or increases head-ache, and may disturb the peace of mind and prevent the effects of medicines." To perceive the relationship of the patients' envi-ronment to the treatment of illness was a concern of the day, but Mother Clark's views appear more advanced and could be included in a histori-cal introduction to a chapter in a modern text on hospital ecology.

Attention to the "holistic" character of treatment was evident in Mother Clark's chapter on new patients. After determining the nature of the illness and the need for a physician, the sister was to be concerned with "many little things that can be done by way of relief without increas-ing the disease or hurting the patient." She suggested a cool or warm drink or "bathing the head." Such "little attentions to a newcomer" may have "admirable effects and make great impressions on these poor suf-fering and dejected beings. Charity carries with it a soothing balm, something not earthly, and can never fail to produce happy results, if not on the body, at least on the mind." She referred to her own experience of the "neglect" of concern for the "newcomer." She refers to the "inexperi-enced infirmarian," one who has not learned "the blessed art of taking care of the sick," as likely to overlook the needs of the new patients. "Oh, for God's sake, if ever you have the care of the sick be kind and attentive to all. Above all to those who are yet unacquainted with the pure motives by which you are actuated. Whenever it was said to our dear Lord 'Such *a one is sick*', how quickly he would reply: 'Let us go to him.'—and would even leave his most important instructions. Do the same and God will bless you."[31]

Sisters were dependent on male employees to attend to the mens' wards but the sisters administered medicines and meals. Mother Clark, conscious of the sisters' vow of chastity, instructed them not even to feel the pulses of the male patients.

Under the title "On the modesty, prudence and religious spirit which should always adorn a person *consecrated to God*," Mother Clark comments on the sisters' responsibilities related to the direct spiritual care of the patients. Indeed they were to be perceived as religious symbols rather than *women* religious. "The eyes of a sister should never rest upon any man's face; she should merely give the look that charity demands of her, and see . . . if the patient looks better or worse and that will suffice. A patient should be able to say, when a Sister leaves his bedside, 'That Sister is more like an angel than a human being:—The very sight of her makes me think of God and love him.'" Purity of intention, a foundational virtue of the sister-nurse, blended with angelic, "disembodied" purity to convey God's presence to male patients, who were potentially subversive to both forms of purity. The angel image, as noted earlier, was imposed on the heroic life of sister-nurses to illustrate their crucial role in the conversion of Protestant patients. Mother Clark implied this role when she noted that the sisters' angelic image would turn men's thoughts to love of God. It is interesting to note that many men's religious communities also stipulated that brothers and priests were to keep "the modesty of the eyes" by never looking directly into the eyes of a woman.

The Sister of Charity was to be ready with a "few words of instruction and encouragement said with piety and in a proper manner"; then patients may be more reconciled with their "miseries" and may sense their religious duties. "A Sister can do a great deal of good when she keeps herself in the presence of God and sees him in all those poor creatures about her." To be assured that Catholic patients receive the "consolations of religion" a sister should greet new patients first with all the physical comforts and then say "'of what religion are you my good friend?' If he says: 'I am a Protestant'—she should say nothing more but give him all the temporal assistance he needs." A sister should not mention the Catholic faith "because some of these poor creatures are very bitter against our holy religion."[32]

In response to a Catholic patient who is critically ill, prudence was to guide the sister's approach. She should be cautious that her references to the afterlife do not emphasize a fear of punishment and thereby cause the patient to experience despair. Mother Clark urged sisters "to speak of the mercies of God, of consolations of our holy religion; and drawing them to God through J. Christ, in pointing out to them the great love of our divine Savior for them; his suffering and death for them; and thus you will neither fatigue nor cause despair and they will be prepared to see the priest when he comes." However, sisters were reminded to respond first to the physical needs of the patient: "Your charity to their bodies will aid them to raise their minds to God." She added the reflection: "The union between the soul and the body is so close that when the latter is suffering a great deal, the other, attentive to its wants, cannot think of anything else."

The final chapter in this instruction manual is entitled "on the meaning *of attending the dying.*" A prefatory note refers to spiritual care of the dying Protestant patient. She is told to "offer silent supplications to the Father of mercies for a death-bed conversion, for a special act of infinite goodness, like that exercised on the penitent thief . . . a last cry for mercy is all she can do for him!" Pluralism tended to inhibit direct convert-making, but "angels of mercy" mediated conversion in compassion and concern for the "little things."

In caring for the religious needs of the dying Catholic, sisters must be always aware of the continuous struggle with the forces of Satan, who are determined to snatch the person from the grips of faith and hope. After informing the priest "of the danger of his penitent" so that the last rites will "not be delayed too long" the sister was instructed to remind the priest of the "*Last Indulgence* which . . . might be entirely forgotten." Mother Clark embarked on a detailed instruction of sisters so that they may "well prepare" their coreligionists for death. It included three pages of prayers to be recited in a solemn tone with frequent pauses to discern the patient's attention and to allow for some respite from the ordeal. Sisters were reminded to light a candle and periodically sprinkle holy water around the bed, "but do not throw the holy water suddenly on the face of the person; it might cause a motion in the nervous system, already agitated enough by the fears and horrors of death." Besides reciting the *Our Father* with a meditation on each phrase, sisters were to join with the patient in an act of "blessed profession of faith" and the baptismal vows. The final prayers included invocation of God's mercy and a litany of particular saints: Mary, Michael, guardian angel, the patient's "holy patrons."

The art of nursing "a person in his last agony" entailed keeping the room quiet, neither praising the edifying life of the patient—lest he become complacent thereby inviting the devil to exploit him in such an unguarded condition—nor admonishing him of his "past faults" that could engender despair. "Oh, who can tell the mysteries of death, what passed these moments!! Prayers only ought to be heard at the couch of the dying." Persons should not "crowd around the bed; it obstructs the air too much; for one who is panting for breath, this must be very painful." When the patient expired sisters were instructed "not to close the mouth or disturb the corpse for a half hour or more because sometimes we think the person is dead and he is not yet. . . . In laying out the corpse make sure there is no exposure."[33]

As a wife and mother who nursed her husband and son, Mother Clark had early experienced care of the dying. The principles of order, efficiency, gentleness, calm sensitivity, and an intuitive sense of nursing (nurturing) were, in one sense, traditional ("other") womanly virtues cultivated in the home. The art of nursing reflected the mother's ingenuity to be attentive to the "little things" and to discern the relationships between the physical and the psychic, the body and the soul, treatment of illness and concern for emotional well-being. Portions of Clark's rendering of the ideal nursing sister were close to those contained in middle-class culture's definition of the ideal mother. The cult of domesticity was not fully developed as an ideology in the first half of the nineteenth century, but characteristics of the ideal mother had been cultivated in the popular press by 1840. According to a French writer, published in the *U.S. Catholic Magazine*, women's calling was to motherhood, and women religious were portrayed as representing "maternity of the spirit."[34] Joseph Menard interpreted strands of the anti-Catholic animus aimed at women religious as derived in part from nascent feminists, such as Catharine Beecher, who considered sisters as slavish papists incapable of independent thought. Menard viewed the male anticonvent rhetoric as rooted in an opposite characteristic; convents were unnatural communities of single women. These males were proponents of the "natural" domestic arrangements, with the woman in the home headed by a man. Despite the complexity of the term domesticity, the hospital was indeed the sisters' home where they formed a family atmosphere within a larger household composed of the working-class staff and the sick poor dependent on the sister nurse, who cared for all their needs as mothers care for their physical families. Mother Clark never referred to the families of the patients; the sick poor had only the people in the hospital or infirmary as their family, and the nursing sister was "the angelic mother." In a sense, this attitude reflects the males' perceptions of sister-nurses as "angels of mercy" articulated during the cholera epidemics and later during the Civil War.

Domestic Medicine, the title of a manual for care of the sick at home, was written by William Buchan and published in Edinburgh in 1769 and in Philadelphia in 1771. Aimed at the elitism of the physician, Buchan's manual was "a general exposition of the causes and prevention of disease, and a detailed description of the symptoms and treatment of specific disorders."[35] According to customs in the domestic economy, women were responsible for caring for the sick, were expected to maintain a supply of medicines, and were frequently dependent on a particular woman in the community who was considered especially skilled. Buchan and others, such as John C. Gunn (author of an 1830 work, *Domestic Medicine*), provided the mother with a simplified guide for nursing the sick, directives that were secular and free from reference to divine causation.[36] As noted earlier, there was a widespread moral interpretation of the degeneration of illness, and such ethical views entered these manuals.

There is no evidence that Clark had any familiarity with these works but relied rather on the collective wisdom handed down from mother to daughter. Her several references to physicians (there were three physicians and four surgeons on the staff of the Baltimore Infirmary in 1823) and her detailed instructions on the preparation of medicines indicate that the sisters were participating in a nursing context that represents a new stage in the nascent professionalization of medicine. There were resident medical students; indeed, the University of Maryland, to which the infirmary was attached, graduated fifty-one students in 1829.[37] Granville Sharp Pattison, the physician in charge of the infirmary, became chair of surgery at the university in 1820 and had published several articles on aneurysm. Born in Glasgow, he received his medical diploma in 1791 from the university of that city in 1820. Pattison was professor of surgery at the University of London for ten years.[38]

The year Mother Clark penned her manual, 1841, the population of Baltimore was at 102,313 with only eighty-two physicians. In February of that year the University College of Pharmacy was incorporated. Perhaps in composing the instruction manual Clark benefitted from the advice of sisters who had been missioned to the Baltimore Infirmary.

II

As will be noted in the next chapter, the cholera epidemic of 1832 expanded the sisters' mission in Baltimore, where they cared for sick and dying in the city almshouse known as Maryland Hospital. After the epidemic the Emmitsburg community and the city of Baltimore agreed that the sisters would remain there and take charge of the hospital, primarily a facility for the mentally ill. The sisters were told that they were responsible for the general administration of the hospital, but, since the agreement was not in writing, there were several conflicts on the spheres of authority between the physicians and the sisters. Sister Olivia McTaggert wrote to Louis Regis Deluol, the Sulpician superior of the Sisters of Charity:[39]

> I do not know when the Board will meet, but am very anxious to have the agreement written, we are subjected to much inconvenience from the Patients, without having the Doctor to contend with & if Drunkards can go in & out without the Sisters' permission I think it a very improper place for us to be—. . .[40]

The physician board approved rules regulating the discipline of the hospital, which, unlike those governing the Baltimore Infirmary, gave the doctors rather than the sisters final authority. This was an intolerable situation for a religious community grounded in self-determination. Consequently, Deluol concluded that the board of physicians "had resolved to make slaves of the Sisters."[41] He gave notice that the sisters would leave at the end of September 1840. In October 1840, Elizabeth Seton's community established their own mental hospital, Mount St. Vincent's, on a ten-acre site west of Baltimore, a facility that housed eighteen patients whose families preferred the sisters' care to that of Maryland Hospital.

In November of 1841, the hospital was visited by a W. G. Read, who was investigating mental hospitals for the State of New York, concerned about the administration and general direction of such institutions. Read's report on this first Catholic mental hospital is a remarkable testimony to the sisters' blend of compassion and "professional" care:

> The sisters never use blows or a strait jacket, which they consider extreme harassment. . . . The usual mode of restraining the violent is with a sort of sleeve, invented by themselves, as I understood, and which is attached to a frock body, made to lace up behind, like a lady's corset. The sleeves are some inches longer than the arm, closed at the end and drawn around the body and fastened behind. Festoons in front support the arms as in slings, and prevent the distressing weariness that would otherwise be experienced. A coat or dress over the whole conceals the restraints, so that other patients are not aware of them, as they find their patients excessively sensitive to the observation and opinion of others . . .
>
> Solitary confinement and precautionary restraints used elsewhere the Sisters say causes the mind to prey upon itself; they prefer, as far as pos-

sible, the restraint of their own presence and companionship to actual bonds. . . .

Treat them as rational beings, converse with them as such, endeavor to conceal every symptom of distrust. Occasionally lead them to converse upon the theme of their derangement, rather than leave this sorrow uncommunicated. Gradually gaining their confidence, endeavor to insinuate more rational ideas. Sometimes let two communicate with each other freely . . . sympathy is thus excited instead of the morbid selfishness of the insane.

Occupation is important; light labor . . . adds to self respect. In cases of sullen withdrawal, under the direction of the physician [the sisters administer] some slight bodily annoyances, as a blister, cupping, mild cathartic to draw attention and prevent the mind from preying on itself.[42]

The report also included favorable commentary on the diversity of activities for St. Vincent's patients, such as bowling, sewing, outings to shops, and an abundance of reading material. He concluded that "the sisters combine natural tenderness with a supernatural motive of divine love, the softness of domestic affection with the firmness of a stranger."[43]

St. Vincent's fulfilled such a growing need that a new building was purchased in 1844, a school with the name of Mt. Hope, which because of its connotation of recovery was kept as the name of the new mental hospital located in a pastoral setting north of Baltimore. In an article on Mt. Hope, published in 1847, just three years after its opening, Dr. W. M. Stokes, the principal physician at the hospital, described the architecture and setting of the asylum, which "commands an extensive view of the adjacent country, the field of vision embracing hill and valley, wood and water in their most gracious combination. . . . We have been particularly anxious to deprive the institution of everything partaking of a prison like appearance, and have aimed to assimilate it, as far as possible, *to any ordering abode of domestic ease and refinement*" (his italics). Stokes emphasized the dual nature of the institution; it was for both the mentally and the physically ill. This was intended to assure the mental patient that he or she had not been entirely removed from social interaction with ordinary people: "Nothing . . . tends more to restore the balance of the disordered mind, than this application to it of the sound intelligent mind. . . . Now the certain offset of their being brought into contact with the same and allowed free intercourse with them, when their condition admits of it, is to call into play, and sustain in vigorous exercise, whatever remains of intellect and feeling in each case."[44] Stokes reflected the general notion that by developing a proper human and physical environment based upon the principles of kindness and employment, there would be a therapeutic and often curative effect on most patients.

In 1847 Mt. Hope cared for one hundred people, fifteen to twenty were charity patients. There were twenty-two sisters on the staff. This community of women religious was, according to Stokes, responsible for the "moral treatment" that pervaded the entire "system of treatment."

> That a spirit of *kindness* and *benevolence* pervades this institution, no one can doubt who is acquainted with the *Sisters of Charity*. These virtues, kindness and benevolence, are the direct emanations and blessed fruits of that enlightened and universal *charity* which they so beautifully illustrate by their lives, and which has its imperishable root in the Christian religion. In possessing the services of the Sisters of Charity, this institution enjoys a lofty and enviable preeminence. This, in truth, constitutes its distinguishing and crowning glory. For, in an institution for the insane, it is impossible to estimate too highly the importance of possessing a corps of faithful and competent attendants. Nothing can compensate for the want of them. However gorgeous and imposing may be the architectural embellishments of its buildings—whatever the ability, zeal and activity of the physician—it is at least, on the character of the attendants that must mainly depend almost every thing relating to the moral management of the patient, as well as his general comfort and well-being. Unless they are humane, cheerful, good-natured, and capable of entering heartily into the views of the physician, the patient will necessarily be deprived of most important aids to his recovery. How is it to be expected that the uneducated hirelings, who, for the most part, enlist in this service in most institutions, can possess these essential endowments of the mind and heart. . . . In the *sisters* we have found associated a combination of qualities admirably adapting them for this responsible and delicate duty. By their exalted piety—by their controlling sense of responsibility to the all seeing God—by their refined taste and cultivated minds, they possess the very attributes most necessary to constitute faithful, efficient and skillful attendants on the insane. In a word they possess, in an eminent degree, all those endowments of the mind and heart, requisite to insure the fulfillment of all the requirements of that *law of humanity and kindness*, which should be the pervading genius of every lunatic asylum.[45]

In 1847 Sister Matilda Coskery was "Sister Servant" or superior of Mount Hope. She was a sister of Father Henry Coskery, rector of the Baltimore cathedral during this time and a representative of the Maryland tradition of openness to the larger culture. In her retirement years Sister Coskery taught the young sisters a course in nursing. This was prior to 1873, the year when the first nurses' training school was established in the United States and many years before the first Catholic training school was opened in 1886. The notes for her class, entitled "A Manual for the Care of the Sick," include a long section on the proper care and treatment of those patients suffering from mania *a potu* (the milder stage of which is delirium tremens) and from other emotional and mental illnesses.[46] Steeped in years of experience, the directives on the care of acute stages of alcoholism include concern that the patients have "no intention of hurting themselves. . . . Insane and delirious persons [have the tendency to destroy] themselves . . . as soon as they find their friends are determined to take them from home . . . but in the mania a potu if the thought or desire to destroy himself exists, he will do it in any manner, even to beat his brains out against the wall if left alone." The "student nurses" were instructed to "never reproach those suffering from intoxication, for their own thoughts are often more than they can bear . . . in most cases it is better to console them saying that others have reformed from this vice or habit." Coskery described the alcoholics' periods of despair: "at times they think hell flames all around them and they reproach themselves and deplore the shame, disgrace they bring upon their friends too; and the loss of their souls." In such cases nurses should respond with kindness and the "mildest persuasion."[47]

Coskery seems to have considered alcoholism both an illness and an immoral habit, but in either case pastoral care was the pressing concern of the sisters.

> For God's sake do not laugh at them or suffer others to treat them with contempt, though this shd be the hundredth time he has been brought to yr. care, you may save the soul the last time, and this done, all is right. Perhaps, crushed by frowns at home, he hopes to find pity from the Daughters of Charity as channels of mercy from Jesus & pity from Mary, & cheered and sustained by you, he may, like Magdelaine rise to fall no more, instead of leaving this life Judas, saying: only hell remains for me.—Tell them to take courage, that this will pass off, and they must now resolve to serve God and pray for grace to avoid falling again.—that they must now do as the Dr. & Srs. tell them and all will soon be right, that they will then go home and give their dear friends great happiness by showing them how well they will do the remainder of their lives.[48]

Under the rubric "A Few Remarks on Insanity," Coskery introduced the students to the contents of printed forms for interviewing the relative or friend of a new admission to the hospital—today's "intake" session. Primarily a series of questions, the form included concern for physical and emotional problems such as:

> What is his age? How long since you first saw a change in him? What was it that made you fear that something was wrong with him? What did he do or say that made you think so? Was he ever this way before this time? How

long ago & how long did it last? How old was he then? What did you think caused it then? Had he had trouble of any kind, or sickness & what sickness & of how long standing. Is he married? Is his wife living or how long dead? Did other deaths occur that distressed him greatly? Had he differences with members of his own family or neighbors? How did he behave during this disagreement? Is he kind in his family? Had he loss of property or injustices done him, or spiteful enemies that talked hard of him? How did he bear these things? Was he disappointed in his affections? What was his general health before this strangeness came on? Are any of his Relations in this way? Was he much with them, & how did it affect him? What was his appetite before this, & how is it now? How much did he use to sleep, & how much now? Was he often from home? Was he a drinking man, & how long & what was his usual condition? How long since he quit it? Has he smoked, chewed or snuffed Tobacco greatly? & how long since he quit it, or is he a great snuffer yet? Did or does he chew opium, or has he used laudanum or Paregoric often? Has he quit these & how long ago? and is there a change in him since? Was he free & pleasant among his friends, or sad & gloomy before this? Does he desire to be alone now? What seems to be his greatest desire? Desire to wander from home? Seen to fear friends? Does he hate or love some one particularly? Who is that one? How long has he had a Drs. care & what was done for Him? Was he bled, cupped, blistered, leeched etc.? How often or has he lost much blood in any way? Has he been dieted, how long & what was the kind of food & how much was he allowed & how much did he take, or did or does he still desire more food than the Dr. allowed him? Was he freely purged? What used to be the state of the bowels & what are they now? Did the Dr. order opiates, how much & how did they seem to affect him & how long did he use them, & how long since he quit them? How was he different in taking or not taking them? Does he or has he at any time since he did so, wished he were dead? Has he tried to hurt others? or himself? and how?[49]

The manual refers to what "best writers on Insanity say: that *kindness* is the *main remedy*, because this method treats them as if they are *sane*; this excites to self-respect, often the poor patient thinks there is something wrong with him. . . . This bright hope makes him try to deport himself in the best manner, he suppresses rising emotions. . . . They forever remember what bitter things were said to them. . . . They are always *depressed* at remembering the contempt or hard things said to them."[50]

With a deep sense of the threads of divine providence woven into the fabric of human life Sister Coskery said that kindness and gentleness will earn respect and the sisters will be viewed as "angels of consolation, and each paroxysm [of severe depression] will be lighter, as they recollect your tender compassion for them. . . . We should bear in mind that God leaves us our reason, whilst he takes it from our patient, but shall we outrage this God of Charity by making a *cruel* use of ours over His poor servant, who without sense, is put under our care by Him? Or will we by anger, add our own violence to theirs?"[51] Once again, the "angel" imagery denoted selflessness, mercy, and compassion—the qualities of the sister-healers in the premodern setting.

To calm the patients the nurse or "attendant," as Coskery referred to care givers at Mt. Hope, should refer to the "paroxysms" of acute illness manifested by "bad speeches and manners toward us," as "fevers." For example, if a patient seeks forgiveness for such "improprieties" the attendant should say "Oh, if I had your fever, I might have done far worse, do not think of it." Obviously the therapy was to redirect the downward momentum of negative feelings by the dynamic of positive responses regardless of the behavior, which is named not "insanity" but "fever." Of course this kindness therapy was not only to calm the troubled "fevers" but to compensate for the abuses to which the mentally ill were subjected in the world outside Mt. Hope. The positive responses are "precious words . . . registered in Heaven, as they are on the grateful heart of your poor patient. How then does the Heart of Jesus view them! And if in the course of time, they, or their grateful friends may come to know or embrace the true Religion, it will be because its truths were written in honey. . . . Happy, happy lot of the Sister of Charity [sic], whose duty is, Service to the Insane!"[52] The invocation of the sisters' devotionalism and their role in conversion were intertwined in the hearts of humanity and the Sacred Heart of Jesus.

Mount Hope became so popular that another hospital for the "sick and insane," Mt. Hope Retreat, was opened in 1860 six miles north of the city on Reisterstown Road. The latter was a large institution in the remote countryside that eventually absorbed the other suburban institution. Sister Coskery nursed during the Civil War, and her "Manual on the Care of the Sick" expands our understanding of the origins of Catholic presence in the treatment of the mentally ill.

Though Sister Coskery did not reveal an understanding of the feminist horizon she represents the transition to the professionalization of nursing. Her manual was observant of the cases of mental illness and highlighted the need for training. It was based on her own experiences, independent of the male physicians' instructions.[53]

Domesticity and medical understanding permeate the manuals of Clark and Coskery, but the manual of Clark seems to emphasize the religious sphere. Her emphasis on "purity of motives" illustrates that a total commitment to God implies care for the sick poor without regard for earthly or personal satisfaction. Purity of motive was also intended to deepen one's sense of duty to tolerate those mean and cruel conditions of the nursing environment to which they may be subjected and which were out of the sisters' control. The religious symbolism of the sisters' garb, their prayer with their patients, their care of the mentally and critically ill and dying, which included a strongly ritualistic culture, conveyed a distinctively Catholic identity, one that was at the essence of their call to serve the sick poor as a praying activity.

Andrew White with the Piscataway, John Francis Moranville with the yellow-fever victims in Fells Point, and Mother Mary Xavier Clark and Sister Matilda Coskery represent four strands of the Catholic blend of caring for bodies and souls. Protestants were equally concerned with the physical and pastoral care of the sick, to whom they brought the comforting words of scripture. The Catholic response was made by persons committed to the vowed religious life with its evangelical counsels of poverty, chastity, and obedience; Catholic rituals, symbols, and prayer mediated the religious experience inherent in critical illness.

In the mid-nineteenth century the Baltimore Infirmary stands at the threshold of a new era in the history of medical care, one characterized by the advance of medical education at the University of Maryland. This first encounter of an American community of women religious with a health-care institution reveals a Catholic minority consciousness in a non-Catholic context, a familiarity and a respect for the condition of religious liberty, separation of church and state, voluntarism, and pluralism. American religious conditions engendered among Catholics, as well as Protestants, Jews, and nonbelievers, an active assertion of their beliefs tempered by civility and respect for the freedom of all to stake out their credal claims. Though the sisters conveyed a strong religious commitment, the instructions of Clark and Coskery also manifest a remarkable degree of insight into the psychological dimensions of all treatment and the interrelationships between the physical, emotional, and spiritual needs of their patients. They seem to have dwelt with ease in a pluralistic setting. Unlike the European model of unity of throne and altar with its strong authority structure, American conditions liberated Catholic nurses to respond to sickness with a religious integrity free from the weight of privileges so central to the European tradition. American pluralism tended to foster both a self-consciously Catholic attitude and a consideration of Protestant sensibilities.

CHAPTER THREE

Epidemics: Responses to the Cholera 1832–1850

I

THE FIRST CATHOLIC HOSPITAL west of the Mississippi River was opened in St. Louis, Missouri, on November 28, 1828. Staffed by four Sisters of Charity of Emmitsburg this three-room log cabin represents the origin of the oldest Catholic hospital in the United States continuously sponsored by the same religious community up to the present day. St. Louis was founded in 1764 by Auguste Chouteau, who was associated with Pierre Laclede, an entrepreneur from New Orleans and the man responsible for choosing the site just south of the confluence of the Mississippi and Missouri Rivers. It soon became a thriving center of the fur trade. With the Louisiana Purchase, St. Louis, named by Laclede in honor of Louis IX, was incorporated into the United States.[1]

In 1812 Archbishop John Carroll appointed Louis William DuBourg, S.S., as administrator for Louisiana and Florida with residence in New Orleans. Because he confronted several ecclesiastical problems, particularly among the clergy, DuBourg went to Rome in 1815 to seek support for his tenuous authority in New Orleans. As a result Pope Pius VII appointed him bishop, and he recruited Vincentian priests to help alleviate a severe shortage of diocesan clergy. Because of continuous conflict in New Orleans the new bishop moved his episcopal residence to St. Louis, where he brought four Religious of the Sacred Heart to establish a school for girls (Sr. Rose Philippine Duchesne founded the first school in St. Charles, Missouri). He also encouraged the Jesuits to settle there where they founded St. Louis Academy, which in 1828 became a university. In 1824 the Vincentian Joseph Rosati, C.M., was named DuBourg's coadjutor. Two years later DuBourg resigned because of exhaustion and returned to France where he was appointed the ordinary of the diocese

of Montauban. Shortly before his death in 1828 he was appointed archbishop of Bésançon.[2]

St. Louis was established as an independent diocese in 1826 with
Joseph Rosati, C.M., as its first bishop. In 1830 the diocese numbered
some forty thousand Catholics in a vast area stretching from the Great
Lakes to the southern border of Arkansas and from the Rocky Mountains
to the Mississippi River. In the vicinity of St. Louis, Catholics numbered
about three thousand out of a population of eight thousand.

The Female Charitable Society, founded in 1823 and, characteristic of
the frontier experience, composed of women of Catholic and Protestant
denominations, had urged the foundation of a hospital responsible for
poor relief in the town. This Society engendered preliminary discussion
between DuBourg and Charles Nerinckx, founder and superior of the
Sisters of Loretto at the Foot of the Cross in the diocese of Bardstown,
Kentucky. Though Nerinckx responded positively, the sisters were too
immersed in teaching to take up nursing. After some delay Rosati
approached Simon Bruté at Mt. St. Mary's in Emmitsburg in the hope
that the Sulpician would personally represent the bishop in his request
for three Sisters of Charity to staff a hospital in St. Louis. In a second letter Rosati enthusiastically informed Bruté that the hand of Providence
had secured financial assistance for the hospital. "Without having said
a word, a very rich man offered a very beautiful piece of ground with two
houses in the city of St. Louis. He will give besides another lot with other
houses that will bring a revenue of six hundred dollars a year. He will
give one hundred and fifty dollars for the journey of the sisters, three
hundred and fifty to furnish the house."[3] The generous benefactor was
John Mullanphy, an Irish-American millionaire, who made his fortune in
the fur trade. This association of a bishop and a wealthy Catholic phi-
lanthropist did not form a characteristic pattern; it rather represents a
minor trend in the history of Catholic health care.

On November 5, 1828 four Sisters of Charity arrived in St. Louis to
take charge of the hospital, which was not ready for patients until
November 28. Officially entitled St. Louis Hospital, it was frequently
referred to as Mullanphy Hospital. Of course Rosati, a Vincentian of the
religious family of Vincent de Paul and Louise de Marillac's Daughters
of Charity, was very pleased to have the American sisters modeled after
the Daughters in his diocese.

The hospital was a three-room log cabin, with the sisters living in the
kitchen area so that the two remaining rooms would be for patients. After
an inauspicious beginning the hospital soon became too small for the

needs of the city. In 1830 Bishop Rosati wrote to the Leopoldine Foundation in Austria, a strong source of funds for American missionary endeavors. He described the hospital ministry of the sisters: "This is the means Divine Providence makes use of in order to preserve the lives of a number of laborers, sailors, negroes and others, who are received gratis, and treated with kindness and solicitude."[4] With the help of John Mullanphy and other benefactors the sisters and patients moved into a brick building that could accommodate sixty patients. The new facility opened in 1832, the year of a cholera epidemic in St. Louis and many cities throughout the nation.

According to Charles E. Rosenberg, cholera was to the nineteenth century what the plague was to the fourteenth century. Originally restricted to the Far East it struck eastern Europe in 1817, and because of economic and social interaction in trade and emigration the disease spread westward. American scientists, physicians, and public health officials studied its trek toward North America but were not excessively alarmed because they considered the United States to be relatively free from the conditions of urban filth and decay prevalent in Europe. However, there was widespread effort to impede its spread by restricting imports and travel from European ports. The largest and most vulnerable city was New York, where public health precautions were too little too late.[5]

Though fatalities from malaria and tuberculosis were more numerous than cholera, the latter struck with a dramatic immediacy; most victims died within a day after contagion. Its cause, a bacteria that attacks the intestinal system, was discovered in 1883; by this time the disease had ravaged American cities during 1832, 1848-49, 1850-54, and 1866. Rosenberg traced the disease within social and religious contexts; he notes that the "most striking of changes in America between 1832 and 1866 was the dissipation of the piety still so characteristic of many Americans in the Age of Jackson. The evangelical fervor of this earlier generation had been eroded by a materialism already present in 1832, but seemingly triumphant by 1866." Simultaneous with the "dissipation of piety" was the development of a "critical and empirical temper" that was not limited to physicians but manifested among journalists and ministers. "Cholera, a scourge of the sinful to many Americans in 1832, had, by 1866, become the consequence of remediable faults of sanitation."[6]

Many physicians, preachers, and lay people viewed the epidemic's cause as a blend of gross misbehavior, particularly among the prostitutes, the Irish immigrants, and African Americans both slave and free. Since these people dwelled in the slums where bacteria thrived, the death statistics verified these social and religious biases. In what Rosenberg calls "the doctrine of predisposing causes" there was a convergence of the popular attitudes and professional opinion that "cholera was a scourge not of mankind but of the sinner."[7]

The *Western Sunday School Messenger* included the following explanation of the epidemic in the editor's weekly column:

> *Drunkards and filthy wicked people of all descriptions,* are swept away in *heaps,* as if the Holy God could no longer bear their wickedness, just as we sweep away a mass of filth when it has become so corrupt we can not bear it. . . . The cholera is not *caused* by intemperance and filth, in themselves, but it is a *scourge,* a *rod* in the hand of God. . . .[8]

Traditional clergymen said that God did not cause cholera, but it was nonetheless symbolic of divine displeasure; "enlightened" ministers stressed humanity's violations of the laws of nature, that is, living in squalor, as the primary cause. Hence, Rosenberg concludes that the doctrine of predisposing causes promoted the belief that both supernatural and natural forces were responsible for the pestilence.

While many civic and religious leaders were calling for fasting and prayer, President Andrew Jackson and the governor of New York refused to support the proposal for a day of repentance on the grounds that it would violate the principle of separation of church and state. Traditionalists viewed their refusals as a sign of moral decadence.[9] In a pastoral letter, dated June 29, 1832, Archbishop James Whitfield of Baltimore provided a Catholic response to the epidemic. Opening with a plea that all Catholics join him "in prayer and supplication that God may avert the scourge from us," Whitfield asked, "who does not see in this plague the finger of God? Yes, it is the scourge of the Lord, whose wrath is enkindled against the nations of the earth. And should we not fear this Supreme King of nations? Are we less guilty than the millions of men the cholera has cut off in other parts of the globe? . . . Unless we do penance we may in like manner perish." Hence he urged all his people to commit themselves to "doing penance, . . . calling for mercy and abounding in every good work."[10] Whitfield's emphasis on the Catholic paths to grace—faith, good works, the sacraments, and the intervention of the saints—were countervailing forces denied by the Protestant reformers, who charted the road to righteousness along the lines of individual virtue and the will of God.

Hence, Whitfield struck a chord of hope: "Christians! if these be days of alarm and terror, they are also days of mercy and salvation, and particularly for sinners. The fear of an attack of cholera, that strikes all of a sudden, and kills in two or three hours, is a powerful motive to persuade men, guilty of mortal sin, to approach the sacraments." The archbishop's pastoral also reflects a common Christian notion of predisposing causes: ". . . a good conscience and a regular virtuous life are, even according to the physicians, the first and best preserve against the cholera." Whitfield urged all Catholics to attend Mass and instructed the clergy to offer one Mass with the intention of "appeasing God's wrath and averting the pest." He recommended that "a public mass be celebrated, if possible, on the fourth of July," in accord with the proclamation of the governor of Maryland that this be "a day of Thanksgiving to the almighty for the great political liberty we have enjoyed, and for all the mercies he has vouchsafed to us, as well as to offer up our prayers for a continuance of same, and that he may be graciously pleased to arrest or mitigate the threatened calamity." Whitfield closed with the statement that before the principal Mass on Sundays and weekdays, the Litany of the Blessed Virgin was to be said, "that through her intercession our petitions may meet with a more favorable reception."[11]

The following October, Whitfield suffered from the cholera. He was nursed by Sister Anthony Duchemin, an Oblate Sister of Providence, a community of African Americans founded three years earlier in Baltimore. Whitfield survived the ordeal, but Sister Anthony was fatally struck by cholera the day after she began nursing the archbishop's housekeeper. Her daughter, Sister Theresa Maxis Duchemin, joined the community before Sister Anthony and became superior. In 1845 Sister Theresa left and subsequently became one of the founders of the Servants of the Immaculate Heart of Mary of Monroe, Michigan.[12] Because she was a woman of color she was forced to leave the latter community.

Sister Anthony had been one of the four Oblate Sisters of Providence who volunteered to nurse at the Baltimore almshouse that was designated as the cholera hospital. A trustee of the Bureau of the Poor and a young doctor explained to Father J. H. Joubert, S.S., the Sulpician founder and director of the community, that they had hoped for eight Sisters of Charity to staff the hospital, but only four were assigned. Having heard of the recent foundation "of a society of religious colored women" they sought four Oblate Sisters to complete their staffing needs. In the diary for that day Father Joubert recorded his response: "I replied to these gentlemen that the Sisters of Charity were by the spirit of their institute obliged to look after the sick, but that the Sisters of Providence were not, as they are obliged to the education of young girls of their color." Hence, he informed them that he would seek volunteers rather

than require sisters to depart from their rule. The entire community volunteered, so Joubert chose four who left for the hospital the next morning. However, he informed the authorities that the sisters should be
assigned to their own sections of the hospital rather than be associated
with the Sisters of Charity.[13] Though the two communities had some con-
tacts, it appears that Joubert was sensitive to the conflict inherent in
assigning whites and blacks to work together on an equal basis.

There were three cholera hospitals in Baltimore. Five Sisters of Charity served at the cholera hospital No. 2, the former almshouse; three
nursed at hospital No. 3 a few blocks south of St. Mary's Seminary, and
four sisters were transferred from an orphan asylum to the new almshouse two miles north of the city. The Oblates nursed at the latter institution, which housed over two hundred cholera patients.[14] The critical
period at the almshouse lasted for about a month. In a letter dated
September 25, 1832, Archibald Sterling, secretary for the Trustees for the
Poor, extended the board's gratitude for the "Colored Sisters of Providence for the assistance kindly and charitably rendered by them in nursing the cholera patients in the almshouse."[15] Rather than write directly
to the sisters, Sterling communicated to them through their director,
Father Joubert. However, the Oblates were still subjected to public abuse,
even from Catholics, who considered African Americans as inherently
unfitted for the religious life.

The Sisters of Charity left the almshouse for the orphan asylum, but
those sisters at the two cholera hospitals remained until late October.
Cholera fatally struck Sister M. Frances Boarman on August 30, 1832.
One of the Baltimore weeklies recorded that her death "caused a lively
sensation. She was one of those ministering angels who had volunteered
their services, under a lofty sense of duty to God and man, to nurse the
sick and comfort the dying. . . . Her remains were attended to the grave
by the mayor and members of the board of health. . . ."[16] (This is the first
reference to sisters as "angels," in conformity to ideals of the "other" sex;
their duties included compassionate, selfless service, the disembodied
ideal or model of virtuous womanhood.)

Sister Mary George Smith died from cholera on September 19. Just
twenty-one years old, she was eulogized in a Baltimore newspaper daily;
"[she is] one of those admirable ladies, who are truly denominated Sisters of Charity. . . . There is a sublimity in the virtue of these pius [sic]
ladies, which we all can and do admire, but which few have the courage
to imitate!"[17] After the cholera epidemic terminated, the mayor and city
council of Baltimore resolved to memorialize Sisters M. Frances Boarman

and Mary George Smith by erecting a vault for their remains upon which was laid a marble slab "with a suitable inscription . . . in testimony of the respect and gratitude of the corporation."[18]

This display of gratitude was no doubt sincere as there were several cities and towns who were compelled to pay high salaries not to angels of mercy but to "mercenaries, who appear to possess as much sympathy or humanity as the walls," as Rosenberg, who was unaware of the Oblate Sisters' role, remarked on the contribution of the nursing sister. "Only the Sisters of Charity could be depended upon to serve faithfully; in Philadelphia, Baltimore, Louisville [the Sisters of Charity of Nazareth, Kentucky], St. Louis and Cincinnati, they staffed the cholera hospitals, working with little sleep or food until the epidemic subsided."[19]

During these cholera years, the home was still the principal place of caring for the critically ill and the lame. Domestic medicine, though normally monitored by the mother of the family, fostered a volunteer network of care givers. The African-American Catholic layman, Pierre Toussaint, was an activist on the domestic medical network in the black community of New York. Born into slavery in the French colony of Santo Domingo (Haiti) in 1766, he was brought to the United States by the Berard family in flight from revolutionary unrest. Privileged status in the Berard household allowed him the opportunity to achieve a modicum of learning so that after he had received his freedom and had passed an apprenticeship as a hairdresser he became an independent man of some means. Though he was unpretentiously very charitable, the abundance of his extant letters testify to the widespread recognition of Toussaint's many acts of charity and kindness. He also nursed those struck by epidemics. In his history of Black Catholics Cyprian Davis cites the following story:

> One lady mentions that when the yellow fever prevailed in New York, by degrees Maiden Lane was almost wholly deserted, and almost every house in it was closed. One poor woman, prostrated by the terrible disorder, remained there with little or no attendance, till Toussaint day by day came through the lone street, crossed the barricades, entered the deserted house where she lay, and performed the nameless offices of nurse, fearlessly exposing himself to contagion.[20]

Toussaint also brought several orphans and sick people into his home, where he and his wife Juliette Noel cared for them. On one occasion they nursed a sick priest in their home. Davis notes that "Toussaint attended Mass every morning at 6:00 at St. Peter's Church. Then he would begin his visits to his clients. People enjoyed talking to him and he became the confidant of many. He always walked because blacks were not then allowed to ride the horse-drawn buses. Slavery was finally ended in New York in 1827, twenty years after his own manumission."[21]

Pierre Toussaint's papers, mostly letters to him, provide a rare glimpse into the life of the African-American community; such evidence is also valuable because one may cautiously generalize that the laity played active caring roles in the premodern phase in the social history of medicine. The persistence of racial segregation that was reflected in the hospitals until recently fostered the continuity of domestic medicine in the African-American community long after it had precipitously decreased in the white community. Without a black Catholic clergy and only the Oblate Sisters in Baltimore and later the Holy Family Sisters in New Orleans, the laity formed a domestic church that included networks of home nursing.

II

Black victims of the cholera were nursed in the Catholic hospital in St. Louis. Without nurses to staff the city hospital in St. Louis, cholera patients were sent to the Sisters of Charity hospital. Four priests and a Vincentian brother ministered to the patients during the epidemic. One anonymous sister recorded her experiences during October of 1832:

> On the 25th and 26th, our city presented nothing but a scene of dismal confusion and horror—people fleeing from the town, many leaving their dearest friends to die alone. . . . Never can we forget October 26th! It was Communion Day for us. Our good Bishop said Mass, but we were too much occupied to hear the whole of it, and could come only after consecration. We found the Holy prelate standing at the Holy Table. . . . Turning toward us he said, "Come, dear Sisters, and receive your God. He will be your strength and your courage. He will go with you all the day long and count your steps." I went with the Sacred Host in my mouth. . . . From that time until the 30th and 31st we heard nothing but the feeble groans of the dying. . . . Our worthy priests were all the time busy . . . our sisters . . . nursed day and night, never taking the least rest until, exhausted, nature forced them to do so. . . . Everyone who had health ran away from us.[22]

Several testimonials by the city fathers and doctors praised the sisters' heroic efforts. Mother Rose Philippine Duchesne wrote to a relative: "The Sisters of Charity have won the people of all creeds by their charity."[23] Nevertheless anti-Catholic prejudice persisted in St. Louis; the Western Catholic Association, a group of laymen dedicated to defend Catholicism and promote the Catholic newspaper *Shepherd of the Valley*, was formed the year after the epidemic of 1832.[24] The sisters' hospital became the city hospital until 1846 when a new city hospital received patients. The latter appears to have been an almshouse. Patients were virtually unattended at night. "The only nurses were middle aged women, most often recruited from City Hall charwomen, or recommended by the policemen on the beat."[25]

Prior to the arrival of the Sisters of Charity in 1845, Detroit combatted the cholera epidemic with the help of the Catholic Female Benevolent Society. It was Father Martin Kundig who initiated the society that year. As early as 1817 the Protestants in Detroit had founded a Moral and Humane Society to aid the "worthy poor." The Catholic women's organization was intended to "remove the stigma attached to the Roman Catholic character by Protestant's [sic] from their want of sufficient energy [i.e. Christian motivation] to follow [the Protestant] example."[26]

Influenced by Kundig the society appointed two commissioners to examine the county almshouse, and who reported on "the deplorable situation of the sick. . . ." The Catholic women's organization offered to take charge of the institution and mobilized to meet the needs of the victims. Kundig was "engaged amid the scenes of the suffering" when he heard from the county board of supervisors who, "observing our exertions, proffered . . . to the association the care and supervision of the county poorhouse."[27]

Along with the Catholic Female Benevolent Society Kundig immersed himself in reform and expansion of the poorhouse. Indeed he became a county Supervisor of the Poor. He also had an infirmary built to separate the sick from the chronically indigent, and he found homes for the orphaned. Subsequent to the epidemic, economic recession, followed by the panic of 1837, precluded paying Kundig a salary or even reimbursing him for his expenditures on the infirmary and the orphans. Because Kundig had borrowed money his creditors broke into his rooms and confiscated everything of value. "They sold even the clothes of the 30 orphans."[28] For five years, 1834–1839, the priest served as Superintendent of the Poor and refused to sue for compensation when he retired. He ultimately paid his debts but only after he moved to Milwaukee where he became vicar general of the diocese.

The women's organization helped administer the poorhouse and held two fund-raising events to pay for an orphanage located adjacent to the county institution. Representatives of the "genteel" class, these women adopted a costume that was, according to Leslie Woodcock Tentler, "a compromise between worldly dress and that of certain religious orders."[29]

The costume was "a black dress, white cape, straw bonnet *fashionable* with black ribbon." The Poor Clares moved to Detroit in 1833 and, contrary to their traditional cloistered life, within two years took charge of the administration of the infirmary and orphanage; the women's society appears to have been discouraged from maintaining an independent reform organization. With participation waning, the organization stopped recording minutes in August of 1836. They seem to have become a ladies auxiliary to the Poor Clares. The Poor Clares left Detroit in 1839, and between that date and the arrival of the Sisters of Charity of Emmitsburg in 1845, two women's organizations surfaced to support Catholic charities. When later epidemics occurred the Sisters of Charity responded as they did in Baltimore, Philadelphia, and other cities. In these areas there were also women's benevolent organizations; it seems that they followed the Detroit pattern, from social activism to philanthropy.

When the first epidemic hit the United States the Catholic population numbered almost six hundred thousand. In the 1840s immigration resulting from the great hunger in Ireland and from famine and revolutions in the Austrian Empire and German States in 1848 greatly augmented the Catholic population, reaching nearly 1.25 million when the second scourge struck in 1849. Urban poverty expanded proportionately; gross neglect of sanitation, exacerbated by overcrowding in the slums, meant that conditions were predisposed to a rapid spread of cholera.

Father Pierre DeSmet, S.J., well known for his missionary efforts among native Americans of the Rocky Mountain West, interpreted the spread of the disease in St. Louis in the summer of 1849.

> Imagine a city of seventy thousand inhabitants [population had tripled in size during the 1840s] crowded and packed together in new brick houses, in the dampest and worst drained prairie in existence, undulating, imperfectly drained and interspersed with stink-holes and stagnant waters. The city has hardly a sewer and in the new streets mostly unpaved, all of the offal of the houses runs out or is thrown in the omnipresent mud. Add to this that outside the corporate limits is a dirty mound, a mile or more in circumference. Around this natural *slop-bowl*, at short intervals, you will find breweries, distilleries, oil and white lead factories, flour mills and private residences of Irish and Germans, into this pond goes everything foul— this settles the opinion as to the real cause of the dreadful mortality here.[30]

In these conditions St. Louis lost ten percent of its population to the deadly disease. Rosenberg notes that "Sextons, undertakers, even the horses in St. Louis were exhausted by the sisyphian task of removing and burying the dead."[31]

The Sisters of Charity cared for nearly 1,500 cholera patients during the 1849 epidemic; over five hundred died including two nursing sisters.[32] The Sisters of St. Joseph, who had arrived in St. Louis from France in 1836, also responded to the cholera victims in 1849. They settled in Carondelet, a small village in the southern outskirts overlooking the Mississippi River, an impoverished area referred to as the *Vida Poche* or "empty pocket." In 1849 they had charge of a day school near St. Vincent's Church. The sisters nursed the sick and dying in this heavily afflicted area of the city. Three of the four sisters died of the disease.[33] When the Carondelet Sisters settled in St. Paul, Minnesota, in 1850 their hospital became an asylum for cholera patients.

Of the sixteen communities of women religious in the United States in 1849 five nursed in hospitals. The Sisters of Charity, who would soon merge with the French Daughters of Charity, were in charge of five hospitals; Bishop John Hughes of New York assumed direct control of the Sisters of Charity in his diocese; during the cholera epidemic the New York community founded St. Vincent's Hospital. The Sisters of Charity of Nazareth, founded in 1812 by Catherine Spalding and John B. David, S.S., had nursed cholera patients in Kentucky and Tennessee during the epidemics. Each of two European communities, the Sisters of Mercy and the Sisters of St. Joseph, had charge of one hospital in Pittsburgh and Philadelphia respectively. The size of these hospitals ranged from the old charity hospital in New Orleans, which was a state institution with five hundred patients that the Sisters of Charity staffed since 1834, to the hospital in Pittsburgh where the Sisters of Mercy could accommodate eight patients. Hence during the 1849 epidemic there was a small but effective Catholic presence in contrast to 1832 when only the Sisters of Charity and the Oblate Sisters nursed in city almshouses and special cholera hospitals.[34]

The religious response of Catholic leaders to the cholera epidemic of 1849 varied. Reverend Charles I. White, editor of *The United States Catholic Magazine*, wrote an article, "Reflections for the Time of the Cholera," in which he interpreted the epidemic as a sign of God's wrath. "Nothing can give us a truer idea of the severity of Divine justice in another world, than the chastisement he sometimes exercises in this world by a general scourge. But, after all, God, in scourging men, has principally in view the salvation of his elect." After a lengthy quote from St. Cyprian, White concludes with an admonition to docility. "To have nothing to fear from the cholera, let us do penance, go to confession as for the last time, make our will, and resign ourselves in the hands of God."[35]

White's *Magazine* also reprinted Bishop John Baptist Purcell's pastoral letter to the diocese of Cincinnati. His biographer, M. Edmund Hussey, states that the Irish-born prelate "was by temperament an ebullient optimist with an enormous amount of energy and a great fund of resourceful pragmatism."[36] His predecessor, Bishop Edward Dominic Fenwick, O.P., had died of the cholera in September 1832.[37] Though Purcell interpreted the epidemic within the economy of divine providence as a chastisement and urged all to confess their sins and cease transgressing the laws of God, he concluded that "all have every reason to hope in the justice and mercy of God that the cholera will cease also."[38] In apparent harmony with President Zachary Taylor's call for a national day of prayer and fasting, Purcell called upon the priests to begin "Novenas and other public prayers for the cessation of the pestilence." He praised the Sisters of Charity and his priests for their ministries to the cholera victims. However, nearly half his pastoral letter was concentrated on the social conditions that gave rise to the disease's contagion. Purcell noted that the "mysterious disease . . . falls with peculiar heaviness on the poor, of whom, always, everywhere the great majority of God's elect are composed. Their poverty, which assimilates them to Him who 'knew not where to lay his head,' leaves them no choice of habitation, clothing, food, or labor. They must put up with the damp cellar, the ill-vented garret, the loathsome alley, the coarse fare, the wet unchanged garments after toil and rain."[39] Of course in the cities most of the poor were Catholic. Nearly eighty percent of those who died of cholera in St. Louis were Catholic.[40]

In contrast to Purcell's embrace of the poor as composing a majority of the elect, a typical nativist anti-Catholic interpretation viewed the disease as striking only the unworthy immigrants who were polluting the pure streams of American life. "A very large portion of the foreigners that have come to this country for several years past are vicious and worthless," was a statement with widespread support.[41] According to the Catholic bishop of Cincinnati one of the sins that may have brought on the pestilence was "oppression and insensitivity to the wants and the claims of the poor." He recalls examples from Scripture "that it is not always for the sins of all the people, but frequently for those of their rulers, sometimes for those of a single individual, that God pours out the vials of his wrath on a doomed city and nation."[42]

To alleviate the desperate conditions of the poor, Purcell appealed to the "hearts of the rich and all who are clothed with the temporal authority that by a united and a generous effort . . . [we may wipe out those] filthy and disgusting hovels where the penniless are compelled to congregate." He pleaded for funds "to build up whole streets of comfortable cottages or houses, in sufficient numbers for all who may require them." He referred to the need for a "creating spirit" and appealed to American "genius and practical good sense" to develop a community that would live "in pure air [and] sound health" that would eventually be self-sufficient and a source of revenue. He believed that a combination of "zeal and benevolence . . . unblighted by sectarianism" was the formula for successful community-renewal efforts. An optimist to the core Purcell was also a pragmatist. He commended the Sisters of Charity for assuming care of additional orphans and "our German brethren" for building a new orphanage. He urged families to give shelter to those children whose parents had died of cholera.[43]

Amid the ravages of the cholera epidemic the bishops of the country, gathered at the Third Provincial Council of Baltimore, issued a pastoral letter that referred to the nursing ministries of "The Sisterhoods." Written by John England of Charleston, the letter opens with the remark, "We would especially commend to your fostering care those pius [sic] and meritorious sisterhoods. . . ." The bishops mentioned the sisters' schools and orphanages and then their commitment to "attend the couch of sickness to moisten the burning lip, to assuage the anguish of pain, to whisper consolation to the raving spirit and to point to the true source of the sinner's hope, when in the dimness of his eye he begins to be sensible to the darkness of the grave." England wrote that the sisters' "godlike charity" was manifested in schools, prisons, "in the maniac's call. . . , in the hospital [and] in the midst of pestilence." Obviously the bishops discussed the cholera epidemics; the letter identified the sisters' scene of nursing the pestilent "surrounded by the bodies of the dying and the corpses of the dead."

John England had referred to the growing anti-Catholicism of the 1830s and the need to heal the wounds of division. Implicitly referring to the pornographic literature that portrayed nuns and priests in illicit unions, he noted that the sisters discharged "their duties of their holy zeal, alike to the professor of their faith and to its opponent, and tending with the same assiduity the wretched calumniator of their creed, their virtue and their sex, as they would their most generous defender."[44] With only a few Catholic hospitals in existence in this early period prior to the mass immigration of the 1840s there was no reference to the development of Catholic hospitals to nurture the faith in a hostile world.

The social mission of Catholic orphan asylums originated with the epidemics, but their religious role developed because the public institutions were dominated by a Protestant ethos of protecting children from the superstitions of popery. In such an atmosphere Catholic priests were not welcomed. Though many orphan homes were attached to parishes, there was an increase in diocesan-wide institutions frequently staffed by sisters, many of whom also founded hospitals. In 1850 Catholic hospitals were serving some six thousand patients. Sisters, priests, and lay organizations immersed in ministry to the sick and dying reflected the dominant missionary model of health care: voluntarism, the separation of church and state, and the relative scarcity of sisters, brothers, and priests.

The following excerpt from the description of Milwaukee's St. John's Infirmary in the 1850 *Metropolitan Catholic Almanac* illustrates the adaptability of Catholic tradition in the American context of religious liberty:

> As the Sisters of Charity are to be the only nurses and attendants in the house, none need fear the absence of sympathy, and eager vigilance. The very title and profession of a daughter of St. Vincent de Paul are sufficient guarantees to the public, that there will be no departure from the strictest order, the greatest cleanliness, and the most unremitting attention.
>
> Any patient may call for any clergyman he may prefer. But no minister, whether Protestant, or Catholic, will be permitted to preach to, to pray aloud before, or interfere religiously with, such patients as do not ask for the exercise of his office. The rights of conscience must be held paramount to all others.[45]

The first wave of immigration during the pre-1850 period had not yielded a strong Catholic institutional fabric in health care. That process would occur in the post Civil War period when medical science, nursing education, and the rise in immigration brought about the proliferation of Catholic hospitals and nursing schools.

The transition from the missionary to the immigrant model, the topic of the next chapter, occurs during the 1850-1875 period and was characterized by Catholicism on the expanding frontier in the West and South, and by the urban Catholicism developing in the East and Midwest. The profound impact of the Civil War on both the urban core and the frontier periphery was not limited to the religious history of the Catholic community, as the war was also the harbinger of significant change in the general developments of nursing and medicine.

·CHAPTER FOUR·

Catholic Benevolence

I

THE CHOLERA EPIDEMIC of 1849 exposed the critical need for hospitals to meet the needs of a burgeoning urban population subjected not only to the vagaries of epidemic illnesses but to the deplorable conditions in factories, railroads, canals, and mines. Hence, immigration, industrialization, and urbanization necessitated the growth of hospitals. For example, in 1850 New York and Boston had only one voluntary hospital. Consequently, many sick, particularly among the immigrant population, were sent to the almshouse with its diversified pauper population. Twenty-five years later New York had eight voluntary hospitals and four specialized institutions. The pattern was replicated throughout urban America during this period, 1850–1875.[1] Had hospitals not kept pace with the increasing need of the "worthy" sick, the "pauperization" process would have been terribly exacerbated. The founders of Hartford Hospital viewed their institution within this process. "One member of the family becomes sick. The watching, nursing, and increased expense impoverished them, in consequence of which they must all be provided for at the almshouse. If the sick person could be provided with a free bed . . . the family . . . would be able to sustain themselves without assistance from the town."[2]

Protestant benevolence was structured into the management of the hospital. The board of trustees was composed of prominent citizens with a deep sense of stewardship; the hospital superintendent was a moral and pious person, and his wife (who would be in charge of the domestic services of the hospital) was also to be of impeccable character. The prevailing spirit of the Second Great Awakening, with its evangelizing thrust, penetrated the general hospital. Catholic patients in such hospitals, particularly those Irish-Americans inflamed by their traditional anti-Protestantism as well as by the increasing devotionalism of the period, felt estranged in the "non-Catholic" hospital. Some bishops perceived these hospitals as antithetical to Catholicism and were eager to establish a Catholic counterpart in the urban centers. The 1851 *Catholic Almanac* interprets the need for Catholic benevolence within the context of Protestant-Catholic tensions:

> [T]he wants of religion are great. The wide-spread heresy of our land, and its vast efforts of propagandism, the mixture of Catholics with Protestants, especially in parts seldom visited by a priest, the growing materialism of the age, which imperceptibly but effectually weans the heart from the spiritual objects of faith, are causes that still operate largely to the disadvantage of religion, and call for the most vigorous measures to oppose their influence. These will be found in the continual accession of pious and learned clergymen to the field of the ministry, in the spiritual retreats for the clergy and laity that are so effectual in renovating the life of the soul, and in the establishment of Catholic schools, under the charge of religious orders or congregations, for the imparting of a solid and virtuous education, and in various other means which the wisdom of the bishops has adopted.[3]

Like all private voluntary hospitals of the period, these Catholic hospitals of the 1850s could not have developed without the cooperation of physicians eager to infuse the trends of medical training and prestige into these institutions. Because many general hospitals of all denominations were still more like boarding houses where the chronically ill, the injured, and the feverish patients came for some rudimentary care as a last resort, nursing was primarily custodial. The Catholic nursing sister was committed to pastoral ministry, which was desperately needed because of the shortage of priests during this period. In contrast to the alienating character of the "public" hospital, the Catholic hospital offered patients the comforts of the church.

For both Catholics and non-Catholics, religious and secular impulses were principal sources of hospital development in the 1850s. The foundation of Hartford Hospital was associated with "benevolent gentlemen" and physicians of "The Society for Providing Home for the Sick." Frequently Protestant women philanthropists, who engaged directly in home nursing, provided the financial basis for the establishment of a new hospital. Such was the case in the foundation of Union Memorial Hospital in mid-century Baltimore.

The Protestant deaconess movement originated in the German towns of Hamburg and Kaiserwerth. Phoebe, referred to in Paul's letter to the

Romans, was a model for single women of service (*diakonia*) to conse-crate themselves to the sick, dying, and the poor. In Hamburg, Amelia Wilhelmina Sieveking (1794–1859) responded to the cholera victims of 1831 and initiated along with twelve other women the Protestant Sisters of Mercy. There were also Mennonite deaconesses in Holland, but the largest representation of the deaconess movement was in the Rhineland town Kaiserwerth. Pastor Theodor Fliedner, a notable Lutheran clergy-man, founded an order of nursing sisters who received some training from physicians and were assigned to a hospital that Fliedner estab-lished in 1836. The Kaiserwerth Institute for the Training of Deaconesses became a model for the movement.[4] Elizabeth Gurney Fry, a Quaker social reformer, achieved fame because of her work in prison reform. She expanded her concern to the sick poor and visited Kaiserwerth. Subse-quently she founded an Institute of Nursing in London. Simultaneously developments occurred in the Church of England, particularly among leaders associated with the Oxford Movement with its focus on the early church. Dr. Edward Bouverie-Pusey, a former associate of John Henry Newman, was one of the principal founders of the Park Village commu-nity in London, the first Anglican community of sisters whose ministry included visiting the sick in their homes and in hospitals.

Pittsburgh, the location of the first hospital of the Sisters of Mercy, was the original home of the deaconess movement in the United States. Pas-tor Fliedner and four deaconesses arrived in 1849 to take charge of the Pittsburgh Infirmary (now Passavant Hospital). Founded by the noted Lutheran clergyman William Alfred Passavant, the infirmary was the first Protestant hospital in America. Passavant was also associated with several movements in Lutheran life, particularly related to immigrant welfare, home missions, and publications.[5] Though the Protestant ethos was regnant in most antebellum hospitals, Passavant's was the first iden-tifiably Protestant institution. Ethnic Lutheran hospitals, particularly among the Germans, were established in midwestern areas such as St. Louis. The most significant group of women religious nurses in the American Episcopal Church, the Sisters of the Holy Communion, was founded in New York by Dr. William Augustus Muhlenburg in 1845. First limited to home nursing, this community staffed the Infirmary of the Holy Communion, opened in 1854, which evolved into St. Luke's Hospital. The religious character of the hospital was pervasive: it was constructed around the Church of the Holy Communion. "The patients lived in the House of the Lord. St. Luke's, as a church, has the chapel for its nave and the wards for its transept."[6] The nursing school's pin displayed its motto, *Corpus Sanare, Animam Salvare,* "to heal the body and save the soul," a theme applicable to religious nurses of all denominations.

Episcopal hospitals included the Church Home and Hospital in Baltimore, Episcopal in Philadelphia, and St. Luke's in Chicago. The Jewish community founded Mt. Sinai Hospital in New York in 1852, and this was followed by Jewish hospitals in several eastern and midwestern cities. As mentioned earlier, these denominational hospitals were founded by women and men philanthropists, benevolent associations and by leading clergymen. The Catholic pattern included philanthropy, such as John Mullanphy in St. Louis, but most of the Catholic hospitals in the antebellum period were founded by bishops.

The development of hospitals was a distant reality to John Carroll. In 1811 he wrote to Elizabeth Seton: "A century at least will pass before the exigencies and habits of this country will require and hardly admit of the charitable exercises towards the sick sufficient to employ any number of sisters out of our largest cities. . . ."[7] The nation's first Catholic bishop was primarily concerned with providing his parishes with priests who could minister to the people imbued with a strong sense of harmony in their American and Catholic identities. His vision of the communal character of the Catholic presence in the United States was based upon his positive incarnational anthropology that all are called to reflect God's compassion by visiting the sick, attending to the needs of the poor, and reaching out to the outcast. Just as all are elevated to compassionate service, so the clergy were viewed by Carroll as "coadjutors of God" and "ministers of Christ."[8] Joseph P. Chinnici remarks: "Always the priesthood was described not in reference to individual status but in reference to Christ. . . ."[9] Accordingly, Bishop Carroll was a model of communal ministry to ecclesial and secular societies. He served with Protestant clergymen on boards of directors of charitable and educational institutions and was a founder of the Baltimore General Dispensary in 1802. Sensitive to the legacy of antipopery in the United States he fostered a spirit of openness to Protestants. Symbolic of Carroll's view of the young republic was a first communion/confirmation certificate of Baltimore that portrayed the Holy Spirit as a dove casting the bright rays of Divine Providence upon that portion of the globe entitled "America."[10]

Though the immigrant church in the United States represents a departure from the ecclesial-cultural interaction characteristic of John Carroll, the leadership of Bishop John Hughes of New York and John Neumann of Philadelphia did not entail negation of religious liberty and pluralism.

In contrast to the Catholic minority of the federal period, the Catholic population of this period was composed primarily of urban poor, with little education and no strong habit of practicing the faith. The cosmopolitan model of the Carroll community gave way to an ethnic and religious particularism intensified by the need to protect the immigrant flock from Protestant domination on the one hand and, on the other, to develop American institutions, to foster catechesis, and to establish roots within the Catholic tradition. Spurts of anti-Catholic and nativist hysteria, manifested in convent burning in Charlestown, Massachusetts, in 1834 and church burning and riots in Philadelphia in 1844–45, cemented Catholic loyalties to their own institutions.

Immigrant Irish slums, such as the Five Points area in New York, where cholera made its first appearance in 1832, engendered an antipauper dimension to the no popery and nativist cant. Protestant benevolence to the immigrants appeared patronizing as well as proselytizing. Of the three million immigrants who entered New York between 1840–1860 about one-half million, mostly poor Irish, remained there, while the more prosperous Germans tended to move to areas within the so-called German triangle, whose points were Cincinnati, St. Louis, and Milwaukee.

There were an array of Protestant societies dedicated to evangelizing immigrants. The Home Missionary Society in 1843 responded to the waves of immigration by stating, "Let them come with good or evil intent, as exiles fleeing from tyranny or as emissaries to spy out and possess the land—let them come. We will meet them on the beach, with bread in one hand and the Gospel in the other. . . ."[11] Catholic novelists such as Mary Ann Sadlier portrayed Irish orphans adopted by Protestant families to rescue them from the superstitious conditions of their Irish-American background.[12]

John Duffe, an Irish-American ward nurse in New York Hospital's Marine House, recorded his experience in his journal. Commenting on the superintendent's religious hypocrisy, he said that it would be "useless to complain because if we do it may offend the religious feelings of our superintendent and he will soon point out the way to the gate." Duffe described the food as "putrefied . . . and our butter is rotten and stinks worse than a skunk but it must be borne with for . . . if we complain our godly superintendent will tell us you may consider yourself discharged for the Lord sent it and you must eat it like a hireling."[13]

The Protestant chaplain at the same hospital, John Moffett Howe, referred to Catholics as "Hardened infidels [and] despisers of the Bible—of the means of Grace." Howe observed the deathbed scene depicting a delirious woman receiving the last rites: ". . . although as insensible as a block he administered to her the Sacrament of the Lord's Supper. . . . The priest dressed in his cossac [sic] on the ground—the ceremony [sic] was inspiring but perfectly unintelligible to the ignorant attendants and to the insane dying woman."[14] In contrast to Duffe's views of the superintendent, Howe considered him to be as kindly as "a father of this large family." With certitude on the relationship between vice and sickness and death, Howe stated that "all diseases, or nine out of 10, are produced by bad habits—or rum."[15] Not all public hospitals permitted Catholic priests to attend to dying patients, as some Protestant chaplains would not allow it.

The focus of nativism and anti-Catholicism generated a response among bishops and priests to develop schools and hospitals that would guarantee the preservation of the faith among the youth and provide devotional and sacramental sustenance to the sick and dying. In the development of hospitals this Catholic benevolence was dedicated to nurturing the immigrant population of the urban ethnic villages. Though they would accept the sick poor of all religious denominations most were founded to serve their own, which included particular hospitals founded for Irish, German, and later Italian and Polish Catholic communities. The missionary model of the earlier period, characterized by an openness to the culture, continued to motivate many communities of women religious, but the immigrant model of Catholic health care in opposition to the patterns of discrimination of Catholic priests in the putatively community hospitals and to the general anti-Catholic hostility of the political, social and economic climate, tended to be motivated by a preservationist impulse.

As will be noted in a later chapter, a revival of devotionalism in Europe in the wake of the French Revolution with its opposition to the thrusts of modern antireligious worldview suited the immigrants' needs for spiritual balm in their confrontation with anti-Catholic hostility. Rather than the Holy Spirit radiating grace over America as depicted on the first holy communion/confirmation card of the missionary era, the portrayal of Mary's Immaculate Conception (proclaimed a dogma in 1854) with the Virgin crushing the serpent as she stands on the globe was in accord with the immigrant's experience of the animus of the prevailing ethos.

Sisters, who were subjected to offensive caricatures, were affected by this devotionalism which particularly underscored the clear boundary lines between the hospital and the community. Even after some Irish- and German-American immigrants assimilated in the latter third of the nineteenth century, the immigrant model persisted. Morris Vogel, a historian of the modernization of health care in Boston, captures the identity of the religious hospital: "The major function of such institutions . . . was to . . . serve quite specific needs within their communities. They were organized and supported without fear and mistrust of the larger society, and because of special services they fired their people. Like churches and fraternal organizations hospitals were agencies of identification for uprooted immigrants, promoting group cohesion." Vogel cites sociologist William Glaser to substantiate the notion that sponsoring religious hospitals "is a way of maintaining religion and religious identity in the face of competition."[16]

II

Of all the bishops promoting strong institutional religious identity for immigrants none felt more keenly the need for competition than John Hughes, Bishop of New York. Well known for his polemical defense of Catholicism, Hughes was the ecclesiastical counterpart to the political boss. "Episcopal authority comes from above not from below . . . [and] Catholics do their duty when they obey their bishop."[17] Indeed, Hughes referred to himself as "bishop and chief."[18] When the Sisters of Charity were anticipating union with the congregation in Paris they decided to follow French customs and terminated care of orphan boys. Hughes reacted by calling a special meeting to allow the New York sisters to decide between remaining with the Emmitsburg community or joining a diocesan community; of the sixty-two sisters serving in New York thirty-three remained in the diocese. On November 9, 1849, St. Vincent's Hospital, under the direction of Sister Angela Hughes, the bishop's sister, was opened in a small building on East Thirteenth Street. Sister Angela, who had been superior of the Mullanphy hospital in St. Louis, later became superior of the diocesan community. St. Vincent's could accommodate thirty patients, and those who could afford to pay were charged three dollars a week. Without running water and other amenities, the hospital was moved to a new site on West Twelfth Street and Seventh Avenue, its present location.[19] From Bishop Hughes's vantage point the hospital provided Catholics with a refuge from the snares of religious prejudice and Protestant proselytism.

The Freeman's Journal, edited by the convert James McMaster but directed by Hughes, noted that the Sisters of Charity of Buffalo had set the example for New York City. Bishop John Timon, C.M., had urged the sisters to establish an orphanage, school and the hospital in his diocese. McMaster emphasized "the necessity for such an enterprise in our city." He stated that "Although the enterprise originated with a religious denomination and is under the supervision of a Religious Order, it is not only open to the poor sick of any denomination but all who resort to it are at liberty to avail themselves of their own spiritual advisers [i.e., ministers] without interferences. In this, and every other respect, the institution is placed on a liberal and truly charitable basis."[20]

McMaster's description resounds with pride in Catholic institutions, an attitude that no doubt reflected the general sentiment. Because Hughes was motivated to cultivate a strong Catholic identity, to liberate his flock from Protestant paternalism and proselytism would be considered a notable achievement. He built over one hundred churches during his administration, 1838–1864, but St. Vincent's was the only hospital. However, the German community, with a population of about fifty thousand, opened St. Francis Hospital in 1868. Staffed by the Franciscan Sisters of the Poor, who originated in Aachen in 1845, the German hospital was relatively small; it served only one hundred patients in 1879.[21]

The foundation of the first hospital in Lowell, Massachusetts, began as a tiny parish institution in the mid-1850s. Under the direction of Father John O'Brien, pastor of St. Patrick's Church, it was first staffed by women of the Sodality of the Holy Family. Though actually a hostel for a few old and infirm women, eventually a hospital was opened, which absorbed the parish hostel, under the Daughters of Charity who had staffed the school. Sister Rose Noyland, the first Sister-Servant (i.e., superior) of the hospital, recalled that the workers in the city's cotton mills were "nearly all Catholic. A large number were young Catholic girls who had no other home than a boarding house, and in case of protracted sickness their condition was deplorable. A Protestant hospital existed, but a priest could not enter its precincts, and a Catholic conveyed to its wards was exposed to dying without the sacraments."[22]

In Philadelphia the Irish-American community allied with physicians eager for a training facility and with Bishop Francis P. Kenrick to establish St. Joseph's Hospital in 1848. Anti-Catholic riots in 1844 galvanized the Irish into promoting a strong institutional response for needy emigrants from the old country. In 1846 Kenrick formed a Council of the Hospital of St. Vincent de Paul. Unlike John Hughes, who been assigned to Philadelphia before his appointment as coadjutor bishop of New York, Kenrick was a scholar whose works in theology marked him as a reflective man.[23]

Kenrick's intention to establish a diocesan hospital never material-
ized. Instead in 1848, the Jesuit pastor of St. Joseph's Church, Joseph
Felix Barberlin, together with several lay persons, founded the "St.
Joseph's Society for the Relief of Distressed Immigrants from Ireland,
and for the Establishment of a Hospital." With a board representing
middle-class Irish-American businessmen and members of the Hiber-
nian Society, the St. Joseph's group had a financial base to initiate an
appeal for funds. Two Catholic doctors, a prominent Irish American and
a convert, provided strong leadership and a sense of prestige. Within a
year the board of the Relief Society became the board of managers of St.
Joseph's Hospital, incorporated in March 1849. Bishop Kenrick was *ex
officio* president of the board, which had responsibility for ownership
and governance of the hospital. It was analogous to the articles incorporating lay trustees of parishes with the exception that the physicians
dominated policy on admittance and the cost of fees. However, there
were several subscription schemes by which individuals and parishes
could prepay for treatment while wealthy individuals could endow a private room or a ward. Prior to its June 18, 1849, opening, the hospital
received $2,700 and furnishings from the Ladies Catholic Hospital Soci-
ety founded the previous January.[24] To staff the hospital the board turned
to the Sisters of St. Joseph, who had just arrived from St. Louis two years
earlier in order to run an orphanage.[25] Archbishop Peter Richard Kenrick
of St. Louis, Francis's younger brother, had encouraged the young
French-American community to expand. With no experience in nursing,
the Carondelet Sisters seem to have never fully adapted to the hospital.
French customs still prevailed in the community; one observer remarked
that patients' needs gave way to those of the sisters' "presumed necessity
of attending religious services." Mother St. John Fournier, superior of
the five sisters, wrote that she had to stay with the young sisters during
the night because they were "so afraid of dying. . . . Little by little these
poor children got accustomed to working for the sick and dying."[26]
Accommodations for the sisters were primitive until they moved into
their own quarters in a house adjacent to the original hospital. In ten
years the hospital had expanded to forty beds, and the community
increased to eleven sisters.

Patients were predominately Irish but, because St. Joseph's was dependent upon paying patients (three dollars per week), charity cases rarely
exceeded thirty percent. Poor immigrants were sent to the Blockley Hospital, a division of the public almshouse; in 1855 Irish represented two-
thirds of the patients and almost half of the prostitutes. Hence, St.

Joseph's, like all voluntary hospitals, admitted only the "worthy poor." Gail Farr Casterline, a student of Catholic health care in nineteenth-century Philadelphia, reports that eighty-three percent of the admissions in 1850 were Irish. Between 1856–58 the "place of birth" breakdown of patients was: 495, Ireland; 90, United States; and 48, Germany.[27] The hospital accepted patients and their clergy from all religious denominations; but chapel services, the patterns of feast days, and the manifestation of piety were rooted in the Catholic tradition. It was an Irish Catholic hospital, a source of denominational pride in a city frequently seized by fits of anti-Catholicism and nativism.

Upon the appointment of Francis P. Kenrick to the see of Baltimore in 1851, John N. Neumann, the superior of the Redemptorists in the United States, became bishop of Philadelphia the following April.[28] Born in Bohemia in 1811, Neumann was the first German-speaking ordinary of the diocese. From 1857 until his death in 1860, Neumann was assisted by the coadjutor bishop, James F. Wood. During his nine-year administration Neumann founded a minor seminary, several parishes and schools, fostered devotionalism, encouraged confraternities and parish missions, and imposed a distinctive character upon the policy and piety of Catholic life.[29] Bishop Wood, particularly responsible for the development of charitable institutions, negotiated diocesan control of St. Joseph's Hospital, which ultimately culminated in 1859 with the removal of the Sisters of St. Joseph and the arrival of the Daughters of Charity with their strong tradition of nursing. No doubt affecting Bishop Wood's decision was his long association with the Daughters and the fact that the new superior of St. Joseph's, Sister Ursula Mattingly, was a friend of some years.[30] By the time the Daughters assumed responsibility of St. Joseph's this rapidly expanding community, composed primarily of Anglo- and Irish-American sisters, ran hospitals in many cities from Buffalo to Mobile, from Norfolk to Los Angeles.

Among the predominantly Irish-American patients at St. Joseph's Hospital, one German patient admitted in 1851–52 was Anthony Bachmann. Three years after he died, his widow, Maria Bachmann, founded the Sisters of the Third Order of St. Francis, a community identified with a wide range of charitable works, which included home nursing. The community's foundation was soon followed by the establishment of St. Francis, a twenty-bed hospital in 1860 which was refounded as St. Mary's, an eighty-bed institution in 1868.

Bishop Neumann, concerned about the lack of charitable works for the German Catholic community, enthusiastically endorsed the new community of women religious. As early as 1852 he remarked that "much care and considerable sacrifice will be required to measure and increase the faith of the very many German Catholics."[31] As a strong preservationist of tradition Neumann understood that recent German immigrants identified Catholicism within the context of German language and customs. He explained the absence of German children in Catholic orphanages as a sign of national prejudice for French and Irish. It was the German Redemptorist pastor at St. Peter's who encouraged the three women to establish the first German community of Franciscan Tertiaries. Within a year the Franciscan sisters were teaching in several cities, nursing in the home and in their own hospital, and maintaining an orphanage.

St. Francis Hospital, located in St. Peter's parish, seems to have originated from several sources: German-American separatism was manifested in myriad confraternities and social institutions; most German-Americans took up skilled trades and could support a hospital; cholera and other epidemics prompted the immediate need to go beyond home nursing. The foundation of St. Mary's Hospital (1866) in the Kensington area, a factory district where Episcopal Hospital was located, fits the pattern of providing a denominational hospital in response to the religious, social, and health-care needs of Catholics from all ethnic groups with Germans determining its primary identity. Gail Casterline's research supports the conclusion that most of St. Joseph's patients were admitted on a charity basis and received good professional health care within a deeply personalist context. (Bishop Wood, a physician, and the sister superior formed the board of St. Mary's.) Casterline remarks on the character of St. Mary's Hospital: "The atmosphere was homelike. The superior knew the patients by name, kept them amply supplied with pillows and blankets, and directed the sixteen sisters, most of them of German background, with no paid help, who did all the work of the institution."[32]

The foundation of the two Catholic hospitals in Philadelphia represents several developments in the burgeoning immigrant Church. In response to Protestant benevolence, associated with anti-Catholic hostility, Bishop Francis Kenrick perceived the need for a Catholic institution to care for many newcomers to the city. The business leaders and women of the Irish parish responded to the call from parish leadership, which was allied with physicians, including a prominent Catholic. Catholic benevolence linked with professional medical interests, comparable to the foundation of all denominational hospitals, to establish St. Joseph's. However, because it represented the predominant Irish-

American community, St. Joseph's projected an English-speaking exclusiveness, and it alienated its German coreligionists. Just as St. Joseph's was founded in reaction to Protestant benevolence, so St. Mary's owes its origin in reaction to Irish-American Catholic benevolence. Such Irish-German tensions existed in Philadelphia since the late eighteenth century, but they were exacerbated by the first wave of mass immigration and would persist until after World War I. Most evident in parish development, ethnic separatism was manifested in religious attitudes in most institutions. Though the Irish forged a religious identity in opposition to Protestantism, associated with three centuries of British imperialism and colonialism, they inherited a relatively restrained liturgical and devotional life in contrast to the Germans, who identified the cultivation of their faith with the preservation of language, culture, and an actively communal and elaborate devotional and liturgical life. The ethnic separatism did not become hostile unless an Irish bishop appeared to ignore the needs of the German community. It was not uncommon for Irish parishes to participate in the festivities associated with the consecration of a German-American church. Most German-American hospitals were founded in the latter third of the nineteenth century, less in reaction to Irish dominance than as one of many institutions to strengthen the cohesion of traditional German self-understanding of the relationship between religion and culture.

As Milwaukee and Chicago passed from frontier towns to cosmopolitan cities during the 1850s, development of the organized charitable institutions was not under the aegis of Protestant benevolence. A general spirit of goodwill was extended to the Sisters of Charity hospital in Milwaukee and that of the Sisters of Mercy in Chicago. John M. Henni, a native of Switzerland, was appointed Milwaukee's first bishop in 1843 during that decade which saw the city's population increase from 1,700 to over 20,000, sixty-four percent of whom were foreign born.[33] Henni served in Cincinnati as pastor of the city's first German parish and was involved in founding the first German Catholic newspaper in the United States, the *Wahrheitsfreund*. In 1850 Milwaukee had two German and one Irish parish, and the Cathedral. Henni invited many German communities to settle in the area, but since the late 1840s the American Sisters of Charity (after 1850 the Daughters) ran a school, an asylum, and St. John's Infirmary, the only hospital. As referred to in chapter two, the sisters described St. John's Infirmary in the *Catholic Almanac* of 1850–51: "The house is large, commodious, and built in the healthiest part of the city." There were three wards, but for an unspecified fee there were private rooms. Since the sisters were "the only nurses and attendants in the house none need fear the absence of sympathy, and eager vigilance." Reflecting the regnant domestic virtues of the era the sisters guaranteed "the strictest order, cleanliness and unremitting attention." By their rule sisters were deferential to physicians "but all food and medicines must be administered by the Sisters." As quoted earlier the sisters' hospital was opened to clergymen of all faiths as long as they were invited by patients, but "no clergymen, whether Protestant or Catholic were permitted to preach to, to pray aloud before, or interfere religiously with such patients [who did not] . . . ask for the exercize of his office. The rights of conscience must be held paramount to all others."[34] Such liberality was not characteristic of the immigrant church but rather appears to reflect the missionary, frontier spirit, particularly sensitive to liberty and pluralism. Of course itinerant preachers could have been exploiting a "captive" congregation in this hospital.

Perhaps this openness is partially explained by the excellent relationship between the city and the hospital; the Milwaukee City Medical Association formally opened St. John's Infirmary, and the city paid a fee to the sisters for each of the mentally ill patients in the hospital. Responsible for the public health of the city the sisters were asked to staff a special quarantine hospital at North Point for immigrants who arrived by ship. Eventually St. John's closed and North Point became the Daughters' St. Mary's Hospital in 1858. While there were clashes among German Catholics, Lutherans, and "free thinkers" the hospital generally remained above these conflicts. Within this predominantly German community the Daughters also maintained cordial relations with its episcopal leadership. Such was not the case with the Sisters of Mercy in Chicago.[35]

In 1833 there were only 350 people in Chicago. Four years later it incorporated as a city with a population of 4,000. Located at the mouth of the Chicago River and on Lake Michigan, the city was a port and a rail center linking western agriculture to the manufacturing East. It reached a population of 30,000 in 1850, more than fifty percent of whom were foreign born. In 1843 William Quarter, an Irish priest of the New York diocese, was appointed first bishop of Chicago. Though educated at Mt. St. Mary's Seminary in Emmitsburg he encouraged the Irish Sisters of Mercy from his homeland to establish themselves in his diocese. In a letter to Bishop John B. Purcell of Cincinnati, Quarter wrote of "the spirit of great liberality . . . toward Catholics in this state, and in this city." Later he wrote that "Protestants show the greatest kindness and liberality."[36] Indeed they gave funds and sent students to the University of St. Mary of the Lake, which Quarter opened in 1845. When five Sisters of Mercy arrived from Pittsburgh in 1846 they soon became the principal source of welfare for the city. Accompanied by Mary Francis Xavier Warde, considered by many as the American foundress of the Sisters of Mercy, the community first founded St. Xavier Academy, which catered to the wealthy; in 1850 twelve boarders paid $150 half yearly and seventy day students paid an unspecified tuition. St. Xavier's predated the city's first public school by ten years. According to the pattern established by Warde this American departure from the rule that limited their ministry to serve the poor was established to fund the sisters' works of mercy.[37]

In 1850, eighteen students attended St. Mary's free school in Chicago, and in the wake of cholera epidemics the Sisters of Mercy operated orphan asylums for boys and for girls. "We rely on Providence for support of them. The Catholics of the city, though scanty [in numbers] are in prosperous circumstances, have generously responded to the call, and our Protestant fellow citizens have evinced great interest and liberality on the occasion."[38] The Sisters of Mercy also taught adults in night school, operated a boarding house for working women, an employment office, and visited the prisoners and the sick in their homes and in the city almshouse, which was only an emergency shelter housed in the same building with the jail, office of records, and the fire department.

The Mercy sisters occasionally served in a dispensary at Rush Medical College at Tippecanoe Inn (1842), a short-lived infirmary, and at the U.S. Marine Hospital. In November of 1850 twelve beds in a private boarding house, the former Lake House hotel, were rented as Illinois General Hospital of the Lakes. Incorporated by the physicians and civic leaders, the hospital's document of ownership in February 1851 was transferred to the Sisters of Mercy, who had been nursing there for two months. Of the four sisters assigned to the hospital Sister Mary Vincent McGirr, sister of one of the physicians on the staff, was superior. In 1852 the hospital was officially named Mercy Hospital and Asylum. From that time until 1863, Cook County, which had closed its almshouse, paid three dollars a week for each indigent patient. In October of 1853 the hospital moved to a new brick building on Wabash and Van Buren Streets. With the medical college of the new Lind University affiliated with the hospital the institution grew in reputation. Among its leading staff physicians was B. Nathan Davis, a founder of the American Medical Association in 1847 and the first editor of the AMA journal.[39]

Bishop Quarter's successors, James Oliver Van de Velde and Anthony O'Regan, experienced economic difficulties associated with the faculty of Our Lady of the Lake University as the beneficiary of the estate of Bishop Quarter. These bishops were also opposed to a diocesan community of women religious possessing title to property in its own name. Indeed Van de Velde placed the property on Wabash Avenue in the name of the diocese, a move that prompted the superior to seek a patron to purchase property for the academy in Carville, then in the country. Bishop James Duggan, who was later certified as mentally ill and forced to resign in 1869, decided to sell the hospital and asylum property. He announced that the girls of the asylum should be sent to the Sisters of St. Joseph and that the Sisters of Mercy should vacate the hospital in two days. Determined to maintain control of this institution, the superior decided to transfer the hospital to the Carville property that housed St. Agatha's Academy; the students were moved to St. Xavier Academy, which made room for the one hundred patients.[40] Located at Calumet and 26th Avenues Mercy Hospital continued its affiliation with the medical school and remained there for a century. In the post–Civil War period Germans and Polish established their own hospitals, a reflection of the ethnic tapestry of the "second city" in the United States.

Social welfare in Milwaukee and Chicago illustrates the midwestern Catholic alternative to the established poor-relief system of almshouses in the East. Catholic benevolence was the principal source of asylums and hospitals within political structures dominated by Protestants and increasingly dependent upon immigrant Catholic voters. Episcopal leadership was at the source of the foundations of Catholic hospitals, but physicians, eager to develop private hospitals for medical education, were a vital force in the development of these hospitals. In New Orleans, where Catholicity was at the core of culture, an alliance between the bishop and physicians resulted in the foundation of a Catholic hospital.

Charity Hospital in New Orleans was a state-owned Catholic institution. Since 1832 the Sisters, later Daughters, of Charity had staffed the hospital.[41] In 1845, five Sisters of Charity were assigned to the private infirmary of Dr. Warren Stone, who had been a surgeon at Charity Hospital. In 1852 the sisters took charge of the infirmary on a lease basis. Opened in 1839 the infirmary was called the Maison de Santé from 1852 until the sisters opened their own private hospital.[42]

At the suggestion of Dr. Stone and an associate, Bishop Antoine Blanc wrote to the mother general in Emmitsburg urging her "not to refuse to gratify the wishes of those two professional gentlemen whom I esteem greatly. The immense good the Sisters . . . are doing at [Charity] hospital makes me more anxious to see the private infirmary conducted under the same moral principles."[43] This was a rare instance of a bishop aligned with physicians for the establishment of a Catholic presence in a private institution. The Maison de Santé was, like Charity, devoted to the care of strangers. Creole customs required home nursing and fostered folk remedies for most illnesses.

New Orleans was subjected to a severe yellow-fever epidemic in 1852–53. Among the thousands who died were four Sisters of Charity. Cholera victims and convalescent soldiers from the Mexican War were also cared for at Maison de Santé. Convinced that they needed a larger facility and urged on by a physician, the Daughters of Charity purchased ten lots along Canal Street for a new hospital, which was opened in 1859 and named Hôtel Dieu. The patients' register for the first year lists 285 slaves, with a few F.M.C. and F.W.C., that is, free men of color and free women of color. To care for African Americans, even in segregated wards, was a drastic departure from custom.[44]

As early as 1842 Henriette Delille and Cuban-born Juliette Goudin, free women of color, entered the religious life in a new community called the Presentation Sisters, later entitled the Sisters of the Holy Family. The sisters cared for orphans and the aged, thereby becoming the first religious community in the United States to provide a residence for elderly homeless persons. Prohibited from wearing religious garb for the next three years, the Sisters of the Holy Family were subjected to severe criticism from white Catholics who considered them inherently unworthy for the religious life. There were traditional hostilities between black and mulatto cultures. Historian Randall M. Miller explains: "Light-skinned, middle- and upper-class French-speaking free people of color occupied a middle-ground between slave and free, black and white."[45] Despite their nursing victims of cholera and yellow fever in the 1850s and wounded soldiers in the Civil War, the Holy Family Sisters never received public recognition even from the clergy and episcopacy. Bishop Jean Marie Odin did not acknowledge their existence even when they were servants in his household. When the Jim Crow system was absorbed by the church in the South, the Sisters of the Holy Family along with former slaves formed a separate and inferior caste in both civil and ecclesial society. Without economic resources and episcopal sanction the black Catholic community did not develop the institutional fabric common to the burgeoning immigrant culture. It was not until the 1930s that a nursing school for black Catholics was founded. Hence, the story of black Catholic health ministry reflects the general trends in culture; the first bishops' letter against racism (1958) followed the Supreme Court's decision, Brown v. Board of Education of Topeka, Kansas (1954).

While racial conflict ran deeply through the Catholic community, sisters of both races were subjected to abuse arising from anti-Catholicism and nativism, which was laced with virulent anticonvent stereotypes. Protestant revivalism of the 1820s and 30s, the threat of an organized Catholic hierarchy in provincial councils, the increasingly strong waves of immigration promoted a rebirth of the antipapist sentiment expressed in the popular press, in public lectures by alleged former priests and nuns, in sermons by preachers of various denominations, in violent anti-immigrant protests, and in convent and church burnings. The anticonvent component included pornography. Maria Monk's notorious *Awful Disclosures of the Hôtel Dieu Nunnery of Montreal* (1836) is replete with stories of illicit sexual behavior. In a Baltimore religious magazine two Protestant ministers stated: "The papist doctrine of celibacy–the unreasoned obedience due to bishops and priests from all nuns and females in holy orders, opens the way for corruptions"[46] (1836). The burning of the Ursuline Convent in Charlestown, Massachusetts (1834), was partially motivated by stories of a woman who was held against her will by tyrannical sisters. Since republicanism and Catholicism were perceived as inherently incompatible, convents were viewed as prisons. Stories by "escaped nuns" substantiated the biases.

Irate at the scene of free independent women self-determining their lives in sisterhoods responsible for social institutions, many men considered convents as deviant and dangerous models contrary to the natural (i.e., patriarchal) order. This was buttressed by exaggerated stories of convents imprisoning innocent young women. Hence when anti-Catholicism gained valuable political coinage in the prominent Know-Nothing period of the mid-1850s, convent inspection laws were passed with the intention of liberating the captives from the clutches of the sisters. Ironically the very domesticity that these lawmakers were protecting was a dominant spirit promoted by the sisters in their schools, asylums, and hospitals. Pornographic anti-Catholic lore persisted even after the sisters served heroically in epidemics of yellow fever, cholera, and typhoid.[47] The Know-Nothing party emanated from the South and East to the midwest, and with the gold rush of 1848–49 Yankee anti-Catholicism was transported to the west coast.[48]

Nursing sisters were subjected to such hostility, but contrary to the public perception then and now they were keenly aware of their responsibility to welcome patients of all religions. However, where there was a choice, denominational loyalties among Protestants and Catholics and ethnic loyalties among coreligionists were strong. In the 1850s hospitals did not house those who could afford home nursing. For the middle classes in occupations unprotected and unregulated, the hospital was the refuge for those many injured on the job. Public perceptions of nursing sisters were profoundly affected by the over six hundred women religious who nursed on battlefields, field hospitals, and hospital ships during the Civil War.

·CHAPTER FIVE·

Catholic Nurses in the Civil War

I

THE ABOLITIONIST IDEOLOGY, the Dred Scott Decision, and the expansion of slavery into new territories culminated in the crisis that from the southern perspective became nonnegotiable with the election of Abraham Lincoln. Francis Patrick Kenrick, the foremost moral theologian in the United States, argued that the origins of American slavery could not be justified, but the descendants of seized African slaves "are not seen to be held unjustly in servitude." To safeguard a tranquil social order Kenrick said "that nothing against the law must be attempted, neither anything by which slaves might be set free.... The prudence and the charity of sacred ministries must be shown in this so that the slaves, informed by Christian morals, might show service to their masters, venerating always God, the Supreme Master of us all."[1] Bishop Auguste Marie Martin of the diocese of Natchitoches—a diocese of all French Catholics in northern Louisiana—and Augustin Vérot, vicar apostolic of Florida, justified the conditions of slavery, attacked abolitionists, and were enthusiastic in their support of the Confederacy. Though Vérot later became an enlightened evangelizer of the freed African American, both bishops represented an extremist position; all southern bishops expressed loyalty to the Confederacy as a legitimate authority.[2]

There were Catholics who publicly opposed slavery, while bishops such as Archbishop John B. Purcell of Cincinnati and John Hughes of New York were deeply loyal to the Union cause. There were many Catholics who believed in educating and evangelizing African Americans as equal to whites, but most Catholics held to the accepted dicta on the inequality of the races. Several bishops and religious communities owned slaves. Because abolitionists tended to be anti-Catholic and nativist in sentiment they alienated Catholics. Some abolitionists linked slavery and Catholicism as "natural allies founded and supported on the basis of ignorance and tyranny. . . ."[3] Many immigrant Catholics, particularly the Irish, considered freed slaves as competitors for jobs. The draft riots in New York pitted Irish draftees against blacks in a bloody attack upon the African-American community. Even though there were strong Union and pro-Confederacy bishops, with a few actively involved in official diplomacy, the Civil War did not fracture the Catholic Church as it did other denominations.

There were only about seventy Catholic chaplains—volunteers and commissioned officers—ministering to both armies of the war. Many were drawn from the religious communities, but most were secular priests, two of whom later became bishops, Lawrence T. McMahon of Hartford and John Ireland of St. Paul. Most Catholic soldiers went unattended by priests, but the 617 sisters from twenty-one religious communities nursed the sick and injured on both sides of the conflict with a strong dimension of pastoral care. This number represents roughly twenty percent of the total 3,200 nurses; there have been three books published on the sisters and the Civil War based on sisters' diaries; yet the widely acclaimed television documentary by Ken Burns on the Civil War completely ignored them in the section dealing with women nurses.[4] Regrettable though this may be, the historical record and eyewitness narratives abound in accounts of sister-nurses. Many of these contemporary witnesses referred to sisters of all religious communities as "sisters of charity" or "mercy." In contrast to other women nurses, sisters were sought after by physicians familiar with their hospitals; or in the case of those nonnursing communities, doctors preferred women religious who were generally capable of following directions with discretion but who were also experienced in initiating independent judgment and managing institutions.[5]

As mentioned in chapter two, Sister Matilda Coskery, a Daughter of Charity who nursed soldiers at Antietam, Gettysburg, and other campaigns, composed a handwritten nursing "text" based on her own experience:

> The office of "Nurse" is one of awful responsibility if its duties be properly considered; for on the faithful discharge of them, will the life of a fellow being, in very many instances, almost exclusively depend.
> How much intelligence, good sense and fidelity are therefore required,

that the patient may profit by her attentions; or that he may not be injured by her self-willedness or neglect! Where there is a Medical Attendant, the duties of a Nurse are reduced to two simple, but highly important rules; the observance of which should be most rigidly insisted upon. First, to do everything that the Physician orders to be done, and this is the strict letter of the commands. Second, to do nothing herself, nor permit any one else to do, that which he has not ordered; for it is fairly to be presumed, that the Physician will direct to the best of his knowledge, whatever he may think is essential to the welfare of his patient.

There are however, exceptions to these remarks, that the Medical faculty admit of, that is: when the nurse is *experienced* and faithful, and has also shown herself equal to her duty, she may, and should, withhold medicines, drinks, etc., which she observes act contrary to the designs or wishes of the Physician, but this liberty is only to be exercised between his visits, and she should relate to him as soon as he comes of what she has done, & why.[6]

This detailed text, which an archivist had transferred to thirty-eight typed pages, illustrates the refined training available to sisters which, when combined with experienced bedside care and hospital administration, justifiably earned them the respect of physicians. By the time Dorothea Dix was appointed by the Secretary of War to supervise women nursing volunteers, there were Daughters of Charity in charge of nursing Union soldiers in Norfolk and Confederate soldiers in Richmond, Sisters of Providence of St. Mary of the Woods in Indianapolis, and the Sisters of Charity of Cincinnati were at Fort Dennison, Ohio. The sisters' response to the cholera and yellow-fever epidemics led to requests for them in the war. The Secretary of War, Edwin Stanton, and General Ambrose Burnside, as well as many local political and military leaders, sought support from the various communities of women religious. Some requests went through episcopal leaders, such as Archbishop John B. Purcell of Cincinnati, or through religious superiors, such as Edward Sorin, C.S.C., superior of the Sisters of the Holy Cross. When placed in charge of a hospital, a deferential attitude on the part of physicians and soldiers was commonly manifested. The Sisters of Mercy of Baltimore, who were assigned responsibility for Douglas Hospital in Washington, were presented with the following:

To whom it may concern.

On application of the Sisters of Mercy in charge of the military hospital in Washington, furnish such provisions as they desire to purchase and charge same to the War Department.

[Signed Abraham Lincoln][7]

Dorothea Dix, a Boston teacher of national repute for her reforms in the treatment of the mentally ill, as the Superintendent of Army nurses, imposed strict qualifications. Volunteers were to be at least thirty years of age, "plain looking," and were to be attired in brown or black dresses. Surgeon General Robert C. Wood imposed further qualifications; besides presenting two certificates from physicians, the nurse volunteers were to be certified as morally fit by two clergymen.[8] Well known for her drive to firmly control the corps, Dix was a controversial figure, who lashed out at bureaucratic obstacles and and imposed her own regulations. Louisa May Alcott, a volunteer for a few months, said that Dix was "a kind old soul, but very queer and arbitrary."[9] One historian remarked about Dorothea Dix's "resolute anti-Catholic feeling."[10]

Physicians gained ultimate authority by convincing the Secretary of War to order all nurses to have the assignments signed by Dix counter-signed by the physician in charge. However, this general order (#381) was not intended to apply to the Catholic sister-nurses.[11] Of course this exacerbated conflicts between sisters and Dix's nurses, another mani-festation of Protestant–Catholic tensions. Several Protestant nurses' post-war memoirs include a pattern of criticism that identified the sisters as mindless automatons. For example, Jane Woolsey wrote: "The Roman Catholic system had features which commended it to medical officers of a certain cast of mind. The order and discipline were almost always good." She added Protestant orders of women could have adopted some of these features, and because they were more attached to "the uses of the country and the spirit of the times" they would "have been better than the Romish by so much as heart and intelligence are better than machin-ery."[12] Jane Woolsey appears to represent a new generation of women in Protestant benevolence. Dorothea Dix was of the old generation with its pursuit of righteousness linked to the improvement of the almshouses and asylums for the mentally ill. Woolsey's generation, influenced by the Seneca Falls convention, the foundation of the American women's rights movement, was driven to make society function more orderly and effi-ciently. Domesticity played a role in curing the social disorders "with heart and intelligence" of enlightened Protestant benevolence. The Seneca Falls movement of Elizabeth Cady Stanton was also more politi-cally active than the previous generation. The Know-Nothings did not permit a women's auxiliary. Because of Woolsey's condescending atti-tude toward Catholic immigrants it comes as no surprise to see her attached to the nativist movement of the 1850s. In this sense Jane Woolsey's critique of Catholic sister-nurses may have masked a more severe criticism of the physicians, whose power was assured by the mechanistic deference of the "Romanists." However she was also derisive of Dorothea Dix.

Woolsey, whose three sisters were also Civil War nurses, as well as many of the women and staff members of the Sanitary Commission, "belong nearly all to the most wealthy and respectable families." Hence, there may be a note of class consciousness in Woolsey's condescending comment on the sisters. Obviously they didn't know of the refined, knowledgeable, and richly experiential manual of Sister Matilda Coskery, a not untypical Catholic sister with a command of nursing and self-possessiveness that was rare in the general history of nursing.[13]

II

Various women's groups mobilized to support the war effort by providing supplies, blankets, food, and clothing for the soldiers. The United States Sanitary Commission was the product of the women's rights movement into medicine and social work, symbolized by Elizabeth Blackwell's New York Infirmary for women and children. The Sanitary Commission was also influenced by Florence Nightingale's emphasis on the significance of cleanliness in preventing infection and contagion among the injured soldiers. Its leadership noted that physicians discriminated against Protestant nurses because of the sisters' putative docility.[14] One such leader quoted a physician who praised the sisters for not reporting to the press on hospital conditions, thereby protecting the doctors from embarrassment.[15] However, Mary Livermore, a leader of the Commission who later became an activist in postwar women's affairs, was aroused from her anti-Catholic attitudes after encountering the Sisters of the Holy Cross at the general hospital in Cairo, Illinois. Livermore lauded Sister Angela Gillespie, who became the superior of the community after the war and is identified with its Americanization, as "a gifted lady, rare in cultivation and executive ability with winning sweetness and a manner. . . . If ever I had felt prejudice against these sisters as nurses, my experience with them during the war would have dissipated it entirely."[16] Later she remarked: "The world has known no nobler and more heroic women than those found in the ranks of the Catholic sisterhood."[17]

Angela Gillespie's brother wrote to their mother about the impact of the Sisters of the Holy Cross, particularly his own sister.

> General Wallace and other officers of the brigade . . . are delighted with the
> sisters. When the Methodist chaplain, who is very zealous in the discharge

of his duties, fails to make an impression on a hardened sinner, he requests M. Angela to pray for the sinner and to talk to him herself. . . .[18]

There were countless stories of heroic service among all groups of nurses during the Civil War: Clara Barton, later of the American Red Cross; Mary Ann Bickerdyke, New England evangelical laywoman fondly referred to as "Mother" Bickerdyke; Harriet Tubman, the famous abolitionist and African-American liberator also nursed the injured; other African-American notable women nurses were Sojourner Truth and Suzie King.[19]

Many made the ultimate sacrifice, including several sisters. Sister Lucy Dosh, a Sister of Charity of Nazareth, Kentucky, a community that nursed Union and Confederate soldiers, died early in the war at Central Hospital in Paducah and received a full military funeral.[20] Daughters of Charity, Sisters of the Holy Cross, and indeed sisters from most of the religious communities died of diseases contracted in the wards of hospitals, prisons, and hospital ships. The nursing days were severely exhausting; besides bedside care, cooking, washing, and housekeeping, there was assistance at surgery, supervising wards, and distributing food and medicine.[21] In a report of the Daughters of Charity in Richmond there were references to lacking the "necessaries of life. . . . For the sisters' table rough corn and strong fat bacon were luxuries. . . ."[22]

There were many documents on deathbed conversions. The sisters' religious motivation tended to sustain them during the war, just as it did during the epidemics. In her recent work on sister-nurses in the war, Sister Mary Denis Maher captures this religious spirit:

Clearly, the sisters were not the only women nurses functioning on battlefield, ships and in hospitals, carrying out a multitude of duties, and often suffering from the consequences of hard work. They were but a sixth of such women, who themselves were but a small part of those who cared for the sick and wounded during the Civil War. What set them apart was the entire context of religious life, which consciously and unconsciously shaped the sisters and their actions. The result of this shaping produced a group of women like no other, willing to serve in a variety of places and doing a multitude of jobs in a manner that exhibited dedication and organization. But no matter what others saw as the value of their nursing services, the sisters saw themselves as missionaries promoting religion, not nursing pioneers opening up new areas for themselves or other women. To them the fundamental purpose for serving was to care for the sick and suffering as Jesus Christ would, bringing sick and dying men to think of God in their suffering and to be baptized if they were not. Often, in their memoirs and letters, the sisters seemed cognizant of the hard work needed to accomplish their job, but they seemed to have no particular awareness that they had a skill that could or should be promoted among other women. Basically, whether the sisters came from hospital service or from teaching, care of children, or some other ministry, the areas in which they served in the Civil War and the duties which they performed simply were viewed as an extension of their ministry of doing good for those in need. As one Holy Cross sister succinctly stated, "we were not prepared as nurses, but kind hearts lent willing hands and ready sympathy and with God's help, we did much toward alleviating suffering."[23]

With the shortage of chaplains many women religious were deprived of a regular channel of eucharistic spirituality. Some bishops and superiors anticipated a severe disruption of their religious routine. The superior of the St. Joseph Sisters of Philadelphia before they began nursing on hospital boats told them: "Go to Holy Communion when you have that favor. . . . Make your meditation in the morning after your prayers and be not troubled if you can say no other prayers of the community, not even if you are deprived of Mass on Sundays."[24] On the other hand, Mother Angela Gillespie assured the Mississippi Fleet surgeon that she would not remove the Sisters of the Holy Cross from the hospital ship, the Red Rover, "as long as they were able to attend Mass." Because the Eucharist was generally available on a regular basis the sisters remained on the Red Rover throughout the war.

The Sisters of Our Lady of Mercy, founded in 1829 by Bishop John England (first ordinary of Charleston, South Carolina), were assigned to the Confederate General Hospital in Greenbriar White Sulphur Springs, Virginia until the advance of Union troops forced the removal of everyone to Montgomery White Sulphur Springs. The sisters experienced a few incidents of anti-Catholic hostility, but the chief surgeon, Dr. J. Lewis Woodville, was very supportive of them. Criticism of Woodville's support became overt shortly after he appointed Father L. P. O'Connell, the Catholic chaplain, to the sisters and patients, as the official chaplain of the hospital. This led to the resignation of the Protestant chaplain, a Reverend Madison.[25] Prior to his departure, Madison accused Sister M. de Sales Brennan of refusing to call a Methodist minister for a patient in need because O'Connell had baptized him. The sister explained the situation to the bishop, John Lynch.

> Dr. Woodville denied that such could have been the case for he knew me to ask him at the Greenbriar White [Sulphur Springs] to send him miles for a Minister. . . . I have sent for Madison himself. The fact is they are frantic at the influence we have over the men and at the number that have been baptized, all of whom have died save one who went of himself to Father O'Con-

nell, became instructed and has received baptism and Holy Communion. There are three others studying the catechism and asked for themselves."[26]

Soon after this incident, exhaustion compelled O'Connell to resign in March 1863. Some four weeks later Bishop Lynch, who became the Confederacy's agent to the Vatican, wrote to the Commissary General of the Confederate States of America. He told him of O'Connell's retirement and of the appointment of Reverend Charles J. Croghan as his replacement. "I write to know if he can be appointed Chaplain, just as the Rev. L. P. O'Connell was. The sisters receive no remuneration whatever, and have asked for none. I have had to spend something for their vesture, etc., and such articles of food as are not comprised in the rations they receive, and the additional expense of supporting a clergyman there would be unreasonable and beyond my means." Within two weeks Croghan was appointed chaplain. No doubt the commissary general's note to the Secretary of War at the bottom of the letter had a strong impact. "The writer is the Bishop of Charleston. The sisters will not remain without a Chaplain. Economy is advanced by yielding to their wish."[27]

At the conclusion of the war the sisters at Montgomery were responsible for three hundred patients from both the Union and Confederate armies. When the hospital closed six weeks later the sisters traveled to Lynchburg to seek means for returning to Charleston. The commanding officer sent them to Washington, D.C., where they were told that as noncombatants they did not qualify for travel subsidies. Father Croghan found resources for travel to New York, where they stayed at the convent of the Sacred Heart on 17th Street. Thanks to the efforts of Rev. William Quinn of St. Peter's parish on Barclay Street, the six Sisters of Our Lady of Mercy and their chaplain received $1,148 for them to travel to Charleston. The story is vividly recounted in the New York *Tablet*, July 1, 1865.[28]

In the process of rebuilding their community during the Reconstruction era, the Sisters in Charleston received financial support from the "carpetbag" city and state governments, and as thanks for their nursing Union soldiers and prisoners, Congress appropriated twelve thousand dollars. In 1882 the sisters opened the only Catholic hospital in the diocese. A small community that numbered less than one hundred members, Our Lady of Mercy Sisters had responded to the yellow-fever and cholera epidemics and to war as an expression of their commitment to pastoral care. The Sisters of Providence of St. Mary of the Woods was another such community that first entered nursing ministry during the Civil War.

Founded in Ruillé-sur-Loire in the diocese of Le Mans, France, the Sisters of Providence originated as a group of pious women who gathered to teach and visit the sick. Under the leadership of a dynamic priest, Jacques François Dujarié, the sisters were officially recognized as a congregation in 1820. At the invitation of Simon Bruté, the first bishop of Vincennes, Indiana, six Sisters of Providence established a house near Terre Haute, Indiana, in 1840. Though there were several conflicts with Bruté's successor, by the mid-1850s the sisters had opened St. Mary's Academy, later referred to as St. Mary's of the Woods, and twelve other schools and two asylums.[29] With the outbreak of hostilities they were asked to serve in the military hospital in Indianapolis. Though the sisters had no hospital experience the author of the community's chronicles did not even allude to this factor.

> The surgeons appointed to manage the military hospital established in Indianapolis, soon felt the embarrassment of having no persons of trust to take care of the sick. Though Protestants they naturally looked to the sisters as the most proper persons to have charge of the suffering soldiers.[30]

When the superior visited the hospital she was shocked by the "miserable state of filth and disorder and the sick in a wretched condition." Nevertheless, the community took charge of the hospital because it allowed them "to begin our career serving the sick in hospitals which we had long so earnestly desired." Three sisters were appointed to what the superior referred to as the "nursing career," which entailed "making it a clean, comfortable house for the sick soldiers. . . . This successful beginning was gratefully acknowledged to our Lord who permits us the happiness to serve him in the person of the sick."[31]

There was no reference to training, as if the sisters' roles as teachers and directors at orphanages had prepared them for the domestic duties of managing a clean "house," as the diarist designates the hospital. Indeed many of their tasks were in the areas of housekeeping, cooking, feeding, and managing personnel. There was some rudimentary training, as every community house included an apothecary, and there were directives in the rule of the community on the care of the sick. With most of the sisters from Irish-American families, they appear to have had experience in traditional domestic medical care. The Sisters of Providence remained behind the lines in the Indianapolis Military Hospital throughout the war and served at two other temporary hospitals. Sister Athanasius was a very astute nurse. Among immense numbers of dead and wounded soldiers sent to the hospital, she noticed one of the supposedly dead move his foot. She struggled to remove the body and placed it in a storage room, where the sisters cared and prayed for him. The man, who was a Dr. Fletcher, revived the next day. In gratitude he sent a twelve dollar check every month.[32] The community was compelled to refuse one hospital because sisters would not have been in charge but rather under the direction of a steward and would have been just a religious minority, which would have inhibited them from setting the moral tone of the hospital.

Anti-Catholic literature had been distributed in the Indianapolis hospital when the sisters were in charge. The diarist explains the atmosphere of the hospital. "They labored under considerable restriction, its Protestant discipline, and the military government to which the whole management was subject, did not give them much liberty for the benevolence and Christian duties of a Sister of Charity [of Providence] who becomes the true friend and the sole comfort of the invalid whom she nurses."[33]

After the war the Sisters of Providence, eager to place their hospital ministry on a permanent basis, opened St. John's Home for Invalids, a small institution for veterans. With only a limited need for a veterans' hospital the sisters reluctantly closed St. John's in 1871. By this time they had received a large gift of land and money from a Protestant benefactor to establish a hospital in Terre Haute. Located on five acres, Providence Hospital, a three-story brick facility that could house seventy-five patients in an emergency, and fifty comfortably, required a forty thousand dollar investment from the community. The chief physician was Dr. J. I. Batty, a French doctor who had studied at the Sorbonne and who had cared for Mother Theodore Guérin, the founder of the American community.[34] The dedication of Providence Hospital included delegations from various cities, many sisters and eleven Catholic societies in a gala parade that included Hibernians, Emmett Guards, Friendly Sons of St. Patrick, and three German societies. However, because it occurred on a Sunday, many Protestants were outraged. One critic wrote in the local newspaper: "Is this a studied insult, or a carelessness hardly less culpable, that at least four of the most prominent Protestant churches were passed by this procession during the hour of services?"[35]

Resentment against Providence Hospital originated among physicians who were opposed to a foreigner as chief of the medical staff and among the general public who renovated the public almshouse or asylum so that the city would not be compelled to send its poor to the Catholic hospital. Indeed the County Commissioners sought to remove all county patients from Providence and to prohibit sending patients without an official letter of permission.

Overt anti-Catholic sentiment was manifested in a public lecture by a putative ex-priest sponsored by the Congregational Church and aimed at Pius IX and the recently promulgated doctrine of papal infallibility at Vatican Council I. A book by P. W. Thompson of Terre Haute, entitled *The Papacy and Civil Power*, was published during the early 1870s. With a total of only seventy-three patients over a nearly two-year period Providence Hospital had been clearly ostracized by the physicians, by the commissioners of the county asylum, and by the general public. It was closed in November 1874, twenty-six months after its auspicious beginning. The building ultimately became an orphanage. Thus ended the health-care ministry of Sisters of Providence that they had "so earnestly desired."[36]

Another French community, the Sisters of the Holy Cross, also entered health care in the Civil War for the first time, but their postwar experience took a more positive direction. As noted earlier Mother Angela Gillespie was a nurse in Cairo Hospital and as superior was concerned about regular religious duties while the sisters served on the hospital ship, the Red Rover. Along with the priests and brothers of the Holy Cross, Father Basil Moreau founded the sisters out of a group of "pious women" attracted to the life of service. In 1841, the year the first four women received the habit from Moreau, Father Edward Sorin, C.S.C., and six brothers set sail for the diocese of Vincennes. Two years later four sisters arrived in the diocese. Under the direction of Sorin the sisters eventually established in 1855 an academy at St. Mary's, adjacent to the property where the University of Notre Dame had been founded in 1842. By the time of the Civil War Sorin had become thoroughly Americanized, and the sisters welcomed many young women from Irish-American and German-American families. Indeed they had grown so rapidly that nearly sixty-five Holy Cross Sisters served in Civil War hospitals as far east as Washington, D.C., and as far south as Paducah, Kentucky. At their Mound City hospital they cared at times for over one thousand patients. It was here that Mary Livermore became interested in Mother Angela Gillespie's administrative and nursing skills.

In a letter to the sisters early in the war Edward Sorin perceived their nursing ministry as modeled on that of the "Sisters of Charity [sic] . . . in the late Crimean War."[37] He invoked the charism of the young community:

> Are we not members of the holy band of the Cross—a company recently formed to meet the chief needs of our time? If the Standard of the Cross,

under which we have enlisted, knows of no enemies among men, if our object, on the contrary, is to rally them all under the precious emblem of our salvation, our little army stands arrayed against the enemy of mankind, the spirit of darkness, and the evils and the wounds which he has inflicted on humanity. Hence, wherever there is a pain to soothe, a pang to relieve, a bleeding heart or limb to treat or dress, there is a field for us to enter, under pain of deserting our noble banner.

Because their heroic ministry was infused with the purity of intention and identified with their roles as convert makers, associated with the angel of mercy imagery, Sorin was confident that the sisters' wartime nursing would dispel religious prejudice so widespread through the 1850s.

A little band of devoted sisters, ministering like angels amidst the soldiery, will do away with prejudices and show the beauty and resources of the Catholic Faith to support man in all possible trials much more forcibly than volumes of argument and evidence.

However, Sorin perceived the sisters' nursing within the context of evangelization.

But, laying aside all terrestrial considerations, there are souls to be saved— souls redeemed by Jesus Christ, and exposed to eternal ruin. Who knows if, after receiving the kind ministrations of these angels of the earth, those poor sufferers will not be willing to listen to the words of salvation; and if thus made to feel the benefit of their devotedness, they will not permit them to prepare their souls for baptism and heaven? If a single soul could thus be gained to God, would it not more than justify the trial? But who could tell how many may thus be sent to heaven?[38]

The Sisters of the Holy Cross continue to thrive in their nursing ministry today. Because they represent, like the Sisters of Our Lady of Mercy and the Sisters of Providence of St. Mary's of the Woods, a community without previous experience in their own hospitals, their stories are worthy of particular attention. Since the Daughters of Charity and the Sisters of Mercy are fully treated in other chapters of this work, it was also a matter of balance that I chose relatively young, inexperienced communities.

III

To say that the sisters' Civil War nursing dispelled religious prejudice is a commonplace consensus among historians, but there are various emphases upon its causation. By demonstrating the practical viability of the vowed life they convinced many Protestant nurses, physicians, and patients that Catholic women religious were well-disciplined, respectful, and loyal nurses; to the patients they brought compassion, consolation and prayer. When one knowledgeable woman was asked whether or not the Catholic sisters were better nurses than other women, she replied, "Yes, they are. . . . I think it is because with them it is a work of self-abnegation, and of duty to God, and they are so quiet and self-forgetful in its exercize that they do it better while many other women show such self-consciousness and are so fussy."[39]

At the American bishops' Secondary Plenary Council of Baltimore in 1866, Martin John Spalding, archbishop of Baltimore, who presided as apostolic delegate at the council, introduced a schema that an ecclesiastic, residing in Baltimore, should be assigned responsibility for the African-American Catholics in the wake of the emancipation of all slaves. Spalding suggested that the ecclesiastic be a vicar apostolic, a bishop under Roman authority rather than possessing ordinary jurisdiction. Augustin Vérot, once the defender of the Confederacy, agreed with Spalding, a former moderate on the Confederacy and the slavery issue. Most of the bishops opposed this proposal, which, in effect, precluded any concentrated efforts at evangelization. Instead pastoral responsibility remained at the discretion of each bishop. There were only six black priests ordained over the next fifty years; and in this age of brick-and-mortar bishops, there were some black Catholic elementary schools, but they were separate and unequal, and there were only a handful of black secondary schools. While there were black annexes or wards within Catholic hospitals, there were no black Catholic hospitals until after World War I. Without a coordinator or a vicar apostolic for African-American Catholics there was an appalling gap between Catholic ideals and social reality, particularly when many other Christian denominations responded vigorously to the needs of the African-American community. Catholic bishops feared that if they followed suit they would be fanning the flames of anti-Catholicism ever smoldering in southern society.

The pastoral letter of the Second Plenary Council did not explicitly refer to the over six hundred sisters who nursed soldiers in camps, battlefields, and prisons. Though there had been a tendency to portray sisters in idealistic terms,[40] the bishops' letter reveals a higher plane in this rhetoric of patronizing gender construction:

> We are filled with sentiments of the deepest reverence for those holy Virgins, who, in our various religious communities, having taken counsel of St. Paul, have chosen the better part, that they may be holy "In body and in spirit." These serve God with undivided heart; and, like Mary, sit at the feet

of Jesus in devout contemplation; or, like Martha, devote themselves to the service of their neighbor, instructing youth or tending old age, ministering to the sick, or calming the remorses and encouraging the hopes of the penitent.[41]

The bishops would not violate their own sense of the humility of the vowed life of women religious by directly praising sisters' wartime ministry, but they seem to imply their pride in the sisters' general contribution to American church and society:

> We discharge a grateful duty, in rendering a public testimony to the virtue and heroism of these Christian Virgins; whose lives shed the good odor of Christ in every place, and whose devotedness and spirit of self-sacrifice have, more perhaps than any other cause, contributed to effect a favorable change in the minds of thousands estranged from our faith.[42]

The impact of the Civil War upon women religious was deeply significant; new communities entered nursing as a permanent ministry; others were encouraged to expand; while all sisters could have claimed a sense of satisfaction in their response to the war effort. The American sisters were activists able to adapt to the most severe tests of human endurance. They drew sustenance from their missionary experience on the boundaries of existence—that sacred condition on the threshold of death.

It was nearly fifty years after the war that a monument, "Nuns of the Battlefield," memorialized the Civil War nursing of the twenty-one communities of women religious. Mary Ryan Jolly, who wrote a history on the topic, and the Ladies Auxiliary of the Ancient Order of Hibernians were responsible for the monument. Erected on Rhode Island and Connecticut Avenues in Washington, D.C., the monument portrays in bas-relief sisters from twelve communities. The year was 1924, during a period when the Ku Klux Klan's organizing principle was anti-Catholicism and when an immigrant restriction law had just been implemented after years of lobbying by the "respectable" representatives of Anglo-Saxon superiority eager to close the gates to immigration from the Catholic and Jewish communities of eastern and southern Europe. The sister-nurses of the Civil War no doubt contributed to the breakdown of religious prejudices, even if only for a short time.[43]

CHAPTER SIX

The Frontier Experience

I

IN RECOGNITION OF the quadricentennial of the United States, the American Historical Association convened in Chicago during the Columbian Exposition (1893), where Frederick Jackson Turner presented his seminal paper "The Significance of the Frontier in American History." In opposition to those historians who viewed the origins of American democracy in the New England town meeting the "Turner Thesis" was based on the notion that the mix of peoples on the western frontier created a distinctive Americanism; its free land, individualism, self-reliance, and "that buoyancy and exuberance that comes with freedom" is the significant environment that nurtured the seeds of liberty.[1] Nearly sixty years later the French philosopher Jacques Maritain commented on Americans as "pilgrims in their own land," always on the move.[2] Though Turner referred to the topic of religion on the frontier he concluded that it was a relatively unexplored area in historical studies.

Among the historians of the Catholic community Thomas W. Spalding, C.F.X., has contributed the most recent study on the topic. In an article entitled "Frontier Catholicism," Spalding expands on the work of Thomas C. McAvoy, C.S.C., and James Hennesey, S.J. He particularly addresses the "Turnerian legacies of the frontier—democracy, individualism, activism; confidence, optimism, simplicity, patriotism, [and] plasticity." Though aware of the blurred lines between immigrant and frontier Catholicism he views the latter as more identifiable with the movement of the laity "who pushed the parameters of American Catholicism outward and dared the institutional church to follow. . . . Catholics on the frontier knew instinctively that they were the Church, the people of God, whom God in due time would endow with whatever institutions their environment demanded. . . . They did not always expect an exact replication of the institutional church they had left behind."[3] Though the frontier was peopled by Catholics of every ethnic group and though there were parishes that reflected ethnic rivalries, there is a distinctive regional flavor to the Catholicism that developed by interaction with the pioneer conditions of the nineteenth century. In this chapter the focus will be on those hospital foundations in mission areas in the small towns and mining communities of the far West, in the remote regions of Oregon and Washington, and in the borderlands of Texas, New Mexico, Arizona, and California.

In contrast to the strong institutional presence in the large immigrant centers in Boston, New York, Baltimore, Philadelphia, Cincinnati, St. Louis, Chicago, and Milwaukee, the church in Vancouver, Portland, Leavenworth, Salt Lake City, and San Antonio was missionary, self-reliant, activist, pragmatic, and open to the plasticity of the culture. In response to the demands of the health-care mission, women religious stressed the active apostolate rather than "passive" contemplative prayer and tended to be more self-determined than their sisters in the structured and institutionalized Northeast.[4] The frontier hospital experience originated in the premodern period with an emphasis on custodial care, cleanliness, order, and a refined moral climate. The eastern voluntary hospital serving the immigrant population according to the model of Protestant benevolence did not take root on the frontier where local idiosyncracies determined the hospital; Catholic sisters staffed mining and railroad facilities with particular insurance schemes, but the ethos was formed by women religious who symbolized the intersection of the sacred and the secular. In many towns the sisters' hospital was the only facility available. Without priests these sisters were as "priest-chaplains" invoking the presence of God in their prayer and ministry. The sisters' pastoral ministry blended with the nineteenth-century women's sphere of domestic life to impose a touch of refinement on the rough edges of frontier existence. This experience, which requires an extensive narrative, added a new dimension to the missionary model of health care.

II

St. Paul, Minnesota, was a frontier diocese in the early 1850s when Bishop Joseph Cretin provided the Sisters of St. Joseph of Carondelet with a suitable building for what became St. Joseph's Hospital. Comprising the entire territory of Minnesota, the diocese in 1854 had a Catholic population of ten thousand, who were served by only thirteen priests. Besides the hospital the sisters had opened St. Catherine's Academy. The *Metropolitan Catholic Almanac* of 1855 included a description of the new location of St. Joseph's: "An hospital, all of stone, three stories and a half, besides the basement, 75 feet by 34, in a fine location on a large block . . . , is nearly completed. It affords room enough in its different divisions, for a Novitiate for the Sisters; for an orphan asylum, and many patients."[5]

Thirty years later (1885), John Ireland had been bishop for a year, his sister Ellen (Sister Seraphene, C.S.J.) was provincial superior of the Sisters of St. Joseph, with 140 members in the St. Paul province. Ireland, who later achieved national status as a leader of the Americanist movement and as a prominent figure in the inner circles of the Republican Party, advocated a policy of aggressive assimilation. At the Third Plenary Council of Baltimore, the then recently installed bishop of St. Paul spoke of the inherent compatibility of American republicanism and Roman Catholicism. "There is no conflict between the Catholic Church and America. I could not utter one syllable that would belie, however remotely, either the Church or the Republic, and when I assert, as I now solemnly do, that the principles of the Church are in thorough harmony with the interests of the Republic, I know in the depths of my soul that I speak the truth."[6]

By 1885, St. Joseph's Hospital had expanded considerably to accommodate seventy-five patients and was at the take-off point to modernity. That year the hospital had its first interns and affiliated with St. Paul Medical School.[7] In Minneapolis, the Sisters of Mercy, who had moved from Grand Rapids, Michigan, in 1879, owned and operated Mater Misericordia Hospital since its foundation in 1882. According to Sisters Helen Angela Hurley, C.S.J. and Anne Thomasina Sampson, C.S.J., historians of the Sisters of St. Joseph and of St. Mary's Hospital respectively, the Sisters of Mercy had experienced such severe financial problems that Archbishop Ireland was compelled to purchase the hospital and turn it over to the province of the Sisters of St. Joseph in 1887.[8] However, in a recent study of the Sisters of Mercy who originated in St. Paul, it was not the financial problems of Mater Misericordia that elicited the intervention of Ireland, but rather it was his disapproval of the fund-raising efforts of Mother M. Joseph Lynch, the superior of the community. As a diocesan community under the direct authority of the bishop, the Sisters of Mercy were prohibited from solving festering financial problems of the hospital. ". . . instead [Ireland intended] to ease the Mercys out of his diocese and replace them at the Minneapolis hospital with the Sisters of

St. Joseph. One of Ireland's sisters was a major superior in the latter congregation. He may have felt that that fact would give him more control over the Sisters of St. Joseph."[9] Inferring Ireland's intention to expel the Sisters of Mercy because they were competing with his sister's community, this interpretation, based on primary evidence, is supported by the general consensus that the archbishop of St. Paul tended to be liberal on large national issues but rather authoritarian at home.

St. Mary's Hospital achieved prominence in the twin cities. The education of the sisters was particularly enlightened. After undergraduate study at St. Catherine's College, the first Catholic institution to be awarded a Phi Beta Kappa chapter, several nursing sisters pursued advanced degrees at Teachers College, Columbia University. By the time St. Mary's was founded, St. Paul was no longer a frontier outpost, but its character had been partially shaped by its interaction with the frontier and its remoteness from the dominance of the Northeast.

The story of the first hospital at Fort Vancouver in the Washington Territory is replete with themes of frontier Catholicism. Employees of the Hudson's Bay Company had made many requests for priests. On November 24, 1838, Francis Norbert Blanchet, vicar-general of the territory, presided at the first Mass in the new mission. Twenty-six Catholics, Canadian and Iroquois, made up the congregation. News of the creation of a vicariate-apostolic for Oregon in 1843 did not reach Blanchet for over a year. The vicariate, which included all the territory north of California and west of the Rocky Mountains, became the archdiocese of Oregon City in July of 1846 with Francis Blanchet as the ordinary while his brother Augustine Blanchet was appointed bishop of the new diocese of Walla Walla—later Nesqually, Washington. Though the number of Catholics did not warrant the establishment of a metropolitan see—there were only five churches in Oregon City and Walla Walla—the great distance from either St. Louis or Quebec was the rationale for its establishment. Because of an incident that ignited native American hostility Bishop Augustine Blanchet moved to Fort Nesqually in 1850. Three years later Nesqually became the see city with jurisdiction over the Territory of Washington, but Blanchet built his cathedral in Vancouver.[10]

In 1856 Mother Joseph Pariseau and four other Sisters of Charity of Providence arrived in Vancouver, where they established a school and a hospital. This community, officially named the Daughters of Charity, Servants of the Poor, was founded in Montreal in 1843. The widowed founder, Madame Emile Tavernier Gamelin, organized a group of seven women who responded to the cholera epidemic of the 1840s and then established a home for the elderly poor. Influenced by the Daughters of Charity of France and the Sisters of Charity of the United States, the Sisters of Providence responded to Bishop A. M. A. Blanchet's request for sisters. Earlier, in 1852 five sisters had traveled six thousand miles to Oregon City only to find it virtually deserted. Two months later the sisters left for San Francisco, and ultimately they decided to be missionaries in Chile.[11]

As superior of the mission to Vancouver, Mother Pariseau became known as "the builder." When her father introduced her to the Sisters of Providence he commented on her qualities: "She can read, and write and figure accurately. She can cook and sew and spin and do all manner of housework. She has learned carpentry from me and can handle tools as well as I can. Moreover, she can plan and supervise the work of others. I assure you . . . she will some day make a good superior."[12] She was indeed appointed to that post and, with four other sisters, arrived in Vancouver on December 8, 1856, the feast of the Immaculate Conception, the patronal feast of the United States. It was on the birthday of the father of the nation, George Washington, that the frontier community moved into their convent, "a small wooden building 16' x 24' with four windows." The sisters lived in the attic. A small room served as a chapel; "with a few boards Sister Joseph built a suitable altar; from a candle box she made a gem-like little tabernacle, painted and decorated with gold ornament."[13]

In a January 14, 1860, letter to the motherhouse the sisters in Vancouver described the population of the town: "some four or five hundred whites and lesser number of half breeds; as for Indians, we see them as seldom as you do in Montreal." There were two hundred soldiers at the fort. The Hudson's Bay Company was thriving and the sisters could "see the wharf where the steamers land. . . . If the place keeps on progressing it will soon become an important city."[14]

Characteristic of the interfaith cooperation of the frontier, Vancouver's first hospital was sponsored by an ad hoc group of Catholic, Protestant, and Jewish women organized in March 1858, by Father John Brouillet, vicar general of the diocese. Based on the Ladies of Charity model of Vincent de Paul, the women raised money for furnishings and a pharmacy for the one-room hospital, appropriately titled St. Joseph's. Mother Pariseau described the women's group to the bishop of Montreal: "They assemble on Wednesdays to sew, since they are not numerous and have little means they are only able to take care of the sick poor of our country. But they allow ten dollars a week, the price which seems to be set up as that for board in this country. We bear only the expense of those that can't pay."[15] In contrast to the densely populated East with almshouses that cared for hundreds of poor and with general hospitals associated with groups of teaching physicians, this first hospital in the Washington Territory could accommodate only three or four patients. By the end of 1858 fifteen patients had been admitted, three of whom had died. In her letter Mother Joseph Pariseau wrote of the religious dimension of the hospital. Deathbed conversions, symbolic of the sisters' mediation of grace, "excite our ardor and . . . make us work zealously for the conversion of so many straying souls." Of the three who died the first year, one was baptized. "Some weeks after he arrived at the hospital he began to realize the truth of the Catholic religion. Realizing his failing strength he asked to be baptized on the feast of St. Vincent de Paul. . . . The edifying death of our first patient appears to have made a favorable impression even among the Protestants of the town."[16]

A young native American familiar with the sisters came to the hospital to "take their medicines" but did not survive. "This poor little one had the happiness of receiving Extreme Unction." The president of the Ladies of Charity, an Episcopalian, entered the hospital, but, because she never regained consciousness, "we were unable to give her religious help. Her death was a great sorrow to us." Unsure of the proper disposition toward Protestants in their last moments Mother Pariseau asked Bishop Bourget to "give us a rule by which to guide ourselves under like circumstances in homes as well as in hospitals."[17]

The superior reported to Bishop Laroque about a patient who called himself an Episcopalian but who was "indifferent about things religious." When his illness inflicted "great suffering" the sisters "asked him to invoke the Blessed Virgin, assuring him that she would not fail to help him. He did so but called her the Mother of Jesus. He had told me some days before that he thought she was a woman like all others." Despite this "insult our Immaculate Mother seemed to accept his invocation. An immediate change took place in him. He wished to be baptized." Before he died he received the last rites. The sisters gave him a medal of the Virgin Mary, and "he kissed it affectionately." Mother Pariseau remarked that since the patient had embraced the faith there was no need to hide the medal "under his pillow," indicating the practice as standard procedure for Protestant patients.[18] (An analysis of the significance of this devotion to the Miraculous Medal appears in chapter nine.)

By 1865 there were thirty-one Sisters of Providence located in the diocese. They had an academy and orphanages—girls' and boys'—in Vancouver, an academy in Walla Walla, schools in Steilacoom, Washington, and St. Ignatius Mission. They would soon establish a mission school at

Snohomish Indian Reservation. In his first tour of the vast archdiocese of Oregon City as coadjutor, Archbishop Charles John Seghers visited St. Ignatius Mission in the summer of 1879. Considered as a model, this Jesuit ministry to the Flathead Indians of Montana flourished as a center of religious and social activity. Upon his arrival on August 2, Seghers was greeted by eleven hundred Indians. In the procession were the Sisters of Providence, and later Seghers toured the sisters' school and hospital.[19] Had they not had a hospital the sisters' school, like the schools of many women religious on Indian reservations, would have been a makeshift hospital. Of course when the occasion demanded all sisters did home nursing.

Prior to the arrival of the Sisters of Providence, two Jesuit priests, Gregory Mengarini and Anthony Ravalli, who had been trained in homeopathic medicine in Italy, nursed the native Americans subjected to epidemics because of their contact with white men and women. Pierre de Smet, founder of the Rocky Mountain Missions, reported: "One of the Fathers each morning visits the sick to furnish them with medicines and give them such assistance as their wants require." Mengarini discovered the religious significance of his nursing ministry. "It is absolutely necessary that a missionary have some knowledge of medicine or the Indians would have turned to traditional folk medicine." Another Jesuit priest, Nicholas Point, noted that "Indians associate the priesthood with medicine. He who is a specialist in medicine enjoys the attributes of the priest, the miracle worker, and the prophet."[20]

The Sisters of Providence also had charge of St. John's Lunatic Asylum in Vancouver.[21] Before this time the mentally ill had been housed in jails. In a letter to John B. Brouillet, Mother Pariseau referred to a contract between the sisters and the Territory of Washington "for the care of the insane." The sisters received $8 a week for each patient to cover the cost of room, board, "laundry and medical care." Apparently, it was a temporary arrangement, as Mother Pariseau stated that the "Governor is kindly disposed in our regard [and] . . . will do all in his power to make the work permanent for us."[22] Such a "small revenue" discouraged Mother Joseph, who had hoped for nine dollars per week income that would have allowed her to pay the travel expenses of sisters from the motherhouse. However, the contract with the government was not renewed, and in 1866 the asylum became the new St. Joseph's Hospital; additions were made in 1869 and 1872. It was still a small hospital, 630 patients were admitted between 1858 and 1881, 490 of whom were charity patients.[23]

Mother Pariseau managed a farm that was owned by Brouillet and tilled by a tenant farmer. It was a precarious enterprise, as the weather ruined all the crops of the 1862 fall harvest. Since the orphanage was entirely based on charity the sisters relied on donations, particularly during periods of crop failure. There were in the mining camps begging tours by priests sponsored by Archbishop Blanchet of Oregon City, but, according to Mother Joseph, the archbishop kept two-thirds of the collection "to pay for the travel of his recruits," that is, priests and sisters destined for Oregon. Though "she disliked to write" this account, she pointed out to Brouillet that the diocese centered in Vancouver is "burdened . . . with works of charity [and] with far fewer advantages than the Archdiocese of Oregon."[24] Mother Pariseau eventually led her own begging tours into the mining camps; there are several extant photos depicting her mounted on a horse and speaking before a crowd of workers.

Mother Pariseau presided over the expansion of the sisters into Portland and Seattle. Without one Catholic hospital in the entire archdiocese of Oregon City the need was obvious. During an 1874 visit to Portland, she received two proposals to establish a hospital, one from a wealthy frontiersman and the other from the St. Vincent de Paul Society of Portland. While both included a gift of property the Vincentians also offered one thousand dollars, a gift the superior accepted. On July 19, 1875, St. Vincent's Hospital was dedicated by Archbishop Francis Blanchet. Four Sisters of Providence staffed this seventy-five-bed hospital. With only about twenty thousand Catholics in the archdiocese served by twenty-three priests the presence of a Catholic hospital was significant not only for the Catholic community but for the frontier Oregon population in general.[25]

In 1877 the Sisters of Providence took care of the poorhouse of King County. Comparable to an almshouse in the East, this institution housed paupers, the mentally ill, and the marginalized sick poor. The following year the sisters moved the patients to a new facility, Providence Hospital, which could care for thirty patients. Mother Joseph designed the new hospital opened in 1882. It was a modern facility, the first to use gas lighting in Seattle. Its most innovative feature, however, was the introduction of a ten-dollar prepaid insurance certificate. In an advertisement for Providence Hospital, this insurance coverage was explained.

> In response, now, to what seems to be popular demand, the sisters will furnish tickets to any person in health who desire them, at $10 each; the holder of which shall be entitled to admission to the hospital, whenever incapacitated from any cause whatever, during the year for which the ticket

is issued. Holders of tickets will be furnished with a pleasant room, board, skilled nurses, tender care of the sisters, medicines and competent medical and surgical treatment, without any further expense to them whatever.[26]

The new hospital could accommodate 125 patients and, according to the advertisement, "It is perfectly non-sectarian in its management. No one, whether Jew or Gentile, Protestant or Catholic has even been turned away from its doors, but all have been welcomed, whether or not they have had the means wherewith to pay."[27]

When Mother Joseph died in 1902 there were Washington and Oregon provinces numbering over 250 professed sisters, many of whom were staffing hospitals in Vancouver, Seattle, Portland, and six other towns in the two states. By this time the Sisters of the Third Order of St. Francis of Philadelphia, founded by Bishop John N. Neumann, were in charge of St. Joseph's Hospital in Tacoma, established for the German community. The Sisters of St. Joseph of Peace, recently founded in Newark, New Jersey, had a small hospital in Whatcom, Washington; the Dominican Sisters also had a small hospital, St. Joseph's in Aberdeen, Washington. By 1902 the hospitals were rapidly modernizing with nurses' training schools advancing gradually toward full professionalization. Since there were as many as fifty sisters nursing in one hospital, convent life had also become more routinized.

Mother Pariseau designed and built relatively modern hospitals in the setting of frontier Catholicism. The mission character of the church in Nesqually (Seattle) and Oregon City (Portland) in contrast to the immigrant church in Philadelphia and Boston is clearly demonstrated in the following statistics for the year 1877. Philadelphia's Catholic population was 250,000 with 227 priests, 14 communities of women religious, and three hospitals; Boston's Catholic population was 310,000; priests numbered 200, while there were eight convents and five hospitals; Oregon City numbered 20,000 Catholics served by 23 priests, two communities of women religious, and one hospital; Nesqually's Catholic population was around 10,000, with 17 priests, 48 Sisters of Providence, and one hospital.[28]

The Sisters of Providence, like the Daughters of Charity, were committed to active life outside the enclosure. The foundress, Mother Emile Gamelin, was closely associated with Bishop Ignace Bourget of Montreal, who is considered the founder of the community. He said that "the principal end for which you have been instituted . . . [was to] be devoted, heart and soul, to your poor and your sick,"[29] ". . . in the homes of the sick or by the bedside of the dying must you immolate yourselves for charity's sake. . . ."[30]

Mother Pariseau, the activist, architect, and artisan, manifested this charism as she established eleven hospitals, seven academies, five Indian schools, and two orphanages. Considered the first architect of the Pacific Northwest by the American Institute of Architects, Mother Pariseau's missionary endeavors were memorialized when she was chosen to represent the State of Washington in the National Statuary Hall in Washington, D.C. Though there had been some controversy during the nominating process the recognition received widespread support when President Jimmy Carter dedicated the statue in May 1980. She was the fifth woman and the first woman religious to be so honored. The other statue representing Washington is of Marcus Whitman, a Protestant missionary. As Wilfred P. Schoenberg, S.J., has noted, "it is ironic that Washington, well known for its large unchurched population, should select two missionaries as its representatives in the Hall."[31]

III

As the Sisters of Providence expanded eastward into Montana in the 1870s there was another congregation, the Sisters of Charity of Leavenworth, pioneering health care on the frontier.[32] This community of women religious had migrated to Leavenworth from Nashville, where they had been formed as a diocesan community of former Sisters of Charity of Nazareth, Kentucky. Founded by John B. David, S.S., a missionary associate of Bishop Benedict Flaget of the Bardstown (later Louisville) diocese, in 1812, the Sisters of Charity of Nazareth's first superior was Catherine Spalding. During her administration the community founded St. Vincent's Infirmary in 1836. By the mid-1850s the infirmary, now named St. Joseph's, became a thriving hospital, the largest private institution in the state. As noted earlier, the Nazareth community was widely acclaimed for its response to the cholera epidemics and to the wounded in the Civil War. At the request of Bishop Richard P. Miles, O.P., the community expanded into the diocese of Nashville in 1842 and soon established an academy, an orphanage, and a small hospital.

Influenced by Bishop John Hughes, who assumed authority of the Sisters of Charity of Emmitsburg, Miles wished to be the superior of the Sisters of Charity of Nazareth in his diocese, but Mother Catherine

Spalding opposed such a separation and recalled the sisters from Nashville in 1851. Of the fourteen sisters six remained in Nashville and were soon joined by two more sisters from Nazareth. Bishop Miles appointed Father Ivo Schacht the ecclesiastical superior of the diocesan community. Under his direction the sisters continued nursing at St. John's Hospital, cared for orphans, and returned to teaching. Schacht purchased property for an orphanage and a sisters' home. The community expanded with the arrival of six Sisters of Charity of Cincinnati and a few vocations from the diocese. However, a conflict between Miles and Schacht culminated in the latter's suspension of priestly faculties, and he left the diocese in 1857. Miles refused to honor the priest's debts so the sisters felt abandoned. The superior, Mother Xavier Ross, a convert and daughter of a Methodist minister, sold all the property to pay the creditors.[33] With a frontier sense of self-determination the community sent Mother Ross to the Provincial Council of St. Louis (1858) in search of an episcopal sponsor for a western mission among native Americans. The famous Jesuit missionary Pierre DeSmet introduced her to Bishop John B. Miège, a Jesuit and a vicar apostolic of Kansas with residence in Leavenworth. Miège offered the sisters a challenging mission, told them he would respect their constitutions derived from Vincent de Paul's rule for an active community, and accepted their request to become their ecclesiastical superior. After Mother Ross made an exploratory visit to Leavenworth, six sisters, one novice, two postulants, and one orphan girl (three sisters returned to the Cincinnati community) journeyed to their new home, thus forming in November 1859 the first community of Sisters of Charity of Leavenworth. Of the sixteen priests in the vicariate apostolic east of the Rocky Mountains in 1860 most were either Benedictines in Atchison or Jesuits in St. Mary, Kansas. By 1860 the Sisters of Leavenworth had opened an "Academy for Young Ladies" as well as a "Day School," which had an enrollment of two hundred students, many of whom were Protestant.[34]

The territory was known as "Bleeding Kansas" during the late 1850s as Free-Soilers and proslavery settlers competed for a majority vote on slavery in the territories. Leavenworth's population was nearing ten thousand in 1858 with several factories and foundries, mills and breweries. In this boom town the sisters opened St. John's Hospital in 1863, the first nonmilitary hospital in Kansas. The hospital was the first institution owned by this young community of women religious. Sister Joanna Bruner was the initial superior of St. John's. With nursing experience in the hospital in Nashville, Sister Bruner, in cooperation with the two staff physicians, provided apprentice training for the sister-nurses. Perhaps it was she who composed a list of twelve rules for visitors and patients, which was placed on the wall of each of the hospital rooms. The list represented a blend of Catholic and domestic life:

1. The Sisters are responsible only for money and valuables given to their charge.
2. Patients are not permitted to enter any rooms except those assigned to them by the Sister in charge: they are particularly requested to preserve order and silence, and not to stand in the corridors and doorways.
3. Patients must be at their proper places either in or about their beds at the visits of the physicians, or at the hours for taking medicine.
4. Patients are requested not to chew or smoke in the rooms or corridors; spitting on the floors or defacing the walls is prohibited, and no one is allowed to throw anything out of the windows. Smoking is allowed only in the smoking rooms.
5. All articles for the use of the patients must be kept in their proper places, clothing not in use should be placed in the wardrobe.
6. No patient who is dressed is permitted to sit or lie on the bed or in any manner to disarrange the same.
7. Passionate conversations should not be carried on and those on Religion and politics are especially to be avoided.
8. Patients are not allowed to get up without the permission of the Physician or to leave the premises without the consent of the Sister in charge.
9. No one is permitted to handle the heating apparatus of the hospital, either in rooms of the patients or in any other part of the house.
10. Visitors are admitted Sundays and Thursdays from 2 to 4 o'clock p.m.
11. Visitors are prohibited to hand eatables or drinks to the patients, such things are to be given to the presiding Sister who will serve or withhold the same by order of the Physician.
12. For the sake of the patients, persons entering the Hospital are kindly requested to avoid all unnecessary noise.[35]

The hospital accommodated patients in charity and public wards and six private rooms. With a majority of charity patients the hospital relied on donations for support. Sister Bruner encouraged a group of laywomen to sponsor a festival and auction that was unsuccessful. But independently they raised money at a ball and auction. However, Sister

Bruner's confessor prohibited her from accepting money earned from dancing, entertainment severely criticized by relatively rigorous clergy of the period. The laity, who had raised much of the money, refused to yield. Groceries were delivered and money was sent from anonymous donors. Such fund-raising activities were necessary, given the voluntary character of hospitals in the United States. The rigorous confessor represented an "old-world" response to American pragmatism and the survival ethic of a pluralistic society.

In the fall of 1869, just ten years after their arrival in Leavenworth, the sisters expanded into Montana at the request of two Jesuit missionaries in Helena, F. X. Kuppens and Leopold Van Gorp, and through the intervention of Pierre DeSmet. Five sisters and a lay teacher departed from the motherhouse for the fifteen-day journey by rail and stagecoach to the thriving Montana city, which numbered some three thousand Catholics, and which the Lewis and Clark Expedition had visited in 1805. Immigrants arrived by wagon train in 1862, but with the discovery of gold in Last Chance Gulch the population grew to 7,500 in 1866. The discovery of silver engendered further growth. Made the capital of the territory in 1875, Helena became state capital in 1894. The vicariate of Nebraska became a diocese in 1884 with a Catholic population of fifteen thousand.[36]

The Jesuits planned for an academy and a hospital. In November of 1870 St. John's Hospital was opened, staffed by sister-nurses sent from Leavenworth. The need was so great that within five years the hospital moved twice, the last move entailed doubling its bed capacity to around fifty patients. Though not included in the *Catholic Directory* until 1877, as early as 1872 it accepted the indigent sick from Lewis and Clark County and Meagher and Jefferson Counties. Hence it was both an almshouse and a private hospital. It was also the territory's first mental hospital until 1877 when the territory placed mentally ill patients in its own facility in Warm Springs. There is evidence that Lewis and Clark County withdrew its indigent sick from the sisters' hospital to the poor-farm ostensibly because the hospital's patient care was so effective that too many of the sick poor applied for admission, thereby increasing public expense. There was historical precedent for such an austere individualistic ethic; the famous 1834 poor-law reform bill in England was designed to be a deterrence to poverty by prohibiting the dole and limiting relief to the poorhouse. In a history of the Sisters of Charity of Leavenworth, written by L. B. Palladino, a noted Jesuit missionary who was an eyewitness to these events, the physician's report for the county board of commissioners included the remark that the sisters were "feeding their patients on pious talk instead of well-prepared and wholesome food."[37] If the food was so poor why would there be so many applying for admission, while a pious conversation, according to many physicians of the day, enhanced treatment of illness. Hence, it appears that anti-Catholic animus influenced the decision. In any event St. John's Hospital in Helena continued to expand with the addition of an orphanage.

In the 1870s and 1880s the Sisters of Charity of Leavenworth founded hospitals in Deer Lodge, Virginia City, Butte, and Anaconda, Montana. Patients were victims of mining accidents particularly at St. Ann's Hospital in the "smelter city," where Anaconda Copper Mining Company required its thousands of workers to pay into an insurance fund for hospitalization. Virginia City went from a boom town of twenty thousand to a much smaller town when the mines failed to yield enough gold. Hence the pioneer hospital, St. Mary's, was closed after four years (1875–80).

Butte, Montana, had a tiny gold rush, but it was silver and copper mining that made it flourish. In November of 1881 St. James Hospital opened with accident cases predominating. Within ten years it doubled its bed capacity to over one hundred, and until 1892 it admitted county patients. St. Ann's Hospital in Deer Lodge was a small fifty-bed facility that grew with the expansion of the Northern Pacific Railroad into the town.[38]

The sisters' move to Wyoming originated with a personal request from a priest. While Mother Xavier Ross was waiting for a train at Cheyenne, a transfer point between Montana and Colorado in the fall of 1875, Father Eugene Cusson, of Laramie City, one of the two pastors in Wyoming, fortuitously identified the superior and told her that the county needed a hospital for its sick poor and that the Union Pacific Railroad also needed care for its workers. Several months later two sisters arrived in Laramie City to establish the first hospital in the territory that was then in the vicariate of Nebraska, which in 1880 had a Catholic population of about forty thousand. The Union Pacific Railroad provided the sisters with their first building, which was renovated for a twenty-four bed hospital. They prepared for its opening by sewing bed clothes and begging for money for supplies. Later two more sisters arrived to help staff St. Joseph's Hospital.[39] To support the facility, begging tours were organized during the summers among the mining camps unaccustomed to women visitors, much less to women religious. Despite the enormous personal and religious commitment to the Laramie community the railroad moved its mills where it made tracks in Rawlins, Colorado, and the county founded its own hospital for the sick poor. With its principal sources of patients removed, it became evident that the hospital could not survive. Hence in 1895 the sisters left Laramie.[40]

Colorado and Utah became a vicariate apostolic in 1868 with the appointment of Joseph Projectus Machebeuf as bishop with residence in Denver. Located at the western rim of the Great Plains the mile-high city, as it is now known, received its name from James D. Denver, governor of the territory, 1859–60. The "Pike's Peak or bust" gold rush of those years brought 150,000 to the Rocky Mountain West. However, many returned frustrated, while those who stayed settled in the mining areas of Leadville, where the Sisters of Charity of Leavenworth founded St. Vincent's Hospital, Georgetown, and hospitals in other mining towns in Colorado, Montana, Wyoming, and Idaho. Machebeuf invited the sisters to establish a hospital in Denver. Arriving in 1872 they moved to four locations before they developed a permanent eighty-bed facility in 1878 at a cost of forty thousand dollars. The *Rocky Mountain News*, Denver's oldest newspaper, reported on August 31, 1891 that "St. Joseph's refuses nobody from its doors. . . . The sisters have hid themselves in the garret in order to make room for the increased number of sick."[41]

The period was one of phenomenal growth brought on by the railroads and manufacturing. Between 1870 and 1890 Denver grew from 4,800 to 107,000; Catholic population went from 12,000 in the vicariate apostolic of Colorado and Utah to 50,000 in the new diocese of Denver. There were no hospitals in 1870, but in 1890 there were ten Catholic hospitals in Colorado, but only 260 patients listed in the *Catholic Directory* for the year. Besides St. Joseph's, the Sisters of St. Francis of Perpetual Adoration (motherhouse in Lafayette, Indiana) had charge of the Union Pacific Hospital in Denver since 1898. Later they opened their own hospital. In Colorado Springs the Sisters of Charity of Cincinnati took over the Albert Glochner Memorial Sanitarium in 1893. They also had a hospital in Pueblo, while the Sisters of Mercy came from St. Louis to Conejos, Colorado, where they opened a storefront infirmary in 1882. Eventually they opened hospitals in Durango and Denver.[42]

The Sisters of St. Joseph of Carondelet also traveled from St. Louis to Georgetown, Colorado. At the request of Bishop Machebeuf they started a small community hospital in 1880. In announcing its opening the *Colorado Miner* noted that "$700 had been subscribed by the mining and mill companies." At first fifty cents a month entitled the individual subscriber to nursing and physician care. However, those workers whose companies did not subscribe would be requested to pay ten dollars a year for health insurance, otherwise board and lodging was eight dollars per week not including a physician's fees. Patients came from the many mining camps in Clear Creek County. Beginning with a bed capacity of fifteen St. Joseph's Hospital rarely exceeded its limit. Eventually the mines gave out, and by the second decade of the twentieth century the area became severely depopulated. Without the prospect of patients St. Joseph Hospital closed in 1914.[43]

IV

Father Lawrence Scanlon, appointed pastor of St. Mary Magdalene parish in Salt Lake City, Utah, inherited the largest territorial parish in the United States, eighty-five thousand square miles, which comprised what is now the entire state, temporarily placed in the archdiocese of San Francisco. Ordained a priest for the latter archdiocese at the Missionary College of All Hallows in Dublin, Scanlon was assigned to the see city; later he served in a parish in a mining area of Nevada before his 1873 appointment to Salt Lake City. In 1887 Scanlon was vicar apostolic of Utah and first ordinary of the diocese of Salt Lake City in 1891. Brigham Young and the Mormon pilgrims had arrived in 1847, and by 1873 there were only about eight hundred Catholics in Utah, most of whom worked on the railroads or in the mines; ninety lived in Salt Lake City. Father Scanlon must have been popular in the community for in 1879 he accepted an invitation to celebrate Mass in the St. George Tabernacle. Later that year the congregation of St. Mary Magdalene parish joined their pastor at the Tabernacle for a liturgy accompanied by the Mormon choir singing "Peter's Mass." Scanlon's text for his homily was appropriate for the unique gathering. "True adorers of God adore Him in spirit and Truth." This remarkable spirit of good will is a clear illustration of the frontier adaptability that was rooted, according to Scanlon, in social benevolence.[44] Scanlon's ecumenism was controversial in the East where denominational lines were rigid, and Mass in non-Catholic houses of worship was considered tantamount to indifferentism. At his request, Mother Angela Gillespie, well-known Holy Cross sister who nursed in the Civil War, sent two sisters to staff a twelve-bed hospital in a rented two-story brick building in Salt Lake City. Opened in 1875 Holy Cross Hospital was in the words of Scanlon "an absolute necessity here as there are a great many poor men of all creeds working in smelters and lead mines which are very unhealthy and cause . . . leaded or lead disease, the effects of inhaling arsenic and other poisonous matters. . . ." He referred to Holy Cross Hospital as "the crowning institution in this territory." He spoke of the many people who "hate the Catholic name, but in spite of themselves, respect and love its philanthropic spirit, its grand broad-hearted character institutions. They may curse the present, but most bless the devoted Sister of Charity [sic] – the angel in human form." Scanlon compared the many priests' sermons on spiritual and dogmatic questions which were ignored as the utterances of "a mere professional man, if not a heretic," but the ministry of the sister-nurse possesses "a logic and an eloquence which the most bigoted and prejudiced can not resist." The pioneer priest listed the ways in which the sisters manifested their domestic and pastoral ministry. He invoked the romantic, heroic role of the sister-nurse, so characteristic of patriarchal imagery of the angel of mercy, though the reality of nursing was severe at best. Scanlon implies their self-determination as well.

> leaning over the bed of the suffering, wiping away the sweat of death from the pale forehead of the dying man, soothing his declining moments, softening his pillow, administering to his last needs, consoling him in his expiring agonies, standing by him as his friend, when perhaps his own desert him, encouraging him to enter with confidence his long and mysterious journey, alleviating his sufferings in life, and closing his eyes in the last long sleep of death – all these performed for no earthly reward, but through love of humanity, irrespective of creed, color or country, and very often to an enemy, are sufficient proof that even the most rigorous and seemingly repugnant maxims of the Gospel . . . are actually realized every day by hundreds and thousands of these devoted creatures in the Catholic Church. . . . The sisters in charge of the "Hospital of Holy Cross" have loudly preached to the public . . . and [have] already exerted a wonderful power in closing the mouths of the many revilers of our holy religion.[45]

Within five years it was evident that a new hospital was needed, and a 125-bed facility was planned for an 1882 opening. In a November 15, 1882, report to the Society for the Propagation of the Faith, the French organization committed to funding foreign missions, Father Dennis Kiley gave an account of the church in Utah. Written on behalf of Lawrence Scanlon, the report includes a commentary on the competition between St. Mark's Hospital of the Protestant Episcopal Church and Holy Cross Hospital. "Public opinion, basing its judgements on the good accomplished by both institutions was to decide which institution was superior. The work of the past seven years [1875 – 1882] had decided the contest; for while the Protestant hospital has advanced but little, the sisters' hospital has extended its salutary influence through Utah and the adjoining territories. The former has nothing save a small brick building never intended for hospital use. . . ; the latter has succeeded in obtaining a whole block of land (10 acres) in the healthiest part of the city, . . . and erected thereon the finest hospital . . . within a radius of a thousand miles."[46] Kiley, no doubt quoting Scanlon, stated that Protestants were boasting of their superiority over the Catholics, but, stated Kiley, "here in Salt Lake we apply the argument, from which there is no appeal, "*contra factum non datur argumentum*," roughly translated, "You can't argue with the facts."[47]

Characteristic of pioneer congregations, the Sisters of the Holy Cross engaged in begging visits in the mining camps and promoted an insurance feature of one dollar per week. However, the major source of funding was a grant from the motherhouse derived in part from tuition at the sisters' academy in Salt Lake City, which they had established shortly after the foundation of the 1875 hospital. The size of the new 125-bed hospital required augmenting the staff; in 1891 seventeen sisters were nursing at the Hospital of the Holy Cross. The sisters, like their episcopal patron, demonstrated a spirit of good will toward the Mormons. Upon arrival in Salt Lake City, they paid their respects to Brigham Young.[48]

There were two short-lived hospitals in Utah staffed by the Holy Cross sisters: in 1879 four sisters were assigned to a small hospital in Silver Reef. Based on an agreement with the miners, Scanlon built St. John's Hospital. With a monthly income at about two hundred dollars and with donations from a fund-raising fair the sisters could afford an addition to the small two-story frame hospital. In 1880 fifty patients were admitted to St. John's. Because of declining silver prices the miners' wages were lowered. Labor-management conflict and a general strike led to the arrest of many miners. The mines reopened for a brief time, but they were finally closed in 1885, which led Scanlon to abandon the mission and the sisters to close their hospital.

It was an agreement with the Union Pacific Railroad that brought the Sisters of Holy Cross to Ogden, Utah in 1887. The railroad company provided the house, fuel, medicine, and surgical supplies, and five dollars a week for each of its patients. In return the sisters provided nursing, food, cleaning, and maintenance of the property. This amicable arrangement lasted until 1898 when the company notified the sisters that it no longer needed the hospital; so the sisters terminated their ministry in Ogden. Named St. Laurence's Hospital, perhaps in honor of the patron saint of the then Bishop Laurence Scanlon, the hospital was a Union Pacific institution with a Catholic ethos.[49]

For three years, 1878 to 1881, the Holy Cross sisters ran hospitals in

Deadwood and Leadwood in the Dakota Territory. Deadwood City was another illustration of an "instant city," when in 1875–76 thousands of prospectors descended on the Black Hills of what is today South Dakota. Despite a treaty between the federal government and the Sioux Indians protecting their sacred space in the area, these miners entered the Black Hills in 1875 without regard for the treaty or the Indians, who after two years of armed struggle were pushed off their lands. A few miles south of Deadwood, gold was discovered in Leadwood.[50]

Characteristic of frontier Catholicism the church followed the people; Bishop James O'Connor, vicar apostolic of Nebraska, which included the southwestern part of the Dakota Territory of the gold rush, missioned a priest to the area and wrote to Mother Angela Gillespie for sisters to staff a hospital, the founding of which had already been begun by the priest at Deadwood, Bernard Mackin. In June of 1878 before five sisters arrived in Deadwood, a "Grand Charity Ball at the Opera house, Central City D. T. for the Benefit of the Sisters' Hospital" raised one hundred dollars to add to the hospital fund of over five hundred dollars. After a two-day stagecoach ride from Cheyenne the sisters arrived in mid-August, 1878. In a notice on "The Sisters Hospital" in the *Black Hills Daily Times* of August 22, civic boosterism was the basis for support of the hospital.[51] "We are confident that the general inhabitants who wish to see Deadwood prosper and also to furnish an occasion of aid to suffering humanity will . . . give their assistance to this undertaking. It should be remembered that these ladies have exchanged an old establishment where all was orderly for the rugged life of the Black Hills."[52] St. Edward's Hospital in Deadwood, the first in the Dakota Territory, was in a rented house. Despite the fact that a new brick building that accommodated twenty-five private patients, miners, and later the sick poor patients on the city and county relief rolls symbolized stability, the sisters could not maintain it on a sound financial base. According to one account the physicians collected the fees from the city and county and did not share them with the hospital. Without such funds the sisters were providing free room, board, and medicine for a majority of the patients; instead of reducing the debt they were increasing it. In 1881 they closed St. Edward's.[53]

A similar situation prevailed in Lead City. The Homestake Mining Company of California—which managed the largest gold mine in the Western Hemisphere and is still operating today—made a four hundred dollar donation for a hospital. Three sisters moved from Deadville to open "the Miners' Hospital" in 1878. The company imposed on the miners a hospitalization fee that was intended for the maintenance of the sisters and the hospital. However, it was collected by the attending physician, leaving the sisters without support. According to a cryptic remark by one priest, the hospital "was meanly taken away from" the sisters, perhaps implying that the company and the physician were in collusion. In any event the sisters left after selling the hospital to the city for a public school.[54]

The Sisters of the Holy Cross maintained a school in Deadwood, St. Edward's Academy, from 1883 to 1897, when it was decided to assign the sisters to a location closer to the motherhouse. The Benedictine sisters of Sturgis, South Dakota, purchased the property for a school in 1892. A typhoid epidemic of that year underscored the need for a hospital, and the Benedictine sisters opened St. Joseph's Hospital in January of 1898. A twenty-six bed hospital, St. Joseph's was staffed in 1900 by ten sisters who had nursed 110 patients in 1898-99. The Benedictines of Vermillion, South Dakota, were in charge of the other hospital in South Dakota, St. Gertrude's in Fort Yates, where in 1900 two sisters nursed ten patients.[55] These were the only two hospitals in the diocese of Sioux Falls (established in 1889), which numbered only thirty-five thousand Catholics.[56]

V

Catholicity in the Southwest—Texas, New Mexico, and Arizona—is rooted in the Mexican experience; the immigrants were the "Anglos," many of whom were unsympathetic if not hostile to Catholicism and contemptuous of Mexican culture. John Marie Odin, C.M., was appointed vicar apostolic of the Republic of Texas in 1841 and bishop of Galveston in 1847. For three years the new diocese encompassed all of Texas, parts of Oklahoma, New Mexico, Kansas, Colorado, and Wyoming.

In 1848 Mexico ceded the territories of New Mexico and Arizona in the Treaty of Guadalupe-Hildago. John B. Lamy, like Odin a native of France, became vicar apostolic of Sante Fe in 1850 and first ordinary of the diocese in 1853. In 1868 it was decided to form the vicariates apostolic of Colorado and Arizona with two Santa Fe priests appointed bishops, Joseph Machebeuf and John B. Salpointe. While the Sisters of Charity of Cincinnati founded the first hospital in Santa Fe, a community founded in France *specifically for hospital ministry in Texas* was the Congregation of the Sisters of Charity of the Incarnate Word.[57]

Upon the promotion of J. M. Odin to the archdiocese of New Orleans in 1861, Claude Marie Dubuis, C.M., succeeded to the see of Galveston, where there were only two communities of cloistered sisters. After attending the Second Plenary Council of Baltimore in 1866 Dubuis made a personal appeal for activist sisters to establish hospitals and orphanages in his diocese, which in 1866 included all of Texas. In response to his many letters to convents in France he received a positive response from three sisters of the hospital community of L'Antiquaille in Lyons. When in Europe he appealed to the superior of the Religious of the Incarnate Word and Blessed Sacrament, founded in Lyons by Jeanne de Matel in 1625 when the French School of Spirituality was flourishing. At the request of Bishop Odin four Sisters of the Incarnate Word community had established a school in Brownsville, Texas, in 1853. While in Lyons Dubuis wrote to the superior: "Our Lord Jesus Christ, suffering in the persons of a multitude of sick and the infirm of every kind seeks relief at your hands. . . . He begs you to accept the mission of corporeal works of mercy by sending sisters to take charge of the hospitals and asylums. We beseech you, then, to form according to the rules of the Order of the Incarnate Word, the . . . [three sisters from the other community] we send you . . . ."[58] Though the French society never entered nursing ministry, the superior agreed to supervise the formation of the three recruits and any others who might have wished to join the new congregation. Two days after his letter the first three Sisters of Charity of the Incarnate Word received the religious habit and soon departed for Galveston, where they stayed with the Ursulines until construction of the hospital and convent was completed in the spring of 1867 in the midst of a yellow-fever epidemic. Hence St. Mary's Infirmary, the first Catholic hospital in Texas and popularly called Charity Hospital, immediately experienced a severe crisis with a hundred patients under the care of three sisters, one of whom died of the disease. The Galveston community was so impressed with their care that the sisters were asked to staff the city hospital.

This public institution in 1868 was an almshouse in terrible condition. Though the sisters had to contend with anti-Catholic and nativist hostility, soon they succeeded in cleaning the hospital and breaking down the animosity. That first year at least one patient, an African-American woman, converted to Catholicism shortly before she died. The following year, 1869, St. Joseph's Infirmary (changed to St. Mary's that year) successfully applied for the status of a federal Marine hospital for sailors, which entailed construction of a new hospital. Then in 1874 the Incarnate Word Sisters opened an orphanage in Galveston to house yellow-fever victims' children who had been living in the hospital for nearly seven years.[59]

With vocations from France and the United States the Galveston community grew from three to twelve sisters in just two years. Subsequently, in 1869 Bishop Dubuis made plans to open a hospital in San Antonio and appointed Mother M. Madeline Chollet, a twenty-three year old woman, as founding superior. After six months at the Ursuline Convent the community of three sisters moved into Santa Rosa Hospital, named after Rose of Lima, the Americas' first saint. In October 1869 the two-story adobe hospital accepted its first patient. Because it had to rely on private patients with no support from the city or county and because the majority of the patients were charity patients, it was in difficult financial straits. The growth of San Antonio necessitated construction of a new three-story hospital at a new location in 1882. However, in 1892 it became the city hospital. In 1874 San Antonio became a diocese with Dominic Anthony Pellicier as first bishop. Vitally interested in parochial education Pellicier encouraged the community to establish schools. Dubuis had envisioned the San Antonio sisters as a separate community, according to the tradition of the Lyons' Incarnate Word Sisters. In 1870 Dubuis approved a separate novitiate for San Antonio.[60] From that time to the present, there have been two communities of Sisters of the Incarnate Word, Galveston/Houston and San Antonio. The ministries of the San Antonio community were more diversified than Houston's. Besides orphanages, schools were established (both for Anglos and separate schools for Mexican Americans), homes for poor aged women, as well as private and railroad hospitals.

The Missouri Pacific Railroad Hospital in Fort Worth was staffed by the Sisters of Charity of the Incarnate Word in 1885. The superior, Mother St. Pierre Cenquir, viewed nursing in a secular institution as an opportunity to influence Catholic immigrants, many of whom had not been practicing the faith. After a fire razed the Fort Worth hospital the patients and staff moved to Marshall, Texas, but eventually a new hospital was constructed in Fort Worth. In 1889 the sisters purchased the hospital from the railroad and named it St. Joseph's Infirmary. They continued to take Missouri Pacific patients and soon contracted with two other railroad companies, while also accepting an invitation from the mayor to care for the sick poor of the city of Fort Worth. The infirmary admitted 456 patients during its first year. The San Antonio community staffed other railroad hospitals in Marshall and Palestine, Texas, St.

Louis, Sedalia, and Kansas City, Missouri, and in the twentieth century founded several sanatoriums. To staff these institutions bishops and superiors recruited candidates in Ireland and Germany.[61] Though many Mexicans joined the community, only a few stayed, because the religious communities were immersed in prejudice. This is substantiated by Sister Maria Louisa Valez, in her article "The Pilgrimage of Hispanics in the Sisters of Charity of the Incarnate Word." At least Mexican Americans were allowed to enter; no white communities accepted African Americans at this time.[62]

The San Antonio community continued to expand. By 1929 they had a house of studies in County Galway, Ireland, dedicated to formation of candidates. There were four provinces, with over one thousand sisters and ten hospitals. In that same year the Galveston community, numbering some two hundred sisters, operated seven hospitals. Without many schools the Galveston community did not have a basis for vocations, nor did they become involved in railroad hospitals; to staff such hospitals the San Antonio community came as far north as St. Louis and Kansas City. The Sisters of Charity of the Incarnate Word are unique; it is the only order of women religious founded in France for hospital ministry in the United States.[63]

The diocese of Santa Fe under John B. Lamy (1851-1884) developed from a small frontier church—beset with conflicts related to the Anglo-American domination of Indians and Mexican-Americans to which Lamy contributed his own pro-Anglo-American biases—to a thriving archdiocese with an array of Catholic institutions. Santa Fe, founded in 1610, is the first political unit in the United States, as it was the capital of the Spanish Province of New Mexico. Sisters of Charity of Cincinnati, including two sisters who had nursed in the Civil War, arrived in 1865 to establish a hospital. As mentioned in a previous chapter, this community originated in 1852 when seven sisters under Mother Margaret Cecilia George separated from Emmitsburg when the American motherhouse affiliated with the Daughters of Charity of Paris. Shortly after ordination for the Clermont-Ferrand diocese in France (1838), Lamy was attracted to Bishop John B. Purcell's diocese of Cincinnati where he was introduced to the Sisters of Charity. He was therefore confident when he appealed to Mother Josephine Hannen—who had expanded St. John's Hospital in Cincinnati and who provided thirty-one sisters to nurse in the Civil War—to establish a hospital in his diocese. Sisters of Loretto at the Foot of the Cross founded three schools, but they had never been involved in hospital ministry.[64]

Advanced one thousand dollars by Bishop Purcell, the Sisters of Charity, after a long journey by rail and boat to Omaha and stagecoach to Santa Fe via Denver, found a twenty-room adobe house, which was the bishop's residence, behind the cathedral. Sister Blandina Segale, the well-known diarist, described the first impressions of the sisters as they reported to her.

> Imagine the surprise of persons coming from places where houses are built with every convenience and sanitary device, suddenly to find themselves introduced into several oblong walls of adobe, looking like piled brick ready to burn, to enter which, instead of stepping up, you step down onto a mud floor; rafters supporting roof made of trunks of trees, the roof itself of earth which they were told had to be carefully attended, else the rain would pour in; door openings covered with blankets; the whole giving you a prison feeling; a few chairs handmade and painted red; a large quantity of wool which they were assured were clean and for their use; no stores, square openings in corners where fires could be built—all those things were to constitute their future home. Where the bare necessities of life were to come from was an enigma to them. Strangers to the country, the customs, and language, do you wonder that a lonesome feeling as of lingering death came over them? Can you doubt that it would have required the presence of an angel to convince them that the preparations made for them were princely? Yes, so they were, for the time and country. This had been the Bishop's Palace, which he had given up, so that the Sisters might have easy access to the Cathedral![65]

The hospital received widespread support; the territorial legislation provided a subsidy of one hundred dollars a month, and the commanding general of the federal troops gave a grant of two thousand dollars to the hospital for medical care of his soldiers. Named St. Vincent's, the frontier hospital cared for forty to fifty patients in 1884, the year Lamy retired. Memorialized by Willa Cather's *Death Comes to the Archbishop*, Lamy had built a new cathedral and had sponsored many schools and several sodalities and confraternities. Sante Fe never developed a strong industrial base but rather became a major tourist attraction particularly as the center of the Pueblo civilization, Mexican-American culture, and the old Catholic sites, including the architecture of the Lamy period when the first hospital was attached to the old cathedral. The Church has been in Sante Fe for almost four hundred years, one hundred and forty of which have been under American "occupation."[66]

The Sisters of Mercy established frontier hospitals in Omaha and Durango, Colorado. They came to New Mexico and Arizona to open schools but soon opened a sanatorium in Silver City, New Mexico. At a height of 6,100 feet the sanatorium, like Glochner in Denver, attracted tuberculosis patients throughout the nation and abroad. At Prescott, Arizona, the Sisters of Mercy began in a cottage, but within four years they were in charge of a general hospital. In Nogales, a United States-Mexican border town in Arizona, the sisters' hospital was a vital refuge in the border struggles of Pancho Villa during the critical years 1910-1915. Another border hospital was in Laredo in the vicariate apostolic of Brownsville. Of all these hospitals Prescott is almost the only extant Mercy hospital today. Hospitals of the Sisters of Mercy in southern California are associated with Mother M. Bonaventure Fox and Mother Milrad Cummings. But these developments were subsequent to the foundation by the foremost frontier Sister of Mercy in the West, Mother M. Baptist Russell in San Francisco.

In 1847 amidst the Mexican War 1846-48, San Francisco received its name and numbered about 450 people. Ceded to the United States in 1848, California elected Peter Burnett, a Catholic convert from Tennessee, as its first civilian governor in 1849, the year that over eighty thousand "gold rushers" arrived in the state, nearly quadrupling the white population. In 1850 Joseph Sadoc Alemany, O.P., the United States provincial of the Dominicans, was appointed first bishop of California. When he arrived in San Francisco, the population had grown to twenty thousand; the discovery of gold had created an instant city based on a thriving port, a manufacturing hub, and a financial center to serve the tens of thousands of prospectors in the mines. To contend with the severe economic, social, and political conditions vigilance committees meted out instant "justice."[67]

The Catholic presence in the area was so meager in 1851 that in the entire state there were only twelve diocesan priests, one Dominican, one Jesuit, seven elderly Franciscans, and seven French missionaries. The Sisters of Notre Dame de Namur entered that year and established a school in San Jose, while at the First Plenary Council of Baltimore (1852) Alemany convinced the Daughters of Charity to mission six sisters for California, two of whom died of fever during the passage through the Isthmus of Panama. They established an orphan asylum and a school.

Thaddeus Amat, C.M., bishop of Monterey (1853-1859 and Monterey-Los Angeles, 1859-1878), which covered the southern half of California, recruited the Daughters of Charity for Los Angeles, where in the mid-1850s they founded the county's first hospital in a four-room adobe home that later evolved into St. Vincent's Hospital. In tracing the sisters' adaptability, their proactive roles in shaping their institutions and negotiating with bankers, politicians, and people of all faiths, Michael E. Engh, S.J., clearly illustrates the frontier character of the Daughters of Charity in Los Angeles.[68] The Sisters of Mercy in San Francisco simultaneously evidenced their open interaction with the culture.

As archbishop, Alemany recruited Hugh Gallagher, an Irish priest who became pastor of St. Mary's Cathedral in 1853, the year that San Francisco became an archdiocese. In desperate need of priests and religious, Alemany sent Gallagher to Ireland to seek missionaries for his archdiocese. As a result, in 1854 five Presentation Sisters and eight Sisters of Mercy arrived in San Francisco. The Presentation Sisters, under Mother M. Theresa Comerford, entered the harbor on 13 November and took charge of a publicly financed school at St. Francis Church in the North Beach section of the city. Committed to teaching the poor, the Presentation Sisters opened a school for native Americans and African Americans, but post–Civil War reaction forced its closure. The Mercy Sisters under Mother Baptist Russell arrived on 8 December, 1854, and immediately initiated their ministry of nursing.[69]

Baptist Russell was only twenty-five when she was missioned to San Francisco. Born in Newry, County Down, of a well-to-do family, Kate Russell entered Mercy Convent at Kinsale, which was led by Mother Mary Francis Bridgeman, who, as noted earlier, had served in the Crimean War along with other Sisters of Mercy and Florence Nightingale. After spending a few weeks with Daughters of Charity on Market Street, Mother Russell rented a house near the State Marine and County hospital where they had begun visiting the patients. When cholera struck in early 1855 the sisters were given charge of the hospital. Having had experience nursing this disease in Ireland, Mother Russell easily adapted to the demands of the crisis. Though their heroic service received several public commendations, the Daughters of Charity were subjected to anti-Catholic invective. There was a Know-Nothing governor of California during the mid-1850s. The superior had known of problems with extremist anti-Catholicism in her home in northern Ireland, but the experience in San Francisco manifested itself not only in attacks on the sisters at the county hospital but also in the county's financial obligations to the hospital during nine months, 1856–57. Forced by circumstances to pay for the "immense outlay to carry on a hospital [for] . . . one hundred and forty patients,"[70] Mother Russell told the county supervisors either to assume their responsibilities or she would consider the contract terminated. In July of 1857 the county patients were sent to the city hospital and the old county institution became the new St. Mary's

Hospital with an attending staff of prominent physicians. Two years later Sister M. Frances Benson reported to the Kinsale sisters on conditions in San Francisco:

> You will perhaps be interested in a few words about this great country. Great it is and wonderful but also great in wickedness. . . . You may grow old and descend in the grave without ever imagining there could be such depravity in human hearts as the Americans have to deplore and work against. . . . The sisters' ministries included a House of Mercy for six hundred working women, an employment office, a "Widow's House," a home for aged women, a Magdalene Asylum with over twenty "penitents," former prostitutes, home nursing and visiting the jails.[71]

Sister Benson considered the county and St. Mary's Hospital to have been "a world in itself. . . . We had under our care persons from every country in the world and all religions too. We have had perpetrators of all crimes and under advice, instruction or care." The sisters' pastoral care included "reconciliation of husbands and wives, rescuing unfortunate creatures from self destruction and exhorting to contrition those who have already fallen."[72] This was an intensive ministry for only twelve sisters in 1860. However, with twelve novices they were soon able to expand. In 1861 St. Mary's moved to a new location at First and Bryant Streets on Rincon Hill, which is now the foundation for a portion of the Bay Bridge. On November 11, 1861, twenty-seven patients moved into the new hospital. The hospital was able to accommodate 120 patients, and the rates in 1861 were $14, $15, and $20 for ward, double and single rooms. There were two physicians in attendance; each received for his services twenty-five percent of all private patients' fees and fifteen percent of those in the wards. Later a resident physician's salary was $150 per month in addition to room and board.

Mother Russell was superior of the San Francisco community from 1855 to 1898 except for three intervals; had there been no canonical limitations she would have served continuously. Besides presiding over St. Mary's Hospital, Mother Russell was actively engaged in other works of mercy. She arranged for sisters to visit the prisoners in San Quentin. In a letter to the San Francisco *Monitor*, the Catholic weekly newspaper (December 1894), one prisoner expressed "sincere and heartfelt thanks to Mother Russell and the Sisters of Mercy under her charge at St. Mary's [Hospital] for the many and varied services rendered the unfortunate inmates." Particular gratitude was extended to Sister M. Baptist Morgan, who had been visiting the prison on a semi-monthly basis for almost forty years. "When the poor, dishonored friendless, helpless transgressor sees nought before him but the gloom of desolation there comes to him as an ambassador of a fairer and brighter sphere, the meek, gentle, Sister of Mercy to cheer, encourage and help him."[73]

Besides the hospital and the prison ministries the San Francisco Sisters of Mercy founded four free schools, a Magdalene home for young girls, referred to as penitents, a boarding home for working women, an industrial school, and a House of Mercy for elderly women attached to the hospital. In 1876 there were seventy sisters in the community; fifty were Irish, twelve of Irish descent, two German and two of German descent, two native-born Americans, one Spanish, and one Canadian.[74]

Russell was particularly active in home nursing. On one occasion she was referred to a sick man who was a Protestant and a Freemason. "When leaving Mother said to the critically ill man, wrote her companion, 'we have a call in this neighborhood; would you like us to call again?' He said yes, but it meant 'I do not care.' Several times again Mother called, and had the pleasure of seeing him die a holy death. . . . he renounced Masonry and offered his life's sufferings and death to God."[75]

In accord with traditions of other hospital communities Baptist Russell recorded deathbed conversions in the annals of the community. One patient of no religion was suffering from an "acute disease of the heart which added to a naturally violent and uncontrollable temper [that] rendered him almost a terror to those around him." When a sister-nurse asked him to consider his salvation he refused, only to remark: "I don't care if I die like a dog, I only wish God would take me out of life this instant." That night while the patient was sleeping the sister placed a "miraculous medal under his pillow beseeching Mother of Mercy not to allow that soul for which Christ died to be lost." The next day he greeted the sister, "Oh! Sister forgive me; I do not want to die like a dog. . . . I don't know what I ought to do. . . . I must have a clergyman." Ultimately the patient converted to Catholicism, and when told about the medal he wore it and later a crucifix and scapulars around his neck. Mother Russell added her own reflection on these events:

> And now, may we not with truth attribute the Salvation of this soul to the power of *Mary* the Refuge of Sinners? and does it not seem as if providence allowed the Sister to forget applying to her till the case seemed hopeless in order to make the effects of her intercession the more striking? but so many were the conversions effected from time to time by means of the Miraculous Medal that the Sisters had unbounded confidence in it and usually had a few pillows in each Ward with a Medal inclosed; this custom originated in the wonderful change wrought in one night in the "Hardened Man" in February 1855.[76]

In the summer of 1868 Mother Russell and Sister M. Frances Benson took charge of the city's pesthouse during the smallpox epidemic of 1868. In a copy of a letter to a B. Cole, M.D., located in the *Annals*, there is a traditional theological reflection on the sisters' mission: "It is one of the privileges of the Sister of Mercy that we attend on our fellow in whatever form of disease it is the Divine Will to afflict them. Therefore if the City Authorities are willing to accept our Services two of our Sisters will D.V. [*Deo volente*, or "God willing"] go to the Pest House and take up residence there until such time as the Almighty wills to deliver the City from this terrible malady. . . . one room is all we require. You know the accommodation of a Sister of Mercy is very simple."[77]

Sister Benson wrote to the Sisters in the Kinsale convent in Ireland:

It is truly a horrible disease, so loathsome, so disgusting, so pitiable. Twice the number of patients with any other disease would not require the care and attendance those afflicted with small-pox require. Not one spot from the crown of the head to the sole of the foot was sound, the eyes of the greater number closed and pus running from them down the cheeks; their throats so sore that to take a drink almost chokes them, the tongue sometimes so swollen that not a drop can pass down; the hands so sore that they are helpless, and the *mal-odour* so terrible that they themselves cry out: "O Sister, I cannot stand the smell." The doctors say it is an unusually malignant type. It is strange that few Irish take it. The majority of the sufferers are Germans, the next in number native Americans, with a mixture of Danes, Prussians, French, Spaniards, Italians, and Portuguese. The greatest precaution is taken to prevent the spread of the disease; all beds, bedding, and clothing are burned. Now I shall turn from the body to the soul. The number baptized is truly consoling; also the number of negligent Catholics brought to make their peace with God. In most cases it is easy for us to get at their souls, because in this dreadful disease they become humbled. Proud men cannot but feel themselves objects of disgust to their fellow-creatures, and even to themselves. They are abandoned by their nearest and dearest, shunned as objects of terror. Therefore, when they see us joyfully attend them, they are astonished and thankful, particularly as they know we receive no money for it. Another thing which draws them to us is, that not a single minister of any denomination ever enters this pesthouse. . . .[78]

This last statement was verified by a report from a local newspaper, which described the "feeling of shame for Protestants that . . . none of our religious denominations have, like the Catholic Church, . . . any organization that could furnish help—competent, intelligent, kind female nurses to enter the home of misery and take charge of its ministrations to the crowd of suffering humanity it contains. Those devoted Sisters of

Mercy willingly presented themselves and entered on a mission of charity from which all others shrink in dismay and affright. That their presence will have a beneficial effect none can doubt. Already the good results of their presence are apparent. Their fearless, self-sacrificing love is an honor to their Church and to their Order."[79]

The Sisters of Mercy served for nine months in the small-pox hospital from the spring of 1868 to early 1869. Though they had no expectations for remuneration, the board of supervisors successfully petitioned the state legislature to authorize a $1,500 grant to the community as a sign of gratitude for the sisters' service.

Commitment to the poor was the principal imprint of Baptist Russell's administrations. She strongly disagreed with Mother M. Francis X. Warde's policy of establishing academies for students of wealthy families. She wrote to Warde: "the difference between the Sisters of Mercy in *Ireland* and the Sisters of Mercy in *America* that strikes *me most* is that in the former we are devoted to the poor suffering members of J. Christ, whereas in America, with the exception of ourselves here in California, and those in St. Louis, New York, Brooklyn and Cincinnati, our Sisters are employed in *Boarding Schools* and . . . *you* get the credit—deservedly or not I can't say—of introducing the change first. I know Londonderry and Down Patrick are exceptions of what I have said about Ireland." Mother Russell thought that once boarding schools were established, the free schools for the poor "will be of secondary importance, consequently won't you be rather servants of the rich rather than of the *Poor?*" She believed in adapting to the customs of the United States, but "The *Spirit* of our Rule is to me sufficiently clear from the very formula of our Vows— The *Service* of the *Poor Sick*, and *Ignorant*."[80] When the Sisters of Mercy of the Union was established in 1929, thirty-nine of the sixty independent congregations amalgamated; the San Francisco community, perhaps inspired by the spirit of Mother Russell, decided not to join the new centralized body. Mother Russell died on August 6, 1898. In an announcement of her death the *San Francisco Call* stated:

> No death in recent years has been heard of with greater regret in this community than that of Mother Superior, Mary Baptist Russell, the sweet woman who watched over the destinies of various charitable institutions in this city during the past half century. The tidings of her calm leave-taking of this life will fill with sorrow the thousands who were fortunate enough to meet her and those who have heard or read of her beautiful deeds of charity since her advent in this State. A more lovable character than hers has been rarely found. Her constant aim in life has been to uplift the suffering and the wounded, and in this she was entirely successful.[81]

Many such eulogies witnessed to the impact of the life of Mother Russell on the social and religious life of San Francisco. One publication described Mother Russell as one of the fifty "Makers of Northern California," the only woman so recognized. Her forty-four years as hospital administrator and superior witnessed the closing of the frontier.

Missionary adaptation fostered an activism among religious engaged in their own hospitals, as well as in city, railroad, and mining facilities, on Indian reservations, and in the town and country life west of the Rockies. Religious traditions took root, but their vitality depended on the sisters' sense of ministry rather than their subservience to tradition. Because of the remoteness of centers of authority and because of the paucity of priests, nursing communities tended to develop their own "western"-style independent ministry, one that was open, expansive, and conscious of doing prayer in action.

Traditions and Transitions

✤ Two pioneering Sisters of Providence in the northwest. Mother Joseph Pariseau, S.P. founded the Sisters of Providence in the northwest. *Courtesy: Sisters of Providence Archives, Seattle.*

✤ The evolution of Saint Joseph's Hospital, Atlanta, GA.
Courtesy: Archives of Saint Joseph's Hospital of Atlanta.

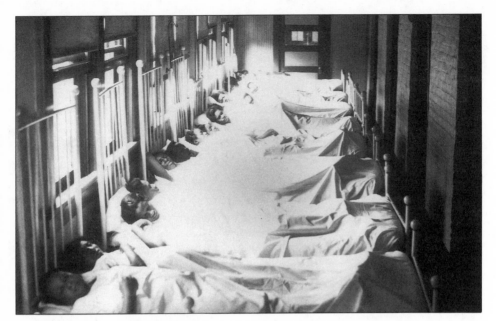

✤ An "overflow" ward with two African-American women to one bed—Charity Hospital, New Orleans.
Courtesy: Louisiana State University Medical School Alumni Affairs files.

✤ A capping ceremony at St. Mary's Hospital College of Nursing, San Francisco.
Courtesy: Archives of the Sisters of Mercy, Burlingame, CA.

✤ This depiction of the religions culture of suffering has been eclipsed by a pastoral ministry based upon the healing process of confronting one's pain within the contexts of scriptural prayer and the Sacrament of Anointing. *Courtesy: Sisters of Providence Archives, Seattle.*

✚ Pastoral care chaplains administer individual and group Sacrament of Anointing.
Courtesy: The Catholic Health Association of the United States, St. Louis.

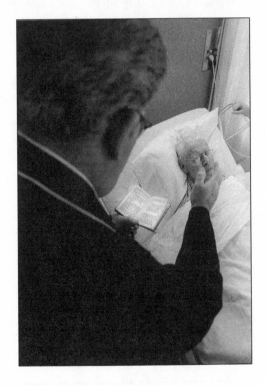

Other Nineteenth Century Ministries

✤ Sisters of Charity of the Incarnate Word smallpox hospital, Houston.
Courtesy: Sisters of Charity of the Incarnate Word, Houston.

Seattle, W?

TO PROVIDENCE HOSPITAL

Hospital Ticket

Valid for   months. from   189   to   189

Delivered to

    From

    By

    Location:

    Date

Sign here:

Let a few dollars of your wages go to Providence Hospital: and when you get sick or injured,
you will find in its wards the best treatment you can get in Seattle.
    This price includes Board, Medicines, Fresh milk, and Liquor, as ordered by your doctor, as
well as the use of Bath rooms and Operating room.
    You choose your own doctor, and settle with him for his services.
    Your own doctor decides when you are to be admitted or discharged.
    You may secure a private room, while at the Hospital, by paying $1.00 a day in advance.
    Present this card (signed by yourself at the time of purchasing), when coming to the Hospital.

TICKET No. **1349**

✤ Prepaid insurance plan.
Courtesy: Sisters of Providence Archives, Seattle.

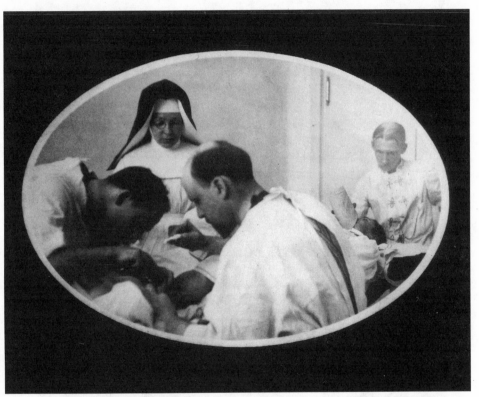

✚ Surgery at St. Elizabeth Hospital, Appleton, WI. Sister Ludwina Weber and Dr. V. Marshall. Notice black veil; no gloves or masks or head covering for surgeon and assistant.
Courtesy: Wheaton Franciscan Sisters Archives, Wheaton, IL.

In Time of War

✤ A Sister of Mercy at Douglas Military Hospital, Washington, D.C., during the Civil War.
Courtesy: Sisters of Mercy Archives, Baltimore.

✤ "Angel of the Battlefield"—Sister Anthony O'Connell, S.C. Painting by Sister Ernestine Foskey, S.C., 1900.
Courtesy: Sisters of Charity of Cincinnati Archives, Mount St. Joseph, OH.

✠ "Nuns of the Battlefield" Washington, D.C., monument to honor the 640 sister-nurses in the Civil War.
Courtesy: The Catholic Health Association of the United States, St. Louis.

✠ The typhoid ward staff—Camp Hamilton, KY, October, 1898. Sister Lydia Clifford (in center) was in charge of all the nurses.
Courtesy: Sisters of the Holy Cross Archives, Saint Mary's College, Notre Dame, IN.

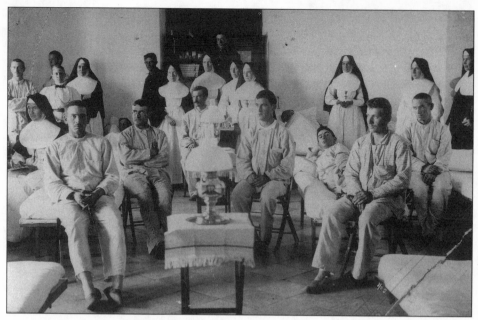

✤ Sisters of St. Joseph of Carondelet nursing in the Cuba Hospital during the Spanish-American War.
Courtesy: Sisters of St. Joseph of Carondelet Archives, St. Louis.

✤ First Red Cross unit at St. John's Hospital, Fargo, ND (1917).
Courtesy: Sisters of St. Joseph of Carondelet Archives, St. Paul Province, MN.

·PART TWO·

Modernization and the Persistence of Tradition 1890–1948 Introduction

REGIONAL AND LOCAL DIVERSITY, so characteristic of Part One, play an integrative role in chapter eight, "The Convergence of Subcultures," which explores the modernization and professionalization processes in the contexts of Catholic hospitals and nursing schools. Because these processes are pervasive in the history of twentieth-century health care, the remaining four chapters focus on national trends, with particular emphasis on the Catholic Hospital Association's (CHA) mission to mediate modernity through the standardization movement, to sponsor professional education for religious and lay nurses, and to promote a strong Catholic identity in what was perceived as an increasingly threatening secular society. The CHA is a prism refracting the trends and patterns in Catholic health care, such as the conflicts between religious and secular values.

Characteristic of the clericalization of most Catholic societies in the twentieth century, priests dominated the CHA; and, in accord with the tendencies of patriarchal governance, the men elaborated on the ascribed roles of women religious in a Catholic hospital. In contrast to Part One, the development of protective canopies is more evident here, especially in the topic of popular Catholicity and illness in chapter nine, which spans more than a century of diverse religious experiences. The myriad devotional practices, prayers, and invocations of divine healing were portions of the cultural infrastructure that supported the separatist mentality so dominant in the institutional edifice. Though Catholics took pride in their modernized institutions, their religious culture in both the popular and elite spheres fostered distinctive religious boundaries. The centralized authority structures in dioceses and the promulgation of the revised code of canon law (1917) added thick layers to the boundaries. Indeed, Mary Ewens, O.P., refers to this period, 1917 to the 1960s, as the era of the "Great Repression."[1] The lives of women religious were profoundly affected by the imposition of convent enclosures; the proactive ministry of the frontier gave way to a strong institutionalization that was based on separation from the evils of modernity. Progressive Americanist bishops in the 1880s and 90s, who perceived the presence of grace in culture, were told by Pope Leo XIII (in the encyclical *Testem Benevolentiae*, 1899) that the source of grace is in the institutional church and that life in the culture is not an occasion of grace but sin. Though the premodern domestic virtues of the ideal woman religious and ideal lay nurse were invoked during the period before the 1960s, the drive for professionalism was in dialectical tension with the persistence of these ideals of women.

In chapter ten, the emphasis is on Catholic idealism or romanticism infused into the separate spheres of health care—e.g., the guilds of Catholic physicians and Catholic nurses—that anchored modernity in traditional religious understanding. However, in the practical quotidian life of the hospital, modernization and professionalization were inexorably affecting the religious ethos. For example, during this period many sisters attained graduate degrees in hospital administration, a countervailing force to the male dominance of the profession. Professionalization entailed social mobility into the middle class and tended to affect self-perceptions and social expectations. The CHA, though founded as a separate religious organization, drove a wedge into the religious boundaries as it promoted widespread participation in professional societies and developed a positive consciousness of the relationship between Catholicism and modern health care. The CHA leadership during the 1930s and 40s tended to fragment this relationship into separate religious and medical spheres, but CHA's mission was emblematic of the advance of modernity in the religious climate of Catholic hospitals.

CHAPTER SEVEN

The Convergence of Subcultures: Medical, Religious, and Ethnic

1890–1915

I

THE INCREASE IN HOSPITALS during the period 1850 to 1875 was, according to Charles E. Rosenberg, "in good measure the response to demographic and economic reality, but it was shaped by a motivating alliance of would-be scientific rationalism, pious commitment, and traditional stewardship."[1] Catholic hospitals, which numbered about 160 in 1875, were animated by these general motivations mediated in a Catholic context subservient to religious and ethnic traditions. The Catholic voluntary hospital at the turn of the century tended to be thoroughly immersed in the modern medical subculture, but as a religious and ethnic institution it was anchored in the traditional Catholic subculture. Competition with Protestant benevolence and the drive to provide religious sustenance to those on the borders of existence persisted as motivating factors in Catholic-hospital subcultures.

Scientific rationalism enlarged the bureaucratic control for orderliness and cleanliness to prevent the spread of disease, particularly after the Civil War, when the reforms popularized by Florence Nightingale were generally implemented in the United States.[2] Though there had been advances in recognizing the relationship among ventilation, administrative control, and the diminution of contagion, Nightingale based her reforms on statistical evidence and infused political commitment and emotional fervor into her movements. Rosenberg summarizes her contribution: "Nightingale's views of disease causation didactically underlined the connection between behavior, environment and health—and thus constituted a systemic program for hospital reform."[3] She perceived the spread of hospital infections according to the analysis of William

Farr, an English specialist in vital statistics, who portrayed infections and epidemics as analogous to fermentation: a process that emphasized the significance of atmospheric conditions. Nightingale aimed to create a climate of cleanliness and orderliness monitored by a disciplined nursing staff trained in nutrition and in the proper procedures of treating wounds, ulcers, etc. Permeating Nightingale's reformed hospital was a "moral universe" (Rosenberg's term) in which illness was a vice that could only be remedied by virtuous behavior according to rigid codes of hygiene.[4]

With the evolution of the germ theory of contagion, illness was removed from the moral realm of cleanliness and placed within Joseph Lister's scientific world of the antiseptic operating theater, the pathology laboratory, and later the X-ray. These innovations in diagnosis and treatment occurred gradually; for example, antiseptic carbolic acid spray to kill germs shifted to aseptic conditions and procedures to inhibit microorganisms in the operating room. Specialties in surgery with resident programs proliferated: for example, gynecology, orthopedics, and ophthalmology.[5] By the turn of the century anesthesiology and clinical pathology were entering the residence specialties in medicine. All of this changed the hospital from a working-class setting for the severely ill and injured—that is, those too poor to be attended at home—to a middle-class institution for curing illnesses no longer perceived as moral vices but as physiological weaknesses.[6]

The precipitous increase in the number of hospitals reflects the developments of medical science, nursing education, and the prominence of new technologies under the control of physicians: 178 in 1872 to four thousand in 1910. During that same period Catholic hospitals increased from about seventy-five in 1872 to nearly four hundred in 1910. Many of these hospitals were founded to serve the nearly five million Catholic immigrants between 1881 and 1910. Schools and hospitals were established by sisters representing the new immigrant groups from Germany, the Austro-Hungarian Empire, and Italy; of the forty-nine new foundations of women religious begun between 1870 and 1900, thirty-nine originated in Europe, eight in Canada, and twelve in the United States.[7] Refugees from Bismarck's *Kulturkampf* dominated the twenty-six foundations in the 1870s. The Franciscan Sisters of the Sacred Hearts of Jesus and Mary founded Pius Hospital (later St. Anthony's) in St. Louis, St. Joseph's in Milwaukee, and St. Mary's in Racine, Wisconsin. Other German communities, such as the Poor Sisters of St. Frances Seraph of the Perpetual Adoration, founded St. Joseph's Hospital in Omaha, Nebraska, and six other hospitals in Colorado, Wisconsin, and Indiana as well as facilities in Columbus and Lincoln, Nebraska. Mother Frances Cabrini, founder of the Italian Missionary Sisters of the Sacred Heart, established New York's Columbus Hospital in 1892, followed by hospitals in Chicago and as far west as Seattle.[8]

According to Paul Starr, there were three principal phases in the development of American hospitals. The first period, 1750–1850, was characterized by the voluntary hospital under the direction of lay trustees and "ostensibly nondenominational but in fact Protestant" and by municipal hospitals, offspring of the old almshouse. It was in the second phase, 1850 to 1890, that "particularistic" hospitals were established; these were ethnic hospitals and institutions organized by religious groups for care of special diseases or for particular groups of patients, women, and children. From 1890 to 1920, the third phase was characterized by "profit-making" hospitals, run by physicians.[9] Starr's division does not neatly apply to Catholic hospitals; as the previous chapters have illustrated, Catholic religious communities staffed municipal and state hospitals and physicians' voluntary hospitals (infirmaries), while many of these communities owned and operated their own voluntary hospitals, some of which were for special diseases such as tuberculosis or for particular groups such as railroad workers, miners, as well as those for women and children. In the third phase the diversity persisted, but the dominant model was the large voluntary hospital with a board of directors most often composed of sisters or brothers. Some boards were dominated by bishops and priests, and some had a few lay persons. There were a considerable number of Catholic ethnic hospitals, particularly German, with a smattering of Italian and Polish facilities. Though Starr's rendering of the "elite voluntary hospital with its strong affiliation with medical school" excluded Catholic hospitals, many of the large Catholic hospitals, such as St. John's in St. Louis and Mercy in Chicago, were affiliated with medical schools. However, Starr's "elite voluntary hospital" was limited to those that treated the wealthy and the poor, for fund-raising and "teaching purposes," respectively. Hence, because they tended to have little or no endowment and because they depended on some paying patients, the large Catholic teaching hospitals were not elite.

II

The famed Mayo Clinic in Rochester, Minnesota, is identified with the apex of the modernization process. Attached to St. Mary's Hospital, it traces its origins to a devastating tornado of August 21, 1882, that left in its wake thirty-one dead and hundreds of injured. The Sisters of St. Francis of Our Lady of Lourdes, founded by Mother Alfred Moes in 1877, were among the many volunteer nurses in the emergency situation.[10] According to Doctor William Worrall Mayo, the father of two physicians, it was Mother Moes who suggested the foundation of a hospital. "I answered Mother Superior, 'this city is too small [ca. five thousand population] to support a hospital.'. . . 'Very well,' she persisted, 'But you must promise me to take charge of it and we will see the building at once. With faith and hope and energy it will succeed.' I asked her how much money the sisters would be willing to put into it, and her reply was, 'How much do you want?' I said 'would you be willing to risk forty thousand dollars?' 'Yes,' she replied, 'and more if you want it. Draw up your plans. It will be built at once.'" Mayo was also concerned that his identity as an Episcopalian might be a problem, to which Mother Moes replied: "The cause of suffering humanity knows no religion or sex; the charity of the Sisters of St. Francis is as broad as their religion."[11]

Mother Alfred Moes was a woman of great energy and determination; she emigrated from Luxembourg in 1851, and during the next twenty-five years she had been a member of the School Sisters of Notre Dame in Milwaukee, of the Marianites of the Holy Cross in Indiana, and founder of the Order of St. Francis in Joliet, Illinois, before she founded a house in Rochester which became an independent community within a year. Her biographer, Carlan Kraman, O.S.F., portrays Mother Moes as an intelligent, committed, and determined woman religious, who was misunderstood by bishops as too independent. When she was subjected to abuses of authority she stood her ground rather than yield to false accusations. With the approbation of Bishop Thomas L. Grace of St. Paul, Mother Moes's community, composed of twenty-five sisters who were allowed to freely leave the Joliet Franciscans, was welcomed into the diocese. The bishop of Chicago, Thomas Foley, had not explicitly authorized Mother Alfred's foundation in Rochester, and when she was elected mother superior of the Joliet community Foley vetoed the election and gave the sisters the opportunity to remain in Joliet or join Mother Moes. Both the Joliet communities were exclusively dedicated to teaching; St. Mary's was the only hospital to be founded by the Rochester Franciscans. Prior commitments to construction of their Rochester academy and the need to impose rigid fiscal policies on all the houses delayed the building of the hospital until the late 1880s.[12]

After the Mayo physicians had gathered information on hospital construction, St. Mary's was opened in 1889. Built with room for only thirty-five patients, it opened on the threshold of the period of modernization. By this time the elder Dr. Mayo was in practice with his sons William Janus and Charles Horace, both of whom became world renown surgeons. W. J. Mayo was a stomach specialist and was active in medical associations and a founder of the American College of Surgeons. C. H. Mayo was well known for goiter and urologic surgery. Beginning in 1912 the Mayo brothers offered graduate courses in medicine at the clinic, and in 1915 the brothers gave $2.8 million to the Mayo Foundation for Medical Education and Research at Rochester.[13] The Franciscan Sisters opened a nursing school which was later integrated into the College of St. Teresa, the Franciscan school in Winona, Minnesota.

The Alexian Brothers' Hospital in Chicago also illustrates this convergence of subcultures. On February 6, 1894, Dr. O. L. Schmidt, secretary of the Medical and Surgical Staff of the Alexian Brothers Hospital, sent to the Brother Provincial, administrator of the hospital, a copy of resolutions of a staff meeting that clearly reveals the advances of the germ theory of infection, aseptic surgery, the general influence of Joseph Lister and Louis Pasteur, and the necessity for a course of instruction for the brothers.

> A motion by Dr. [John B.] Murphy to recommend to the Brothers, that there should be two Brothers assisting during operations and that these two should wear white gowns. Also that no Pus cases should be kept or dressed on the first floor.
>
> Also that the Pasteur filter ought to be used to furnish drinking water to the patients.
>
> The chair appointed Drs. Schmidt, Hoelscher, Henratin, & Oswald, to report at the next meeting, a plan for lectures on nursing to the Brothers.[14]

Many of the hospital's staff physicians had been trained in German universities well-known for advances in microbiology and other medical sciences. The medical staff had formed a society with a constitution in February of 1893, a relatively early date for the formation of a board that symbolized the physicians' control of the modernization of the hospital as well as the hospital's control of admissions.[15] A year later it approved a course of instruction of twenty-four lectures for nursing brothers, equally divided between medical and surgical lectures, but the hospital's school was not incorporated in the State of Illinois until 1898. The high demand for well-trained nurses necessitated expanding the school to include laymen. Since admissions to the hospital were limited to men so was the nursing school. It acquired the services of a graduate of Bellevue

Hospital's Mills Training School for male nurses to be the superintendent of the Male Training School. The first two-year program began in 1899; twelve students were enrolled each of whom was required to be between the ages of twenty-one and thirty-five, and to be of "good moral character."[16]

The first Alexian Brothers Hospital was a frame building founded in 1866 by Brother Bonaventure Thelen, "Rector of America." With room for only six patients it was actually an infirmary. Brother Bonaventure found his first patient on the street and carried him back to the humble facility on Dearborn and Schiller Streets. According to their traditional charism to the diseased outsider, the plague victim, the brothers almost instinctively responded to those struck by cholera in a Chicago epidemic in late 1866. By 1868 the brothers moved into a new building on Franklin and Market Streets with room for seventy patients. Mercy Hospital, the only other Catholic facility, could accommodate three hundred patients.[17]

In the articles of incorporation in Illinois this first community of nursing brothers in the United States described their traditional charism. They viewed themselves as dedicated to "an active exercise of Charity, particularly in times of war, the gratuitous nursing and taking care of the wounded soldier on the battlefield, the gratuitous burial of the dead in times of epidemics, the establishing and conducting of hospitals, the nursing of sick male persons, and the nursing and taking care of idiots and lunatics of the male sex."[18]

In an 1885 edition of Alfred T. Andreas's multivolume *History of Chicago* the author reveals a deplorable ignorance of the brothers' European roots ("founded by St. Alexius in Rome in honor of Juan de Dios de Hispana").[19] However, he did indicate a grasp of the brothers' local history. He cited a newspaper which reported that at the Alexian Brothers' Hospital "any sick person who desires the solace of his religion can send for any representative of his faith, . . . whether they be a Protestant preacher, a Catholic priest, a Jewish rabbi or deacon of the Mormon church. The fraternity exacts payment from those who are able to pay; but receive the poor gratis, making no distinction on account of religious belief, or irreligious unbelief, of a prospective patient."[20] (According to an 1886 report of the Chicago hospital, the religious breakdown of the patients was "669 Catholics, 526 Protestants, and 26 Hebrews.")[21] Though the reporter criticized the brothers' tradition of excluding women from the hospitals, a practice he said originated "from monastic dogmatism partaking of misogamy [sic]," he nevertheless concluded, "But to those who obtain access to their hospitals and asylums, the Alexian Brothers prove kind, gentle, scrupulously careful nurses and many poor men have reason to bless this philanthropic organization."[22]

Many women religious were remote from the care of men, which would compromise or challenge their vow of chastity; the presence of women in a male religious hospital would be, according to the traditional notion of women as descendants of Eve, inherently challenging to the brothers' commitment to chastity. However, Catholic hospitals, where religious tended to live, usually on the top floor, were considered the homes of women and men religious. It is significant to note that Andreas's description of the Alexians included remarks on the "kindness and gentleness" of the brothers, hints of the brothers' blend of domestic virtues with the general calling of nurses to be particularly sensitive care givers. The brothers' new Chicago hospital, which cost $100,000 and opened in 1868, was completely destroyed by the great Chicago fire of 1871, but the patients were safely evacuated.

The third hospital, which opened in 1873 on the same property, was considerably larger with space for 150 to 175 patients. Because the Northwestern Elevated Railroad required the hospital grounds for construction of its line, a new hospital was opened in 1898 on Beldon Avenue with room for 260 patients.[23]

The architect described the physicians' concern with proper ventilation to prevent germ contagion:

In each of the wards there is an opening behind each bed, removing the air around each separately, so that it cannot pass on to the adjoining beds. The opening and ducts are so proportioned that it will not be possible for the air to pass from one room to the other; each patient will have ample and fresh supply of air at all times, or as nearly perfect as possible. . . . The operating department . . . contains rooms for administering anesthetics, for convalescents, instruments, bandages, sterilizing rooms for visiting surgeons and the surgeon's locker room.[24]

Also in the official 1898 report of the hospital the brothers proudly informed their public of the new hydro-therapeutic department. As adjuncts to the water treatment were the uses of electricity, massage, and physical therapies. The latter included "therapeutic gymnastics" required for "Swedish movements and German training exercises." During 1898, 4,562 treatments were administered, 1,697 of which were for charity patients. Though steam baths, massages, and physical therapy would be listed under a fitness or wellness program today, these treatments were for physical and functional disorders of the "nervous system and of the constitution such as fatty degeneration, gout, rheumatism and similar ailments," as well as for muscular injuries.[25]

This new department symbolized the evolution of the private hospital from a refuge for the injured and sick poor people to a middle-class treatment center. By the turn of the century the Chicago Alexian Brothers' Hospital had experienced the "take-off point" into modernity. The advances in germ theory required a full-time pathologist with a laboratory and a physician to administer X-rays, both of whom were critical to diagnosis and treatment.

Monastic tradition inhibited the development of modernity. Two years after the foundation of its nursing school a newly appointed provincial, in accord with the directives of the superior general, dismissed the lay superintendent of the nursing school and limited its enrollment to brothers. It is ironic that a community founded by anonymous laymen on the fringes of church and society so rigidly applied the principle of separation between the brothers and "seculars."[26]

Encouraged by Archbishop Peter R. Kenrick and by the increase in the community from American vocations and brothers from Aachen, Brother Bonaventure and two other brothers settled in St. Louis in 1869. They lived with the vicar general for the German, Polish, and Bohemian Catholics of the archdiocese, Monsignor Henry Muehlsiepen, a Rhinelander who may have known of the brothers' mental hospitals in Cologne and Essen. On September 21, a week after their arrival, the brothers purchased an old mansion located on five acres. Soon they occupied a "neat little house," but their "entire belongings consisted of a tea pot, a wash basin and $23,000 in debt." After begging from door to door, the Alexians gradually transformed their house into a hospital. On April 12, 1870, they admitted their first patient, a Father Strombergen. Because the brothers were to become the unofficial nurses of the St. Louis clergy, it was very appropriate that their first patient was a priest.[27]

The authorities in Aachen bristled at the rapid rate of indebtedness by the American houses, not only because they appeared to have been fiscally irresponsible but also because they required excessive contact with the secular world that could undermine the religious life. In the letter of appointment of the first provincial of the United States, Brother Clement Walrath, the superior general, warned the brothers against the American spirit of individualism and independence, "it would be . . . pride if any member would wish to direct the order . . . according to his own head and short-sighted spirit. All of us . . . would protest against this, we would say to such a party, We have no need of you; we shall adhere to the past; we want no innovations!"[28]

Located in a German-American section in south St. Louis not far from the Mississippi River, the Alexian Brothers' Hospital expanded to a capacity of 250 beds by 1900. That year a free dispensary was opened for those who could not afford medical care. In a golden jubilee booklet of the St. Louis hospital the author records the significance of the free clinic. "How much charity is done for poor suffering humanity the world will never know, nor will the brothers receive much credit from the city for the burden taken off its shoulders by this free establishment but there is One who knows and repays, and the good people will ever be grateful for the noble work."[29]

The St. Louis hospital developed a major psychiatric ward that was well known throughout the area. In 1879, the first Alexian hospital, which eventually became a facility for the mentally ill, was opened in Oshkosh, Wisconsin, with its origins entangled in relations between Paul Polleg, a strong-willed, very personable brother, on the brink of expulsion by the authorities in Aachen, and Bishop Francis X. Krautbauer of Green Bay, Wisconsin. Concerned with establishing a third house, as required by the Holy See in its approval of provincial status, Brother Clement accepted responsibility for a mansion, a gift from the bishop.

Once again begging was an effective source of funds, but a public fair yielded $1,085.10 in 1880, nearly twice the amount collected from begging. In his introduction of the brothers, Bishop Krautbauer said that the new facility would be devoted to caring for priests unable to fulfill their ministry. Since the hospital gained an identity as a refuge for alcoholic priests, perhaps the bishop's statement of intention was indeed accurate.[30]

After purchasing more property and enlarging its building, the Oshkosh institution altered its character from a general hospital to "the Alexian Brothers' Asylum for Insane, Idiotic and Nervous." In 1891 the Sisters of the Sorrowful Mother opened a hospital that by 1900 had a bed capacity of four hundred. A thriving lumber town, Oshkosh was able to support these hospitals.[31]

In 1894 the brothers opened a general hospital in Elizabeth, New Jersey. Prior to its opening the Alexians did home nursing, which had been a traditional aspect of their ministry. With room for only forty patients, the new hospital was strongly rooted in the immigrant community. The general pattern of expansion and modernization was manifested in this the only eastern outpost of the Alexian Brothers. As in all their hospitals the brothers did all the work; they nursed, fed, bathed the patients as well as attended to every aspect of the physical plant and also managed a small farm adjacent to most institutions. As one reporter stated, "The service of the Alexian Brothers is very severe and fatiguing. On an average day they are engaged in their calling during seventeen hours out of twenty-four, an undisturbed night is unknown to the Alexians. No wonder therefore that few of them reach their 40th year."[32]

The provincial statutes codified the proper procedures, ranging from admitting to releasing patients. The brothers were instructed to admit any male person "not incurably sick unless suffering from a contagious disease [regardless of] class, nationality, religion, race or color." Needy patients were cared for without charge, others were to pay per week "in advance." Regimentation and standardization were the pillars of efficient modern Alexian hospitals. Though there were twenty nationalities represented on the Chicago hospital's patient list of 1885, each hospital possessed a decidedly German imprint. "The kitchen shall be furnished and conducted in the German style."[33]

Because the community prohibited lay students from the nursing school it was entirely dependent on brothers to staff the four Alexian institutions: Chicago, St. Louis, Elizabeth, New Jersey, and Oshkosh, Wisconsin. In its *Golden Jubilee* souvenir book the St. Louis community appealed for vocations.

We need young men who are willing to lead a life of self abnegation and heroic charity to continue the great work of Mercy to suffering humanity and, alas! few only comprehend the invitation of Christ: "Come, follow Me!"

For the guidance and direction of those who may feel inspired to embrace the great vocation of Brothers in nursing the sick, God's chosen friends, we submit for their kind consideration the following rules the applicant to the Order is to be guided by:

1. A good intention and pure motive (principal condition).
2. Between 18 and 33 years of age.
3. Certificates of Baptism and Confirmation.
4. Recommendation from the parish priest or some other priest.
5. Certificate of health, no apparent deformity.
6. A good, ordinary elementary education.

The confidence and esteem shown the Alexian Brothers on the part of the physicians and the public prove to a certainty that they are up to date in their noble and important calling, to relieve the suffering of the sick, and also that, by the quiet and sure way in which they go about performing their duties as nurses, they know how to gain the faith and confidence of their patients. Careful preparation for their vocation, firmness of character, knowledge of men, quiet dignity, and also, to a certain degree, knowledge of medicine, and above all, unselfish devotion to their calling, all these are factors which characterize the Alexian Brothers ideal nurses of the sick.[34]

The 1893 World's Columbian Exposition was a tribute to Chicago as a railroad, shipping, and manufacturing center of the nation. Over twenty-seven million visitors witnessed a "veritable encyclopedia of civilization."[35] By 1900 Chicago's population exceeded one million, thus becoming the nation's "second city." Chicago became an archdiocese in 1880; by 1900 it numbered about 660,000 Catholics in an area of 10,379 square miles, 168 of which comprised the city. Of all the states reporting to a survey in 1903, Illinois had the largest number of Catholic hospitals; of the 118 hospitals, 43 were Catholic.[36] The majority of the Catholic hospitals, many of which were staffed by German-American sisters, were in small towns. For example, in the diocese of Peoria there were nine hospitals located in Bloomington, Danville, Kewanee, LaSalle, Lincoln, Macomb, Peoria, Rock Island, and Streator. Patient capacity ranged from 15 to 175. The Catholic population of the diocese was about 123,000, which implies that these institutions, like most private hospitals, served the general population. According to the *Catholic Directory* of 1903, the Archdiocese of Chicago had a population of one million but had only seven hospitals.

Mercy Hospital, the oldest Catholic facility, grew with the city. By 1910 it had three hundred beds and was affiliated with Northwestern University's School of Medicine. It also ran its own three-story clinic. Dr. John B. Murphy, who left Alexian Brothers' Hospital because it excluded women patients, joined the staff of Mercy Hospital. Known for innovative surgery—the Murphy button, a device for suturing the large intestine—Murphy gained a national reputation for his scholarly productivity and his pedagogical skills. Dr. William J. Mayo described him as "the surgical genius of our generation."[37]

University affiliation fostered the continuous modernization of the hospital. As early as 1892 two lay nurses and five sisters graduated from the two-year course of Mercy Hospital's nurses' training school. The practical spirit of the Sisters of Mercy, with their various ministries ranging from prisons to homes for working women, allowed them to cultivate a nurses' training school free from the confinement of rigid tradition. However, Chicago possessed a strong Catholic presence, manifested in five hospitals and in a strong parish life with schools and orphanages representing a rich mix of ethnicity and religion. For example, Patrick A. Feehan, the first archbishop of Chicago, 1880–1902, established fifty-three ethnic parishes for Germans, Slavs, Italians, and Poles.[38]

The Franciscan Sisters, Daughters of the Sacred Hearts of Jesus and Mary, originating in 1859 in Paderborn, Westphalia, settled in St. Louis, Missouri, in 1872. Two years earlier, laymen of St. Boniface parish in the German section of Carondolet, on the southwest periphery of the metropolitan area, had written to their pastor, Ernest Andrew Schindel, requesting that he consider "establishing . . . a hospital."[39] Reacting to recent industrialization in the area the laymen appear to have been persons of some means, perhaps employers who wished to provide for their workers and fellow parishioners. "The many late accidents, in our midst, among the employees of the railroad as well as the foundries and furnaces, the constant increase of this class of men—most of them without family and without facility for relief or comfort in cases of accident or sickness, most urgently appeal to our humanity and demand that proper steps be taken to accomplish this object."[40] After receiving permission from Archbishop Peter R. Kenrick, Schindel purchased property and wrote to his godfather in Muenster of his concern for locating sisters to staff the hospital. This led to the archbishop's approaching the young Franciscan community, which, because of the *Kulturkampf*, responded favorably. Eventually they founded St. Boniface Hospital, which was opened in December of 1873. By this time there were eleven sisters in St. Louis, and on December 5, 1875, four more sisters departed from Bremerhaven on the ship the *Deutschland*. Struck by a storm off the coast of England the ship eventually sank, with forty-five of the over two hundred passengers perishing at sea. The sisters denied themselves life preservers in deference to those more in need and commenced to pray. Their heroism was immortalized in the poem of Gerard Manley Hopkins, "The Wreck of the Deutschland," dedicated "To the happy memory of five Franciscan nuns. . . ."

Though they successfully begged for funds in the German areas of several midwestern cities and towns, the Franciscan sisters experienced an early tragedy when fire burned down their hospital. Its replacement was called Pius hospital; in 1900 they opened St. Anthony's, which became a modern facility. Henry J. Spaunhurst, a prosperous German-American businessman, publisher, politician, and a national figure in lay Catholic movements of the 1880s and 90s, was a valuable patron of the sisters, responsible for fund-raising and for their investments and mortgages. Though they founded some schools, they eventually concentrated exclusively on hospitals, orphanages, and homes for girls. Over the years they founded six other hospitals in addition to St. Anthony's in St. Louis: St. Francis in Cape Girardeau, Missouri, St. Joseph's in Milwaukee, Wisconsin, St. Mary's in Racine, Wisconsin, St. Andrew's in Murphysboro, Illinois, St. Elizabeth's in Appleton, Wisconsin, and St. Francis in Waterloo, Iowa. Since their motherhouse is in Wheaton, Illinois, they now are referred to as the Wheaton Franciscans.[41]

In her unpublished history of the Franciscans Sisters of the U.S. Province (St. Clara Province), Sister M. Berenice Beck describes the evolution of medical care from their origins in 1873. At St. Boniface (1873–77) the staff represented general practice, surgery, eye and ear, throat and lungs, skin, nervous system ("including insanity") as well as drug and alcohol habits, and women's and children's diseases.[42] Pius Hospital (1877–1900) could accommodate twenty patients. In 1887 thirty beds were added. According to Sister Phillippa Breidenbach, who nursed there from 1887–94, surgeries were performed in patients' rooms, until a small operating room was placed in the addition. The physicians did much of the work later assigned to nurses, but because it was the motherhouse of the congregation there are no criteria for discerning the sisters assigned to nursing.[43] It appears that the religious community was steeped in German Catholic traditions. Of all the hospitals in St. Louis in 1915, only St. Anthony's did not list lay nurses on the staff.[44] Prayers were still recited in German, and the vast majority of the sisters were from Germany or at least were German speaking. Without an organized medical staff in 1915 (Alexian Brothers in Chicago was formed in 1893) and without an X-ray machine (a physician at St. John's in St. Louis, run by the Sisters of Mercy, introduced one before 1907), it appears that St. Anthony's was a cultural lag in modern Catholic health care. Old world tradition with its strong devotionalism and its rootedness in surrounding ethnic neighborhoods were significant compensations for St. Anthony's moderately slow adaptation to the modernization and professionalization processes.

The oldest German-American women religious community founded in the United States, the Sisters of the Third Order of St. Francis of Philadelphia, was founded in 1855 amid the flowering of devotionalism promoted by their episcopal patron, Bishop John N. Neumann. As mentioned in chapter four, the sisters entered hospital ministry to serve the burgeoning German-American community. In 1864 the sisters accepted the donation from Catherine Eberhard of three houses along Caroline Street in Baltimore which were to be used for the care of the "sick and infirm."[45] In making plans for this charitable bequest Mrs. Eberhard had worked closely with the Redemptorist pastors of the three German parishes (St. James, St. Michael's, and St. Alphonsus), and it was through this association that the sisters' hospital received its name, "St. Joseph's German Hospital." With three Redemptorists and six laymen representing the German parishes on the board of trustees of the hospital it seems that the parishes' sick benefit societies were intended to send their members to the hospital, which in its first year also housed some wounded and sick soldiers at the Civil War's final stages. The demands for health care in East Baltimore's only Catholic hospital necessitated purchase of a tract of land of a little over four acres, located along Caroline Street. According to a handwritten "History of St. Joseph's German Hospital," which appears as a chronicle with copies of the minutes of the board of trustees, "a temporary building was erected capable of accommodating about fifty patients at a cost of $5,800 and more sisters were [assigned]."[46] In 1871 the construction was laid for a new wing of the hospital designed by Dr. Oscar Coskery, who became its chief of the medical staff. Opened in December 1872, shortly after the death of Archbishop Martin John Spalding, who had welcomed the community to the nation's premier see, the new wing could accommodate seventy-two patients and cost nearly $50,000. Mrs. Eberhard in accord with an understanding moved into the hospital as a resident in 1873. Incorporated as simply St. Joseph's, and listed in the *Catholic Directory* as "St. Joseph's General Hospital," the Redemptorist pastors and "one or two of the social led [sic] Lay Trustees prevailed upon Rev. Mother General to change the name and call it St. Joseph's German Hospital."[47] However, few German physicians were on the staff and non-Germans dominated the medical board. Perhaps the German-trained physicians gravitated to those facilities attached to universities where they could blend research and practice, such as Johns Hopkins and the University of Maryland.

The hospital's medical board, founded in 1910, completed the modernization of the hospital. It almost immediately took charge of the operations of the dispensary, separated its staff from that of the hospital, and designed rules for its governance. The dispensary was a facility where patients were treated at no cost. Young physicians who for various reasons were not incorporated into the recently established intern program, could gain experience at the dispensary and could attract private patients to their offices. Eventually some would be appointed to the hospital staff, thereby allowing them to admit patients. Apparently some staff physicians wanted to close the dispensary, but the sister superintendent,

Sister Zita, insisted that it remain open. Concern for the poor was her principal motive. Since 1881 St. Joseph's had been designated as one of the hospitals to care for indigent patients by both the city of Baltimore and the state of Maryland, and private charity patients represented a sizeable figure.[48]

Evidence of modernization included the appointment of a lay surgical nurse, the requirement of resident physicians to pass an examination, the concern for proper patient records, separation of consumption (tuberculosis) patients into their own ward; and eventually a pathologist and radiologist were appointed to the staff.[49] Because of the inability of the twenty-four sisters to keep pace with the accelerated changes of the hospital there was an obvious need for a training school. The Franciscan community assigned a "special sister" to be superintendent of the school. In November of 1901 five students were enrolled in a three-year program, which eventually included sister-students as well. A new wing was added to the hospital in 1901, a portion of which housed the students until a separate residence was opened in 1925. This first class did not reflect the prominence of the German community; except for perhaps Mary Cloman, the other four were Irish Americans: Bronley, Cavney, Boyle, and Cunningham.[50]

But the German-American character of the Franciscan community persisted. In 1900 the community published an edition of its *Rules and Constitutions* that included the general rule of the Tertiaries of St. Francis. While the latter was steeped in traditional notions of penitential practices, the particular rules of the Philadelphia community (its motherhouse moved to Glen Riddle, Pennsylvania, in 1896) were also quite rigorous, particularly for a community dedicated to an active apostolate. For example, on Wednesday and Friday the sisters were to "take the discipline [self-flagellation] . . . whilst reciting five Our Fathers and Hail Marys." They were also to abstain from meat on Wednesdays, Fridays, and Saturdays. There were many fast days throughout the year but teaching and nursing sisters were exempted from most fasting regulations.[51]

The chapter "On the Care of the Sick" opens with a general statement on the significance of health-care ministry. "One of the chief means by which the members of the Congregation endeavor to acquire perfection, consists in cheerfully rendering consolation to the sick in hospitals attached to their convents and in private homes." The sisters were urged to respond to the poor, the sick, and the dying with Christian charity "and in so doing walk in the footsteps of their heavenly Bridegroom who 'went about doing good and healing all.'" Their primary concern was the "spiritual welfare of the sick . . . while they work for their bodily recovery let them try to win their souls to God." Though the sisters were expected to lead the patient to the significance of religious duties they were instructed to "teach them the easiest way of affecting their conversion, raise them to confidence in Divine Mercy, and urge them to make no delay in procuring their eternal salvation."[52]

One sister was to be in charge of the hospital, and no one was admitted without her permission. Professional nursing procedures had not reached the level of community regulations: "No sister is allowed to interfere in those things that have been ordained regarding the care of the sick. The sisters shall conduct themselves in a dignified manner and maintain the best order and cleanliness in the discharge of their duties. All unnecessary conversation in the dormitories [i.e. wards] and rooms of the sick is forbidden, whether it be with the convalescent or the physicians, much less with the servants and other outsiders who work around the building and the yard."[53]

By the time this rule was printed in 1900 the community ran nine hospitals, seven in the East and the other two in the far West: Tacoma, Washington, and Baker, Oregon. Like the Baltimore foundation these hospitals were strongly rooted in the German-American community. St. Joseph's German Hospital, within a mile of the Johns Hopkins University Hospital, remained the only Catholic facility in East Baltimore. The Sisters of Mercy owned and staffed City Hospital in the downtown area. Called the City Hospital because of its proximity to the city gardens, the institution accommodated two hundred patients. Located in west Baltimore was St. Agnes Hospital, a Daughters of Charity institution with 289 beds. The Daughters were no longer located at the Baltimore Infirmary, but they operated the only Catholic hospital for the mentally ill, Mt. Hope Retreat, with sixty-three sisters and 930 patients. The Bon Secours Sisters were located in the western section of the downtown area; their apostolate, traditionally limited to home nursing, now included hospital nursing.[54]

The persistence of the German character of St. Joseph's was manifested in its devotional life. Each of the wards was named after a saint, a custom rarely evident in other hospitals. Forty Hours of eucharistic adoration, vigorously promoted by Bishop Neumann, was also an annual devotion in all Glen Riddle Franciscan hospitals. The constitution's directive that the sisters prepare the patient for "conversion" was analogous to the Redemptorists' parish-mission apostolate aimed at turning the laity away from indifference and toward the fullness of religious practice, particularly penance and communion. The directive to render assistance and consolation "cheerfully" illustrates the principal motif of Catholic hospitals, to bring the hope of Christ's redemption to their patients. Though St. Joseph's continued to be referred to as the German Hospital, World War I brought an end to that identity, but by that time the hospital was fully integrated into modernization.

The Philadelphia Sisters of the Third Order of St. Francis was the major German-American hospital community founded in the United States. Five of the communities of women religious in the post-*Kulturkampf* period were principally engaged in health care: the Franciscan Sisters of St. Louis, later Wheaton, Illinois; the Sisters of the Third Order of St. Francis of the Holy Family, who settled in the Midwest; the Hospital Sisters of St. Francis of Springfield, Illinois; the Poor Sisters of St. Francis Seraph of Perpetual Adoration of Lafayette, Indiana; the Franciscan Sisters of the Sacred Heart, who first settled in Joliet, Illinois. The Poor Handmaids of Jesus Christ settled in Fort Wayne, Indiana, after the *Kulturkampf* and still have several hospitals in the Midwest. The German hospitals flourished in the so-called German triangle—Cincinnati, St. Louis, and Milwaukee.[55]

There were relatively few communities identified with health care for Italian Americans. Because of impoverished conditions in southern Italy over 4.5 million Italians emigrated to the United States in search of economic and social security between 1880 and 1924. Mother Frances Xavier Cabrini (1850–1917), canonized a saint in 1946, established hospitals in New York, Chicago, and Seattle. The youngest of thirteen children of a farming family in Lombardy, Frances Cabrini was allowed to join a nascent religious community in charge of an orphanage in 1887 after some years as a teacher and a committed servant of the poor. When the orphanage closed, Cabrini formed the seven sisters into a new community, the Missionary Sisters of the Sacred Heart, and the local bishop appointed her superior. In 1888 the society received the approbation of the Congregation of Religious; Cabrini had hoped to establish a mission in China, but by 1888 she had been advised to go to the United States by Bishop John Baptist Scalabrini of Piacenza, founder of the Missionary Society of St. Charles Borromeo (Scalabrini Fathers and Brothers), and by Pope Leo XIII.

For many years the Holy See and several American bishops had been deeply concerned with the plight of Italian immigrants. Indeed the origin of Scalabrini's religious community was a response to the desperate need for pastoral care among their people so subjected to prejudice and

discrimination in American church and society. Their blend of Catholicity and folk religion, prevalent in the peasant villages of southern Italy,
was transplanted into the "Little Italys" in urban America. With a tradition of alienation from the institutional church and fierce loyalty to the
local village and its patron saints, the Italian Americans tended to identify with the neighborhood rather than parish or diocese. With few
diocesan clergy following the immigrants to the United States, the Scalabrinians were founded "to go to America to do missionary work among
the immigrants and sustain their Faith."[56] Archbishop Michael Augustine Corrigan enthusiastically invited the new missionary society to
work in his archdiocese of New York. When Mother Cabrini heard that
a wealthy Italian countess in New York City wanted to open an orphanage in the city she seized the opportunity and was soon on her way to the
United States. Though there were misunderstandings among everyone
involved, the orphanage was eventually opened in 1899, a month after
Cabrini and six Missionary Sisters of the Sacred Heart arrived in New
York.[57] The sisters' pastoral care of the Italian immigrants included
schools and visitations in homes, prisons, and hospitals.

Columbus Hospital, owned by the Scalabrinians, was opened in 1891
in response to the need for a facility to accommodate the needs of the
growing Italian community. Preceded by a dispensary, called Garibaldi
Hospital and later the Italian Hospital, Columbus Hospital was founded
with the approval of Bishop Scalabrini and Archbishop Corrigan.
Though another Italian community of women religious, the Sisters of St.
Anne, who had hospital experience, was intended to staff the hospital,
the Missionary sisters took charge because, unlike the Sisters of St.
Anne, they could directly participate in begging for funds so crucial to
the success of the hospital. Because Mother Cabrini had experienced the
lax administrative style of the Scalabrinians she negotiated a strong contract that stipulated among other conditions the responsibility for
appointing physicians and nurses and allocating half of the funds raised
for the living expenses of the sisters, who were to be provided with a residence separate from the patients. The hospital was so poorly managed
by the superior of the New York Scalabrinians that it was placed on auction; hence, Mother Cabrini, with the permission and financial support
of Archbishop Corrigan, opened a new Columbus Hospital. With room
for fifty, Columbus Hospital's first patients were transferred from the old
facility. In 1895 Columbus moved again to a newly constructed facility
designed according to specification of the hospital's medical board,
which included at least one Italian-speaking physician. With sixty of the

eighty beds designated as charity beds it was particularly significant that there was a facility for poor Italian Americans that respected their language and culture. Between 1896 and 1904 Italian patients ranged from sixty-six percent to ninety percent. Those paying "Full Board" never achieved five percent. Besides keeping stride with modernization, the hospital also had a full dispensary.[58] In a proposal for funds from an Italian Emigration bureau, Mother Cabrini quoted a report of the Medical Board of New York's Columbus Hospital in which the physicians noted that the Board of Charities sends its Italian patients to Columbus Hospital "because of the knowledge of the language, character, habits, customs and tastes of Italians, in addition to the excellent service rendered to their patients."[59]

In her report to the Sacred Congregation for the Propagation of the Faith, Mother Cabrini referred to Columbus Hospital: "with a capacity of 160 beds, [it] offers free hospitalizations and can particularly [respond] to Italian immigrants." By this time there was a second hospital in Chicago, where the sisters cared for 1,400 patients annually—"not only Italians, but Slavs, Poles, Germans and Spaniards." With characteristic clarity on the pastoral foundation of their hospital ministry Mother Cabrini described the community's health-care presence.

HOSPITALS

The principal goal of the hospitals is to assure that the poor who have come to the end of their lives and resources find not only alleviation for their corporal misery, but principally help for their souls. Experience has shown that the majority of these people have been far away from the Church for many years. Others, even though adults, have not been baptized, nor have they received their First Holy Communion. There are also many who were not married in church.

It is a consolation to see that many patients leave the hospital having been reconciled with God as well as having been helped physically.

By means of the hospitals and dispensaries, the sisters meet thousands of immigrants who are not only Italian, but of other nationalities. These poor, sick people, grateful to those who assisted them at the moment of their greatest need, that in which sickness added its toll to the rigors of poverty, are very well disposed to listen to sister's words about God, and the conversions are many and edifying.[60]

VISITS TO HOSPITALS AND PRISONS

The sisters visit the immigrants in public hospitals, poor houses and prisons. Here the results are most gratifying. Since the chaplains often do not know foreign languages, the sisters have an advantage over them. Since they come from various nations, they not only know Italian, but other languages as well, so they can better communicate with the patients and prisoners and dedicate themselves to the spiritual welfare of their immigrant compatriots with consoling results.

For example, at the bedside of patients, where a priest is often unwanted, the sister, with some fruit or a book, or a religious article, gains easy access, and with the grace of God finds a way of preparing these poor souls for the priest's visit and their return to God. In fact, the zealous chaplain of the prison in Oregon told our sisters in Seattle a few weeks ago: "You do more good in one visit [to] these prisons than I am able to do in a month."

The sisters go regularly to the American prisons to visit the inmates and to teach them Christian doctrine. They take special care to prepare the unhappy ones, who have met their death with resignation and edification. Even desperate cases become tranquil and reconciled with God when they are assured by the sisters that they would take care of their children and their families.[61]

With a strong sense of religious and ethnic identities Mother Cabrini's self-understanding was deeply preservationist, just as the neighborhood devotional *festa* was intended to preserve the folk culture. The cultivation of old-world religion and culture in Columbus Hospital and "Little Italys" buffered the Italians' encounters with religious pluralism and urban modernity, thereby providing some sense of continuity in the adaptation to American life.

III

The Sisters of Mercy and the Daughters of Charity were identified with ministries to the English-speaking people, that is, the Irish-American community that dominated the hierarchy of the church. More fully assimilated into American life, their hospitals cultivated a Catholic identity free from old-world traditions but nevertheless deeply conscious of the religious tradition.

The Sisters of Mercy opened Atlanta Hospital in 1880, which was called St. Joseph's Infirmary in 1903 when it boasted an increased capacity to fifty patients. An offspring of the Savannah Institute (later St. Joseph's) of the Mercy Sisters, St. Joseph's was founded at the initiative of Bishop William Gross of Savannah. The *Atlanta Constitution* of May 2, 1880, reported: "Atlanta has a hospital at last. It is a permanent institution which will grow in importance and usefulness as the city's needs increase. The new institution . . . is controlled by the Sisters of Mercy whose beautiful ministrations to the afflicted are known to all. . . ." With a clear notion of the Victorian ideal woman the reporter continued, "The hospital will be in charge of Sister Cecelia [sic] whose noble conduct during the yellow fever epidemics, has made her name synonymous with all that is womanly and devoted." The name "Atlanta Hospital" conveyed to the reporter of the *Constitution* that "the hospital will have no special religious character, though it will be conducted by the Sisters of Mercy, they will consult the slightest preference of any patient, and will send as quickly for a Protestant minister or a Jewish rabbi as for a priest of their own faith."[62]

With its origin in the 1840s tied to the railroad—it was a terminus from Chattanooga—Atlanta had a population of sixty thousand in 1881; the one Catholic parish in the city was primarily Irish who were originally railroad workers. The Catholic population of the diocese of Savannah, which comprised the state of Georgia, was twenty-five thousand in 1880. Like most areas in the South, the diocese was poor, with few priests and religious and primarily rural in character.[63] The first hospital in the diocese originated in 1875 when Sister M. Cecilia Carroll was placed in charge of the United States Marine Hospital in Savannah, a federal facility for sailors, during a yellow-fever epidemic. With an untrained staff of one elderly white woman and a equally old black man, the two physicians at the hospital had sought the sisters through the intercession of Bishop Gross. The four sisters assigned to the hospital were untrained, but at least they had been educated to teach school and were young and energetic. Originally Sisters of Our Lady of Mercy, founded by Bishop John England in Charleston, South Carolina (see chapter five), these pioneer sisters were soon experienced care givers, who needed to climb a rope-ladder to the attic, where the black patients were housed. After some ten months the Sisters of Mercy moved into a former Catholic orphanage, which they named St. Joseph's Infirmary. Here were housed the patients of the Marine Hospital as well as "a number of destitute poor old men and old women."[64] It was a mix of almshouse and Marine Hospital with the federal and city governments covering the costs of the sailors. Shortly after they had moved into the "new" facility, yellow fever struck the town; two physicians, four priests, and three sisters died of the disease. The infirmary became a hospital in 1901, the year the sick sailors moved into a new separate Marine Hospital opened that year in Savannah.[65]

The Atlanta Hospital of 1880 was a converted home purchased by Father James M. O'Brien, pastor of Atlanta's Immaculate Conception Church. Sister M. Cecilia Carroll and the other three sisters took charge of the ten-bed facility; according to oral tradition, their funds totalled fifty cents. Charitable donations, city funds for indigent patients, and the sisters' own frugality allowed the hospital to survive. Two major donations were sufficient to construct a three-story building, and in 1896 a surgical wing was added. The latter was a gift of Dr. R. D. Spalding of the Catholic Spaldings, originally from Maryland. The new wing also included a chapel, symbolic of the Catholic character of St. Joseph's rather than the generic Atlanta Hospital. However, it remained a cosmopolitan institution with Catholic, Protestant, and Jewish physicians on its staff and patients from many religious traditions. In a 1903 brochure the sisters introduced "the best equipped and most modernly appointed Medical and Surgical Sanitorium in this section of the country." They were particularly detailed in the description of "Operating Department," which was "constructed along strictly aseptic lines, walls and floor of tile and marble, round corners, and an arrangement for flushing the room at will." These conditions, combined with a "sterilizing room . . . an anaesthesia room, a surgeon's dressing room . . . constitute one of the most complete operating suites in the nation." In the tradition of the Sisters of Mercy there were several charity patients, who paid little or no hospital fees. However, St. Joseph's Infirmary was without an endowment and therefore dependent on paying patients.

In the 1903 brochure of the Atlanta Hospital the sisters "gratefully acknowledged the professional services of the gentlemen comprising the medical and surgical staff," not only because of their skills and "their devotion to patients" but also because they "have sent and treated patients in our institutions." Without the admitting physicians there would be no paying patients to help defray the rising costs of health care. Weekly rates ranged from fifteen dollars to twenty dollars per week, "according to the location of the room." Cost of surgical supplies was not included in these rates nor was the "fee for professional attendance, which must be arranged with the physician employed by the patient."[66]

This market arrangement between patient and physician is at the core of the development of modern medicine. Essential to Paul Starr's work, *The Social Transformation of American Medicine,* is the thesis that scientific knowledge of the physician was "transformed into authority, and authority into market power before the gains from scientific advancement can be privately appropriated by a profession." Central to the transformation is the authority bestowed upon the profession by "lay deference [i.e., patients] and by institutional forms [i.e., hospitals and later insurance companies and local governments] of dependence."[67] The Catholic hospitals were being transformed within the context of private markets; their religious self-understanding was rooted in the traditional soil of Catholic religiosity, but in the modernized hospital such devotionalism tended to be privatized in a predominantly Protestant area such as Atlanta. Indeed, it was imperative to convey a cosmopolitan image to counter the anti-Catholic hostility so deeply situated in southern culture. For example, during the first decade of the twentieth century, disillusioned populists and progressive political activists, such as Tom Watson in Atlanta, manifested a strident anti-Catholicism, as if a papal conspiracy had been responsible for the failure of the populist movement to break down the concentrations of economic, social, and political power.[68]

The Daughters of Charity hospital in Boston experienced modernization within a strong Irish-Catholic environment. Carney Hospital owes its origins to Andrew Carney (1794–1864), who in 1863 purchased the property on which was a large home, and presented it to the Daughters of Charity. Two years later Carney's estate contributed $75,000 toward the $100,000 needed for a new hospital of almost one hundred beds. In 1891 a new building doubled the capacity but imposed a heavy burden of indebtedness on the Daughters of Charity. Seventeen years later there was $81,000 left on the mortgage. In 1901 Carney opened a new "outpatient" department housed in its own building adjacent to the hospital. Nevertheless, Carney Hospital asserted its "nonsecular" character and "makes no questions as to the race or creed of any applicant." Located in the South Boston district, which in 1908 numbered ninety thousand, the hospital served this predominantly Irish-Catholic area of Boston. Because many working-class people had no one at home to care for the sick, "they must usually seek shelter of a hospital when ill or incapacitated for any length of time." Of the 2,500 patients treated in the wards during 1908, "a larger percentage pay nothing whatever for their care." Without an endowment and without state or municipal assistance the operating budget was consistently in the red; an $11,000 deficit of 1907 was met from "popular subscriptions."[69]

Despite these financial difficulties the hospital maintained high standards; twelve interns trained there in 1908. According to the annual report of that year, "Carney Hospital has shared with others in Boston in advancing the medical knowledge of the community. This was first demonstrated to the medical profession of New England . . . the possibility of operating successfully upon ovarian tumors." Another innovation at Carney that became common throughout the profession was "the continuous service for a hospital staff and the placing of each department under one responsible chief."[70]

As mentioned earlier, the growth in the number of patients and the gradual advances in medical and surgical sciences and technologies interacted to make the hospital and not the home the central locus for treatment. Hospital literature abounded with references to moderniza- tion; instead of creating a "homelike" atmosphere the annual reports focused on the medical and surgical advances of the institution. In the previous period, what Joan E. Lynaugh referred to as the "domestic era," Catholic hospital reports conveyed a sense of religious domesticity.[71] For example, the 1872 report of St. John's Hospital of Lowell, Massachusetts (a Daughters of Charity facility), composed by a physician, conveys this domestic tranquility.

> There are two or three other classes of sick persons who are greatly bene- fited by this Hospital. Those single individuals and operatives who have no homes or friends here, when taken sick, need just such accommodations as this Institution affords. The great number reported every year on the Register, between the ages of twenty and forty, shows that this class has been largely represented among its patients.
>
> Then, there is a class of most worthy persons in the city, of very limited means, or none at all, who, when they fall sick, cannot find decent or com- fortable accommodations anywhere. What these persons want most are rest, quiet, wholesome air, nourishing food, good nursing, together with some medical treatment. These are just the accommodations this class needs, and who will and must suffer without them. It should be stated that every year witnesses a goodly number of patients here from this class. In fact, the leading, the most prominent feature in the Institution, is one of Christian charity, of pure humanity.[72]

Though this report is a public-relations effort to dispel fear of the hospi- tal and to gain more admissions, it clearly reveals the domestic era.

Just as in the Baltimore Infirmary of the 1830s, St. John's of 1872 was staffed primarily by sisters, along with a few hired assistants. By 1908 the language has changed from "domesticity to efficiency,"[73] symbolizing the patterns of modernization. For example, the Carney Report of 1908 referred to the following statistics: 1863—five sisters, 1908—twenty-five sisters and fifty-five nurses; there were four physicians in 1863 and sev- enty in 1908. "At one time the Sister of Charity [*sic*] was the best and, as she still is, the most devoted nurse, and her assistance was eagerly sought by all hospitals. Later nursing became more a profession among the laity and gradually the hospital-trained nurse has displaced all others." At Carney's Training School, opened in 1892, the sisters "cheer- fully" attended classes with the lay students.[74] A strand of domesticity continued to dominate the sisters' lives as the hospital remained if not the patient's home the sisters' home, where they lived, prayed, and nursed. The Daughters of Charity were the trustees, administrators, and department heads. Lay professionals were expected to practice their religion, but the sisters' lives were immersed in the religious.

Contrary to the trend of modernization and professionalization was the establishment of the Servants of Relief for Incurable Cancer, a diocesan community of Dominican Sisters founded in New York City by Rose Hawthorne Lathrop (1851-1926), whose religious name was Mother Alphonsa. The daughter of the famous literary figure Nathaniel Hawthorne, Rose and her husband, George Parsons Lathrop, converted to Catholicism in 1891. It was appropriate that they were instructed in the faith by Alfred Young, C.S.P., a Paulist, who, in the tradition of Isaac Hecker, represented an apologetic based on a synthesis of American culture and Catholicism.

Alienated by her husband's erratic behavior (perhaps due to alcoholism) Rose separated from George Lathrop in 1894. As an extension of her conversion she decided to serve the poor, a religious self-understanding that entailed a life of service to those suffering from incurable cancer but too poor to receive proper care. During the winter of 1895-96 she studied nursing with the Grey Nuns of Montreal followed by several months of training at the New York Cancer Hospital.[75] She rented a two-room apartment on the lower east side of Manhattan, an impoverished area that was central to her mission "to be of the poor as well as among them."[76] For over a year she nursed the sick poor in her home; in 1899 two women joined her to form a community that was at first recognized as a Third Order of St. Dominic, but they were soon permitted to make public vows as women religious in the Dominican family. Home visits and referrals required a larger facility; in 1901 the community and residents moved to an old hotel with sixty rooms located on nine acres.

The Servants of Relief only accepted incurable cases among the poor. They self-consciously referred to their place as a home, not a hospital. Though they adapted treatments used in the cancer hospital the sisters' home was to emphasize personal care; as Mother Alphonsa wrote in 1899: "Our peculiar trait will be that we dwell closely among the poor, sharing as much as possible, if that expression can be permitted, their deprivations, and also their cold and heat, their laborious effort to exist, and their old-fashioned harshness of convenience in order that these things may be remembered and done away with. We trust that our laborious effort will help elucidate the difficult question of how a charity hospital may be a kindly home."[77] The founder later noted the trend among teaching hospitals: "Incurable cancer is now a matter of general and exhaustive study, and the poor supply the principal material used. This cause is of deepest concern to those who are really devoted to destitute misery." The sisters' home was to be a countervailing symbol to "the interests of science propagated by autocratical estimation by persons of inferior judgement."[78] The Servants' home was also intended to be a model for parish volunteers, who would care for the poor cancer patients in their homes. The Servants' homes became large charity facilities in several cities, but their care remained a blend of commitment to poverty, traditional spirituality, and a religious domesticity.[79]

IV

The convergence of modernity and religion was paralleled by that of professional nurses' training schools and religious tradition. The early history of nursing education is so replete with religious themes that the Catholic story is just one thread in the general pattern of religious sensibility. As a result of the Crimean War, nursing in England experienced a social transformation. The legendary heroic service of Florence Nightingale (1820–1910), a woman from an upper-class Unitarian family with solid connections to the "aristocracy of wealth and brains," meant that nursing would no longer be associated with Sarie Gamp, the promiscuous charwoman, a home "nurse" in Charles Dickens's *Martin Chuzzlewit*, but would be identified with Nightingale's "Lady of the Lamp" image: selfless, courageous, educated in the science and art of nursing, and committed to infusing order, efficiency, hygiene, and moral refinement into the ecology of the hospital. With over forty thousand pounds in the Nightingale fund she established a training school at St. Thomas' Hospital, London.[80]

In 1837, many years before the Crimean War, Nightingale had sensed a call from God, who "spoke to me and called me to His service." After some conflict with family over her intention to enter nursing she visited the Kaiserwerth Institute of Protestant Deaconesses and later spent some time in a Daughters of Charity hospital in Paris. In 1853, a year before the outbreak of war, she accepted an appointment as matron of the Institution for the Care of Sick Gentlemen of Distressed Circumstances, where she introduced minor reforms, but wholesale reform was dependent on a trained nursing staff. Here she followed in a tradition of reform but her postwar prestige earned her the commonly perceived image as the first reformer of nursing education. In 1857 she published her one-thousand-page report on the need for hospital reform in the army, which was based on a vast array of statistical evidence on the relationship between hospital conditions and the spread of disease.[81] As noted earlier in this chapter, Charles E. Rosenberg places Nightingale's notion of nursing and illness within the contexts of her moral universe. "[S]ickness was understood by many of her contemporaries to be a general state of the body, a failure of adjustment to its environment. But that environment could be manipulated and the patient aided in the process of readjustment which constituted healing. This was a persuasive point of view in a period when holistic assumptions characterized medical thought, when lay persons and physicians assumed that every aspect of the individual's physical and psychic environment could interact to produce health or disease."[82] A reconstructed hospital environment and trained nurses were central to maximizing the process of healing.

The moral imperative of the Nightingale system, which justified "an autonomous female role in the hospital," sought nurses committed to relieving the "apprehension, uncertainty, and fear" inherent in the patients' illnesses.[83] St. Thomas' School opened on July 9, 1860 with an enrollment of fifteen students, called probationers, in a one-year hospital-based program. Under the direction of a nursing superintendent, a woman of refinement and class accountable only to the trustees supervised the program, which was based on the apprenticeship principle, by which students were trained in the wards, buttressed by lectures from the physicians and matrons (i.e., head nurses later called sisters, a title still used today, which is derived from Anglican communities of women religious dedicated to nursing, each of whom held a position of authority over the lay staff). The school was administered by a matron who lived in the students' residence. Rosenberg succinctly captured the significance of these reforms: "The Nightingale program wedded intuitive moral capacity and intellect, piety and efficiency, and promised hospital administrators a stable and relatively inexpensive labor force along with improved internal discipline and lower mortalities."[84] Though at first controversial, St. Thomas' School became *the* model of nurses' training.

Nightingale was consulted by members of the Sanitary Commission during the Civil War, but there had been pre-Nightingale educational endeavors in both England and the United States. In 1800 a series of twenty-six lectures to nurses by Dr. Valentine Seamon was published. In 1839 the Philadelphia Dispensary developed a plan of training women for obstetrical home nursing. As a result of the organization of nursing during the Civil War and the success of the Nightingale system, the American Medical Association established a Committee on Nursing

Training Methods. The committee's report described nursing as comparable to the profession of medicine but deplored the appalling fact "that not one nurse in a thousand is prepared to be a good nurse, either in the home or in institutions." The report referred to the American Catholic experience: "So far as the information of the committee goes, little has been done in the United States in regard to the training of nurses outside of the Catholic Church."[85] It is unlikely that these physicians knew of Clark's or Coskery's instructions (see chapter two); no doubt it was the physicians' experiences of the nursing skills of women religious during the Civil War that led the committee to report this finding.

The AMA committee recommended that each "large well-organized hospital establish a school, and district schools" should also be formed and placed under the direction of county medical societies "in every State and Territory of the Union." Regarding the place of religion in the "art and science of nursing" the committee recommended that "while it is not at all essential to combine religious exercises with nursing, it is believed that it is highly desirable, and such a union would be eminently conducive to the welfare of the sick in all public institutions."[86]

In 1873 nurses' training schools opened in New York, New Haven, and Boston. Prior to the opening of the Bellevue School in New York former members of the Sanitary Commission and a representative of the physicians consulted with Florence Nightingale. Georgianna Woolsey, sister of Jane Woolsey, referred to earlier as an illustration of Protestant-Catholic conflict among nurses in the Civil War, founded the Connecticut Training School in New Haven. The school at Massachusetts General in Boston was also founded by women who had experienced nursing during the war. The military model gained currency, as the rules for schools emphasized unity, discipline, obedience, honor, and commitment.[87] On the other hand, the domestic virtues lingered, as the literature portrayed nurses as refined women, sensitive to the patients' needs for compassion, tenderness, and other female arts of healing derived from a cultivated intuition.

The convent metaphor was not uncommonly invoked to foster the idealism of heroic religious self-sacrifice. The Connecticut Training School promoted such an image in its published appeal for women "who in other countries would be inmates of a convent" to reflect on their vocation to minister to "suffering fellow creatures." The Bellevue Training School even invoked variations on the famous dictum of St. Vincent de Paul: "We wish our pupils to be religious women . . . [but] we impose no vows. We say to all in the words of the holy founder of the order of the

Sisters [*sic*] of Charity: 'Your convent must be the house of the sick. Your cell, the chamber of suffering. Your chapel the nearest church. Your cloister the streets of the city or the wards of the hospital. The promise of obedience, your sole enclosure. Your grate the fear of God; and womanly modesty, your only veil.'"[88]

The religious permeation of the nursing school was in accord with Florence Nightingale's sensibilities. Among the many notations, letters, and addresses that include spiritual reflections, the following collection of quotes reveals the religious themes of nursing.

> If then we have the *end*: viz that to work out God's purpose is all we had to do, what is the means? We have said that we must first find out God's purpose—and by altering a little Ignatius Loyola's formula, indeed the Christian formula, we may arrive at a pretty good definition. This formula is: that the *end* of man is "to praise and honour the Lord God and to save one's own soul by serving him." Is it not to "save" oneself and the world (oh "save" is indeed a good word—"save" from this slough of vice and misery, of judgement and desolation, of indifference and selfishness and stupidity) to save the world and oneself by observing, finding out and keeping the laws of the Perfect Being to bring every one of us to perfection. . . .[89]

However, Nightingale repudiated a preoccupation with conformity with the will of God.

> To unite with the passive life of absolute conformity with God's will . . . this is the whole end of life . . . it is not for a nurse to be always striving to maintain in herself a state of absolute indifference in neither wishing her patient to live nor wishing him to die, except in fulfilling God's will. On the contrary. Every action must be performed as if the patient's life depended on it. Yet without anxiety—anxiety of course defeating its own end.[90]

A friend of Cardinal Henry Manning, archbishop of Westminster, and attached to the devotions of Thomas à Kempis, Nightingale cultivated a spirituality of nursing that appears to have been congenial to her Unitarian background.

> And I pray God that He will make through you, every Ward into a church: and teach us how *to be* the Gospel [which is] the only way to preach the Gospel: which Christ tells us is the duty of everyone of us "unto the end of the World" every woman and nurse of us all: and how a collection of any people trying to live like Christ is a church. Did you ever think how Christ was a nurse: and stood by the bedside and with His own hands nursed... the suffering?[91]

The American nurses' training schools that incorporated Nightingale's religious dicta were located in hospitals that, unlike St. Thomas' in London, were not endowed nor did they form a separate board of trustees but were under the hospital administration. As these voluntary institutions experienced modernization, their nursing schools provided an inexpensive labor force with twelve-hour-day apprenticeships contracted for a one- to an eventual three-year term (1870s to 1890s) for a diploma. Prior to the development of graduate programs in nursing education in the twentieth century, hospital physicians dominated the faculties of training schools. Crucial to the blend of classroom and bedside education was the cultivation of character formation, that mix of religious, domestic, and military ideals identified with the "calling" to nursing. There was, and still is, a potentially inherent conflict between the well-trained professional motivated to provide patients with good medical care and the refined sensibilities of the person dedicated to responding to patients with empathy and compassion. It is analogous to the conflict among physicians and hospital administrators motivated by economic and social power and idealism.

The religious motivation of sisters and brothers engaged in health care precedes the character formation of nurses' training, but the religious dimension of the ministry was cultivated at the bedside of patients. Sisters Mary Xavier Clark and Matilda Coskery blended the "science" and the religious art of nursing. It was merely a matter of time before the modernization of Catholic hospitals, as was evidenced in the Alexian Brothers' Hospital in 1893, that Catholic institutions would require professionally trained nurses.

The first Catholic nursing school in the United States was opened in 1886 at St. John's Hospital, Springfield, Illinois. A German community, the Hospital Sisters of the Third Order of St. Francis, founded in 1844 by a Benedictine priest in Tilgate near Muenster, had established the hospital in 1878 after three years of home nursing in this the capital of Illinois. Twenty-one sisters, refugees from the *Kulturkampf*, had responded favorably to Bishop Peter Joseph Baltes's request for sisters to nurse the poor of his diocese of Alton, Illinois. In 1875 one group stayed in Alton, while a second was missioned to Springfield.[92]

As the city's first hospital—the sick poor had been housed in bunk beds at the police station—St. John's Hospital was dedicated on September 22, 1879, with nearly 1,500 in attendance (the population was almost 19,000), including the mayor, governor, the bishop, and an African American, William McMurray of St. Louis, who addressed the gathering in German. The new hospital included two wards and sixteen private rooms. Since St. John's was considered a "charity hospital" the sisters supported it by soliciting funds on begging tours. In the early 1880s the hospital benefited from an insurance program based upon railroad-employee premiums, and in 1884 the community staffed St. Luke's, a small Wabash railroad hospital in Springfield. Sisters continued to engage in home nursing, a duty that augmented the community's finances.[93]

When Father Louis Hinssen became director of the community (since the time of their foundation in Germany a priest had been a director) he met with the leadership of the community about the need for training the sisters to keep pace with modernization and in the process foster a sense of public confidence in the hospital. According to one source the sisters at St. John's established their school because "they were giving their best, and the best was falling short; they felt a need of education along nursing lines, and they would have it."[94]

This first Catholic training school was limited to sisters. Notions of the religious life precluded undue contact with "seculars," particularly among the young students, the "candidates and novices" not fully grounded in the way of life of this hospital community. The leadership of the German Americans in a church dominated by Irish-American bishops tended to cultivate an ethnic-Catholic separatism with an emphasis on old-world customs, an identity based on faith, language, and culture with a rich sense of devotionalism and of liturgy. It is not coincidental that the Hospital Sisters and the Alexian Brothers excluded lay people from their schools, the former until 1912, the latter until 1939.

At St. John's Training School Father Hinssen and some nursing sisters composed the first Catholic textbook in nursing published in the United States in 1893, *Handbuch der Krankenpflege*, which was replaced in 1899 by *The Nursing Sister*, composed in a question-and-answer style comparable to a catechism. In the preface to the 252-page "popular guide in the art of nursing," Hinssen noted his method had been an effective way of introducing the theoretical side of nursing education. He was particularly concerned that the candidates and novices should be "activated by the holiest motives which religion inspires, to devote their lives to the alleviation of suffering humanity for Christ's sake but [who] are often without much experience of practical life and with no knowledge of hospital work whatever." Because of the severe challenges of nursing education many candidates and novices lose "courage before the first year of the probation is ended."[95] Hence, the simple catechetical methodology, with which most Catholic students were familiar, was intended to be easily memorized. Those students who failed the school examination were assigned to nonnursing occupations in the hospital, such as the laundry or other domestic services.

The first question on page one is: "What are the essential qualifications of a Sister of Charity?" The answer is:

1. Love of God and fellow-creature.
2. Good religious and secular education.
3. Purity of intention: all for Jesus.
4. Strength of body and mind.
5. Cheerful disposition.
6. Cleanliness to perfection.
7. Equanimity of mind.
8. Patience and perseverance.[96]

Though "purity of intention" is the only point that is traditionally associated with the life of a religious, the first fourteen pages dedicated to the virtues of nursing refer to particular customs of the religious community, such as a sister nursing in a family home taking her meals alone, doing the needlework assigned to her by her superior at the hospital, and avoiding "private friendships for they are forbidden by the rule and dangerous to virtue. . . . Every woman, and more so a religious, will injure her reputation for life, if she associates with unworthy persons, men or women, or with those to whom the slightest suspicion attaches."[97] At the time of a patient's death the sister-nurse is called upon to "show all courage of a Christian soul" because "death is a relief for many a weary wanderer on earth and it will be a consolation for him that he will soon be released through death from his sufferings. . . . Without a quiet, cheerful Christian faith no woman is properly fitted for a nurse, especially not when a patient is dying."[98] Besides extolling the ideal woman-religious nurse Hinssen was also concerned that sisters adapt their religious habits to the aseptic conditions of surgical wards and operating rooms by wearing a "clean cotton or linen overdress with sleeve."[99]

In 1910 there were twelve Hospital Sisters at St. John's. Since many had received diplomas from the school most were missioned to the communities at other hospitals in Illinois and the railroad hospitals the community staffed in Kansas City and Moberly, Missouri, or Sacred Heart Hospital opened by the Springfield community in Eau Claire, Wisconsin, in 1890. One sister wrote in 1910 that the twelve sisters at St. John's were responsible "for all the nursing with the exception of the nursing of male patients for which we have a trained male nurse."[100] By this time it became apparent that to adequately staff a hospital with a two-hundred-bed capacity it was necessary to expand the nursing school by opening enrollment to lay students. Three such students attended in 1912; by 1914 the school was approved by the state of Illinois, and all alumnae of the school were allowed to take the state nurses' examination. Julia Donnelly, an instructor at Mercy Hospital's School of Nursing in Chicago (founded in 1889), was hired to prepare the sisters for their exams, a challenging task because the nursing sisters at St. John's had not rotated among the services and because three of the six sisters were German-born. The alumnae sisters passed their state exams, but still the school did not flourish with high enrollments until after World War I.[101]

As early as 1893 Cardinal James Gibbons of Baltimore noted the foundations of Catholic nursing schools:

> There is today in the management of many of our Sisters' Hospitals an important feature that cannot but commend itself, even to the most indifferent. It is in the system of training as nurses intelligent young woman who are desirous of adopting nursing as a profession. Under the guidance of Sisters, from whom they learn the principles which underlie the intelligent treatment of the afflicted, they become skillful in the hospital wards, and acquire that gentleness and ease of manner, that devotion to duty so much appreciated by the physician and patient.[102]

The mix of professionalism and domesticity succinctly captured by Gibbons was a rather remarkable insight for 1893, as there were only fourteen such schools in the nation. However, seven of these were run by the Daughters of Charity, whose motherhouse, St. Joseph's in Emmitsburg, was located in the archdiocese of Baltimore. Between 1893 and 1904 the Daughters opened twenty-three nursing schools.[103]

Cardinal Gibbons's reference to the direction of the sisters rather than that of the physicians, who formed the faculties of Catholic nursing schools in 1893, reveals the Catholic influence on nursing education. Because of the twelve-hour day and because physicians held their classes at night there was no time nor consideration to introduce courses in Catholic moral teaching, catechesis, and the religious dimension of nursing. Student nurses at St. Vincent's Training School in New York City worked an eighty-four-hour week from the school's opening in 1892 to 1916 when the weekly hours were reduced to fifty-nine, but eighty-four remained normal for night-duty student nurses until 1927 when it was lowered to seventy. The Standard Curriculum for Schools of Nursing, introduced by the National League of Nursing Education in 1917, engendered reforms in St. Vincent's course of instruction. However, it was not until 1927, when the Standard Curriculum was revised, that History of Nursing, Ethics, and Professional Problems were introduced. With the second revision of 1937, Apologetics and the History of Western Religions, along with other related liberal arts courses, were incorporated into St. Vincent's program. Five years earlier, 1932, the school's admission policy first required a high school diploma.[104] However, one presumes that apprenticeship in Catholic hospitals included sisters' oral presentations along the lines of Mother Xavier Clark's 1841 Instructions for nursing sisters with an emphasis on the religious sphere of nursing. Sisters understood that sphere as primarily the concern of the women religious and priests, but they no doubt passed on the significance of nursing as a vocation within the Catholic tradition.

Amid the early professionalization of nursing, hundreds of sisters, representing several communities, served during the Spanish-American War. Late nineteenth-century American imperialism, buttressed by a jingoistic press and the emotional patriotism of the Gilded Age ("Remember the Maine!"), led the nation to declare war on Spain on April 25, 1898. Ten weeks later the war ended, and eighty-eight percent of the deaths during this conflict were from disease, especially typhoid, malaria, dysentery, and yellow fever.

The Daughters of the American Revolution were responsible for implementing the government's policy to contract volunteer nurses, including men, by organizing the process of contracting with the volunteers. Dr. Newcom McGee and Miss Ella Elaine Dorsey were in charge of this effort. To qualify, volunteers were to be trained nurses. However, Dorsey, a Catholic, wrote to superiors of the religious communities encouraging application and notifying that hospital experience would qualify sisters without diplomas from a training school. As a result of this effort nearly 250 sisters were under contract: 196 Daughters of Charity, 12 Sisters of Mercy of Baltimore; 12 Sisters of the Holy Cross of Notre Dame, Indiana; 11 Sisters of St. Joseph of Carondelet (St. Louis), Missouri; and 4 American Sisters of Fort Pierre, South Dakota.[105] The latter community, composed of native Americans, was founded by Mother Catherine Sacred White Buffalo, a young Sioux woman who died at age twenty-nine. The community of five sisters, all Sioux, taught school, nursed in the homes, and staffed a small hospital. Four nursed in Jacksonville, Florida, moved to Savannah, and ended up in a Havana, Cuba, hospital.[106]

Several communities volunteered in hospitals but were not under contract: the Sisters of the Holy Names of Jesus and Mary in Key West, Florida; the Sisters of Charity of Nazareth, Kentucky; the Daughters of

Charity, and the Sisters of Mercy in the San Francisco area; the Sisters of St. Francis of Philadelphia; and the Sisters of St. Joseph of St. Augustine, Florida. Many letters of commendation from patients, physicians, and government officials comparable to the Civil War testimony are located in the archives of these communities. Besides nursing in hospitals in the United States, Cuba, Puerto Rico, and the Philippines, some sisters' communities turned over their schools and hospitals to care for the sick and injured soldiers.[107] Some physicians complained that the sisters' woolen habits were overly ascetical for the heat of the Southeast and were potentially dangerous because such cloth fostered germs, thereby endangering patients and nurses; one physician noted the sisters' tendency to self-sacrifice.

> The only fault I had to find with the Sisters was that they would not rest, would not take care of their own health. After the long hours which their hospital service demanded, they devoted a portion of the time needed for rest to religious exercises. They arose so early in the morning for this purpose that they deprived themselves of necessary sleep, and by thus lowering their vitality, exposed themselves to disease.[108]

An early scholar of the sisters' contributions concluded from an examination of the War Department documents:

> even those surgeons who are most enthusiastic in their praise of the work of the orders, express their regret that the Sisters have not fallen into line with the system of training pursued in the best modern hospitals. This course may or may not be in every respect an advantage, and is often compensated for by the Sisters' long experience in their own hospitals, and by their discipline, their fidelity, and their self-forgetfulness. But it is nevertheless regarded by many surgeons as a misfortune that the Sisters have not had this method of training. . . .[109]

A surgeon at Camp Wikoff on Long Island emphasized the sisters' experience as far more valuable than trained nurses.

> Whatever may be the case in civil institutions, in the field hospital the Sister of Charity is far superior. Sisters do good work. There is with them no bickering with the ward doctor, no fussiness, no refusing to perform menial work when necessary, no desire to "shine" as is the case with the "trained nurse." The Sister of Charity has no ambition but duty; she obeys all orders quietly, with a prompt, orderly and willing manner. No sacrifice is too great, no service too menial. . . .[110]

The Holy Cross sisters, particularly Sister Angela Gillespie, had first gained prominence when they originally entered nursing during the Civil War. At the outset of the war with Spain, Mother General Annunziata responded to the call for nursing sisters. Her letter to a Sister Lydia in charge of the Holy Cross sisters at Camp Hamilton, Kentucky, reveals the religious perspective of wartime nursing.

My dear Sister Lydia:

To you and all my dear Sisters who are now under your care, my heart goes out in prayerful affection, bearing God-speed to your new field of labor. May God be with each one of you!

Let me impress upon you, once again, the importance of being true to your high and holy vocation; and this, each of my Sisters, I am sure, will bear in mind, while kindly caring for the sick and dying, exposing her own life, if need be, for the salvation of the souls for whom our dear Jesus suffered and died.

Be kind to every one under your care, but interfere not with what does not concern you. Be very kind, good Sisters to all; true to your God, your country, your fellow-men, your own selves. Let there be no distinction of Cuban, Spaniard or American, but let all be one before God.

How much I hope for the good you will do for theirs; you will not disappoint one, I know. God bless you all, and keep you well and strong for this great work of charity. . . .[111]

The persistence of religious traditions amid the modern medical advances during the war was also illustrated by Mother Mariana Flynn's letter to the sisters at Carney Hospital, Boston, designated to nurse the wounded soldiers. As the superior of the Daughters of Charity [i.e., the Sister Visitatrix] she placed the sisters' service in the context of religious ministry. Mother Flynn told the sisters that God "permitted the sickness [yellow-fever epidemics were common] which calls you to minister to the wants of the good soldiers, and in doing so, you lead them back to the Father, from whom they had strayed, and souls that Jesus loved so much, are saved and all are the chosen instruments. O my dear Sisters, let us be very humble and keep close to our good God. You are the . . . joy and the delight of Providence for upon you the community depends for the reputation it will have with the powers of the land." The superior had received reports from the various camps where the Daughters of Charity were nursing. "Their modesty, gentleness, prudence, and fidelity to duty, have commanded the respect and approval of all who have worked with them. All this is not our greatest ambition. No, the smile of our sweet Jesus, is all we crave. But the work is our own and souls are being brought back to him; so if we are faithful He will smile with delight upon the success of the poor little instruments he has selected."[112]

Conscious of the hardship of camp nursing, Mother Flynn urged the sisters not to be discouraged and warned them that "the enemy of souls [i.e., the devil] will not let this work go on without an effort on his part to spoil it, and to rob you of the merit of perseverance." She urged the sisters "to be on your guard against vanity, a selfish motive and discouragement. . . . Renew your good intentions every morning, and base your courage and fidelity on the will of God."[113] Perhaps this exhortation assumed an implicit understanding of the nurse's training as well as the explicit religious art of nursing, particularly since Carney's Training School had opened in 1893. However, one could also conclude that Mother Flynn's view of nursing was limited to the sisters' dutiful deference to the physicians' instructions. Though several Daughters of Charity and Sisters of Mercy served in World War I this Spanish-American conflict represents the last general recruitment of sisters as wartime nurses.

At the time of this letter there were twenty Catholic training schools. The war was a catalyst for the proliferation of such schools. For example, the ten Sisters of St. Joseph of Carondelet contracted to serve in the war had so depleted the nursing staff at St. Joseph's Hospital in Kansas City that the personnel crisis led to the foundation of the hospital's nursing school. After dispensing "with the services of women who were paid to assist in caring for the sick," the training school was opened in 1901 under the motto *Ad Aegros Dei Lavandos,* "For the Relief of God's Suffering."[114] St. Joseph's was one of the 203 training schools opened between 1893 and 1913. The motto of St. Joseph's illustrates the principal religious motivation for the foundation of Catholic nursing schools. For example, the Daughters of Charity of Carney Hospital in Boston stated their school's purpose in 1893: "The ideal and aim of carrying the charity of Christ to the masses of the people through a scientific training which has God for its beginning and end."[115] As mentioned earlier, training schools were opened not only because of the need for educated "professional nurses," but also because the hospitals' increasingly expanding patient capacity required proportionate increase in trained nursing personnel. Sisters alone could not fulfill these needs, so nearly every Catholic nursing school enrolled lay women, and Providence Hospital in the District of Columbia opened a men's school in 1909, fifteen years after the opening of its women's school in 1894.[116]

Providence Hospital was founded in 1861 as a Civil War hospital. With Washington Infirmary unable to keep pace with the casualities of war, Dr. Joseph Toner, representing the infirmary's physicians, successfully appealed to the Daughters of Charity to establish this first hospital in the nation's capital. The Daughters had been in the city since the 1825 foundation of their orphanage and school. Opened to the public in 1866, this hospital's private patients were admitted by their physicians. It housed the first surgical amphitheater in 1882, which allowed students from medical schools as well as nurses to view operations. In 1894 a two-year training school was opened, in 1895 a third year was added. In 1900 there were twenty sisters in Providence Hospital with a total patient census for the year at 2,596. As a community hospital, with a Marine ward for sailors, the Federal Government subsidized fifty thousand dollars of the construction costs of a student nurses' home in 1901.[117] (In 1898 the Supreme Court decided against a challenge to the federal funding of Providence Hospital building for contagious diseases. The decision said that the subsidy did not violate the First Amendment separation clause as any eleemosynary institution such as Providence was allowed government funds as long as it acted in conformity to its charter to admit patients without regard to race, creed, or color. The case established a strong precedent for federal subsidies for religious institutions.)[118]

In 1898 fifteen student nurses were enrolled in the Providence Training School's Sodality of the Children of Mary, which fostered spiritual exercises and monthly conferences, Mass, and communion. For example, at the end of the second meeting the Sodalists' "office," a set of daily prayers, was said and two weeks later a "general Communion was held." The first retreat for the Sodality was not until November of 1906. The retreat master was the Vincentian priest-founder of the Missionary Servants of the Holy Trinity, Thomas Augustine Judge.[119] As mentioned earlier, daily Mass and Communion, fostered by Pius X, and annual retreats were not common until later. Many schools did not organize sodalities until much later. For example, Sisters of St. Joseph of Carondelet introduced them at St. Joseph's Training School (Kansas City, Missouri) in 1917[120] and St. Mary's School (Tucson, Arizona) in 1925.[121]

The origins of Chicago's Mercy Hospital Training School was typical: "the sisters alone could not attend to the growing number of patients." Sister Mary Ignatius Feeney, the first woman registered pharmacist in Illinois (1889), was one of the original faculty members of the school, which opened in 1889. Because the hospital was affiliated with Northwestern School of Medicine the students had laboratory science classes, which marked the school as the most advanced Catholic training school in the United States. Even before the school's affiliation with Northwestern (1905) it had a demanding course of studies. In 1901 five students in a probation-period class of thirty-eight received their diplomas.[122] Sister

Mary Veronica Ryan, superintendent of the school, stated: "This school has succeeded . . . because it required high standards, high rating in previous schools, lady-like behavior and required very special references. . . ."[123]

There were over thirty communities of women religious sponsoring about 220 nursing schools at their hospitals in 1915, the year the Catholic Hospital Association held its first annual convention. As founding member of the association and a member of the board of directors for six years Sister Veronica Ryan of Chicago represented the professionalization of nursing education as it passed into a new era. The College of Physicians, also located in Chicago, had launched a standardization movement that was aimed at evaluating hospitals along the lines of modern criteria of organization and of scientific basis for diagnosis and treatment. Catholic hospitals responded to this movement, but these institutions grounded their religious identity in modern local and national structures that were permeated by a traditional spirit.

CHAPTER EIGHT

National Structures and Hospital Standardization

IN CATHOLIC HEALTH CARE modernization and professionalization were anchored in religious and ethnic traditions. The inexorable drive to modernization proceeded at a pace that elicited a response for progressive nurses' training and graduate education for leaders of nursing schools and hospitals. Because many communities of women religious were mired in old-world rules that governed their relationships with the secular world, sisters in key positions found it difficult to keep pace with the changes and to deal with physicians' demands for new technologies and other reforms. The Catholic Hospital Association (CHA) filled the need for national medical, religious, and social education. Because the Sisters of St. Joseph had established a strong Catholic presence in hospitals in the Midwest it was appropriate that the CHA's origin occurred in this context.

I

On July 19, 1914, Charles B. Moulinier, S.J., and fourteen Sisters of St. Joseph of Carondelet met in Minneapolis, Minnesota, on the porch of a cottage overlooking the Mississippi to discuss Father Moulinier's idea of establishing an organization of Catholic hospitals. As regent of the medical school of Marquette University, Milwaukee, Father Moulinier had clearly perceived the need for a strong and prompt response to the growing public demands that hospitals raise their standards of health care. Some Catholic hospitals were keeping pace with the rapid advancements in medical science, but sister-administrators (superintendents) and heads of departments needed continuing education so that they could deal effectively with physician demands for significant changes in hospitals as well as with the national movement for reform.

The sisters at this historical meeting, each of whom was involved in hospital ministry, were convinced that a unified Catholic effort to meet the needs of modernization was imperative and deferred to Father Moulinier to lead a movement for a general organizational meeting the following year. After receiving the strong endorsement of Archbishop Sebastian G. Messmer of Milwaukee and the approval of his Jesuit superiors, Moulinier gathered thirty-five sisters from the upper Midwest to attend a meeting on April 8, 1915, at Marquette University. Thus was born the Catholic Hospital Association, today's Catholic Health Association (CHA).[1]

Reflecting on the trends of the times, Moulinier was particularly concerned that Catholic hospitals become advanced institutions and meet the standards established by accrediting agencies such as the American Medical Association and the American College of Surgeons. The Flexner Report of 1910 had exposed the desperate need for medical education reform. Although now considered the culmination rather than the cause of a reform movement, this report reverberated through the health-care system.

Abraham Flexner's report became "both the bible and the symbol of medical reform." Vital to the development of scientific medicine was the symbiotic alliance between the medical school and the large hospital with its clinical laboratory and its outpatient dispensary.[2] Research and clinical professors could conduct experiments and teaching within a context increasingly dependent on scientific or secular classification of case histories of patients, analysis of diverse diagnoses, and experimental use of new drugs and other treatments in the free dispensary with its large supply of lower-class patients. In 1906 over half of the medical schools in the United States had no affiliation with hospitals. Between 1906 and 1915 the number of medical schools declined from 162 to 95, the vast majority of which had access to hospitals. Armed with the Flexner report, the American Medical Association Council on Medical Education and other reformers had an obviously significant impact.[3]

Hospital administrators during this formative period were referred to as superintendents; those designated *medical* superintendents were physicians, and until the 1920s many of the superintendents were nurses. The American Hospital Association, founded in 1899, was under the dominance of the physicians when in 1913 it agreed "in principle . . . to the inspection, classification and standardization of hospitals."[4] The

American College of Surgeons, founded in 1913, also supported hospital standardization. The latter group, with a good record of accrediting surgeons, particularly in its efforts to maintain autonomy in confrontation with reforms eager to place surgeons under the monitoring authority of administrators, received a grant from the Carnegie Foundation to initiate hospital accreditation. Under the direction of John G. Bowman, founder of the Foundation, the College of Surgeons, located in Chicago, embarked on a national standardization program of evaluating hospitals. As regent of Marquette University's medical school Charles B. Moulinier, who had arranged the school's affiliation with St. Francis Hospital, was deeply influenced by these trends.

Held in Milwaukee from June 24 to 26, 1915, the first CHA convention was attended by two hundred sisters, lay nurses, and doctors, representing forty-three hospitals from twelve states. Participants discussed such topics as "The Trend of Modern Hospital Service," "Significance of Hospital Rating," "Staff Organization," "The Training School," "Social Work in Hospitals," "The Hospital's Equipment." Contributors included an architect (who explained principles of hospital construction), medical school faculty, hospital administrators, and nursing superintendents.[5]

A constitution and bylaws for the Catholic Hospital Association of the United States and Canada were adopted at this first convention. Among CHA's stated purposes was "to advance the general interests of all hospital work, to encourage the spirit of cooperation and mutual helpfulness among hospital workers, to promote by study, conference, discussion, and publication the thoroughness and correct moral tone and practice of medicine."[6]

The delegates elected Moulinier as the first president of CHA, a position he held until 1928. A native of Cincinnati, Charles Moulinier was born on December 6, 1859. After completing Jesuit formation, scholasticate, and theological studies, he was ordained on June 25, 1895. Between then and his 1908 appointment to Marquette University, he taught philosophy at St. John's College, Toledo, Ohio, and was academic dean of the University of Detroit. At Marquette he first taught philosophy and lectured on medical jurisprudence at the medical school. After a year of lecturing on ethics in the schools of dentistry, law, and pharmacy, he was appointed regent (the Jesuit superior's representative) of all professional schools, but in 1913 his assignment as regent was limited to the medical school.[7]

Moulinier was a dominant personality in the early years of the association. Primarily an educator, he developed convention programs that included a series of seminars on every aspect of hospital life. Moulinier's speeches and writings focused on the interrelationships among hospitals' technological, scientific, social, ethical, and religious dimensions. At the 1918 convention in Milwaukee, he reminded his audience that the association had in previous conventions "repudiated any . . . thought that the hospital is a mere boarding-house, a place where the surgeon merely operates, where the internist merely prescribes medicine or treatment, where the nurse is little more than a cheerful attendant on whims."[8]

As welcome as they were, recent advances in the techniques of diagnosing and treatment threatened to create an impersonal cultural gap between the hospital staff and their patients, and Moulinier saw it as part of his role to remind the audience of this danger. In 1918 he noted, "there was always one overmastering controlling point of view, *service to the patient*. We never lost sight of the great fundamental, ethical principle that the patient has a right to all the most enlightened, self-sacrificing, scientific, philanthropic, and conscientious religious service that body, mind, and soul of man craves for, needs, and has a right to."[9]

From the outset the CHA was recognized primarily as a "sisters' organization." Indeed, Moulinier himself was of the opinion that a sister would be the best choice for association president. Because bishops and superiors did not wish to change those rules of the sisters' religious communities against travel and attendance at night meetings, their eligibility as full-time officers of a national organization was prohibited; hence, priests occupied CHA leadership positions until the 1960s. Nevertheless, since 1915 the sisters have been well represented among the officers, the executive board, and the leadership of the various committees that planned the convention. Thus, from its origins, CHA has provided a unique forum for women religious representing the communities engaged in health care. (It was not until the 1940s that a brother, Roy Godwin, C.F.A., was elected to the executive board.[10]) Further opportunities for sisters arose when the 1915 convention established a summer school at Marquette University. At first only two courses were offered: clinical pathology and radiology. In the summer of 1916 a grant from the Carnegie Foundation allowed the school to offer seven courses; enrollment increased from twenty-two in 1915 to ninety-nine (sixty-nine of whom were sisters) in 1916.[11]

As early as December of 1914, Moulinier and Louis Jermain, M.D., dean of Marquette's medical school, brought the plan for the CHA to Archbishop Messmer, who recalled that the Jesuit and the M.D. "were principally concerned [that] they should act in harmony with ecclesias-

tical authority."[12] Messmer was so supportive that he sent a circular letter to the superiors of women religious inviting them to a preliminary
meeting to discuss the agenda of the CHA and requesting that each
Catholic hospital in the archdiocese send four sisters—the superior of
the community and the sister superintendent of the hospital if they were
separate offices; the head of nurses and the training school; and one
other sister selected by the superior. In an April 1916 article in *The Ecclesiastical Review* the archbishop quoted his entire circular letter in which
he referred to precedents for national organizations of "Catholic schools
and colleges, Catholic teachers and Catholic charities. The thought,
therefore, naturally occurred to Catholic physicians, nurses, and hospital sisters . . . [to establish] a similar authorization for Catholic hospitals." He referred to the standardization movement challenging Catholic
hospitals to maintain the "high standing for proficiency and competency
which they now hold in the eyes of unprejudiced Americans."[13]

After gathering at the archbishop's residence the Milwaukee group lis-
tened to the presentations of Moulinier and Jermain. Messmer had been
convinced of the need for the CHA, but after this meeting he "felt it a
sacred duty to lend the movement all the help I possibly could give it in
virtue of my ecclesiastical offices." Hence he urged "the bishops and the
priests of the country to lend their hearty encouragement and strong
support to the work now happily begun."[14] In his form letter to the bishops of the United States Messmer reiterated the pressing need for the
CHA but also indicated his concern that "unless they [i.e., superiors of
religious communities] get a hearty approval and encouragement from
their ecclesiastical superiors, many of these good religious will greatly
hesitate to join the Catholic Hospital Association and to take part in its
annual conference, much less . . . to follow a medical summer course
though it last but a few weeks." He informed the bishops of the grant
from the Carnegie Foundation for the CHA summer program, listed the
courses, and concluded with a plea for the moral support of the hierarchy for "this Catholic movement which is to keep our Catholic hospitals in the front rank of the charitable institutions of our country."[15]

The sisters' attendance at the summer school raised doubts concerning the propriety of women religious attending courses taught by non-
Catholics and attended by the laity. Questions arose regarding the
propriety of attempting to lead a religious life outside the convent, the
possibility of finding proper housing, and the necessity of modern training outside the hospital routine. Messmer responded to these questions
in a candid yet respectful style. Assuring the doubters that the sisters'

spiritual welfare would remain a crucial concern, he defended the non-Catholic lecturers as "gentlemen, and therefore kind and considerate of the sisters." He added that he considered the "intermingling of Sisters of different orders . . . to be a most excellent stimulant in all works of charity and religion." Moulinier, the narrator of the proceedings quoted by Messmer, cited several non-Catholic sources supportive of the sisters' organization and concluded:

> If its future development does not come up to the expectations of these gentlemen, I am bold enough to say that it will not be the fault of our hospital Sisters, but of the Hierarchy and the spiritual superiors and chaplains of those Sisters. Our good sisterhoods naturally shun the public hall and platform; they are shy of a closer contact with a crowd of M.D.s, especially when many of these are not Catholic; they are afraid of irregularities or interruptions in the routine of their holy rule, and other similar things. But when it is a question, after all, of promoting God's greater glory by a more effective and fruitful service of Christian charity in the care of the Lord's sick and suffering brethren [sic], why should these angels of charity not come out for a little while from their sacred solitude?[16]

Moulinier was conversant with the trends in hospital administration that were veering away from elevating nurses to the position of hospital superintendent, the prevailing model among those progressive communities in Catholic health care. Hence, it was particularly important that the future sister superintendent be well versed in medical science in order to deal intelligently with physicians on her staff. Because in many of those large modern facilities lay nurses far outnumbered sisters, the latter tended to be department heads or floor supervisors, positions that required continuing education provided by the CHA summer sessions and later in correspondence courses. For example, the CHA's 1916 summer school offered courses in laboratory technician work, X-ray technique, dietetics, anesthetics, hospital record keeping, and massage.[17]

In a six-page letter to the editor of *The Ecclesiastical Review* Father Stanislaus Waywood, O.F.M., responded to Archbishop Messmer's article with a précis on canon law and papal statements regulating the life of women religious. He was particularly concerned that Messmer's invitation to the 1916 CHA convention of superiors of all hospital communities (most of whom were under the direct authority of their ordinaries) was overstepping the boundaries of the law that required sisters to seek their bishops' approval for attendance at meetings. Waywood was also distressed with the introduction of training schools and maternity wards. A strict constructionist on the interpretation of canon law, he was in opposition to sisters being trained in obstetrics.[18] Historian Mary Ewens, O.P., cites the appropriate papal directives on "works which ill befit 'virgins consecrated to God' . . . the care of babies, the nursing of maternity cases, the management of clerical seminaries, and the staffing of coeducational schools," directives Ewens concludes "reveal Jansenistic attitudes prevalent at the time."[19] Each of these areas beyond the pale of propriety was observed more in the breach, particularly in Catholic maternity hospitals such as in Troy, New York, and Boston. However, as will be noted later, obstetrical nursing for sisters gained recognition during the 1920s. Father Waywood was not looking forward but backward as he concluded his remarks with a blend of idealism and nostalgia characteristic of the angel imagery.

> Whether, finally, in view of conditions in the United States, it is advisable to have Catholic hospital training-schools for nurses and maternity wards, let others decide. So much is sure, that whatever may be said in favor of these departments in a Catholic hospital, there is also occasion for scandal, as experience proves. The best of care on the part of the Sisters is not always enough to preclude happenings that are harmful to the interests of the church. Moreover, from the standpoint of Catholic charity, it is to be regretted that the nursing of the sick in many Sisters' hospitals is no longer done by them in person but almost exclusively by the young ladies of the nurses' training school. Angels of charity, the grand title which the Sisters engaged in nursing the sick have earned by hundreds of years of patient toil, seems to be more and more in danger of being lost through the employment of secular professional nurses. The great love and esteem which the Catholic Sisters as nurses of the poor and afflicted have always enjoyed, seems to be a sufficient guarantee that the Sisters have served the public well. As a rule they have done all in their power to acquire the necessary knowledge for their work and are bent on keeping up with the present progress in their particular science of intelligent and loving care of Christ's poor and unfortunate. The Catholic Hospital Association will be very helpful in that direction.[20]

The foundation of the CHA was generally well received among bishops and theologians. However, the association's six-week summer sessions to which Archbishop Messmer had invited women religious throughout the country were controversial. In a letter to *The Ecclesiastical Review* (June 1916) Messmer responded to eight principal doubts about the necessity and propriety of the sisters' attendance at the school. Several doubts related to sisters associating with secular students and teachers and living outside of their convents, without a routine spiritual life, and with sisters of other religious communities whose traditions may conflict. The content of the courses, particularly massage, seemed to be offensive and unnecessary because sisters no longer do "hands on" nursing but limit their roles to hospital and department administration. Two general criticisms were particularly severe; one challenged the need for "chasing after modern ways and secularism," and the other invoked fear of religious indifferentism: "this whole movement with its Protestant and Jewish lecturers, will gradually turn over our hospitals to control of non-Catholic bodies, such as the American Medical Association."[21]

Messmer dispelled most of the doubts by referring to the care and concern of all who manage and staff the summer school for the general spiritual and social welfare of the sisters. He elaborated on the CHA's centralization of the continuing education process, which was preferable to the fragmented curricula on the local level. To those who doubted the need for massage, Messmer said that the sisters would only be introduced to the principles of the procedure. The archbishop lauded the intercommunity character of the CHA's school as a positive contribution to communication and mutual respect.[22] To accusations that the CHA fostered Modernism, Messmer responded with his idealism of "mother" church:

> Let it not be forgotten that the same great Popes who condemned Modernism and the false novelties of the age, have as often admonished the Catholic people "to be up and doing" and to keep abreast of the times in all that is for the good of religion, morality, and the higher things of life. While the Catholic Church is of necessity conservative, she is by the same necessary law progressive. There can be no stagnation in her own self, though portions of her body may by their own fault sink into a state of moral coma or lethargy. She bears in her womb the strongest forces of true progress and advancement, forces not from the earth below, but from heaven above. . . . who can deny the wonderful progress and development of Catholic hospitals, even within our own days, within less than a hundred years? I do not refer to the growth in number; that follows necessarily with the large diffusion of the Church. But I refer to the hospital work, its character, its ways, its methods, its work. Are we now going to fold our arms, sit down and rest where we are, while all around us, in secular and denominational hospitals, the good work is still advancing and taking on new means and forces? Can this be the wish of our Holy Mother Church? Then let us go ahead, though the road on which we travel be of modern build.[23]

Messmer had little toleration for the sister who feared that learning anatomy and physiology would compromise her virtue: a sister who "has not vocation for hospital work . . . ought to gain entrance into another order or ask the superiors to send . . . thence to the kitchen, where she may study the anatomy of the chicken."[24] In response to those who contended that sisters were remote from direct patient care he simply said that "such is not the general practice and custom in Catholic hospitals. Our good sisters don't 'play the lady,' but are truly the humble servants of all patients and physicians."[25] Of course the archbishop emphasized the need for sisters to be well versed in modern medical science.

Messmer answered those who saw the religious pluralism of the faculty leading inexorably toward the capitulation to forces outside the control of Catholics by stating that "State control of Catholic and other hospitals will come, whether we like it or not; it will come without the Catholic Hospital Association and without our employing Protestant and Jewish lecturers. The American public will demand it."[26]

To illustrate the need for standardization, Robert S. Myers, M.D., assistant director of the American College of Surgeons, recalled that "hospital patient care in the first decade of the twentieth century was chaotic." Physical conditions were "antiquated, unclean and unsafe," while medical records were poor, critical evaluation of treatments almost "unheard of," and "diagnostic facilities were grossly inadequate and unused; the majority of the medical profession was hostile toward any effort at reform.[27]

The founder and secretary general of the American College of Surgeons, Franklin H. Martin, realized that the success of the standardization movement was dependent on cooperation of the Catholic hospitals, which he said "contained more than fifty percent of all the beds of the continent." Martin was grateful for the leadership of the "statesmanlike" president of the CHA and commented on their agreement that "as we viewed it, hospital standardization, to succeed, must be viewed as a spiritual as well as an educational movement."[28] To garner support among the Catholic hierarchy Martin turned to the dean of the American bishops, Cardinal James Gibbons, who in 1917 was in his thirty-ninth year as archbishop of Baltimore. After an interview with Martin, Gibbons wrote to him an endorsement of the standardization movement:

> It is a pleasure to assure you of my interest in and approval of your plan as explained to me for this standardization of the hospitals of the United States. We should make every reasonable effort to reach the highest state of efficiency possible in each hospital; bend every effort to bring about uniformity as makes for progress. This plan gives promise of better results in the immediate future and prepares us for any contingencies that might arise that would throw a tremendous burden on the hospitals.[29]

Moulinier, who led the CHA in anticipation of the movement, was invited to attend the organizational meeting of 350 leading surgeons of the nation. Held at Chicago in October of 1917, the meeting launched the hospital reform movement. Father Moulinier became a member of the general hospital committee of the American College of Surgeons in late 1917 with responsibility for visiting "leading Catholic hospitals" and other facilities as well as meeting with state committees on standards and local medical societies "in furtherance of all the aims of the college."[30] So deeply committed to the college's standardization movement, which actually began in April 1918, Moulinier with the enthusiastic support of Archbishop Messmer (from its origin, honorary president of CHA) dedicated the CHA's 1918 convention to the college's reform movement. Messmer invited the bishops of the United States and Canada to send representatives to the meeting so that they would be alerted to the significance of standardization and gain the support of the hierarchy in the investigation of their hospitals by a national non-Catholic accrediting agency.

The primary goal of the 1918 convention, Moulinier told his audience, was to come "as nearly as we can to a uniformity of view on certain great phases of hospital work." He explained that this "is what standardization means" and argued that the ability to set and maintain standards determined the vitality of the Catholic hospital. The three-day deliberations were aimed at understanding what Moulinier called the "soul" of the hospital. "I beg of you never to forget," he told his audience, "that the hospital has a soul, a spirit, a breadth, and a life which is distinctive, which is vulnerable and which can be killed. There are today strong, living hospitals; there are dying and dead hospitals." The vital signs were measured by the standards of the American College of Surgeons and by the hospital's commitment "to make this mortal life of ours a healthier, a more enjoyable, and a better life morally and religiously."[31]

At a special meeting of the bishops' representatives Moulinier called upon all concerned with Catholic health care to unite in the march of medical progress.

Now, think of that, gentlemen [The percentage of beds in the country belonging to Catholic hospitals]. If we organize ourselves so that, with the hierarchy as the background of authority, we the delegate or delegates from each diocese cooperating with this great army of devoted women of the sisterhoods, we can get to thinking all alike, having similar motives, working for the same great end, there will be a dominating force, a controlling and directing of the use of right means that will be simply irresistible.[32]

Dr. Bowman and other physicians met with Cardinal Gibbons, who once again endorsed the movement.[33]

The CHA established a standardization committee, which distributed literature and questionnaires to prepare Catholic hospitals for official representation from the College of Surgeons. Such an official visit occurred in Baltimore's St. Joseph's Hospital in late 1918. In a report included in the minutes of a meeting of the medical board, the visit resulted in the need for improvements in the laboratory in such areas as record keeping and listing procedures, and for the purchase of a new transfusion unit, a trained person to administer the procedure, and the need for "the laboratorian to live in the hospital."[34] Without further remarks it is apparent that the physicians, with the approval of the sister superintendent, implemented the standards imposed by the College of Surgeons. Another visitation in 1924 resulted in proposals for improved record keeping, modernized technology for urinary testing, a new elevator, and increase of interns to ten for a 275-bed hospital.[35]

Fee splitting, the practice of a physician paying a portion of the patient's fee to the referring physician, had been condemned by the American College of Physicians, the CHA, and other organizations monitoring the professional propriety of physicians. On June 23, 1920, the medical board of St. Joseph's Hospital agreed that "this hospital will not permit fee-splitting in any form, and pledged itself to expel any member found guilty of this offense."[36] Though this decision may not have been influenced by the CHA, St. Joseph's was a member of the association. As an example of the CHA's influence, the medical board minutes referred to Moulinier, to contributions for summer institutes, and to Archbishop Michael J. Curley's appointment of a priest to "supervise in a measure to the work of Catholic hospitals in the diocese and bring about a closer cooperation with the authorities representing the Catholic Hospital Association . . . ."[37] Hence it is apparent that Moulinier's commitment to standardization and the CHA's continuing education program had a strong impact on the local level.

In 1919 the association's summer school was transferred to the medical school of Loyola University in Chicago. The CHA's summer schools allowed many sisters, some of whom had a wealth of experience but only an eighth-grade education, to attend medical courses for the first time. As noted earlier, a number of communities of women religious had already been training their sisters. The St. Paul province of the Sisters of St. Joseph of Carondelet, which operated four hospitals, had a progressive education program. During the later period of Mother M. Esperance Finn's administration of St. Mary's Hospital in St. Paul (1906–1918), two sisters of St. Joseph attended Teachers' College at Columbia University to train in nursing, nursing education, and administration.[38]

One of the founding members at the historic Minneapolis meeting in 1914, Finn was elected a second vice-president of the CHA in 1916. At that year's convention she presented a paper on "What the Sisters Should Contribute to the Team-work" of a hospital. After elaborating on the analogy between teamwork in sports and in other areas of life, she focused on the sisters' role in relation to the doctor and the chaplain. The former, she argued, was the "director of our team-work," but the latter "holds the highest honor and worth in the team-work of a Catholic hospital. He stands for the patients' spiritual interests, which we sisters are eager to promote."[39] Although many consider the term health-care "ministry" to be of recent origin, Finn identified the sisters' role as one that included pastoral care. "With God's anointed priest, we are seeking to save the souls of men, and, though our ministry in this respect is indirect and secondary, it is frequent, and we know how effective it may be made, through Divine help, by prayer, unlimited kindness, and the word in season."[40]

In addition to sisters and priests, physicians played a significant role in the CHA from the beginning. Maude R. Williams, M.D., of Milwaukee was elected the association's first secretary. In 1916 Bernard F. McGrath, M.D., held that post, and in 1917, when the secretary and treasurer positions were combined, the executive board appointed McGrath to the new position. Because the United States had recently entered World War I, the convention did not meet that year. At the 1918 convention the executive board, which had comprised the officers and two separately elected members, was enlarged. In addition to the posts held by Moulinier and McGrath, women religious held the positions of three vice-presidents and five of the six memberships on the executive board.[41]

At the 1919 convention the organization's structure was expanded to include a director of diocesan superintendents to act as the liaison among those priests appointed by their bishops to oversee hospitals. Bishop Joseph Schrembs of Toledo agreed to direct the division of diocesan superintendents, and Rev. Michael Bourke of St. Joseph Sanatorium in Ann Arbor, Michigan, was appointed acting director. Through the good will of Archbishop Messmer and Bishop Schrembs, the CHA easily gained official recognition by the recently organized National Catholic Welfare Council (changed to "Conference" in 1922).[42]

Also at the 1919 convention, Maurice Griffin, chaplain of St. Elizabeth's Hospital in Youngstown, Ohio, successfully proposed that the CHA establish a division of state and provincial conferences. He argued that such subsidiary organizations were necessary to influence state and (in Canada) provincial legislation "and in the end have a code of hospital laws entirely satisfactory or at least not objectionable to the [Catholic] hospitals." Griffin was appointed the first director of local conferences, a major responsibility because it planted the CHA in the various states and regions of the nation where the membership could gain from workshops and cement their loyalties to the association. Michael Bourke was an expert in canon law as well as in the history of the nation's common law and its relationship to medico-moral issues. His convention paper, "Some Medical Ethics Problems Solved," which dealt with a number of issues, including moral questions related to protecting the fetus and the life of the mother during problem pregnancies, became the foundation of the Surgical Code, which was officially adopted by the CHA in 1921.[43] The 1919 convention also passed a resolution to establish a monthly journal, *Hospital Progress*, which began publication in May 1920. The twenty-two-member editorial board included seventeen physicians. McGrath conceived of the journal, its title, and its general thrust, but Moulinier was the major force behind *Hospital Progress*.[44]

As the CHA approached its fifth anniversary convention, in St. Paul, it had firmly established itself as a part of American Catholic life. With 412 hospitals in the United States and Canada enrolled—nearly two-thirds of the total number of Catholic institutions—the association's effort to improve the scientific, technological, moral, and spiritual character of Catholic health care had clearly gained enormous support from religious communities, including the predominant men's nursing community, the Alexian Brothers. The CHA numbered 1,290 individual members in 1920, and the membership included a significant percentage of physicians, lay nurses, and priests. Under Moulinier, who by this time had served on accreditation teams of the American College of Surgeons for two years, the CHA had achieved prominence in continuing the modernization of its institutional members.[45]

Shortly after promulgation of the new Code of Canon Law (1917) the apostolic delegate to the United States, Archbishop John Bonzano, wrote to Charles B. Moulinier to gratefully acknowledge receipt of "Extracts from the Transactions of the 1918 Convention," which included a "Resolution of Purpose" that dealt with the change of the sisters' habit while on nursing duty. With characteristic sense of male "responsibility" for the lives of women religious, Bonzano stated: "It is well that you made this matter dependent upon the approval of superiors and upon the sanction of ecclesiastical authorities; still it seems to me that it would have been better to ascertain the opinion of authority before making the matter a question of public discussion." Bonzano noted that the issue had already "become subject of complaint and alarm among some of the sisterhoods" and concluded that "Novelties have a disturbing effect in almost every walk of life . . . particularly [in] religious communities."[46]

In his response three days later Moulinier assured Bonzano that the change "is perfectly harmless and leaves the whole matter in the hands of each religious order, their superiors and ecclesiastical authorities. . . . It will be well to note that there is no thought of a change of form in the habit, but only a change in material and a slight curtailing of the veils." Moulinier told Bonzano that he had been told by several sisters that the changes could be made easily and that they would "satisfy all scientific purposes not in the least interfering with community traditions, and be more economic in the long run." He also informed the delegate that Archbishop Messmer had brought the matter to the 1918 annual meeting of the archbishops in Washington (this is prior to the formation of the National Catholic Welfare Conference and its annual meeting of bishops) and that "their attitude was one of hands off, because they feared the flutter it would cause among religieuses [*sic*]."[47]

II

At the 1920 CHA convention in St. Paul there was a special meeting for sisters to discuss a paper presented by a Rev. J. V. Bacci, D.D., chaplain of St. Joseph's Hospital, Mason City, Iowa: "Remarks Concerning: Diocesan Superintendents, and Wearing Washable Habits While on Duty." Sister Alexandrine of St. Joseph's Hospital, Cleveland, run by the Sisters of Charity of St. Augustine, reported that her community had decided to wear a white habit because they had been told to have a clean habit every morning, "sometimes two or three a day."[48] Sister Veronica Ryan of Mercy Hospital in Chicago explained that Dr. Murphy (mentioned in chapter seven as the inventor of the Murphy button) "gave us a choice of wearing washable dresses in the operating room or not be present." With permission from their ordinary and at the suggestion of the sister superintendent of Mercy Hospital the sisters voted on the issue, and "the majority ruled and decided to wear white dresses in all departments and are still doing it without friction or question. . . ."[49]

The principal points of the discussion centered on the interpretation of canon law. If the sisters were a diocesan community then the bishop may allow changes in the habit, but a papally approved community had to appeal to the Vatican for such changes. This of course was jarring to the Sisters of Mercy, who though under the direction of their bishop did have their constitutions approved by the Vatican. Father McMahon considered the requirements of asepsis to necessitate a change to washable habits to be enough to allow a reasonable change in habit. Griffin supported McMahon and added that the change to a washable habit is not a fundamental change that would require any more than the bishop's authorization. "One who is responsible for the observance of the law in a given section of the church and that is the ordinary of the diocese, and the Sisters of Mercy Hospital have the permission from their Ordinary and I believe . . . that [they] will have no further conflict in [their minds] about the washable habit."[50] Bacci retorted that there would be a conflict until there was Vatican approval of the change. McMahon reported that hospital sisters in London and Dublin had been wearing washable habits.[51]

The major antagonist was not Bacci but Father Joseph C. Straub, director of St. John's Hospital in Springfield, Illinois, and spiritual director of the Hospital Sisters of the Third Order of St. Francis, whose American motherhouse was in Springfield and who operated fourteen hospitals in Illinois and Wisconsin (see chapter seven). As will be noted later, Straub was an opponent of the standardization movement because it was in the hands of secular authorities. He articulated an excessively separatist view of the church in modern society. He explained that there were three thousand Hospital Sisters all under the motherhouse in Germany and that when he was in the old country before the war, the physicians "were insisting on the change into a washable habit as explained this evening. The question has not been settled to this day."[52] While the Vatican's Sacred Congregation for Religious had acted in asserting prohibitions against obstetrical nursing in Germany, it had not responded positively to the habit change which would have been proposed by the bishops on behalf of the physicians. Straub explained his own views: "Personally I am opposed to the change because the habit is the expression of the different sisterhoods and if the habit our sisters wear is changed we will have nurses who are wearing a habit, but not sisters. Some time ago a nurse happened to be in my office and saw the [CHA] magazine *Hospital Progress* on my table. There was a picture in this magazine of sisters in white washable habits and she made the remark 'Don't you think that this will have an influence on sisters? Look at those white shoes.' The fact is, sisters, that the patient wants to see sisters not nurses. Non-Catholics want to come into our hospitals and beg to be taken care of by sisters, not nurses. They want to see sisters."[53] Fathers McMahon and Griffin asserted their liberal understanding, thereby defending those sisters who had changed their habits without feeling that they had compromised their religious identity to the profession of nursing particularly since they still wore a veil, cross, and other religious symbols of their communities' traditions.[54]

Sister Veronica Ryan, apparently frustrated with the discussion dominated by men, concluded: "We have discussed this question for six years and where are we now? We are puzzled, this is beyond us; we are not canonists. I make a motion that this subject be taken out of the Association and referred to the superiors who counsel sisters who have to wear this dress."[55] Clearly the issue was not so easily or immediately solved as Moulinier had told Bonzano. Straub's opposition was grounded on the preservationist understanding that there was an inherent conflict between the traditions of religious life and modernity, which was not only godless but also adrift without a moral compass. In a discussion with other priests involved in health care Straub said that at St. John's Training School "we refuse to take engaged girls and refuse visitors. We insist that they go to religious services and dismiss them if they do not. They are not allowed to be out longer than 8:30 evenings unless chaperoned. We also urge daily communion and have a rule that every Catholic girl shall go to Mass every morning. We find that if a girl goes to daily communion there will be better work done in every line. The benefit and encouragement of daily communion helps in daily work." When one priest said that because the school with which he was associated had students from all parts of the country, "We permit them to go to dances and have visitors and callers," Straub responded, "We do not permit girls to go to dances or keep company with any man." In contrast to Straub's authoritarianism, a Father Ryan of Fargo, North Dakota, came down on the side of liberty, which "achieves more splendid results." A priest from Omaha said that "the more liberty is given the more the girls appreciate their responsibilities."[56] Such was the dominant role men played in attempting to regulate the lives of women in Catholic nursing schools.

Moulinier, who had initiated a vocation program within the CHA because of the decrease in hospital sisters, tended to stress the synthesis between the positive character of modern medicine and the traditions of religious life; he said that "hospital sisterhood, by reason of their religious life and consecration to the service of the sick [may] exert their great and sanctifying influence in a most intimate, vital and abiding way, upon all the those who come to those institutions for the care of their health."[57]

In a letter to Moulinier (December 16, 1923) Archbishop Pietro Fumasoni-Biondi, the apostolic delegate who succeeded Bonzano in 1922, asked the president of the CHA for "information requested by the S. Congregation for Religious." The curial office was concerned with "the conditions under which sisters labor in hospitals, clinics, homes, etc., in caring for the sick; what limitations are placed to the sisters' participation in operations and of other care of men and women. What safeguards surround them as Religious."[58] As early as 1909 the Vatican had asked Cardinal Gibbons to report on the care of men by sister-nurses. He merely replied that "the hospitals directed by sisters are a true blessing."[59] Moulinier responded generally with assurances that the conditions "are all the Church would desire or the Sacred Congregation of Religious would desire." He drew on his personal visits to "most of the hospitals in the United States and Canada" as a basis for his particular points: the sisters had a "separate dwelling place carefully secluded"; they were served by "zealous chaplains" who ministered the sacraments; and there were safeguards for their home nursing. Lay nurses, young physicians on the house staff, or male orderlies performed such functions as would be improper for sisters; a lay superintendent of obstetrical departments "relieves the sisters in charge from any direct or objectionable contact with the patients in time of delivery." Moulinier concluded by extolling the "superiors, chaplains and the hierarchy under whose vigilant care hospitals are conducted [who] are gratifyingly solicitous about the religious lives of the sisters."[60] Since there is no evidence of continued concern, the apostolic delegate must have been satisfied with Moulinier's rendering of the structural protections of nursing communities. But the correspondence still clearly reflects the Romanization of the church in the United States.

The vast majority of the CHA membership praised Moulinier's leadership in promoting high standards (Catholic hospitals were being accredited at a consistently higher rate than were others); but other movements severely challenged the president's identification with the American College of Surgeons. The first serious opposition to the CHA'S ties with the college came in 1920–1921 from Joseph C. Straub. Because Catholics did not participate in the formulation of the college's hospital standards, and because the college demanded that accredited hospitals allow only board-certified physicians on the staff, Straub concluded that the sisters' autonomy was threatened. His resistance to secular involvement in Catholic health-care facilities represented a strong tendency of religious separatism, then characteristic of American Catholic life. Straub protested to Bishop Peter J. Muldoon, the episcopal chairman of the Social Action department of the National Catholic Welfare Conference. And for a few months Straub published a *Monthly Hospital Letter,* in which he challenged the direction of the CHA under Father Moulinier's leadership. After an executive board meeting attended by Archbishop Messmer and Bishop Muldoon, Father Moulinier's policies were vindicated.[61] To forestall future complaints about secular control of Catholic hospitals, Father Moulinier championed a move to establish a separate set of CHA standards, which included guidelines for moral and spiritual dimensions of health care and ensured accreditation by the American College of Surgeons.[62]

A second major challenge came at the 1921 convention in St. Paul, Minnesota, just a few months after the resolution of the Straub crisis. A group of physicians led a movement to dissociate the CHA from the American College of Surgeons. In a circular distributed to sisters attending the business meeting, the physicians claimed that the college wanted to dictate policy to Catholic hospitals and to American physicians. For the sisters to submit to the college's accreditation program, they argued, would be to cede control of their hospitals.[63]

The physicians were also concerned that Catholic moral principles could be jeopardized by the secular accrediting agency. Well organized in advance of the convention, the physicians cited their constitutional right to speak from the floor as they accused Moulinier of forcing the sisters to accept the college's standardization program. Breaking with parliamentary procedure, Moulinier overrode the arguments from the floor on the grounds that his position was in the sisters' best interest.[64]

To further defuse the physicians' challenge—and to calm fears that a commitment to standardization threatened to erode Catholic morality— Moulinier urged the CHA to officially adopt the code of ethics set forth by Father Michael Bourke, Ann Arbor, Michigan, in his 1919 convention paper "Some Medical Ethics Problems Solved." (As mentioned earlier, this code dealt with moral issues related to surgery, particularly when life-threatening procedures were involved.)[65] The move did not, however, settle the conflict. Between the 1921 and 1922 conventions, the dissidents rallied around Bernard F. McGrath, M.D., secretary-treasurer of the CHA, as a potential candidate for the office of president, one who would not be closely allied to the American College of Surgeons. Once again

Father Moulinier managed to control the meetings. To obviate the challenge from individual physicians, he adopted the suggestion of Florence Sullivan, S.J., New Orleans, to amend the constitution to limit voting to the institutional membership, effectively placing sovereignty in the hands of the religious communities that held the votes for each of the member hospitals.[66]

The McGrath challenge must have been a blow to Moulinier. They had been colleagues at Marquette University; as president and secretary-treasurer of the CHA, respectively, Moulinier and McGrath were the principal editors of *Hospital Progress* and formed the association's administration. Although there was an attempt at reconciliation, Moulinier led the executive board to ask for McGrath's resignation, which was tendered in May 1923. The crisis had forced the president to go beyond the constitutional basis of his authority, but his motivation had been to maintain high standards for Catholic hospitals and to protect the CHA's primary constituency, the women and men religious in the hospital apostolate.

In 1923 the CHA decided to establish a series of summer institutes to replace the convention. Several factors motivated this decision. The political agitations of 1921–1922 had led to a disillusionment with the annual convention. In addition, Moulinier and others had come to believe that the three-day convention schedule was far too brief for an effective educational experience. Finally, the president had been a strong advocate of establishing central headquarters for the CHA to foster research and training in medical science and engender an appreciation for Catholic moral and spiritual traditions. Spring Bank, Wisconsin, location of the midwestern Catholic summer school, was a country estate owned by the archdiocese of Milwaukee and located on the shores of Lake Oconomowoc; it seemed an ideal site for the CHA's central office and for the annual conferences that replaced the convention. The CHA arranged to lease the site early in 1923.[67]

Convened from the middle of June to the end of August, the seven three-day conferences began with meetings of the national, provincial, and local superiors of religious institutes in the hospital apostolate. Each of the six other conferences was organized for separate groups of hospital personnel. The following year (1924) Moulinier offered two eight-day retreats for hospital sisters, an innovation intended to emphasize their common ministry rather than the particular traditions of each religious institute. Also in 1924, Marquette University opened its Hospital College, the nation's first academic program in hospital administration. Moulinier had encouraged the president of the university, Albert C. Fox,

S.J., to initiate the program, which also included short courses for women religious who had hospital experience but not the requisite undergraduate degree to pursue graduate studies.[68] About this time Father Moulinier, who suffered from diabetes, began to experience poor health. In January 1925 he wrote to the Jesuit provincial that he was "no longer physically or mentally able to do all the work which falls to one of my position." He pleaded for a full-time assistant. Although no assistant was appointed, Moulinier continued to be an enthusiastic leader.[69]

In 1926, after it had become evident that the Spring Bank experiment had not generated strong interest, the annual convention was restored. It was held in Chicago immediately before the International Eucharistic Congress, which drew tens of thousands of Catholics to the archdiocese. Convened at Loyola University, the CHA's convention had the general theme of religion and science. The Spring Bank conferences had included a clinical congress featuring exhibits by manufacturers in medical science and technology. A persistent innovator, Moulinier incorporated the clinic-congress notion into the convention programs for 1927 and 1928.[70]

According to Moulinier, as the Catholic hospital achieved the requirements of the American College of Surgeons and as the sisters experienced the CHA's continuing education programs and later entered its graduate programs in hospital administration, Catholic health care not only embraced modernization and professionalization but it became more Catholic in the process. He continued to extol the sisters' way of life as grounded in the "motivating power [and] . . . interior grace of the Holy Spirit through prayer, religious exercise and the reception of the Sacraments. . . ." However, Catholicity permeates the institution particularly when the interior life of the sisters as well as the brothers is manifested in the struggle for "the better things . . . for self—for neighbor—for civilization."[71] Moulinier's articulation of progressive synthesis of religion and health-care culture appears to have been grounded on a positive anthropology, as if religion and medical care were mutually transformationist.

Included in the "better things" were the continual vitality of the organization in teamwork and its advances in modern medicine in achieving high professional and ethical standards: "the fundamental spirit of harmony and teamwork become more pronounced and all pervading . . . and the hospital becomes more worthy of its name [when] helpfulness to all becomes the actualizing motto. . . . Patients, doctors, and nurses who may not believe in the deep religious dogmas that make up the religious convictions of Catholic sisters still see and feel and appreciate that deeper, stronger, all pervading *something* which is so unmistakable in the sisters' hospital where Christ and His doctrine live and move and actuate to holiness the lives of the Catholic sisters."[72]

In his description of twentieth-century hospitals, Charles E. Rosenberg notes that because the hospital's "transactions involved pain, sickness, and death as well as the public good . . . an insulating sacredness surrounded the activities. . . ." As a result, the hospital's "products were, in a literal sense, beyond material accounting."

Central to the theme of this work is that those who respond to the limit situation of critical illness and death are conscious of dwelling in sacred space; here the Catholic tradition is mediated in particular rituals and symbols as well as the chaplain's particular witness. As noted earlier, this witness was manifested in unofficial chaplains, those sisters and brothers and lay nurses who attended the dying. However, according to Rosenberg the twentieth-century hospital "intensified expectations of scientific medicine [that] were both material and transcendent. Americans hoped and expected that the new institution would provide a refuge from . . . sickness and premature death. . . ."[73] Mouliner's synthesis of the modern hospital and traditional faith fostered these expectations but included that "something special" reflecting the religious character of the refuge.

The leadership of the communities of women religious and of the sister-superintendents were provided a forum within the structure of the CHA, one that allowed them to articulate religious idealism in hospital administration. A 1922 report of the CHA Conference of Mothers Provincial and Superior and (hospital) superintendents illustrates their concerns in a list of resolutions/suggestions for improving the quality of Catholic hospitals. In accord with the strong emphasis on technology they considered it "advisable to install all labor-saving devices from point of view of economy, time, labor and material." Though they recognized the "sentiment opposed to osteopaths or medical cults having entry to our hospitals in any capacity," they nevertheless urged their medical staffs to "give more attention to the value and possible use of therapeutic measures employed by them." The conference evinced a concern for small hospitals, particularly related to their nurses' training schools, which were "obliged in justice to nurses to seek affiliations with other hospitals" to provide clinical practice in areas too specialized for small facilities. The conference proposed to deal with the topic of small hospitals for the 1923 CHA convention. To achieve high standards in nursing education the group suggested that each religious community that supervises several hospitals "should have a Sister directress of hospitals" and that each hospital "apply uniform [clinical] methods . . . throughout every department." The sisters' organization recommended "comfortable living quarters . . . surrounded by a cheerful homelike spirit" for the workers in their hospitals. Since religious dedicated to poverty may tend to be too rigorous in budgets for workers and nurses, the report concluded that for nurses' training "economy should never be practiced to the detriment of efficient service" and that for workers "it is a mistake in policy to employ cheap help." Explicit references to the religious ethos of the hospital included the opposition to the use of "collecting agencies . . . for delinquent accounts"; instead hospitals should credit "such losses to charity."[72]

The most emphatic point of the entire report dealt with the Catholic hospital's religious identity: "Committee considers it of extreme importance that patients coming to our hospitals should be impressed through a Christ-like spirit of charity and cheerful sympathy and understanding that they have every reason to expect." They also considered it their "sacred obligation to provide hospital facilities for expectant mothers." To improve the climate of the hospital the report recommended a hospital library as "essential to an up-to-date hospital" and the "elimination of noise and of too many visitors."[73]

This report reflects not merely a conference in the structure of the CHA, but, because provincials, local superiors, and hospital administrators were chairs and members of the corporate boards governing many Catholic hospitals, these recommendations appear to have reflected existing and prospective operating principles and policies. Hence through the structure of the CHA the concerns of the leadership of women religious circulated, and, one should recall, the committee structure of the entire association, including the chair and membership, was dominated by sisters. The president of the CHA accurately described the CHA as a sisters' organization.

Moulinier recalled the original charism of the CHA when in 1914 the Sisters of St. Joseph in Minneapolis, Minnesota, "while making a retreat in July of the year 1914 were brought to a realization such as they had never had before, that 'hospital work was God's work' and that the present organization [i.e., CHA] was needed in order that *God's work might be better done*." He then referred to the other sisters and physicians who made the CHA flourish. He reminded the delegates to the 1922 convention, most of whom were sisters, that "four million patients each year are receiving help for soul and body in six hundred and seventy-five sisters' hospitals at the hands of seventy-five thousand members of the medical profession, twenty-five thousand lay nurses and at least one-thousand priests. Who can count or begin to measure the wounds and burdens of soul and conscience that are healed and made light by the administration of sisters and chaplains. Who will count the number of souls brought back to the knowledge and love of God? Who will tell us how many of those four million patients, who pass into eternity owe their salvation to the prompting of a sisters' hospital?"[74]

Moulinier then linked the religious character of the hospital to its ethical commitment to bring the finest quality of health care to their patients. "The movement for better hospital service called standardization . . . surpasses anything recorded in the annals of medical practice." He referred to the thousands of unnecessary or criminal surgeries that are prevented each year because of standardization. The medical profession's "ethical standard and professional courtesy are rising month by month to a higher plane." He applauded the "Sisters' hospitals and the Catholic Hospital Association of the United States and Canada" for playing such a large part in the movement for better standards.[75]

For Moulinier the standardization movement almost entailed a transcendental quality, which achieved its optimal embodiment in the Catholic hospital because that "particular something" pervades the atmosphere. The inherently sacred character of caring for the sick and dying, so thematic to this work, had been incarnated in Catholic benevolence of the mid-nineteenth century with its personalist mission in a homelike setting. The traditional Catholic rendering of the sacred character was reconfigured in the modern hospital with its accelerating changes in diagnoses, surgical and medical treatments, so dependent on advanced technologies and bureaucratic organizational structures. The transformation of the hospital profoundly changed the ways in which Catholics understood the traditional call to identify with the compassion of Christ; the religious men and women engaged in health care mediated their call in modern contexts. The modernized hospital reduced the traditional homelike character of the facility while the revision of the Code of Canon Law (1917) imposed upon the lives of men and women religious regulations that emphasized the monastic enclosures which tended to draw a line between prayer life and hospital ministry with the former often assuming a priority. Though demands of the hospital could take precedence over attendance at prayer in the chapel, sisters and brothers could become torn between these responsibilities in contrast to missionary nurses in the ethnic urban villages and the frontiers and rural towns of the country. To mediate the call in modernized structures represented a continual dialectic between the cloister and the ward. From interviews with sister-nurses active in the 1930s and 40s the strongest source of spiritual sustenance was the ministry, without which prayer life tended to be only routine. The membership in the CHA brought the sisters and later the brothers across the threshold into modern professionalism, which would gradually yet profoundly affect their worldview.

Moulinier perceived the CHA in a symmetrical configuration based on a synthesis of religion and medical science:

> Thus the Catholic Hospital Association of the United States and Canada is a religious, ethical and scientific body, aiming at the highest ideals that grow out of its nature and belongs, essentially, as inspiring motives, to the medical profession, the nursing profession, the hospital profession and to the vowed profession of the nun as expressive of the finest flavor of organized woman's service to the sick brethren of Christ.[76]

Moulinier's health continued to decline, and in 1928 the Jesuit provincial urged him to resign. As early as 1925, when Moulinier was seeking an assistant, he had told the provincial that the "one man who stands out unquestionably . . . is Father Schwitalla."[77]

At the 1928 convention Alphonse Schwitalla, S.J., dean of the Medical School of St. Louis University, became president of the CHA. To provide continuity, the position of executive director was established so that Moulinier could remain as president while Schwitalla held executive responsibility. Moulinier moved CHA headquarters to 612 N. Michigan Avenue in Chicago.[78]

In April 1929 the Jesuit provincial removed Moulinier from the office of executive director. This apparently precipitous action was motivated in part by allegations of impropriety. Two nurses in Milwaukee had attended to Moulinier during his bouts with diabetic comas; when he moved to Spring Bank, they took up residence there to assist him. When the summer conferences were discontinued, the nurses remained on the estate both as caretakers and as part-time CHA staff. Because the rumors about Moulinier's relationship to the nurses (which had no basis in reality) might be a source of scandal, the Jesuit provincial acted.[79]

Without an executive director to administer the association, it became necessary to move the CHA to St. Louis, where Schwitalla could oversee the office while he maintained his position at St. Louis University. This transfer was announced in July 1929. To regain influence and to prevent the transfer to St. Louis, Moulinier supported John P. Boland, a priest of the diocese of Buffalo, for the office of president. At the 1929 convention Father Moulinier called a special meeting of the delegates. In retaliation, Schwitalla initiated a meeting with Cardinal George Mundelein of Chicago, who ordered the delegates to hold their regular meeting, thereby preempting Moulinier's strategy. Father Schwitalla was reelected and transferred CHA headquarters to St. Louis.[80]

Despite Moulinier's failed attempt to retain some role in the CHA, few forgot his enormous contribution to its origin and development. Malcolm T. MacEachern, M.D., a dominant figure in the American College of Surgeons, described Moulinier as "a fighter, not of the grim, defiant type but of that rare number of history makers who battle joyously and welcome obstacles as exciting incentives to greater effort." Like a founder of a religious community, Moulinier possessed a particular charism without which the CHA may not have progressed as a thoroughly Catholic professional association. His gifts enabled him to synthesize the demands of both religious tradition and hospital modernization.

By way of a postscript, some four years before his death in 1941, when Moulinier was living in St. Joseph's Hospital in Phoenix, he became interested in a plan devised by a small group of his friends who called themselves "The Companions of the Forgotten Women."[81] As a lay group, the companions aimed to construct and develop residences and nursing homes for single women and for sick and convalescent women. In declining health and nearing eighty years, Charles B. Moulinier was still creating new projects in the spirit of his role as a founder of the CHA.

·CHAPTER NINE·

Illness and
Popular Devotion

THE CATHOLIC HOSPITAL ASSOCIATION promoted a religious identity congenial with the progressive character of modern medicine. As we have
seen, Charles B. Moulinier, S.J., perceived the association's Catholic
character in terms of a traditional medical-moral code; however, its principal identity was as a sisters' organization. Moulinier was not merely
referring to the sisters' need for continuing education, but he was also
implying that the purity of intention and the dedication of the sisters permeated the hospital with a distinctively Catholic ethos.

In contrast to this blend of progressive medicine is the articulation of
popular religious response to illness that may be viewed today as alternative sources of healing, areas that anthropologists and historians have
recently explored. For example, the work of Robert Orsi on the devotion
to St. Jude entails anthropology, spirituality, history, and gender studies
to elucidate this distinctive cult in the popular mentality.[1] This chapter
focuses on popular manifestations of Catholic culture as they illuminate
the intersection of faith, illness, and culture. In the prologue to this work
there are references to popular understanding of sacraments, saints, pilgrimages, and shrines as symbols of meaning and sustenance in the condition of physical suffering or as sources of supernatural healing. Recall
that since sin was the most commonly accepted source of human illness
there was a tendency to seek some means of expiation usually through
the merits of the cross and/or one of the family of saints. The American
context of the immigrant church fostered cultivation of traditional devotionalism as a means of claiming the Catholic area of legitimacy in the
fields of religious pluralism so dominated by the Protestant ethos that
thrived on tagging Catholic devotionalism as old-world superstition. In

the twentieth century, traditional Catholic identity was articulated in opposition to American secularism and with a strong residue of competitive anti-Protestantism. Amid a thriving Catholic school system dominated by women religious imbued with Catholic devotionalism, strands of popular religion continued to be woven into Catholic life with patches of ethnicity persisting well into the twentieth century.[2] Many nurses, physicians, and particularly patients in modern hospitals reflected in various ways and with a wide range of intensity the predominantly popular religious culture that gave meaning and hope to the suffering, the severe crises, and the anxiety and grief of patients and their families. As Robert A. Orsi has pointed out, the culture of suffering was constructed as much if not more for those healthy Catholics who for various social and cultural reasons needed to embellish the devotional sources of expiation and meaning.[3] The methodology of this brief exploration into the devotional environment is eclectic, as it will deal with purported miracle cures in secondary literature, devotion to particular saints, as revealed in holy pictures and popular pamphlets, and pieces of religious culture associated with social and cultural meanings and understandings of illness and suffering. Though there are a few references to personal encounters with miraculous intervention and a glimpse at Protestant faith-healing, the focus is on verbal and visual renderings that reveal a Catholic sensibility of care givers and patients on the boundaries of existence.

I

In an article entitled "The Finger of God Is Here . . . ," Robert Emmett Curran, S.J., noted seventeen "miraculous cures and wonders" between 1824 and 1838, most of which occurred in conjunction with the intervention of Prince Alexander Leopold Hohenlohe-Waldenbourg-Schillingfürst, an Austrian priest well known for the many cures. Prince Hohenlohe's directives for those seeking divine favor included a novena in honor of the Holy Name, confession, communion, and a faith-filled disposition to the efficacy of the devotion. Ann Carberry Mattingly, a forty-year-old woman subjected to seven years of severe suffering—breast tumor, evidence of blood in coughs and nausea, high fevers and chills—was entirely relieved of all symptoms of illness when she received holy communion on the final day of the novena. Stephen Dubuisson, S.J., said Mass at two A.M. that morning, calculating the time when Prince Hohenlohe was saying his Mass in Europe. Ann Mattingly was a prominent Catholic in Washington, D.C. with a brother in the Jesuits and another mayor of the District. Her cure received widespread notice particularly in the capital, where over two hundred persons participated in the novena. Pierre Chatard, a leading Catholic physician in Baltimore, did not examine Mattingly but, though skeptical of stories of the miraculous, surmised that it was indeed "a wonderful thing and I would betray my conscience were I to say that I do not see the finger of God in it."[4] Those who promoted the miracle appear to have represented a romantic drive to integrate religion and culture. They immediately seized upon the miracle as a means of winning converts. The Catholic opponents of the cure tended to have been critical of "miracle hysteria." They professed an enlightened confidence that Catholicism thrived on its own inner resources.[5]

Mattingly's experience of 1825 was followed by seventeen putative cures among fifteen persons, all but one of whom were women and thirteen were members of religious communities. Even the enlightened Bishop John England of Charleston defended miraculous cures in his address before a joint session of Congress.[6] Though most cures were attributed to Hohenlohe, in the 1830s devotion to the Immaculate Conception of Mary gradually took prominence over novenas with the German priest. The new devotion was derived from the 1830 apparitions of Mary Immaculate to Catherine Labouré, a French Daughter of Charity. In accord with a visionary appearance of Mary, Catherine Labouré designed a medal that depicts Mary standing on the globe with the serpent crushed by her foot. "O Mary conceived without sin, pray for us who have recourse to thee" is the inscription around the Virgin, whose hands beam rays of light. On the reverse side are the hearts of Mary and Jesus, the one suffering from a sword piercing through it, the other from a crown of thorns. The medal, first struck in 1832, became immediately popular and because of the wonders associated with it became known as the *miraculous medal*. The young Sulpician John Chanche brought the first medals to the Sisters of Charity of St. Joseph at Emmitsburg, where a cure was attributed to the medal.[7]

Associated with the popularization of the cult of the miraculous medal was its promotion by the Sisters of Charity and by the priests and bishops devoted to the Immaculate Conception, the patronal feast of the United States.[8] As mentioned in chapter four, the medal's depiction of Mary crushing the serpent seems to have signified to the devout immigrants the portrayal of the Catholics' Queen crushing the evil of nativism and anti-Catholicism. The suffering hearts of Jesus and Mary were easily incorporated into the immigrants' experience of social injustice and economic discrimination. Those bishops who were immersed in mediating Catholicity amid the sufferings of immigrants extolled the institutional church, parishes, schools, and hospitals as refuges from the hostile world, as places where the sacred presence of Jesus was a vital sign of Christ's own suffering. Many of the Hohenlohe cures and those of the miraculous medal occurred with the reception of holy communion. Several scholars have noted that just as Christ was a new Adam so Mary was a new Eve, triumphant over the serpent; the renewed Catholicism of the immigrant church will be triumphant over nativism and anti-Catholicism, the serpentine evil in the American garden of religious freedom.

Traditionally, the sick were urged to attach their sufferings to the agony on the cross. The following prayer was recognized by Pius IX and the Raccoltà, the official list of indulgences:

Prayer for the Faithful in Their Agony
O most merciful Jesus, lover of souls, I pray thee by the agony of the Sacred Heart and by the sorrows of Thy Immaculate Mother cleanse me in Thy own Blood, the sinners of the whole world, who are now in their agony.[9]

Though this anthropology of human suffering may appear macabre to sensibilities imbued with a communal sense of the liturgy of anointing and the positive character of contemporary prayer such as *centering*, the agony of Jesus and the sorrowful heart of Mary were intended to give meaning to the suffering of the sick and dying, as well as emphasize the sinfulness of the world that has rejected the healing agonies of the Sacred Heart.[10]

In her study of mid-nineteenth-century devotionalism in the United States, Ann Taves captures the personal relationship between the devout and the heavenly holy family and community of saints in a popular metaphor in the devotional idiom: "The bourgeois family or household in which the mother played such a prominent role was frequently used as a metaphor for the relationships between Catholics and the inhabitants of the other world."[11] Orestes Brownson, who with Isaac Hecker was arguably the most prominent intellectual convert to Catholicism of the era, wrote of the communion of saints as "present with us . . . present to our hearts, and we can speak to them, pour into their open and sympathizing hearts our joys and griefs, and ask and receive their aid, as readily and as effectively as when they were present to our bodily senses."[12] Taves examines the prayer books of the era, which manifest the familial or at least personal relationships between the prayerful Catholic and Mary, Jesus, and the saints; the efficaciousness of these relationships was dependent on the open heart of the faithful during novenas and other particular devotional practices of faith; the cultivation of the devotional subculture was fostered by Brownson and others as romantic renderings of Catholic identity in a non-Catholic world.

Taves's study of such popular Catholic periodicals as *Ave Maria* (published by the Holy Cross Order at Notre Dame, Indiana) and *The Messenger of the Sacred Heart* (published by the Jesuits of Boston) contained letters of gratitude for favors and cures received through the intercession of Mary or patron saints. Saintly founders of religious communities and other holy persons whose causes for canonization were in process were identified as the sources of cures, particularly associated with relics. The Passionist Fathers in their Brooklyn and Hoboken ministries were popularly known for cures attributed to their founder, then Blessed Paul of the Cross. There was a famous cure of the child of a prominent St. Louis family, the Bakewells, attributed to the founder of the Religious of the Sacred Heart of Jesus, Madeleine Sophie Barat.[13]

In his book, *Catholic Revivalism*, Jay P. Dolan notes that healing ceremonies occurred during the parish missions of the late nineteenth century, particularly those led by the German-American Jesuit Francis X. Weninger. In Weninger's ubiquitous mission activity he frequently exhibited the relics of Peter Claver, to which many cures were attributed. Dolan remarks that he did not wait for parishioners to seek cures but "solicited the presence of the sick and the lame at his revivals."[14] Weninger directed the faithful to pray thus: "Blessed Peter Claver, help me, if it be the will of God, if it be better for my salvation, that I be cured; if not, O then obtain for me the patience to bear my sufferings meritoriously." Weninger recorded that "For nearly forty years cures followed cures without interruption."[15] Dolan places the perceived intervention of the miraculous within the "popular assessment" of a parish mission or revival. "People did believe that this was a special moment when God was present in their midst in an extraordinary manner."[16] Hence, many attended these revivals in anticipation of healing. Perhaps Weninger considered these healings in the parish-mission context as fostering reconciliation with the true faith in contrast to the heretical sects in the pluralistic nation.

Shrines or holy places, many of which were memorialized by miraculous cures, have an ancient tradition in Europe. In the nineteenth century none is more significant than Our Lady of Lourdes, a devotion that was appropriated by French nationalists eager to promote traditionalist anti-republican sentiment. Replicas of the Lourdes shrine were constructed as grottoes in churches and on ecclesiastical properties throughout the United States and attracted pilgrims seeking miraculous healing.[17] Our Lady of Lourdes Church at Aberdeen and Broadway in Brooklyn is an illustration of such a shrine where cures were reported.[18] The National Shrine of the Miraculous Medal was established in 1945 at the then Vincentian Fathers' house of studies in Germantown, Pennsylvania.[19]

There are many places of pilgrimage in the United States, but most are not so identified with cures as those of Lourdes. The Ursuline Sisters' shrine, the National Shrine to St. Anne, Our Lady of Prompt Succor, and Saint Paul Chapel are located in New Orleans. Only the latter shrine is entirely associated with protection against disease; during a yellow-fever epidemic it was reported that no member of the congregation in prayer to St. Paul was struck by the deadly contagion.[20] The most popular shrine to Mary's mother is Sainte Anne-de Beaupré in Quebec, Canada. Under the care of the Redemptorists the shrine is composed of a group of buildings as well as the main basilica.[21] So many physician-certified cures have been identified there that the shrine is referred to as "The Land of Miracles" and "canes, crutches and other paraphernalia of illness bear out the testimony of the doctors," most of whom were associated with the hospital close by.[22]

Most North American shrines in churches are in some way attached to the regular practice of the faith in a parish church or at a designated chapel. This represents a trend that originated at the end of the Middle Ages and was revived in the nineteenth century, one that was aimed at absorbing into established parish life places, persons, and practices that had religious meaning in a popular nonecclesial setting.[23] During the pontificate of Pius IX (1846–1878) the centralization of ecclesiastical life proceeded at a greatly accelerated rate; devotions, litanies, novenas, and special prayers were approved by the Holy See and were cultivated in opposition to what Pius IX perceived as the inherently anti-Catholic ethos of the liberal agenda. Papal indulgences were generously granted to the devout practices with the understanding that they would occur within parish life monitored by the clergy, particularly as indulgences frequently required confession and communion.

II

Protestant faith healing, which rivaled devotional Catholicism, originated in the holiness or perfectionist wing of evangelicalism during the postbellum period. Perfectionism evolved from a social focus on pietis-

tic and pentecostal manifestations particularly evident in holiness associations, revivals, and camp meetings; "faith cures" or "healing by faith"
was "a charismatic 'gift'" among the holiness sects.[24] One of the principal proponents of the faith cure was Charles Cullis, who was a homeopathic surgeon in Boston. He founded several social missions, including
nursing and medical institutions, which he called "Faith Work," symbolic of his having received "the second blessing." Influenced by the popular scriptural passage from the epistle of James (5:14–15) that is the
"basis of all prayers and anointing of the sick" and by the example of
European healers, Cullis embarked on a healing ministry. Soon after the
1879 publication of his book *Faith Cures*, Cullis became thoroughly
immersed in prayer and healing services in Boston at Faith Cure House,
which he founded in 1882.[25]

The faith-cure movement gained momentum in the 1880s, but it also
experienced an impassioned controversy among ministers and physicians frightened by what they perceived as its inherently fanatical tendencies. Raymond Cunningham, a scholar of the movement, quotes one
leader's defense of faith cures as a new sign that "regeneration . . . [is]
indeed a miraculous communication of the divine life."[26] He also refers
to those adherents eager to combat the advances of historical criticism of
scripture and the popularity of natural science in religion with "a fresh
display of signs, wonders to keep the church alive and open to God's
immediate visitation." Though Cunningham notes the relative weakness
of the movement he underscores its significance within the context of the
Christian Science's "mental therapeutics" and other sects concerned
with mind cures.[27] Both religious and mental therapies influenced the
integration of religion and health, "while the healing ministry would
transform Protestant pastoral work in the twentieth century."[28]

III

Catholic hospitals incorporated devotions, such as the Forty Hours of
Eucharistic Devotion and special feast-day liturgies of the sisters and
brothers, but as medical science gained prominence as the principal
source of all treatment there appears to have been a tendency to refer to
miraculous cures in hushed tones. A cheerful atmosphere of hope in the
positive character of medicine infused with a strong sense of compassion
was the regnant ethos in all modernized hospitals. However, strands of
Catholic tradition were persistently cultivated and were also manifested
in the material culture of the hospital; the central location of the chapel,

the display of statues (even the Johns Hopkins Hospital features a figure of Christ greeting visitors at its principal entrance), a crucifix, and pictorial renderings of the Sacred Heart of Jesus, Mary Immaculate, and popular saints associated with local devotions. Holy water fonts and the aroma of incense and burning candles were common features of Catholic life. The sound of a bell signified the chaplain's carrying the ciborium with holy communion for patients. Sisters' and brothers' religious garb displaying rosaries, crucifixes, and medals added greatly to the religious character of the hospital, but more importantly their presence was a living witness to the immanence of God. The Catholic culture was a soothing balm for those suffering physical and psychic pain and a source of strength and hope for care givers and for families and friends of the sick and dying.

The manuscript manuals of Sisters Clarke and Coskery and the letters and house diaries of Mother Joseph Pariseau, S.P., in Seattle and Mother Baptist Russell, R.S.M., in San Francisco abound in references to compassion for the suffering patients and prayers for deathbed conversions.[29] The sister-chronicler of Troy Hospital, a Daughters of Charity facility, noted that "several conversions and baptisms gladdened the hearts of the sisters, especially during 1890, and 1892 . . . all due, the writer thinks, to the miraculous medal, sewed in the corner of each pillow. Oh that the medal of your Immaculate Mother might be more lavishly spread all over the earth, forming a net work [sic] to draw in poor wanderers during life, or in the hour of death!"[30] The chronicle also included a miraculous cure of a young girl suffering from a massive tumor. A Vincentian priest, retreat master for the sisters, "told her to make a novena to St. Vincent, which she would make. . . and, at the veneration of the relic, on the feast day," the girl's tumor disappeared and she exclaimed, "I am truly cured." Though the sisters and the family marveled at the miracle the priest "charged the subject of it, *not* to speak of it at all so it was scarcely mentioned within the walls of the hospital."[31] No doubt he was concerned with engendering rising expectations of miraculous healing. Conversions continued to be a deep concern among the sisters and would be passed on to the lay nurses in their schools.

The Archconfraternity of the Holy Agony, founded by a priest of the Congregation of Mission (a Lazarist or Vincentian after the founder, Vincent de Paul) in 1862, was popularized in Europe and the United States in the 1890s by Lazarists and the Daughters of Charity. Dedicated to honoring the mental anguish of Christ in the Garden of Gethsemane at the threshold of his passion and death, the confraternity's members recited daily prayers and were encouraged to attend Mass on Fridays and participate in other devotional practices. They were urged to be particularly responsive to the needs of the dying for a priest and for sacramentals such as candles, oils, and holy water. Members distributed medals depicting Jesus in the Garden on one side with the seven sorrows of Mary on the other.[32] In their hospital, where they experienced the sorrows of nursing the innocent suffering of their patients, some Daughters of Charity promoted the devotion to the Holy Agony. For example, a sister at St. Vincent's Hospital in Bridgeport, Connecticut, wrote to the sister director of the archconfraternity that "the Holy Agony is doing wonders in our midst. Cures, conversions, holy deaths, etc., etc." She wrote of a seminarian who was dying, anointed without "a shadow of hope. . . . A nurse rushed to me for a Holy Agony medal and placed it around his neck, his beloved family were summoned to his bedside in tears while departing prayers were said . . . when to the surprise of all he recovered. . . . Think you this a miracle?" Two other recoveries occurred after the patients received Holy Agony medals, one also had a miraculous medal. "I shall try to send you a list of our conversions for the Bulletin, also a number of remarkable cures."[33] As mentioned in an earlier chapter these cures and devotional expressions of hope were evocative of the culture of pluralism; the Catholic devout not only needed to assert their difference from Protestantism but they also appeared to have needed the hope and the miraculous to sustain their own faith.

Hence, in a sermon entitled "Sickness, a Season of Divine Mercy," Cardinal James Gibbons focused on the blessings associated with illness. Catholic "hospitals and sanatoriums [are] a record of the loving mercy of our Heavenly Father brought upon souls that have been purified in the crucible of long and painful physical suffering." He spoke of sickness as "a salutary penance . . . [that] God in His mercy visits us with [as] a remedial penalty of His own selection. This consideration should prompt us to accept ailments and other corporal pains with patience and cheerful resignation." Of course God does not cause our illness but rather "permits" a person to be afflicted, and indeed the affliction may be "a season of grace, not only to the patients themselves but to the other members of the family as well. When the angel of sorrow presides over the household the voice of anger or ribaldry and profanity is hushed; a solemn religious atmosphere pervades the domestic circle." Responding to this grace are the women in the family, whom Gibbons viewed as representing Christ's healing presence. "There is no one stronger, more unselfish, and persevering than that exhibited by the female sex in the hour of domestic mourning. Their untiring ministration is no labor to them or if it is a labor the labor is loved. These devoted women, in performing miracles of mercy, are imitating our Blessed Redeemer, as far as human infirmity can imitate Divine Power, and never does Our Lord appear to us so amiable and attractive as when he is healing the sick, restoring sight to the blind and strengthening the paralyzed limb."[34]

Gibbons's ideals are parallel to those in the classic handbook of Catholic domesticity, *The Mirror of True Womanhood: A Book of Instruction for Women in the World* (original edition 1876) by Father Bernard O'Reilly. In a chapter entitled "Culture of the Heart" O'Reilly urges mothers to give "reverence and worship [to] the sick and infirm in your home."[35] With characteristic idealism laced with Victorian strands of romanticism the author states:

> We have seen religious communities where the room of a member afflicted with chronic disease was a kind of sanctuary to which all sought, as a special privilege, the permission of paying a daily visit,—and with what exquisite refinement of politeness and charity! We have known homes where the presence of some such incurable disease or life-long infirmity was hailed by parents, children, and servants as a priceless favor of the divine goodness: and how every act and industry that the fondest love could devise was practiced for years and years to render the lot of the stricken one bearable, to make the sick-room bright and cheerful; to fill it with the most pleasant sights and sweetest sounds! The most delicious fruits were sought for the sick one, and the most beautiful and fragrant flowers,—and we have known the master of that home to permit no one but himself to bathe the feet of the sick man,—and on bended knees, as if Christ himself were there. We have seen high-born ladies permitting no hand but their own ever to make the sufferer's bed, or decorate the room with gay colors, or wash and dress the disgusting sores. Think you the children of such parents will fail to inherit this sublime spirit of faith and piety? Or that peace and contentment, deeper than the ocean and sweeter than all joys that can be tasted outside of that vast bosom of God which is to be our home, will not flood such hearts and such households forever?[36]

In Cardinal Gibbons's work he refers to the ill as "patients," symbolic of the role of the physician in the context of modern hospital care. "A spirit of confiding and humble prayer should go hand in hand with nursing of the sick, and . . . [along with] the skill of the physician . . . the aid of the Divine Physician should not be overlooked. The prayer of Mary and Martha to Jesus during the illness of their brother is a model worthy of imitation. . . . I know that whatever Thou will ask of God, God will give it to thee. Let these be your sentiments when you administer to the sick.

The Lord will restore your patient, if it is expedient for his salvation, or if the sickness is unto death he will give you interior grace to bear the cross."[37]

Cardinal Gibbons's reference to the Divine Physician represents a traditional image in a modern context. Tertullian, the early church father, was the first to invoke the Divine Physician with an emphasis on Christ's healing body and soul. Recall his cure of the leper, followed with the admonition, "Go and sin no more." There are many artistic renderings of the theme; among Rembrandt's portrayals of the tenderness of Christ is the 1642 painting "Jesus Healing the Sick." In accord with the rising social status of the medical "profession" the Divine Physician achieves its own place in art under the Latin rubric, *Christus Coelestis Medicus*. The precursor is "Christ as Apothecary," a 1510 Dutch painting depicting Jesus at the counter "surrounded by the paraphernalia of the druggist's profession."[38] The devotion to Christ the Divine Physician in modern medical context appears to have a moral as well as a healing dimension that is related to the almost mythic status of the physician. The most common artistic rendering in the twentieth century depicts Jesus in a white robe, in the background comforting the patient, radiating divine compassion, a healing presence in the modern medical setting with its cold calculus of diagnostics and treatments. The Divine Physician is also the model for the medical doctor to bring the healing balm of empathy to the bedside.

The traditional patron saints of doctors are Cosmas and Damian, third-century physicians, who, because miraculous cures were associated with their ministry and because they refused to deny their faith, were executed by Roman authorities and later were recognized as saints. Dedicated to the study of Hippocrates and Galen these physicians were not self-conscious faith healers but rather were virtuous men who witnessed cures they could only attribute to faith. Extant sculptures of Cosmas and Damian retrieved from late medieval hospitals reveal the ancient veneration of these saintly physicians.[39]

Twentieth-century Catholic medical doctors revived the tradition of "my beloved Luke, the physician" as Saint Paul stated. William Harvey of England, noted for his study of the circulatory system, reported that during his first year (1598) as a student of medicine at the University of Padua the academic year opened on October 18, with a special Mass on the feast of St. Luke. Herbert A. Ratner, a member of the Guild of Catholic Physicians, wrote that the era of Harvey and Galileo "was characterized by fearless scientists who were God-fearing men. . . . Today many of our fearless scientists are not God-fearing men. The marvelous advances of modern science have sometimes functioned to produce darkness and unhappiness. The celebration of the feast of St. Luke focuses more than ever the need for guidance and governance that comes with a true love of God and the Son of God, the Divine Healer."[40] Ratner cautioned that "mass specialization, mass building programs, mass medical centers, mass medical research" may displace the recognition of "the human dignity possessed by each individual patient."[41] He concludes with a quote from the Gospel of Luke, in which Christ did not engage in mass healings but rather, "He, laying his hand on *every* one of them, healed them."[42] Devotion to Sts. Cosmas and Damian and to St. Luke appear to have been subservient to the regnant presence of the Divine Physician, the model for the personal source of healing in the impersonal context of the modern hospital. Perhaps more significantly Ratner was implicitly extolling the freedom and autonomy of the physician so sacred in a medical context and threatened by national health schemes that were proposed by reformers during the New Deal.

In her book *Handmaid of the Divine Physician* Sister Mary Berenice Beck, O.S.F., a registered nurse and a Ph.D. in nursing education, invoked Mary, the handmaid of the Lord, as the patron of nursing. Her dedication page reads:

> To Mary, immaculately conceived, who nursed the Divine Physician in His infancy and who, at her shrine in Lourdes, now serves as his chief hand-maid, as he ministers to the sick and suffering members of His mystical body on earth.[43]

Beck's book is a blend of general Catholic catechesis and a manual of religious directives for Catholic nurses (topics that will be further explored in a later chapter). However, in a section on "Private Devotions," she includes such prayers as "My Uniform" and "My Nursing Career." The former is a plea for the garb of faith, hope, and charity; the latter is more explicitly related to the religious vocation of the lay nurse.

> I am thy own, great healer,
> help thou me
> To serve Thy sick in
> amiable charity
> and lead them to Thy feet with
> shining cord
> of ministrations done for Thee . . .

I ask not thanks, nor praise,
but only light
To care for them in every
way aright
My words and works the
fairest, all are Thine
By mistakes—each one alas,
is mine![44]

Beck's chapter on the "Care of the Dying Patient" includes several catechetical lessons, but she also encouraged nurses "to pray with him [sic] as much as time permits. . . . Eliciting frequent short acts of faith, hope, charity, and contrition, or saying them for the patient too weak to do so for himself, is desirable. The patient should be wearing his [sic] scapular or scapular medal, if he has been enrolled. Holy water should be handy, also a lighted blessed candle, unless oxygen or inflammable anesthesia is being used . . . . A crucifix with the indulgence for the dying is placed in the hand of the patient, or pinned to the gown where the hand can reach it, so that he may die holding it."[45] Beck lists several suggested prayers as well as the Litany of the Dying, traditional prayers for dying, and the Seven Penitential Psalms. She noted that "it is customary for Catholics to gather about the bed of the dying in prayer—so surround him, as it were—so that the enemies of his soul may not come near to molest him."[46] This description of an elaborately devotional setting or boundary situation appears as the modern Catholic hospital's simulation of the rituals of taming death in the home.

Characteristic of the Catholic attitudes of the immediate pre-Vatican II period, the nurse was reminded that it was not permissible for Catholics to "help another [ill non-Catholic] person in the practice of what she believes is not entirely true." However the nurse was encouraged to "emphasize articles of belief held in common, as well as common practices that promote adoration, praise, thanksgiving, and petition to our true God." When treating the dying non-Catholic the nurse "can comfort and console him [sic] by praying with him, begging God to grant him unlimited blessings and graces; also, remain with him in prayer, or see that others do so, until the end comes." Several pages of suggested prayers follow that resound in hope, faith, love, and contrition. There were conversational prayers such as "God talks to me" and "I talk with God," replete with love and petition.[47] Over one hundred years before this 1953 book was published (first edition was 1948), Clark composed her manuscript manual on how to care for the dying patient. Though Beck's catechesis and her directions for bedside religious care are more elaborate than Clark's, both articulated the religious meaning of sickness and dying as well as the religious understanding of the nurse's vocation. Sister Beck's manual is remarkable for its strongly traditional character within the context of modern nursing so subjected to professional demands of record keeping and other time-consuming activities. However, Beck's manual is more highly stylized in structure and content illustrative of her professional status as a Ph.D. nurse-educator. Because the modern setting threatened to eclipse religious traditions, and because lay nurses far outnumbered siters, Beck's manual represents the nursing sisters' concern for the preservation of Catholic traditions and the need to pass them on to lay nurses so easily distracted from their responsibilities for the "Catholic soul" of the hospital.

There was also a strong strand of romantic idealism permeating Catholic culture during this period from World War I to Vatican II. Such idealism was characterized by a sense of moral certitude grounded in a philosophical and theological neoscholastic synthesis that united faith and reason in natural and divine law categories, and these provided Catholics with what they considered as an accurate compass in a secular world beset by skepticism, pragmatism, and a code of medical and family ethics that permitted sterilization, abortion, birth control, and euthanasia. Imbued with devotion to the Divine Physician and his handmaid, physicians and nurses brought moral truths and religious prayers to the bedside of their patients.

Chaplains brought the sacraments and devotional means of religious sustenance. Their manuals of pastoral theology emphasized the proper sensitivity in sick calls. "Be prudent in your relations with the physicians" stated William Stang (later bishop of Fall River, Massachusetts) in his *Pastoral Theology*, the first manual composed specifically for priests in the United States, published in 1897. "Entertain a sincere respect for him, and try to gain his esteem. Never interfere with his work unless absolutely necessary—as for instance, when it is your duty to protest an immoderate use of anesthetics, against craniotomy and abortion." He urged priests not to utter opinions on the disease or its prescribed treatment. "On the contrary, induce people to send for a physician in time, and urge them carefully to observe orders and prescriptions." In the event that the priest had an inflated sense of his calling Stang reminded him that though "the physician may not be the shining light in his profession, he generally knows more about sickness than the average priest."[48]

In accord with the class biases of the late Victorian era, Stang told his priest readers not to be concerned about telling a poor dying patient the truth of his or her critical condition: "death does not alarm them; it is often a great relief. . . . But with rich and worldly people a priest must be prudent when he has to tell them that it would be better that they receive the last sacraments. He must do it in the kindest and least alarming manner, apparently suggesting rather than ordering. He should not take every hope of life from anybody. His task is to prepare the sick person to die well, to be resigned to God's holy will and to make his sufferings meritorious for heaven."[49]

Aware of the need for priests to be conversant with the advances of modern medicine, Stang advised priests to consult works in the area of pastoral medicine. To explore this genre in detail is beyond the scope of this work, but it is important to place pastoral medicine in the context of the mutual responsibilities of the Catholic physician to provide a basic text on hygiene. Recent advances in classification, diagnosis, and treatment of physical and mental diseases fostered the need for seminarians and priests to incorporate this knowledge into the application of principles of medical ethics. In a 1905 text on pastoral medicine by Alexander E. Sanford, M.D., the author divides the material into three parts: Hygiene, Pastoral Medicine (The Relation of Man in His Bodily Condition to Religion and Morality), First Aid to the Injured. In an appendix by the moral theologian R. W. Drum, S.J., there is a treatment of the Moment of Death, the Fifth Commandment, and Neuresthenia in its Pastoral Psychiatric Aspects.[50] Since pastoral medicine is primarily concerned with the relationship between medicine and moral theology and parish ministry, it is only remotely related to devotionalism and spirituality, except in the physician's explanations of the validity of hypnosis and suggestion, as an antidote to some disorders; Sanford states that "as an explanation of miraculous cures it is entirely inadequate."[51]

Central to the theme of this chapter is that religious understanding of sickness was in some way related to sin or a fall from grace with subsequent reliance upon the rituals of sacraments and the practices of devotionalism. Subjected to severe sickness and pain, patients could be helpful in their own spiritual healing—perhaps physical curing—by reciting the prescribed prayers especially to a patron saint. As cancer was becoming a more commonly diagnosed disease, devotion to St. Peregrine, "the cancer saint," rapidly increased in popularity. Born in 1265, Peregrine, converted from a profligate life by a prominent member of the Servants of Mary (Servites), dedicated his life to prayer, penance, and care of the sick as a Servite brother. Afflicted with an incurable disease that required amputation of his leg, he made his way to the Servite monastery where he prayed to Christ and was soon miraculously cured. His own cure became identified as a healing of a cancerous growth on his leg. Later many cures were associated with devotion to Peregrine, who was canonized a saint in 1726.

The Servites in the United States promoted devotion to St. Peregrine, and in the 1930s and in 1941 the following prayer was approved by Archbishop Samuel Stritch of Chicago:

> O God, who gave to St. Peregrine an angel for his companion, the Mother of God for his teacher, and Jesus for the Physician of his malady; grant we beseech Thee through his merits, that we may on earth intensely love our holy angel, the Blessed Virgin, and our Savior, and in heaven bless them forever. Grant that we receive the favor for which we now petition. Through the same Christ Our Lord, Amen.

The devout cancer "victim" is to identify his suffering with Peregrine but not to pray directly to him but rather to the Divine Physician.[52]

The proliferation of mental hospitals during the period of modernization fostered revival of the medieval devotion to St. Dymphna, a woman of various legendary origins, whose body was found in a cave near the Flemish town of Gheel. Putatively murdered by her father because she denied his lustful passion, cures of many suffering from epilepsy and insanity were associated with her intervention. Indeed, the "ship of fools" motif in medieval lore and literature derives from ships of mentally ill persons seeking a cure at St. Dymphna's shrine in Gheel. Twentieth-century devotional literature published by the Franciscan Mission Associates of Mount Vernon, New York, sponsored a perpetual novena to invoke the aid of St. Dymphna, "patroness of those afflicted with Nervous and Emotional Illness." By joining the associates, one was enrolled in the novena and with an offering a vigil light representing the devout would "burn day and night . . . at St. Dymphna's feet . . . reminding her of your intentions even though you can't be there."[53]

All those afflicted with any form of sickness or injury, those invalids or handicapped who experienced suffering or pain, were invited to join "The Apostolate of the Suffering," which "performs the noble mission of educating the sick to patience, of training the soul to high virtue while the body suffers severe pain and agony or is wasting away by a slow fatal malady." The anthropological basis of the pious union is clearly revealed in the statement contained in one of the apostolate's promotional brochures: "The dearest friends of Christ are those whom He in his love chastises." The afflicted's agonies are transformed in the recognition of Christ's love in chastisement. "Sufferings sanctified by love are precious jewels that can purchase immortal souls; suffering is the most powerful of sermons, the greatest of prayers, the most fruitful of apostolates. The apostolate resembles a precious censer into which the combined sufferings of the members are placed and from which their fragrances arise as sweet incense to the throne of God and descend again in a shower of graces on all mankind." Members of the apostolate were to resolve "to accept all suffering in harmony with the holy designs of God and bearing them in a spirit of resignation." Membership included the "Spiritual Benefits" of remembrances at seventy Masses a month and on special feast days, of remembrances during novenas and other special prayer days for those enrolled, and the plenary indulgence at the hour of death granted by Pope Pius XII, some fifteen years after its 1926 foundation. The members received the quarterly publication *Our Good Samaritan* for the "spiritual welfare" of the sick and those who enrolled as patrons to pray for the afflicted. The apostolate's president in 1942 was a lay woman in Milwaukee.[54]

There were several local communities of religious engaged in promoting novenas, prayers, and meditations for the suffering. The Grey Nuns' Studio in Montreal published a simple holy card depicting Christ's glorified presence with a muted cross in the background and a hospital patient and nurse in the foreground. Inscribed in the left corner was the Latin phrase *Caritas Christi urget nos* ("the charity of Christ urges us"), and at the bottom was a quote from St. Paul's first letter to the Colossians: "I now rejoice in my sufferings for you, and feel in my flesh those things that are wanting in the sufferings of Christ." The "Prayer for Those in Suffering," in contrast to the description of the "Apostolate of Suffering," is restrained and free from baroque exaggerations:

> Grant me, O Lord, thy grace to unite my sufferings with yours so that I suffer as your true follower. I do not ask to be freed from afflictions since these are the reward of Saints, but I crave of you to make me find in calmness and resignation the true use of trials.
>
> Give me faith and hope. Take from me all that can displease you. Restore my health if such is for thy glory, and grant that I may adore thy Holy Will in all that comes from Thee. Amen.[55]

Robert Orsi captures the cultural significance of these devotions:

> The devotional ethos of suffering and pain failed actual sick people. It deepened the silence already threatening persons in pain with its constant injunctions to be quiet, denying them even the dignity of crying out in dis-

tress or unhappiness. It intensified the isolation and claustrophobia of the sick. Devotional writers castigated sick people for asking to be positioned more comfortably on beds that such writers liked to see as miniature calvaries rather than as the lumpy, lonely places of human suffering they actually were. The ethos confronted the sick with an image of the suffering Christ and then, in a perverse inverted Christology, told them that this image mocked any suffering of theirs: Did Jesus ask for a pillow on the Cross? Furthermore, by making pain a challenge, or test, of spiritual capacity, devotional culture added a layer of guilt and recrimination to the experience of bodily disease, as it proclaimed that most humans would fail this test. The ethos denied the social, communal, and psychological consequences of illness.[56]

The offering of the pains of sickness to the majesty of God also reflected the situation of the suffering of a church in a world hostile to the faith. Catholic separatism and the suffering-servant model of the church, energized by devotionalism, sustained the faithful, the sick, infirm, and the shut-in, but particularly those who needed the sick to suffer in silent submission.

IV

German immigrants of the second half of the nineteenth century tended to cultivate a rich devotional and liturgical life. A rare glimpse of the devotional character and the religious culture of a German-American hospital is included in a general letter written by a "student pupil" at St. Anthony's Hospital in St. Louis on the occasion of the religious dedication of a new wing of the hospital in September 1928. Archbishop John Glennon presided at the ceremony:

His Grace went through the entire house and blessed each room separately. Wasn't that a great honor to be conferred on our new institution? When they came to the X-Ray room some one of the Rev. Fathers suggested that it needed a special blessing; so the Archbishop went in and gave it several blessings. It will surely work better now. His Grace said he never enjoyed going through a new place so much as he did this one. He noticed everything was so immaculate, (as he expressed it), and remarked about the beautiful sets of furniture in the sun parlors. Each floor has a different set and this also did not escape his notice. The house really was beautiful.

. . . The nursery is almost the most attractive spot in the building. The thirty-six little white beds were decorated with pink, blue and white crepe paper and the statue of the Infant Jesus was placed at the headend of the cribs,—His baby hand raised over them as for a blessing. On each floor there is a beautiful statue: Christ the King, Blessed Virgin, St. Jude,

Guardian Angel and the Sacred Heart respectively claim the places of honor on the five floors. The statues rest on imitation marble stands. The dainty colors and perfect features were certainly admired. These statues were all donated by our good benefactors, and the ferns and flowers that were received during this week for the new place and the chapel were very abundant.[57]

Twentieth-century immigrants with old-world fears that hospitals were places to die needed an intensified relationship with saints, shrines, relics, medals, rosaries, and holy pictures of saints identified with Italian, Polish, and Bohemian or Slavic villages. In his penetrating analysis of the Italian-American *festa* to Our Lady of Mount Carmel, *The Madonna of 115th Street* in Italian Harlem, Robert Orsi notes women's response to the Madonna's healing of sick children by giving the child's best clothes to the poor as a way of linking the cure with a gift to those most in need. At the end of the procession were the penitents, usually women who had vowed to perform acts of self-sacrifice for a favor received. As one of Orsi's sources remarked: "You see, these elderly women would make a vow . . . maybe for five Mount Carmels they would march with the procession without shoes . . . to repay for the good they had gotten."[58] There were elderly women in the community who "were respected for their skill in healing with traditional cures and that knowledge of southern Italian magical rituals. . . . In the earliest days these women also served as midwives."[59] Folk tradition tended to react against modern medicine as almost devilish deviance from traditional ways of dealing with crises of illness and to prescribe curative practices derived from village life in southern Italy. In his chapter on "The Theology of the Streets," Orsi views the devotion to Our Lady of Mount Carmel as a means of transforming suffering and penitential sacrifice into a redemptive sense of self-respect as immigrants. By asserting their faith in the streets they defined themselves in the process of acculturation but with a strong sense of dignity rooted in tradition within the context of religious and ethnic pluralism.[60]

Folk tradition among Mexican Americans reveals the *curandos*, charismatic healers, usually men, who blended Catholicity and traditional folk cures according to divinely granted intuition.[61] Based upon her research on "Catholic Domesticity," Colleen McDannell describes a Holy Saturday (*Sabado de Gloria*) ritual-healing practice presided over by the grandfather of the family who attempted to cure his grandson with a special folk rite for the day before Easter. These Italian- and Mexican-American traditional prescriptions for healing created "a sacred space in the home." McDannell concludes: "It was not important that children learn the doctrines of the institutional church by memorizing the catechism. What was essential was that they respect the extended family and their traditions."[62]

After Pope Pius X reduced the age of first communion and fostered daily reception of the Eucharist, Catholic hospitals attempted to accommodate patients' wishes for communion. Last rites included confession, anointing, and Viaticum, the communion of passage. Though sacramental ministry and the evolution of the hospital chaplaincy will be treated in another chapter, it is appropriate to note that the traditional devotional life of the early modern hospital also included vital symbols of the Real Presence in the chapel and in communion, beliefs that provided Catholics with a strong sense of identity and beliefs that set Catholics apart from other religions in American pluralistic society.

Hence the Catholic culture of illness, suffering, and pain included three principal motifs: the attachment to the saintly members of the household of faith such as Peregrine and Dymphna; beliefs in the efficacy of types of prayers, medals, scapulars, relics, shrines, holy water, and iconography of Mary Immaculate, saints, the Divine Physician, and the Sacred Heart; the enrollment in pious unions to join one's sufferings to the cross as an offering to God, almost as a communal holocaust to God's majesty; the hope in the Catholic physician, dedicated to Cosmas and Damian and to St. Luke, in the Catholic nurse, the handmaid of the Divine Physician, and the sisters and brothers wearing crucifixes, hearts, and rosaries symbolic of the purity of their intention to serve God in the service to Christ's suffering. The modernization of the hospital and the professionalization of nursing meant that patients were subjected to increasingly scientific, technological, and bureaucratic structures. As Father Moulinier eagerly promoted the standardization movement he consistently lauded the special character of the Catholic hospital. Though the Catholic culture of suffering did not dominate the hospital, lay and religious nurses, physicians, and chaplains were influenced by and even dependent upon that culture; and for those on the boundaries of existence, popular piety and religiosity could have satisfied the need for meaning, for disclosing the sacred, and for participating in the healing mysteries of Jesus the Divine Physician.

CHAPTER TEN

Catholic Idealism:
Hospitals, Physicians, Nurses

DEVOTIONALISM FORMED several popular religious motifs of meaning supportive of those suffering from physical, mental, and spiritual illness and alienation as well as supportive of those lay and professional care givers. Though hospital administrators, physicians, and nurses were imbued with popular religiosity, they were simultaneously articulating in idealistic or romantic terms the religious identity of institutions and professions associated with Catholic health care. The Catholic professional associations of hospitals, physicians, and nurses blended a devotionalism with their identities as they continued to invoke patron saints and extol traditional practices of Catholic culture. However, the prevailing professional self-understanding was articulated in the defensive rhetoric separating Catholic idealistic motivation from what was perceived as the crass motivation of the secular world. The acceleration of modernization and professionalism entailed a corresponding drive to continuously interject Catholic ideals not only to foster a religious identity but also, because nursing was increasingly the professional preserve of the laity, to promote the Catholic ideal of nursing as a vocation in opposition to secularism as well as a means of fostering a submissive nursing staff rather than one composed of self-determined professional women.

This chapter explores the idealism incarnated in the Catholic hospital, the Catholic physician, and the Catholic nurse as it was articulated in the leadership of their national associations and guilds. It is bracketed by the ends of each of the World Wars, ca. 1920–1948. Because of the abundance of material related to this topic, Catholic separatism and idealism act as principles for selecting and organizing this material into themes, trends, and patterns. Once again the CHA's history provides a prism refracting rays of illumination on these general themes.

I

The postwar disillusionment, endemic in intellectual and literary circles, sounded the death knell to the idealism, romanticism, and sense of innocence characteristic of the optimism that had persisted from the Gilded Age to the experience of World War I. The shallow ostentatious twenties were embodied in the Babbittry of bourgeois decadence. The secure moral universe founded on the rational certainties gave way to relativism, pragmatism, and instrumentalism, which, viewed from the lens of a later Victorian, appeared to be an age that had jettisoned principle and consensus only to be replaced by narcissism and individualism. Irish-, German-, Italian-, and Polish-American Catholics were not absorbed into the Protestant crusade "to make the world safe for democracy"; they did not perceive the war in terms of American virtue and European decadence but rather had close genealogical ties to the old countries. There was a tendency among patriotic and thoroughly Americanized Catholics against an embrace of the illusions of the crusade, so they did not experience disillusionment. A Protestant minister after the war noted with a hint of disdain: "Romanist Joe, the mechanic . . . went to France not to make the world safe for democracy but to see Paris."[1] Instead, leaders of Catholic professional groups nurtured the American idealism of the prewar period, a theme central to William H. Halsey's work *The Survival of American Innocence: Catholicism in an Era of Disillusionment.*

Edward Garesché, S.J., editor of *Hospital Progress* (1922–28) and a spiritual director and founder of the International Guild of Catholic Nurses, represented a Catholic perception when he noted that young American veterans were "fresh, immensely moved, matured, instructed, disciplined and inspired. . . . The thrilling opportunities of the time should stir us to the deeps [sic] of our soul's capacity for enthusiasm, energy and sacrifice."[2] As we will discuss later, Garesché wrote a series of articles published in book form, *The Soul of the Hospital.* The leading Catholic historian, Peter Guilday, with characteristic optimism, concluded that the war had prepared Catholics to be "soldiers of a new pilgrimage. . . a war for Christendom [in opposition to] the new paganism." Herbert Hoover said that the Knights of Columbus were "disciples of cheer, apostles of joy, sympathy, help, kindliness. . . ."[3]

According to Halsey, "The multiple movements of Catholic culture," those national Catholic associations of education, charities, history, library, the Catholic Hospital Association and many more, may be understood as voluntary societies that represent "Catholic adaptation to the American democratic genius for forging members into political, cultural, or professional power centers." Another motive for forming societies parallel to the secular professional organizations was placed in the control of competition: "the Catholic spontaneous response to life was different from, if not hostile to those non-Catholic associations."[4] As mentioned earlier, in a pluralistic society there is the persistent tendency to emphasize differences between "them" and "us," among those driven to draw clear boundaries among denominations and between religious ideals and secular ideologies. There were also boundaries drawn within the Catholic communities between the second generation Americanists, who perceived the Holy Spirit's movement in society as well as the church, and the separatists determined to oppose nativism and secular paganism. The clash of public theologies reveals the defensive motif characteristic of the Catholic's confrontation with modernity, as well as a sense of fair play based on religious liberty.

As founder of the CHA, Moulinier manifested a charism to organize, educate, and inspire women religious in health care to develop in their hospitals a meaningful symbiosis between medical progress and American Catholicity. In opposition to those who viewed the American College of Surgeons as a secular threat to the sisters' hospitals Moulinier's idea of the CHA was not in terms of opposition to the drift of American society. On the contrary, his speeches and writings resound a rhapsody on positive themes of medical, social, and spiritual progress. In a 1922 address entitled "Fundamentals of Medical Activities," Moulinier forged his synthesis of science and religion with a strand of logic that begins with scientific knowledge as "the palace of the mind," and ends with the ideal hospital:

> [It] must be a place not only of service to the sick but through this service and by its increasing intelligent and conscientious fulfillment a school of research, wherein knowledge grows and a deeper sense of duty takes possession of all. In one word, the hospital must become the laboratory, the home, the asylum and the shrine where God's laws prevail, where these observances become a sacred obligation and where science and religion join hands in the enlightened conscientious and pious worship of God and His creatures, where the nature and laws God has made for body, for mind and for conscience receives intelligent and worshipful care, and administrations become a consecrated service, elevating real and sure science to the high place of ethics and religion.[5]

Moulinier's "Fundamentals of Medical Activities," a clear illustration of the deductive methodology of neo-Thomism, was derived from natural reason and applied to all hospitals on the path to standardization. Moulinier's theological reflection on the specific Catholic identity of the hospital was a simple fusion of the ideals of the vowed life of the sister-nurses and administrators into that religious space mentioned in the "Fundamentals. . . ." Motivated by a selflessness based on faith and gospel imperatives, sisters' and brothers' hospitals add a sacred dimension, that "something special" Moulinier referred to so frequently.

William Halsey's remarks on the literary world of Catholics illumine a portion of Moulinier's mentality. "Since World War I Catholics had succeeded in creating a literary world-within-the-world which reflected similar efforts in philosophy and general social outlook. There was a world of certainties where nature was malleable to human control, a man was free and unperplexed by either exterior or interior complexes."[6] Though Moulinier was an activist well aware of the realities of health care, he never alluded to injustice, individualism, or the cynicism of the marketplace, but as a descendant of the Americanists he persistently promoted the inherently progressive and providential character of medicine on which the superstructure of civilization inexorably ascends to higher reaches. His associate Edward Garesché represents an alternate trend in Catholic health care.

As mentioned earlier, this rather maverick Jesuit was a representative of Catholic idealism in the post-war era and was a prolific writer on various topics related to Catholic health care. Born into an old Catholic family in St. Louis in 1876, he studied and practiced law before entering the Jesuits. His first full-time assignment was to promote the Sodality of Our Lady on a national scale. In 1912 he was the founding editor of the Sodality publication, *The Queen's Work*, which in eight years had a circulation of 180,000.[7] From 1922 to 1927 Garesché was editor of *Hospital Progress*; he then joined the staff of the Catholic Medical Mission Board in 1927 and two years later became its director until his death in 1960. Active in forming sodalities among nurses and local guilds of Catholic nurses, Garesché founded the International Guild of Catholic Nurses in 1928 and became its permanent spiritual director. While his guild activism will be treated later, it is his book *The Soul of the Hospital* that so clearly reveals a distinctive rendering of the Catholic ethos of the hospital, an idealistic portrayal but not based upon an overt hostility to the spirit of the age.

In the chapter "Culture in the Whole Hospital" he describes the scene upon approaching this hospital, which he refers to as "Christian" rather than Catholic.

... the singular repose and grace of its architecture impress us. It is not lavishly decorated, its exterior does not give us the notion that it has been extravagantly expensive but there is a gentle beauty of proportion, a simplicity and grace of outline about its structure which is restful and soothing as Christian charity itself. It is not the cost of material nor the profuseness of decoration which makes a model hospital building. Rather it is the exquisite fitness of the style, the chaste simplicity of the design.[8]

On entering this ideal hospital one experiences "an atmosphere of kindliness and tranquility." On the walls are "excellent reproductions of great masterpieces, which express at once the sublimest beauty of art and deepest piety. . . . The most plentiful and delightful furnishing . . . is the abundance of books."[9] Garesché's sister superintendent is almost a romantic caricature of the woman religious. Her disposition and "ideals of personal culture" were derived from her vowed life. Indeed her gifts were by no means remarkable. Garesché describes her as having had "a certain natural bluntness, and even rudeness of manner, which rather repelled than attracted." Early in this sister superintendent's experience in religious life, "she learned the lesson that the culture, Christian culture, can overcome almost any natural defects and so she set to work from the very beginning of her career, to remold her personality to fit herself for a life of apostolic charity." Upon this high pedestal Garesché places sister-nurses dedicated to "culture and piety"; after the "long discipline of her training," she almost exudes "sweetness and charity." As a sister becomes a superintendent, these virtues are cultivated: "refinement and goodness gradually strengthen into a second nature, more firm and reliable than mere natural inclinations would have been."[10]

This is a highly melodic rhapsody on the theme of Catholic domesticity. When the superintendent was first assigned to the hospital "the beauty of hospital service dawned upon her. She saw the hospital not as a mere hotel for patients but as a true home of Christian charity and culture. The tenderness of Christ, His perfect courtesy, His love of true learning, His desire to bring out what was best and noblest in mankind was her inspiration in the care of the sick." The sister matures into the superintendent and of course, the hospital "is an expression of her personality but her associates work with her in charming concord . . . as you look into each room you seem to see the impress of a woman's mind and heart on everything. Every room is like a corner of home."[11]

Garesché was no doubt motivated to dispel fears of hospitals and to foster a refined hospitality among women religious. In contrast to the drabness of modernity and the "standardized institutionalism so unpleasantly striking" in many hospitals, the Catholic homelike atmosphere was a refuge, almost an idyllic retreat house for the sick. While Moulinier's synthesis of Catholic health care was the fusion of medical progressivism with the religious commitment of those vowed to serve selflessly, Garesché fashioned his as a blend of middle-brow culture, domesticity, and the sisters' refined sense of service derived from the training of women religious in the art of Christ's charity. Though Garesché was deeply committed to the Sodality, these ideals of Catholic health care did not reflect the devotionalism of popular Catholicity.

Moulinier's successor, Alphonse Schwitalla, dominated the CHA for twenty years (1928–47) and in the process imposed his own imprint on the association. Born in Germany in 1882, Schwitalla immigrated to St. Louis with his family at age three. He entered the Jesuit community in 1900, received his bachelor's and master's degrees from St. Louis University, and was ordained in 1915. After three years of teaching he studied zoology at the Johns Hopkins University, receiving his doctorate in 1921. When he was elected president of the CHA, he was associate professor of biology at St. Louis University, dean of the medical school, regent of the school of dentistry, acting dean of the graduate school, and dean of the school of nursing. Also, by 1928, he had organized the university's department of medical social service, had supervised the rebuilding of the school of medicine, and had helped establish the St. Mary's Group of Hospitals at the University Hospital.

II

Before and during his presidency Schwitalla wrote more than one hundred articles and papers on biology, medical education, and hospital administration, as well as many articles and editorials in *Hospital Progress*. He was elected associate fellow of the American Medical Association in 1932 and served as president of the North Central Association of Colleges and Secondary Schools in 1936.[12] Schwitalla brought to the CHA a singularly deep familiarity with the modern Catholic hospital, along with a critical intellect, a strong will, and a powerful personality. A president who could negotiate well within the CHA, he was also a strong—at times, a dominant—force in the spheres of medical education and ecclesiastical life. A professional and an activist, Schwitalla represented the prevailing idealistic ethos that was manifested in his attitude toward the inherently superior character of private Catholic health care.

Shortly after he assumed office, Schwitalla and his executive board began work on a new CHA constitution that would place ultimate authority in the hands of the hospitals and the religious communities involved in health care. They agreed to refine the committee structure to improve the CHA's effectiveness as an educational and professional agency.[13]

Schwitalla shared leadership with a loyal set of officers who served with him during most of his nineteen-year administration. Monsignor Maurice F. Griffin, of the diocese of Cleveland, was vice-president; Mother Mary Irene Hogan, S.S.M., of the St. Mary's Hospital group in St. Louis, treasurer; and Sister Helen Jarrell, R.H.S.J., of St. Bernard's Hospital in Chicago, secretary. These four officers and two other elected members formed the executive board, which met annually and, according to the new constitution (adopted on a trial basis in 1933–1934 and amended during the next six years), was responsible for arranging the program for the annual meeting and for "general direction of the policies and activities of the association." The board was elected from a slate of candidates presented by the nominating committee. Decisions of the executive board were subject to review by the general membership at the annual convention.

The new constitution stipulated that the executive board form committees, with members appointed by the president. Temporary committees, for example, on nominations, were responsible for the business of the annual convention. Most standing committees, such as those on membership and the editorial board of *Hospital Progress*, had administrative responsibilities, whereas the vocation committee was a professional standing committee limited to making recommendations to foster vocations among religious institutes sponsoring health-care facilities.

The constitution also established councils to deal with particular areas of education or hospital departments. Over the years the CHA formed councils in hospital administration and nursing education, which eventually sponsored regional continuing education institutes, tasks that required CHA staff support. These refinements in CHA structure evolved over the years and had a profound impact on the CHA's character as a professional educational and service agency.[14]

Moulinier's activism was in the areas of hospital reform and continuing education for Catholic hospital personnel. Confronted with the Great Depression, the New Deal, and World War II, Schwitalla vigorously pursued a role in public policy either to harness reform to the aims of private hospitals or to oppose reform as antithetical to what he perceived as a Catholic philosophy of life. In a real sense, he was an idealist on Catholic identity; his pursuit of modern lobbying efforts and modernization of hospitals was subservient to Catholic idealism. This entailed working with other national hospital associations, the National Catholic Welfare Conference, and the National Conference of Catholic Charities. In his strategic defense of Catholic health care in these contexts Schwitalla articulated religious identity with clarity, precision, and a pastoral commitment that marks him as a major figure on the national scene.

The downward economic spiral subsequent to the 1929 stock market crash was energized by a revolution of decreasing expectations. By the time Franklin D. Roosevelt began his famous one hundred days of the New Deal in 1933, consumer spending had decreased by almost forty percent; unemployment rose at an alarming rate; and, as the numbers on the relief rolls expanded, savings and funds for charity constricted; charitable funds for hospital outlay dropped fifty-four percent, for capital improvement, eighty-four percent.[15] Recession engendered increased demand on hospitals, but the Great Depression meant that there were high numbers of nonpaying patients in private hospitals but low revenues and sources of funding. In the process of promoting the social contributions of the private hospital, Schwitalla and others distinguished their institution from private "for profit" hospitals owned by physicians and from city- and county-owned hospitals by emphasizing voluntarism, conveying the notion that these institutions were rooted in democratic voluntary support among the community. (Someone recently remarked that private hospitals refer to their community identity during periods of economic crisis.) According to Rosemary Stevens, the voluntary democratic ideal became a "major unifying rhetoric" that allowed hospitals in the private sector to forge a "common front against increased government intervention. The language of the voluntary way became the antithesis to 'socialized medicine.' . . . Voluntarism [was] an anti-political idea [that] became an organizing and a political ideology for a disparate group of hospitals."[16]

Alphonse Schwitalla became one of the most forceful proponents of the voluntary idea, particularly after 1932 when the Catholic Hospital Association joined with the American Hospital Association and the Protestant Hospital Association to form a joint committee concerned with the formation of public policy and to protect voluntary hospitals. Their common interests were: the promotion of their institutions as vital to the common good; the protection of their hospitals in opposition to tax-based health-care institutions, which the joint committee perceived as having an unfair advantage; the rationalization for increased income from public funds for care of the indigent and those on government-sponsored relief projects such as the Civilian Conservation Corps; and opposition to government regulation of wages at not-for-profit voluntary hospitals such as the codes established by the National Industrial Recovery Act.[17] Rosemary Stevens comments on Schwitalla's significance; he was a "diplomat and a canny politician . . . , a persuasive spokesman in the 1930s for the moral superiority, privileges and liberties of private voluntary hospitals compared with governmental institutions. Schwitalla brought to the political debate on voluntarism an important reminder of the religious and charitable roots of nonprofit institutions as they corrected their twentieth-century course from the consumerism of the 1920s to the political realities of the New Deal."[18]

Throughout the 1930s, CHA member hospitals were experiencing the effects of the most severe economic dislocation in modern times. In his address to the 1933 CHA convention, Schwitalla touched on some of the economic problems of Catholic hospitals. There had been a notable decrease, he pointed out, in professional improvement and progressive development; at the same time, hospitals were beginning to focus more energy on solving economic problems than on improving patient care. And although no Catholic hospital had yet defaulted on its loan payments and occupancy rates had been maintained at almost sixty percent, small rural Catholic hospitals were experiencing great difficulty.[19]

Another focus of Schwitalla's convention address was the need to protect Catholic hospitals from commercialization. Obviously concerned about the acute financial crisis of the time, he warned that money might become an end rather than a means: "We have allowed business interests and other forms of lay interests to inject themselves into the administration of medical service and hospital service," he cautioned. Implying that medical doctors were not motivated by business interests, Schwitalla concluded: "If the physician is not a master voice in medical service, sooner or later medical service ceases to be medicine whatever else it may become."[20]

Regarding hospitalization insurance, Schwitalla restated his commitment to physician autonomy as crucial to the justice of any plan. He was opposed to all insurance contracts that would foster competition among doctors and wished to see contracts limited to bilateral agreements between insurance company and patient, patient and hospital, or patient and physician; rights and obligations in such contracts, he argued, are clear, in contrast to those in multilateral contracts, which create confusion and severe administrative problems.[21]

Alphonse Schwitalla articulated a synthesis of religion and medical progress that was unlike Moulinier's and Garesché's because he reiterated the traditional motive of health care: the imitation of Christ in the culture of healing. Nevertheless, the rhetoric and meaning of his synthesis resounds in the idealistic optimism so characteristic of Catholic culture of the era. In an address at the 1938 convention held in St. Louis during the time of a Eucharistic Congress, Schwitalla spoke of "The Charity of Christ in the Eucharist—An Inspiration to Charity in the Nurse."[22]

In his introduction Schwitalla elaborated on human suffering and why those who dedicate themselves to the science and art of relieving the suffering of the sick are "worthy of man's deepest reverence. For suffering is close to us; the lot of every human being; the daily food and drink of countless thousands." Though we seek the voices of happiness and shun those of grief, "sorrow outweighs joy and life cannot be but a trial in a shadowy vale of tears." In the light of faith Schwitalla exclaims: "If grief is omnipresent, so is joy, for in the world today, the Eucharist is everywhere." The real presence of Christ in the eucharistic sacrifice of the Mass symbolizes Christ's gift of Himself as "food that would make him one with us . . . so that He may transfuse us in our sorrow with the joy of the Real Presence."[23]

Such eucharistic devotionalism, with its emphasis on a high Christology and a suffering lowly humanity, reflects strong denominational boundaries. It follows that the Catholic nurse, who reflects eucharistic gifts to suffering humanity, is clearly distinguished from her secular counterpart. The nurse, called to dwell in the squalor of the tenements and in the most modern aseptic operating room, can only find what she needs to maintain "her sublime elevation . . . at the tabernacle door of him who has shown her the way, the truth and the life." Schwitalla describes the passion and death of Christ as the model for the nurse's selfless courage in dealing with suffering. "Through the Eucharistic Christ . . . can she achieve . . . that synthesis between Science and Faith without which she fails of her highest achievement." Without Christ she will not receive the necessary "grace for herself and those she serves." Schwitalla's synthesis emphasized the progress of nursing as "nothing but the highest professional achievement . . . worthy of the work of Christ." Just as Christ walked through the streets of Galilee "lined as they were with those who wished and prayed . . . that they might be cured . . . [so the nurse] walks with Christ through the wards of our hospitals, through the gangways of our clinics, through the alleyways of our slums, . . . she searches for those whom Christ sought out." Schwitalla's nurse was the laywoman, the dominant figure in the wards, but he expected her to understand her calling in terms of daily Mass and communion and frequent visits to the chapel. Characteristic of the spirituality of the era Schwitalla's message was in opposition to the hostile world so given to secularism. The promotion of the heroic calling of the nurse required sustenance not in the human experience of ministry; only through eucharistic devotion and frequent communion could the nurse struggle with a life of suffering humanity. Moulinier's and Garesché's idealism perceived the character of the progressive Catholic hospital in terms of transcendent qualities, as if the ministry in these conditions was inherently more effective than in the premodern period. Schwitalla's synthesis seems to rely more on the devotion to Christ's presence not in the action of ministry but in the active reliving of the Calvary event in one's own life as the nurse's source of meaning. Such spirituality underscored the ideology of gender construction: the nurse was not the angel of mercy of the premodern period but rather the woman who must cultivate meaning in eucharistic devotion rather than in professional spheres. The physician was master; the nurse was submissive. To isolate nurses' spirituality from human experience illustrates what Joseph Chinnici refers to as the "fragmented inheritance"; this condition resulted from a breakdown in the late nineteenth-century synthesis promoted by some leading Americanists influenced by Isaac Hecker, who articulated a spirituality grounded in human experience, American liberty, life in the spirit, and Catholic sacramentality. It is also emblematic of the separatist mentality, the "cultural conflict between the Catholic and secular worlds."[24]

At the 1940 convention on the silver jubilee of the CHA, Alphonse Schwitalla articulated Catholic identity within a context of "the latest and best triumphs" of modern medicine. He was concerned that amid the demands for continuous advancements—that is, naturalism—"the supernatural viewpoint in hospital activities is apt to be drowned." In response to those who claimed that "a Catholic hospital is only a hospital," Schwitalla elaborated on three distinguishing marks of Catholic identity.[25] The first entails a philosophy of life that was a reiteration of the Catholic understanding of suffering "in the supernatural economy of God's dealing with men. . . . It sees in suffering an opportunity for supernatural grace . . . [and] for increasing Christ likeness. It accepts the principle that the kingdom of heaven suffers violence, and, therefore that self-discipline in suffering brings a patient closer to the dear Lord's Sacred Heart and makes the patient . . . more Christ-like." The president of the CHA emphasized that this appreciation of the graces derived from suffering actually "accentuates the zeal" to cure and prevent illness, "not only because it supplies the highest possible motivation but also because [Catholic care givers] . . . feel a new dignity in the thought that they are serving as ministers of an all loving God in the working out of the destinies of those whom they have under their care." In accord with the neo-scholastic rationale so dominant in the philosophical and theological trends of the day, Schwitalla articulated his understanding of the "accentuated zeal": "Faith does not destroy reason; it builds upon reason and faith itself must be reasonable."[26]

The second distinguishing mark of a Catholic hospital was its insistence that "all those who serve the sick in the institution, do so under the sanction of an obligation in conscience." He answered the criticism which points to the fact that sisters cannot be dismissed as salaried personnel in a secular institution by stating its validity in fact, but "the implication is entirely false. . . . The obligation of the officials of a Catholic hospital are binding not under the pain of loss of salary or the loss of preferment or the loss of professional standing but they are binding under the sanctions of conscience and the sanctions of conscience mean sin and sin may mean hell and hell implies God." He admitted that many fall short. "We are all human and the impact of the physical is so strong "that we fail to see the 'place of faith in the giving service is of its very nature supernatural."[27]

The third area of identity is the Catholic hospital's understanding that "all human activity must be considered as means to the supernatural and, namely, the salvation of souls, then surely the functions of the hospital must be so considered." He recognized republican pluralism by stating that the hospital was not "a church and the bed is not a pulpit; the sick room is not a classroom and the nurse is not a teacher of religion." However, essential to the hospital is its emphasis upon the care of the sick derived from "motives which are implied in its Catholicity."

Schwitalla concludes on a note of militancy and triumphalism grounded on his certainty of faith and the clarity of his Catholic philosophy of life.

> And so . . . the trends of the day, the trends towards magnitude and wealth and comfort and remuneration for the indigent and a hundred other trends which promote naturalism . . . might endanger, if not destroy that supernaturalism which alone is worthy of a Catholic institution. The Catholic institution towers there upon earth but its purposes are in heaven.[28]

Schwitalla's promotion of the joint committee's interests entailed several visits to Washington, speeches, and articles. His Catholic idealism was frequently lodged within his articulation of the voluntary idea and the sacred character of the physician–patient relationship in opposition to the threat of state encroachments. For example, after attending the July 1938 National Health Conference he warned of an increasingly popular national health insurance scheme replete with numerous state regulations that would lead to the ultimate demise of the voluntary nonprofit hospital. The proponents of a national health scheme articulated their concerns within the economic crisis and pointed to the crying needs for health care, particularly the inability of the indigent and the working poor to have access to quality health care and noted the failures of taxed-based and voluntary hospitals to respond to these needs. Schwitalla concluded that though the proponents have amassed "elaborate and convincing data some theses are built upon probabilities" and others "are more or less doubtfully valid conclusions from existing laws, customs, practices, conditions, etc." Schwitalla would agree "to revolutionize a nation's procedures with reference to a matter as deeply personal as medical care, on a basis of mingled certainties and uncertainties, possibilities and probabilities," only if there was a "national emergency of overwhelming magnitude." Because of the "deeply personal character of medical care" reforms needed to be evaluated "in terms of one's basic philosophy of life." Schwitalla's principles were affected by the "stress [on] the economic factor in disease" because it seemed to quantify in a market context the "intangible values in the human needs of a sick person."[29]

The president of the CHA then launched into a Catholic theological reflection on the unsuitability of the singular focus on the economic factor: "[F]rom the motive of faith, sickness and all that is implied in it has a supernatural significance in the life of man [sic]." Of "physical, mental, and spiritual care," only the physical is related to economic factors. "Therefore to plan a national Health Program and to neglect adequate stress upon other phases of human life is to ignore essential issues." In contrast to the Catholic view was the naturalistic and "pagan attitudes toward life [which] are nowhere more easily detectable than they are in the attitudes toward human suffering. The attitude toward the problem of physical evil has become the touchstone of the adequacy of a philosophical system in meeting the contingencies of life."[30]

With the obvious implication that a philosophy based on the economic factor inadequately dealt with the problem of physical evil, Schwitalla elaborated on the CHA's theology of ministry: "Our Association's character of service, our dedication to that service under a perpetual vow to

God, our constant insistence that our lives must be Christlike, so that they may be worthy of the common sublime service which is given to the sick—all these and many other considerations which have been so frequently repeated by the Catholic hospital sisters and by those serving the sick in our institutions, become matters of prime importance to the nation's health, as well as being the guiding principles for influencing our own personal lives."[31] With an absolute certainty so characteristic of the Catholic ethos of the era, Schwitalla infused the Catholicism of the CHA into the mission to protect the voluntary character of the hospital. The president of the CHA also articulated a personalist perspective on the sacred encounter of the healing physician and the sick patient. The enemy was the economic nexus that threatened to dominate health care and subject the indigent patient to a system that was inherently impersonal. This personalism could easily be interpreted as the individualism of medical practice that allows the free market to set the fees for service.

Through the joint commission, voluntary nonprofit hospitals did achieve subsidies for indigent patients in their hospitals as well as immunity from the NRA codes of minimum wages. However, patient census in Catholic hospitals decreased throughout the Depression, and capital investment was considerably lower than in state and city hospitals. Despite all the hardships confronting voluntary institutions only eleven percent of religious sponsored hospitals closed during the Depression; most of these were in rural areas.[32] Because the joint commission had championed the principle of "subsidy without regulation" and promoted the voluntary way, Schwitalla and others eventually accepted Blue Cross as an acceptable form of insurance. As dean of St. Louis University Medical School the president of the CHA rooted his idealism in the alliances between church, medical education, and the hospital.

In response to the military build-up preceding World War II, such as the Selective Training and Service Act of 1940 and arms manufacturing, Schwitalla warned that "Never before has our Association met in a moment of greater uncertainty, tenseness, and anxiety. . . . The possible problems confronting us are overpowering. . . ."[33] Catholic nurses and physicians were absorbed into the war effort, but, unlike the previous war in which some sisters served (in World War I the Mercy Sisters of St. Louis and the Daughters of Charity of New Orleans nursed soldiers in Europe), the quality of lay nurses available obviated the necessity for sisters' participation. In 1943 the Wagner-Murray Bill was introduced in Congress, which was a national health insurance proposal attached to Social Security. Influenced by reports on the poor health of many draftees, Senator Claude Pepper of Florida remarked, "We still have a long way to go to improve the distribution and quality of medical care which our citizens receive."[34] Once again Schwitalla and the joint committee reiterated their opposing arguments based on the warning of the demise of the voluntary hospital and the fear that the system's patients would be wards of the state.

Wartime austerity had an adverse effect on capital improvements of hospitals experiencing an increase in patients and advance in medical technology. Clearly there was a need for quantitative growth and qualitative improvements of health care facilities. The answer came in 1946 with the passage of the Hospital Survey and Construction Act, which was known as the Hill-Burton bill. Even before the latter was introduced in Congress, the joint committee had promoted hospital construction legislation, which, in Schwitalla's words "would separate . . . the extension of hospital construction from other problems,"[35] that is national health insurance. The president of the CHA testified in support of the legislation, which was to be based on health concerns rather than financial need and was to incorporate the local level in planning and coordinating the construction of new facilities and was based on a mutuality of interest and trust between voluntary and public hospitals with the federal government and private interests. These principles guaranteed funds for the construction of Catholic facilities and protection of the religious character of sisters' and brothers' hospitals. The act had a profound impact upon medical care in the U.S.; between 1946 and 1960, 707 new not-for-profit hospitals received some Hill-Burton support for their construction. Congress rejected an amendment to the bill that would have disqualified funds for hospitals that discriminated against physicians because of race, color, or religion.[36]

In pursuit of the aims of the joint commission, Schwitalla was in continuous communication with the staff of the National Catholic Welfare Conference, particularly William F. Montavan, head of its legal department. Established in 1919, four years after the CHA, the NCWC and Moulinier worked out a loose arrangement that placed the association under the Social Action Department. Shortly after Schwitalla became president the Depression and New Deal legislation engendered the need to formalize the relationship between the association and the Conference to achieve unified response to public policy. As mentioned earlier, local bishops were urged to appoint diocesan superintendents of hospitals, analogous to the diocesan officer in charge of schools, to act as the bishop's representatives in coordinating policy. After the standardization process had gained acceptance among Catholic hospitals, however, the status of the superintendents of hospitals became rather vague. By the 1930s the diocesan director of Catholic Charities, a member of the National Conference of Catholic Charities (NCCC), had the primary responsibility for overseeing health care policy in many dioceses. Because the director was not a member of the CHA, the latter often had no official link to local episcopal authority. To rectify this problem, the leadership initiated constitutional revision to grant *ex officio* associate membership not only to diocesan directors of hospitals (a provision that had been added to the CHA constitution during the 1920s) but also to any clergy with responsibilities in health care matters. This status gave the clergy a voice in CHA affairs but did not give them voting rights.[37]

This constitutional change, however, failed to satisfy many of the local bishops' representatives. Diocesan directors of charity often resented the fact that CHA officials visited hospitals under their jurisdiction without first clearing the visit with them; some appeared to want to create a section on hospitals with NCCC. CHA vice-president Maurice F. Griffin, who frequently met and corresponded with diocesan bishops' representatives around the country, believed that directors of charity wanted voting rights in the CHA. Clearly some sort of understanding would have to be reached to avoid duplicating functions and responsibilities between the CHA and NCCC and to ensure that the CHA would continue to honor local episcopal prerogatives. Between 1934 and 1939 Griffin and Schwitalla had several meetings with NCCC leaders to explore ways to more effectively incorporate them into the CHA. There appears to have been a consensus among the women religious that, if full membership were granted to NCCC, clerical domination and the demise of the CHA as a sisters' organization would result. Schwitalla was himself convinced that the diocesan directors of charity wished to absorb the CHA into their organization.[38]

The conflict became acrimonious when an anonymously authored article appeared in the *Acolyte* entitled "The Hallucinations of Hunty," a severe critique of the CHA as if it were dominated by a cabal of Jesuits and in violation of diocesan autonomy through its vocations' program, promotion of its nurses' guilds and sodalities on the local level. Obviously aimed at Schwitalla, the article was ignored by the CHA board. However, in the revision of its constitution the Board included a section that stipulated its submission to ecclesiastical authority and that in pursuit of the CHA's policies and programs on the local level individual hospitals shall in all cases be subject to the approval of the ordinary of the respective diocese.[39]

Father John O'Grady, head of the School of Social Service at the Catholic University and NCCC director in Washington, was a dominant figure in the conflict between the National Council of Catholic Charities and the Catholic Hospital Association. The Schwitalla and O'Grady encounter entailed correspondence, a personal meeting, and consultation with the NCWC. It appears to have been not only a personality conflict but also a clash of worldviews. Though Schwitalla was an urbane diplomat and politician, he was preservationist on religious issues. O'Grady also excelled in diplomacy and political strategy, but he was open and expansive in his views on religion and culture. While Schwitalla extolled Catholic separatism as a means of dealing with what he referred to as naturalism and paganism of the world, O'Grady implicitly associated himself with an activist ecclesiology based on positive interactions between church and culture. Hence, in contrast to Schwitalla, O'Grady was not fearful of national health reform.[40]

The CHA board, Monsignor Maurice Griffin, and the diocesan NCCC leadership proffered several resolutions to the conflict, which was ultimately solved at a special meeting of personal representatives of the bishops convened by Archbishop Samuel Stritch of Milwaukee during the CHA convention in his see city. The bishops' group formed an executive committee that negotiated with Griffin and Schwitalla. Simultaneously, CHA leaders met with representatives of the NCWC. The first result of these meetings and negotiations was that the position of director of hospitals was reestablished throughout the country, a move that effectively removed the NCCC threat to CHA autonomy.

Father Edward O'Brien, diocesan delegate of the archdiocese of Baltimore, reported on the Milwaukee meeting. He told the chancellor of the archdiocese, Joseph Nelligan, that "This thing has turned out to be a rather sensible and effective meeting. Representatives from sixty dioceses are here and Schwitalla seemed much pleased that Baltimore was among them." He noted that the bishops' delegates had been incorporated as a "permanent feature of the CHA setup and the priests saw to it that Schwitalla himself had no official job in the group." O'Brien was impressed that the president of the CHA had "shown more sense, and a better grasp of the whole thing than I expected."[41]

Two years later, in 1941, a new level of governance was created, the CHA administrative board, which would help organize its activities more efficiently. Composed of the CHA executive board and the executive committee of the bishops' representatives, the board was to coordinate general policy, to direct public relations, and to propose legislation related to health care. CHA would retain full responsibility for conducting its business and continue to operate its many educational programs. In April of 1942 Bishop Karl J. Alter of Toledo became the first episcopal chair of the board.[42] Schwitalla was strongly authoritarian and cherished the respect he received from bishops and superiors. During his negotiations on several fronts he wrote to the general secretary of the NCWC, Monsignor Michael J. Ready: "Next to Almighty God's approval for the work of the Catholic Hospital Association, nothing is more important to me than the approval of ecclesiastical authority." Ready had paid tribute to the CHA and its president, which, Schwitalla said, "conveyed a spiritual significance which could not but affect me personally."[43]

Concurrent with the disputes with O'Grady and the NCCC Schwitalla encountered problems associated with leaders in nursing education. The Goldmark Report on nursing education, issued in 1923, helped bring about a shift from nurses' training schools to academic nursing schools, many of which were affiliated with medical schools. The report called for a greater emphasis on nurses' educational needs. The majority of nursing schools at the time were actually departments of hospitals, and nurses' training often focused on the needs of a particular hospital rather than on the students' need for a well-rounded education. Thus, as Edward A. Fitzpatrick, dean of Marquette University Graduate School, claimed in the September 1926, *Hospital Progress*, there was "considerable justification for the conception of the school of nursing as a separate institution affiliated with the hospital, with a separate budget, a separate endowment, and controlled primarily by educational considerations." In the same article, Fitzpatrick, a member of the National League of Nursing Education's (NLNE) grading committee, listed sixteen problems an NLNE study had found to be typical of even the best U.S. nursing schools.[44] In 1931 there were 403 Catholic nursing schools, some of which were small training schools in rural towns.

In 1930 the convention passed a resolution that urged nursing schools to separate from the hospitals with which they were affiliated. The resolution also endorsed the aims of the Committee on the Grading of Nursing Schools, established by the NLNE, and called for a thorough study of Catholic nursing schools. The CHA's support for the NLNE's grading committee's authority was not destined to last, however. In 1931 a rumor spread that the committee was planning to publish a list of one hundred nursing schools that met its standards, of which only one was Catholic. Sister-educators were understandably alarmed. Five of them sent a letter to superintendents of Catholic nursing schools asking that they meet in June to take action on the matter.

Meanwhile, Schwitalla was taking steps to convince CHA members of the benefits of the NLNE program. He arranged for Sister Mary Domitilla, O.S.F., of St. Mary's Hospital and the Mayo Clinic, Rochester, Minnesota—a member of the grading committee—to present a paper at the convention explaining the committee's activities and why they were not a threat to Catholic nursing schools. At the same convention, however, the CHA circulated a questionnaire soliciting members' opinions on the kind of agency they would like to see evaluating these schools. A majority voted that the association should set up its own nursing-school evaluation program. This response appears to have led the CHA executive committee to reverse its position. The committee now decided that the CHA should withdraw its support for the NLNE's grading committee and begin making plans to create its own set of procedures for evaluating Catholic schools of nursing, a decision that ignited a heated controversy.[45]

Many sister-educators of nursing schools had joined the NLNE (making up ten percent of its membership) and had formed the Sisters' Committee within the league. The chairperson of the committee, Sister Mary Olivia Gowan, O.S.B., was teaching nursing courses at Catholic University of America, Washington, D.C., and would become dean of the university's newly established School of Nursing later in the decade. Sister Olivia Gowan, who like Sister Domitilla had a master's in nursing education from Teachers College, Columbia University, believed that the NLNE was better qualified to evaluate Catholic nursing schools than the CHA's program, which was not composed of professional educators. She also considered the CHA's determination to establish its own evaluation teams as symbolic of a form of Catholic separatism, one that rejected the secular world, unlike the Sisters' Committee, which attempted to cooperate and provide a Catholic influence in a secular, professional organization. She was influenced by Moulinier's progressive and providential synthesis of religion and medical science and nursing education.[46]

In a confidential report to the executive board of the CHA Schwitalla defended the apparent contradiction between his openness to secular agencies' evaluating Catholic colleges and universities and his anti-NLNE position. One educator, supportive of Sister Gowan, "expressed surprise that Father Schwitalla should be advocating a separatist program for the schools of nursing while at the same time identifying his activities so intimately with such organizations as the North Central Association, The American Council of Education and similar so-called neutral educational interests." Schwitalla responded that he had attempted to work with the NLNE but discovered that its grading committee would "at least endanger strong Catholic attitudes with reference to education" of nurses. He also pointed out that the objectives of nursing education, including the religious welfare of patients, were so different from those of general higher education that these distinctions justified the Catholic evaluation of nursing education and secular accreditation of colleges and universities. He also doubted the Nursing League's neutrality, a view that seemed to have been based on his interpretation and was at variance with many sisters' views of the NLNE.[47] Hence Schwitalla reconciled the apparent dilemma. His deeply held views on the sacred character of the hospital, the eucharistic dimension of Catholic nursing ministry, and the inherently conventlike character of the atmosphere of the Catholic nursing school precluded a secular agency's evaluation of Catholic nursing education. The conflict must be understood within the spheres of gender relations: Schwitalla's ideal nurse was based upon the submissive and the putative natural nurturing qualities that needed to be cultivated in a separate Catholic environment. Olivia Gowan represents a cosmopolitan, professional woman of stature, so threatening to traditional ideals.

Schwitalla was not, however, without some support from women religious nursing educators. One valuable associate was Sister Berenice Beck, O.S.F., who in 1931 suggested that the CHA develop a permanent council to evaluate and vote on issues related to nursing. The result was the CHA's Council on Nursing Education, on which Beck served through most of the 1930s. During this period, she also helped establish Marquette University's College of Nursing. However, she became a colleague of Gowan at Catholic University.

The dispute between the CHA and the Sisters' Committee would, however, continue throughout Schwitalla's tenure as president. In 1937 he asked the NCWC, whose Social Action Department had approved the CHA, to officially endorse the association's evaluation program. The NCWC did reconfirm the CHA's affiliation with the Social Action Department, a move Schwitalla interpreted as an endorsement. But although the NCWC had, in fact, officially recognized the validity of the CHA's program, its statement did not imply a repudiation of the Sisters' Committee.[48]

In a letter explaining the NCWC's position, the general secretary,

Michael J. Ready, told Schwitalla that the NCWC had "no legislative power." Hence, it could do no more than commend the CHA's evaluation policy for bishops' consideration. "Ordinaries, however, seem divided in their views. Religious groups representing many training schools seem opposed to your association's plan; and even within the association there appears to be a decided minority difference of opinion. Fears and hopes rather than facts are stressed on either side."[49] In his response Schwitalla was deferential to Ready and promised to continue to be "most scrupulous in stressing facts only."[50]

Sister M. Laurentine, O.S.F., a member of the accrediting committee of the NLNE, kept Monsignor Ready informed on the conflict from the sisters' point of view. Associated with a training school of nearly two hundred female as well as male nursing students, Sister Laurentine had been in attendance at a meeting in Boston of the sisters associated with the NLNE, all of whom were opposed to Schwitalla.[51]

Sister Conchessa Burbridge, C.S.J., of St. Joseph's Hospital in St. Paul (who was close to those Sisters of St. Joseph present with Moulinier when the CHA was proposed), responded to Sister Olivia Gowan that at the 1937 meeting of the CHA there were only three dissenters out of three or four hundred sisters present at the meeting to discuss the merits of the association's evaluation plan. She was a moderate on the NLNE: "It is by no means proven that non-Catholics will oppose our plans for running our own hospitals." However, she supported the CHA plan because it guaranteed "that we shall be free to teach and to practice our own Catholic doctrine and follow principles with which we are heartily in accord. . . ." She also told Gowan that the St. Paul provincial and the superior general of the Sisters of St. Joseph of Carondelet, Missouri, supported the CHA plan.[52]

Sister Gowan had become a national figure in nursing education and was appointed dean of the School of Nursing at the Catholic University of America in 1936. She received her nursing diploma in 1912 from St. Mary's Hospital in Duluth, operated by the Benedictine Sisters. In 1917, the year after her religious formation as a Benedictine sister, she was appointed superintendent of St. Mary's Hospital during the period of the standardization movement. Representing Charles B. Moulinier's views on the need for continuing education and for collegiate education for nurses and more importantly her own drive for professional and intellectual improvement, she received her B.A. from St. Scholastica College and an M.A. in nursing education at Columbia Teachers College. Long active in the NLNE she was convinced that the grading program would not threaten the religious identity of Catholic schools of nursing anymore than the standardization teams threaten the Catholicity of hospitals. She was convinced that Catholic University could provide the leadership in both religious and professional areas of nursing education.[53]

Opposition to the evaluation program put Schwitalla in an increasingly defensive position. His arguments, which many found unconvincing, generally stressed the importance of ensuring (as he put it in the September 1938 *Hospital Progress*) that nursing schools maintain "the viewpoints of Catholic education" and "the motivation supplied by Catholic thought." According to Schwitalla, these were among "the special reasons why the Catholic schools of nursing "cannot and should not accept any guidance or supervision except from those who fully appreciate and value" the needs of the Catholic nursing student.[54]

Despite the controversy, the CHA's Council on Nursing Education began to put its evaluation program into effect. The CHA conducted its first inspections in September 1934, and by the 1935 convention had already filed some 160 reports with the CHA's central office. It was not until 1938, however, that the association began to accredit Catholic nursing schools. And less than a year later Schwitalla faced yet another difficulty when the Catholic University of America extended its already well-established affiliation program for colleges and night schools to include Catholic nursing schools. Sister Gowan, now dean of Catholic University's School of Nursing, was a leader of the NLNE accreditation program.

Although attempts were made to reconcile the Catholic University program with that of the CHA, nothing was resolved. In 1942 the CHA published its first list of approved schools; it published another list in 1943. But as wartime demands drained the CHA of key personnel and made travel for sister-examiners difficult, the accreditation program stalled. After the war the CHA began to look for a position that would better answer earlier criticisms and would reopen the possibility of one accrediting agency for all nursing schools in the United States. In 1946 the CHA administrative board resolved that evaluation should be considered an activity distinct from accreditation and that the CHA's Council on Nursing Education should continue its evaluation function. The board left open the possibility that the council could recommence its accrediting activities.[55]

The conflict over accrediting procedures was finally resolved in 1949. In 1947 the CHA had formed the Conference of Catholic Schools of Nursing (CCSN), which studied trends in the nursing profession and in nursing education. In the same year Father Schwitalla, who had suffered two heart attacks, gave up the CHA presidency. Under the leadership of John J. Flanagan, S.J., the CHA moved closer to acceptance of a single national accrediting agency. At a 1948 meeting in St. Louis, the CCSN endorsed this idea, but its members remained divided on whether the CHA should continue its evaluations. Early in 1949, with CHA support, the National Nursing Accrediting Service (NNAS) was organized. It published its first list of accredited schools in October of the same year. In general, Father Flanagan was a consensus builder, whereas Father Schwitalla's personal identification with the CHA and his defensive posture on the issue of nursing education had been strong impediments to reaching an amicable solution.[56]

III

In his opposition to the national health program of the Wagner-Murray bill, Alphonse Schwitalla's views appeared in the *Linacre Quarterly*, the official publication of the National Federation of Catholic Physicians' Guilds.[57] Founded in 1931 the federation was named after Thomas Linacre, a graduate of the famous medical education program at the University of Padua. He was physician to Kings Henry VII and VIII of England, founder of the Royal College of Physicians and its first president. Linacre became a priest in 1520 and died four years later.[58] The St. Luke's Guild, one of the first local groups of Catholic physicians, was organized by Cardinal William H. O'Connell, Archbishop of Boston.[59] A thoroughly committed ultramontanist with a strong determination to consolidate hospitals under archdiocesan ownership, he seized control of St. Elizabeth's Hospital and tried to take over Carney, but because the Daughters of Charity's provincial council composed the board of directors his attempt was frustrated.[60]

The first organizational meeting of the St. Luke's Guild, June 20, 1910, was at O'Connell's home,[61] but the regular meeting did not commence until the following October 18, at which time Dr. Thomas Dwight presented a paper on "Living and Non Living," followed by "a very forceful and eloquent address on the aims and purposes of the guild, calling attention to the growing tendencies of our institutions to divorce science and religion and to secularize everything in life, and showing it to be our duty as Catholic physicians to devote ourselves to the educational work in which the Catholic Church is engaged to endeavor to contribute our share to the task of rescuing medical science from the materialism into which it is falling."[62] Guilds had formed in France as early as 1884, but it may have been the Medical Guild, founded in London in 1910, that prompted O'Connell to initiate the St. Luke's Guild.

The Philadelphia guild, founded in 1911, held its organizational meeting at the request of James J. Walsh, M.D., then dean of the Medical College at Fordham University, "who was familiar with the European guilds."[63] One of the organizers was Dr. Lawrence Flick, who became its first president. A principal aim of the guild, according to a later president, was "to bring before the professional man or woman those Catholic moral principles which apply to everyday work." At quarterly meetings the chaplains and physicians discuss such moral-medical topics as "mercy killings . . . the rights of the unborn child . . . [and] the use of anaesthesia—dispelling the false idea that the church forbids the relief of pain . . . we try to make ourselves better Catholics and better doctors."[64] By the 1930s guilds were associated with the lay retreat movement, as it was noted that the Philadelphia guild made an annual retreat. James J. Walsh and Lawrence Flick, both born in Pennsylvania in the 1850s, achieved national repute; the former not only as a physician—he did his training under the renowned German pathologist Rudolf Virchou—but also as a medical historian and a Catholic apologist and generalist. He wrote five hundred articles and forty-five books, including *Thirteenth, Greatest of Centuries*, which he discussed with President Theodore Roosevelt in the White House.[65] Flick became an authority on tuberculosis, founded a national and an international society and conferences for the prevention of the disease. Flick was also interested in church history; he was a founder of the American Catholic Historical Association and its first president in 1919. However his three books were related to medicine rather than history.[66] Of the two physicians Walsh was more actively engaged in the Federation of Catholic Physician Guilds. He was editor-in-chief of the *Linacre Quarterly* the last two years of his life, 1940–42; he served as contributing editor of *Commonweal* as well.

Dr. Joseph A. Dillon of New York City was president of the federation in its first years. In a posthumously published article entitled "The Catholic Physician and His Sphere of Influence," Dillon commented on the "innuendoes and religious ridicule" encountered by Catholics in non-Catholic medical schools. He urged young Catholic physicians to intern in Catholic hospitals, where "the patient is considered a fellow human being, spiritual as well as physical. Unconsciously, the doctor brings a different approach, a sympathy with suffering, which is not universally the experience of the ordinary hospital case."[67] Besides sensing when it is necessary to prepare the patient for the last rites, the Catholic physician should be active in his parish, "visit the sick poor," act as a consultant on school health, examine candidates for religious orders on their physical, mental and emotional suitability, give opinions on proof of "miracles at shrines," and various other services for church and community.[68] Dillon was particularly concerned with medical ethics and wrote vigorously in opposition to those physicians "who perform ovariectomy after Caesarian section, induce abortion for causes which they call justifiable, use immoral methods for diagnosis of sterility, narcotize dying patients even at the risk of shortening life, recommend contraceptive methods, perform mutilating operations under the guise of eugenics." He concluded that Catholic physicians were "often respected, not because of their faith, but by reason of their sterling principles which imbue their personalities."[69]

Dillon's article represents the ideals of the only national organization of Catholic physicians in a world it characterized as "increasingly pagan."[70] With headquarters in New York, the federation's annual meeting was held in conjunction with the convention of the American Medical Association. Only as strong as the numbers of local affiliates and based on volunteers among a profession subjected to long hours, the federation appears to have been in a precarious situation during its first ten years. Indeed in 1942 it was "threatened with extinction."[71] It therefore sought affiliation with the NCWC in the hope of establishing an office in Washington, D.C., that would provide resources and stability. In 1944 the administrative board of the NCWC asked the board of the CHA to consider negotiating an arrangement with the CHA. In 1945 the association became responsible for the business management and administration of the federation with Schwitalla as editor, manager, and spiritual moderator. Though the federation grew in membership and local affiliates, it never came remotely close to representing a majority of Catholic physicians. However, the *Linacre Quarterly*, which included articles by leading physicians and moral theologians, was found in many Catholic libraries in hospitals, seminaries, and universities. The guilds also promoted Catholic clubs and Newman Associations at medical schools and sponsored seminars for medical students and nonguild members, and the federation affiliated with the Guild of Catholic Psychiatrists aimed at infusing Catholic moral teaching in that area of specialization. The federation also reflected trends within the Catholic community; for example, Catholic action, the lay retreat movement, the Cana conference for the preparation of marriage, medical missions; and the *Linacre Quar-*

terly published forthright articles on medical care for African Americans and the need to break down racism several years before the bishops' 1958 letter on racism. Though its members were intended to assimilate into the culture of medicine, the guilds served to reflect a mentality of Catholic separatism.[72]

IV

The International Guild of Catholic Nurses was founded at the 1924 annual meeting of the CHA. Edward Garesché, S.J., then editor of *Hospital Progress*, was its principal founder and author of its constitution. With its motto "Christian Love in Service" the organization had three major objects:

1. To unite its members for the increase of their personal excellence of character and service, for deepening of their friendship toward one another, and for the expression of Catholic charity in their service to others.
2. To contribute to the strengthening and elevation of the nursing profession in its social, cultural, ethical, religious, economic, and technical aspects.
3. To promote such activities as are most effective to raise the grade of professional service in nursing, to stimulate the initiative and right ambition of nurses to achieve eminence and leadership in their profession; to increase their reasonable and well instructed faith, their ethical correctness and professional devotion.[73]

Garesché's influence was clearly manifested in the ways in which it achieved these objects: annual retreat, lectures on religion, ethics, social service, public speaking, on history, science, art, and literature and a social life based on musical and theatrical entertainment. The guild invited Catholic and non-Catholic graduates of Catholic nursing schools, which numbered sixty thousand in 1927 with projections of five thousand graduates annually. Besides its openness to non-Catholic nurses in accord with its ideals the guild encouraged its members to take an active role in other professional societies. Garesché stated that there was a "great need to encourage Catholic nurses to aspire to the service of leadership." The most practical aspect of the organization was its employment service, matching nurses' credentials with openings in Catholic hospitals. It was hoped that local chapters, composed of ten or more members, would be formed throughout the United States and Canada; it met in conjunction with the annual meeting of the CHA.[74] Garesché's idealism and his posi-

tive attitudes toward the trends in American society illustrate his conge-
niality with the leadership of Charles B. Moulinier and his implicit conflict with Alphonse Schwitalla's separatist mentality. Indeed, the
International Guild's endorsement of secular professional societies fostered support for the National League of Nursing Education. Though we
have no statistics on the Catholic lay nurses in the NLNE there were 317
sister members, 90 of whom were members of committees.[75]

The ideals of Catholic nursing were clearly articulated in the catalogues of schools of nursing. For example, Mercy Hospital's school in
Baltimore captured the motivation of the candidate for admission as a
woman willing "to bend her energies to render service to mankind and
to relieve suffering." Because the nurse "holds a unique position in the
field of medicine . . . her post demands the very highest type of young
womanhood." The vocation was portrayed as a call to heroic virtue identified with "sacred duties," which demand "constant, laborious self-sacrifice and service."[76] The religious calling was essential to Mercy's
understanding of the nurse's way of life. "The sacredness of the profession [entails] the proper appreciation of the chastening value of suffering as well an oblation of herself upon the altar of devotion, with a keen
understanding of God's laws and proper observances of them." At
Mercy's School of Nursing, "religion is in the atmosphere . . . like a sweet
balm purifies the very air we breathe . . . preparation for this noble calling is spent in the shadows of religion—the natural medium for the development of character."[77] Hence, the devotional character of Catholic
nursing was assimilated into the Catholic culture of suffering.

The curriculum in the late 1920s did not include religion or theology
courses but there was a course in professional ethics. The diploma
course was three years and there was an option to complete a B.S. in nursing in the five-year curriculum at the University of Maryland. There was
a separate building, which had its own chapel, for the school of nursing.
"The school is non-sectarian. Catholic students have every opportunity
to practice their own religion, while those of other denominations are left
entirely free. Morning prayers are attended by all."[78]

In a statement on the state of Catholic schools of nursing addressed to
the bishops of the Administrative Committee of the NCWC, Schwitalla
provided statistical breakdowns gathered from a survey sponsored by
the CHA. In 1933 there were 1,068 approved nursing schools in the
United States; 413 were conducted under Catholic auspices. The first
Catholic school to offer a B.S. in nursing was St. Xavier College of
Chicago, which had merged with Mercy Hospital School of Nursing. Sev-

enty-eight other schools of nursing were affiliated with forty-two Catholic colleges and universities while twenty, including Mercy in Baltimore, were affiliated with non-Catholic institutions of higher education. The percentage of Catholics in the 413 schools ranged from one hundred percent (because twelve percent of the Catholic schools accepted only Catholics) to around fifteen percent. About 280 schools offered courses in religion in 1933.[79] The CHA, as well as the leadership at Catholic University, had been actively promoting degree programs, the teaching of religion, and the sponsoring of religious activities in Catholic schools of nursing. During the 1930s Catholic higher education was influenced by the Catholic revival in Europe with its emphasis upon the neoscholastic synthesis of reason and faith, the natural and supernatural. This synthesis was promoted by theologians and philosophers and was identified with "the mind of the church."

These trends were reflected in nursing education. Mercy Hospital's nursing school catalogue of 1941–42 illustrates the prevailing trends in church and education. The objectives of the school open with a quote from Pope Pius XI on the "ultimate" end of all Christian education: "to cooperate with divine grace in forming the true and perfect Christian, that is, to form Christ Himself in those regenerated by Baptism. . . . The true Christian product of Christian education is the supernatural man who thinks, judges and acts constantly and consistently in accordance with right reason illuminated by the supernatural light of the example and teaching of Christ; in other words, to use the current term, the true and finished man of character." The heroic call to nursing expressed in the 1927–28 catalogue as an "oblation of herself upon the altar of devotion" had been replaced by a Catholic professionalism infused with contemporary neoscholastic idealism. The institution is characterized by "religion and philosophy," and its philosophical and educational principles control "all aspects of school life" so as to affect the student not only as a prospective professional woman, but also a woman of character and conviction, prepared as the occasion arises in her life to give emphatic evidence of her Catholicity in thought, work, and action."[80] This is not a docile, self-sacrificing woman but an independent proactive, professional nurse ready to assert and to defend her Catholic principles.

A religion course was required of all students in each of the three years. The dominant theological synthesis is embodied in this curriculum. The orientation course during the first year "treats the purpose of the Catholic professional school and the natural and supernatural virtue of the nurse. The different lectures constitute a survey course in Catholic philosophy, devotional life and dogma." "Catholic Life and Worship," the second year's course, emphasized "the power of the sacramental system in the development of the Christian character and in the promotion of Catholic Action."[81] In the 1930s two forms of Catholic action were promoted: the participation of the laity in the apostolic work of the hierarchy is Pope Pius XI's definition; Specialized Catholic Action, that is, the Young Christian Students, the Young Christian Workers, and later, the Christian Family Movement, extolled personal sanctity and the tripartite formula for apostolic action—think, judge, and act.[82] Pius XI emphasized the authority structure of the church while the latter movement tended to empower the laity to be proactive in specific apostolic areas.

The third year's course, "Catholicism, Revelation and the Modern Mind" had four principal goals: "To establish the rational foundation of Faith; to establish the fact of the Divinity of Christ; to establish the truth of the foundation of the Church; and to present some important teachings from the life of Christ by a study of the Gospels."[83] The course in ethics was infused with religion and philosophy: "The Rule of Human Conduct; Conscience, the Subjective Norm of Human Conduct: Duties to God, Self and to Others." Practical moral topics included "Birth Control; Marriage and Divorce; Character; The Nurse and The Souls of Her Patients."[84]

The 1948 catalogue of Baltimore Mercy Hospital's School of Nursing, entitled "The Mercy Approach to Professional Nursing," included the statement of Pius XI and the objectives quoted above. The only major difference was the removal of the third-year course in religion.[85] Research in several other nursing-school catalogues during this period reveals comparable articulation of idealism and curriculum development.

Concurrent with these developments in the late 1940s were foundations of diocesan Councils of Catholic Nurses, which sponsored monthly lectures and discussions on religious and moral topics for both lay and sister nurses. Authorized by the bishop and organized by the diocesan directors of hospitals and nursing leaders in the area, these councils appear to have been intended for an elite, while local guilds of Catholic nurses, influenced by the International Guild, gradually surfaced among the grass roots in several dioceses in the 1930s and 40s. The Baltimore Catholic Nurses' Communion League, founded in 1928, formed itself into a Catholic Nurses' Guild in 1939 with the approval of Archbishop Michael Curley. The principal organizer explained the advantages of a guild: "activities could be broadened, . . . [with] more frequent meetings, . . . the development of intellectual activities and additional social affairs."[86] A year later Curley published a letter to all Catholic nurses in the Archdiocese of Baltimore and Washington encouraging "an organization of Catholic nurses, regardless of where they have been trained." He referred to the formation of the guild, the president's name and address and stated that such an organization was "desired by the Holy See." He articulated the purpose of the guild with a characteristic blend of idealism and practicality: "[It] would keep before our nurses the high ideals of their profession and by their unity to gather strength to carry on their great work for the sick and many times for the indigent with whom they have to come in daily contact."[87]

In Washington, D.C., the nurses organized the Archdiocesan Council of Catholic Nurses, a unit of the National Council of Catholic Nurses. A committee composed of two sisters and three lay nurses, the council was approved by Curley and within a year had enrolled 155 nurses. The council established a program to instruct women on nursing in the home. In a letter to the chancellor of the archdiocese the president, Mary Alice Suburt, an instructor in the Red Cross Nursing Service, explained the cooperation between the Red Cross and the Archdiocesan Council of Catholic Nurses. "It has authorized us to give its course in Home Nursing . . . but it [also] allows us to preface and (or) conclude the lessons with instructions pertinent to the Catholic religion." The programs were held in the parishes in Washington. Suburt outlined the religious topics included in the instructions: "the historical aspects of the care of the sick and the preservation of health in which Catholic contributions are emphasized; the administration of Baptism in emergencies; preparation . . . in anticipation of the visit of the priest to administer the sacraments; and the spiritual care of the dying." Suburt said that the council "felt assured that there is a wide field of Catholic nurses in this work of Catholic action. It may well be considered Apostolic since we plan to accept non-Catholic women in these classes."[88]

The National Council of Catholic Nurses, formed in 1948 and replacing the International Guild, affiliated with the NCWC and the CHA and met biennially. At its 1952 meeting the national episcopal director, Archbishop Richard Cushing, initiated its quarterly publication, *The Catholic Nurse*, became its editor and published it in his see city of Boston at no cost to the NCCN. That year there were 772 Catholic hospitals in the United States. With 111 special hospitals and 271 "homes for invalids and the aged" the total was 1,054 Catholic health-care institutions.[89] Catholic nurses' training schools numbered 366 with 31,755 students. The first issue of *The Catholic Nurse* included a copy of an address by

Pope Pius XII extolling the scientific, moral, and spiritual requirements for the profession of nursing.[90] Sister Mary Ransom, a Sister of Charity of Nazareth, Kentucky, placed nursing in the context of the Mystical Body of Christ: "Today we find nursing choked with ceaseless cares of industrialism and the evils of secularism. Although at this point the atmosphere is dark and the path obscure, the piper still blows on his pipe our theme song, 'The Branches have thrust thin roots deep into the heart of Christ, our Lord, who is the Vine.'"[91]

Ellen C. Stark, a lay woman involved in nursing education, wrote on "The Spiritual Care of the Patient." Echoing the frequently stated principle to attend to the "body-mind-soul entities" Stark's article presages our contemporary wellness programs based upon the mind–body–spirit connections. However, she demonstrated an ecclesiastical class consciousness within the context of spiritual care; the lay nurse "has a right to be allowed to minister to the spiritual need of patients insofar as she does not encroach upon the work of the chaplain and sisters, but works as an assisting member of their team."[92]

Catholic idealists frequently responded to the challenges of professionalism manifested in schools of nursing and hospitals. At the 1947 baccalaureate liturgy for graduates of five nursing schools in Boston, Archbishop Cushing spoke to the 291 graduates on how the Catholic nurse represents a synthesis of professional motivation and religious vocation: "Our nuns have prepared these girls for a noble profession, say better, for a holy vocation." After extolling the nurse's scientific training he referred to the profession's "legendary place in popular thought. . . . The nurse embodies all that is best and noblest in womankind. Her work is characteristically feminine, yet it is not soft nor passive. It is masterful and scientific, yet it calls for qualities not usually associated with cold mastery or with routine, impersonal perfection of science." Cushing, then listed the characteristically "feminine" virtues, "sweetness . . . compassionate understanding . . . tolerance and tact in lifting despondent souls from listless despair to living hope." He said that the Catholic mind prefers vocation to profession, "a call from God to do the work of God in soothing pain by which the world is constantly reminded of God." Though he said he did not intend to "demean the prestige or security of the progress of nursing as a profession" Cushing found that "nursing as a secular profession may absorb nursing as a divine vocation." He extolled all the professional qualities of nursing but Catholic nurses have a "vocation of serving Jesus Christ in the person of his poor."[93] In a postwar world in which women were organizing professional societies, Cushing's articulation of the "feminine mystique" appears as a defensive strategy to counter such trends.

Cushing's peroration on the religious vocation that separates the nurse from the secular world was echoed in the theme of the 1952 NCCN convention, "The Nurse—A Citizen of Two Worlds." In a summary of that meeting an anonymous member stated that the theme "was developed in many ways. We were left with the thought that we as Catholic nurses, true to high ideals and living lives always on the side of Christ, are not only making a powerful contribution toward the principles of life . . . but of *equal* importance, to Christian principles in nursing."[94] Catholic idealism was so strongly stressed in the post-World War II era because Catholics were rapidly assimilating and the hospital was so central to the confidence of secular progress that it became necessary to cultivate strong Catholic identity to negotiate religious faith in that public culture.

The struggle between profession and vocation among sisters and lay nurses was resolved in nurturing an affective religious idealism and devotionalism as countercultural to secularism and a nascent-feminist consciousness in professionalism. There was a consensus among idealists that without this infusion of Catholicity into the profession the prevailing spirit of world-centeredness with its promotion of birth control, abortion, and euthanasia would dominate the modern nursing profession. Another persistent theme, symbolized by promotion of the religious dimension of nursing, was that modernity and professionalism tend to remove the sense of the sacred from the place and the people involved in health care. The structural ambiguities and tensions in a *private* religious, modern hospital serving the *public,* accredited by *public* agencies and partially funded by *public* funds, challenged Catholics to infuse the sacred into the public spheres embodied in rituals and symbols of the Catholic culture, in the chaplain's sacramental ministry, in the medical/moral principles enunciated by chaplains, physicians, and nurses, and in the religious idealism of the CHA, and the guilds of Catholic doctors and nurses. When Catholic culture shifts from idealism to a critical self-understanding rooted in historical contingency rather than in philosophical categories and in the devotional subculture, there is a corresponding shift in religious identity, one based upon an open-ended missionary model to integrate women's experience, religion, and health care; this is the contemporary quest for meaning in the ever-changing character of the ministry.

Founders

✤ LEFT: St. Elizabeth Seton, founder of the Sisters of Charity.
Courtesy: Sulpician Archives, Baltimore.
✤ RIGHT: Mother Xavier Clark, D.C., author of a manuscript manual for sister nurses, ca. 1840, and her superior during the origins of the ministry in the United States.
Courtesy: Daughters of Charity Archives, Northeastern Province, Albany, NY.

✤ LEFT: Mother Catherine Spalding, S.C.N., co-founder of the Sisters of Charity of Nazareth, KY.
Courtesy: SCN Archives, Nazareth, KY.
✤ RIGHT: Mother Baptist Russell, R.S.M., founder of St. Mary's Hospital San Francisco, and a dominant figure in Catholic Charities in the Bay area.
Courtesy: Sisters of Mercy Archives, Burlingame, CA.

✤ LEFT: St. Frances Cabrini, founder of the Missionary Servants of the Sacred Heart.
Courtesy: Catholic News Service, Washington, D.C.
✤ RIGHT: Mother Rose Hawthorne Lathrop, founder of the Dominican Sisters, Servants of Relief for Incurable Cancer.
Photo used with permission of The Franciscans, St. Anthony s Guild, Paterson, NJ .

✤ LEFT: Brother Bonaventure Thelen, C.F.A., founder of the American Province, Alexian Brothers.
Courtesy: Archives of the Alexian Brothers, Immaculate Conception Province, Elk Grove Village, IL.
✤ RIGHT: Mother Alfred Moes, O.S.F., founder of the Rochester, Minnesota, Franciscans and of St. Mary's Hospital, near the Mayo Clinic.
Courtesy: Archives of the Sisters of Saint Francis, Rochester, MN.

Leadership

✤ Cardinal Joseph Bernardin, Archbishop of Chicago, with a resident of Bonaventure House for persons with AIDS.
Courtesy: Alexian Brothers, Immaculate Conception Province, Elk Grove Village, IL.

✤ Rev. Charles B. Moulinier, S.J., first president of the Catholic Hospital Association.
Courtesy: The Catholic Health Association of the United States, St. Louis.

✤ Rev. Alphonse M. Schwitalla, S.J., (right) president of the Catholic Hospital Association, confers with Bishop Karl J. Alter (left) of Toledo, episcopal chairman of the Catholic Hospital Association Administrative Committee, and Archbishop Richard Cushing, Archbishop of Boston during the C.H.A. s 1947 convention.
Courtesy: The Catholic Health Association of the United States, St. Louis.

✤ LEFT: Sister Olivia Gowan, O.S.B., first dean, The Catholic University of America, School of Nursing, Washington, D.C..
Courtesy: The Catholic University of America.
✤ RIGHT: Sister Berenice Beck, O.S.F., a dominant figure in the education of nurses, 1930s–1950s.
Courtesy: Wheaton Franciscan Sisters Archives, Wheaton, IL.

✤ Pope John Paul, II, greeted in Phoenix, AZ, by John E. Curley, Jr., and Sister Mary Eileen Wilhelm, R.S.M., president and chairperson, respectively, of the Catholic Health Association of the United States, in September 1987 during the pontiff s trip to the U.S.
Courtesy: The Catholic Health Association of the United States, St. Louis.

✤ Members of the Executive Committee of the Board of Trustees of the Catholic Health Association of the United States met August 15, 1994, with President Bill Clinton and Hillary Rodham Clinton to discuss health care reform. From left to right: Judith Pelham, Sister Bernice Coreil, D.C., Dan Russell, Hillary Rodham Clinton, John E. Curley, Jr., President Clinton, Bill Cox, Sister Maryanna Coyle, S.C., Alexis Herman (assistant to the President for public liaison), and Dan Wolterman.

Courtesy: The Catholic Health Association of the United States, St. Louis.

PART THREE

Toward the Contemporary Experience: The Acceleration of Social and Religious Change 1948–1993 Introduction

THE SECOND VATICAN COUNCIL represents a shift to a new religious consciousness rooted in historical understanding of scripture, theology, ecclesiology, and the distinctive character of the religious life. Religious involved in health care experienced renewal chapters or general assemblies which were extended constitutional conventions that composed fundamental documents delineating new understandings of community, governance, spirituality, and ministry and entailed a commitment to respond to the poor, oppressed, alienated, and marginalized. Gradually many sisters and lay women involved in health care absorbed a feminist perspective into the new religious consciousness that profoundly affected the critique of society, church, and educational and health-care institutions. Concurrently, during the years 1965–75, there was a precipitous decline in vocations to the religious life and a rising awareness of the value of the laity in leadership positions.

In the United States, the opening of the Second Vatican Council marks the final hours of the so-called "ghetto church." By the 1960s Catholic institutions had become quite modernized and their personnel highly professionalized. Hence there were large groups of Catholic sisters, brothers, priests, and lay people ready to respond to the call for adaptation, reform, and renewal of the 1960s. The social changes, symbolized by the rise of suburbs, the proliferation of a college-educated middle class, and the popularity of lay Catholic action, portended the developments of the 1960s. Since there were several signs of change during the immediate pre-Vatican II period it is appropriate to refer to the era 1945–1965 as "the making of the modern church."

The accelerating rate of social and religious change of the past four decades is paralleled by the velocity of the medical, technological, and structural transformation of the hospital/medical center. If one would have visited an urban Catholic hospital in 1950 and then again in 1990 one would have been immediately struck by several features of the contemporary scene: the quickened pace of activity, the dominance of lay personnel with many women in positions of authority, the racially integrated character of the facility, the change from priest chaplaincy to an ecumenical, pastoral-care team of men and women chaplains, the creation of an ethics committee, the lay board of trustees, the new office of mission effectiveness, recently established bereavement and other support groups concerned with physical, emotional, and spiritual crises of patients, families, and staff.

To narrate and analyze these changes entailed dividing this era into two periods: Chapter eleven is concerned with the transitions to the mid-sixties with particular focus on such topics as the reform-minded leadership of the CHA, the church's meager responses to the African-American community, the professional and spiritual concerns of women religious, the new religious consciousness of Vatican II, and the social reform climate that influenced the creation of Medicare and Medicaid. Chapter twelve deals with the formation of a new spirit and structures of religious life and of pastoral care, the proliferation of health-care ministries outside hospital contexts, new forms of sponsorship and the development of hospital systems, and the theological, spiritual, and ecclesial identities of Catholic health care.

The Catholic subculture, with its ethnic and devotional foundations so dominant in the pre-Vatican II world, is barely visible in the contemporary hospital. The unraveling of these patterns of traditional meaning was occurring as the new religious consciousness was on the ascendancy. However, the charismatic movement, holistic health care, and the general popularity of wellness with a spirituality component represent trends in the affective dimension of contemporary caring and curing that have filled the void in the decline of devotionalism.

Chapter thirteen, the epilogue, based on the methodology of the journalist, reports on the significant trends in the ministry particularly as the agenda of John E. Curley, Jr., president of the CHA since 1979, reflects these trends: to strengthen ecclesial affiliation, to initiate a trans-formationist model for leadership, and to clearly articulate Catholic identity within the contexts of health-care reform.

In the public place of the hospital, with its paucity of traditional religious symbols, a missionary consciousness, rooted in new understandings of ecclesiology, scripture, pastoral care, and the roles of the laity, is infused into the ethos of Catholic health care. The book ends as it began with the formation of new missionary identities of Catholic health care not with the mix of European tradition and republican ethos but rather with a blend of religious renewal and health-care reform mediated in a climate of American pluralism.

CHAPTER ELEVEN

Transitions in Church, Society, and Health Care

1948–1965

HISTORIANS OF THE 1960S have tended to focus on the cultural changes symbolized by such events as the civil rights movement, student unrest, the rock concert, the moon walk, the war on poverty, consciousness-raising women's groups, the New Frontier, and the Great Society. Religious historians have captured change by focusing on the election of Angelo Giuseppe Roncalli as Pope John XXIII, the Second Vatican Council, and the election of John F. Kennedy as symbols of the demise of religious separatism and the end of anti-Catholicism. Theologians perceive the changes flowing from the council in the positive character of ecumenical dialogue, pluralism in theology, new models of ecclesiology, historical criticism of scripture, liturgical reforms, an ethic of social reform and a historically conscious and inductive methodology in Catholic thought. There is a growing consensus that there were several developments in the ostensibly quiescent and conformist fifties that presaged the changes of the sixties. From both today's vantage point and the point of view of the participants the sense of significant change is becoming quite evident.[1]

The chapter opens in 1948 for several reasons: John Flanagan, S.J., a progressive educator, was completing his first year as the executive director of the CHA; the Hill-Burton Act was having its initial impact on hospital construction; Dixiecrats bolted from the Democratic convention because Harry Truman had allied himself with antisegregationists. The school system of the archdiocese of St. Louis implemented Archbishop Joseph Ritter's desegregation policy, and in the diocese of Kansas City, Missouri, the first hospital founded as a racially integrated facility was established in 1948.[2] The GI Bill provided the opportunity for Catholics to enter colleges and universities, giving them access to middle-class occupations and to housing in the new suburbs; the Christian Family Movement, symbolic of a more assertive laity, was founded in 1948. Shortly after 1948 women religious initiated the Sister Formation Conference that blended higher education with the professionalization of teachers and nurses, and prepared women religious to initiate reform and renewal within the context of the Second Vatican Council. The year 1965 is suitable for terminating this chapter because it marks the closing of Vatican Council II, the election of the first woman religious as president of the CHA, the first year of the desegregation of hospitals following the Civil Rights Act of 1964, and the passage of Medicare and Medicaid legislation.

The voluntary ideal, which had gained a considerable victory in the Hill-Burton Act, continued to dominate both the hospital lobbies in Washington as well as the legislators in Congress. But slow progress in dealing with racial discrimination illustrates the pull of tradition. Indeed the forces of continuity were so pervasive in vast areas of social and ecclesial life that the threads of change appear as pinstripes in the cloth of tradition. Originating in the period of tradition and concluding in a period of profound change this chapter will focus on the Catholic Hospital Association, Catholic responses to the health needs of African-American communities, the Sister Formation movement, and the relationship between Vatican II and the religious self-understanding of Catholic care givers.

I

The postwar years brought rapid growth to the health-care field. In the mid-1940s there were nearly 700 Catholic hospitals in the United States; by the mid-1960s the number had climbed to about 860. Over the same period bed capacity increased from around 100,000 to approximately 150,000.[3]

When Alphonse M. Schwitalla, S.J., retired from the CHA presidency in 1947, the association was poised to enter a new era. Having evolved into a complex professional association, the CHA now needed revised bylaws to more effectively distribute power and responsibility. Gone were the days when the president could also be the administrator and chief executive officer, editor of the association's journal, Washington lobbyist, and the CHA's chief public spokesperson.

Before the 1947 convention Monsignor Maurice Griffin of Youngstown, Ohio, who had been a member of the executive board throughout Schwitalla's tenure as president, proposed a series of changes in the association bylaws. Among these were a one-year term for the presidency and establishment of the office of executive director to supervise the CHA central office and be accountable to the administrative board. Later that year the CHA and St. Louis University signed a contract stipulating that the Jesuit provincial nominate two Jesuits to become the association's executive director and assistant executive director. In addition, St. Louis University would provide faculty and facilities for CHA educational programs; the association would compensate the two officers (no assistant executive director was actually appointed until 1966), and the university faculty engaged in the programs. The CHA also agreed to remain in St. Louis for the life of the contract, which could be terminated by mutual consent at the close of the annual convention.[4]

With the approval of the CHA administrative board, the provincial of the Missouri province of the Society of Jesus nominated John Joseph Flanagan, S.J., as the association's executive director, a new title representing the professionalization of the office. Born in Paton, Iowa, in 1901, Father Flanagan received his law degree from Creighton University, Omaha, in 1926, the year he entered the Society of Jesus. Ordained ten years later, he was administrative dean of St. Louis University's College of Liberal Arts in 1938 and 1939. From 1939 to 1947 he was dean of the College of Liberal Arts and then president of Regis College, Denver.[5]

Monsignor Griffin was the first CHA president to serve with Father Flanagan. Aware that the CHA could no longer depend on the leadership of one person, Monsignor Griffin worked with Father Flanagan to develop a strong central office. Having recently acquired and renovated a three-story house near St. Louis University as CHA headquarters, the association was now in a position to build up a sizable permanent professional staff. This, in turn, enabled the CHA to greatly expand the number of its standing committees. During Griffin's presidency, the CHA also organized the Conference of Catholic Schools of Nursing and, in conjunction with St. Louis University, established a graduate program in hospital administration.

In the early years of his administration, it was clear that Flanagan was leading the CHA in new directions. Symbolic of the new leadership and philosophy was the CHA's decision to take over the management and publication of the association journal, *Hospital Progress*, founded in 1920. In addition to assuming responsibility for its publication, the CHA also began publishing instructional manuals, editions of the Code of Ethics, and the Linacre Quarterly (the journal of the National Federation of Catholic Physicians' Guilds).

As the central office grew, the CHA developed a complex administrative structure. The Special Services division included programs devoted to medical ethics, legislation, and education. In the area of Professional Services were the departments of nursing service, hospital administration, voluntary guilds and auxiliaries, public relations, and financial management. In addition to programs offered at the annual convention, the CHA sponsored workshops and institutes throughout the year. Nearly 3,400 religious and laypersons attended thirty-one such regional meetings between 1948 and 1953.[6]

One of the CHA's priorities in the early years of Flanagan's administration was the development of a revised code of ethics for Catholic hospitals and health-care workers. The original code, published in the first issue of Hospital Progress (May 1920) and officially adopted by the CHA in 1921, had been obsolete for some time. For example, medical advances had made certain surgical procedures safe that had been unsafe (and therefore deemed unethical) in 1921. In addition, Catholic hospitals now were working more closely with local, state, and federal agencies, which made it imperative to articulate clear positions on issues such as birth control and contraceptive methods.

The introduction of a regular section on "Medico-Moral Problems" in the January 1948 issue of Hospital Progress was the association's first step toward a revised code of ethics. The editor of this section, Gerald Kelly, S.J., professor of moral theology at St. Mary's College, St. Mary's, Kansas, also headed a committee that reviewed ethical codes developed locally in dioceses throughout the United States and Canada. From this material and from their own contributions, the committee composed a preliminary draft of the code, which was sent to physicians and ethicists for criticism.[7] Published in 1949, the CHA's code for medical ethics, Ethical and Religious Directives for Catholic Hospitals, was a sophisticated sign of Catholic identity during the period of cultural prominence of the church in the United States.

In 1958 a grant from the Kellogg Foundation enabled the CHA to establish a Department of Continuing Education. The aim was to provide in-service refresher courses for experienced health-care professionals and basic courses for new workers. With many faculty members from St. Louis University and the CHA, the program sponsored sixteen sessions, with a total enrollment of 1,156 in 1958–1959. Another Kellogg grant in 1960 allowed the CHA to add correspondence courses, offered in conjunction with St. Louis University.[8]

The reforms of the CHA's structure reflect the considerable administrative understanding Flanagan brought to the position as executive director. Though his gracious warm personality distinguished him from his predecessor Alphonse Schwitalla, Flanagan's worldview within the context of health care places him in the tradition of Charles Moulinier rather than Schwitalla. As noted in a previous chapter Flanagan brokered a consensus in the conflict between the CHA and Sister Olivia Gowan of Catholic University. He was not a rigid Catholic separatist but rather focused on what health-care ministry can bring to its public rather than on the dangers of secular society.

In two 1959 addresses to a community conference of the Franciscan Sisters of Philadelphia, John Flanagan revealed his progressive perspective of church, hospital, and society. In the first, entitled "Spiritual Aspects of Personnel Relations," Flanagan emphasized the apostolate of Catholic health care in which "each religious seeks to sanctify herself." The apostolate attempted to reach the hundreds of thousands of patients "through the spiritual care of the chaplain and the religious." After noting that ninety percent of the hospitals' personnel are lay people Flanagan listed the public spheres encompassed by the apostolate: "salesmen, relatives of patients, business representatives, those that are met in meetings, hospital councils, state associations, national associations." He was particularly concerned that "in our dealings with our patients . . . lay personnel, . . . members of the public" that sisters and brothers be faithful to the virtues of charity and justice and "to that beautiful doctrine of the Mystical Body of Christ which we study so faithfully in the chapel. . . ."[9] Flanagan centered on social-justice issues to underscore the need to apply the religious ideals in personnel and public relations. "We can influence people in our institutions . . . and our personnel by the example we give in showing we are really and seriously interested in the welfare of patients and not just in the collection of money. And I am saying that, not in the spirit of criticism but to point out an area of interest." He referred to the social encyclicals of Popes Leo XIII and Pius XI, *Rerum Novarum* and *Quadragesimo Anno,* and "wondered why our institutions are not more zealous" in applying these principles to the wage scales of their employees. While whole hospitals have extended charity to poor patients and have "boasted that our rates were lower than others . . . we are sometimes asking our employees to underwrite the charity that we give to others" by paying them lower wages. Flanagan did not indict the sisters as callous employers; they were following "a pattern and a tradition." With characteristic candor he placed the wage question within the context of the religious life:

> Have any of you any problem with financial security? Do any of you have problems of paying rent? Do you have to worry about doctor bills for children? Do you have any idea really of the cost of living that every family has to face? You and I live in the greatest security in the world. We have no financial worries and because we have lived in that financial security, we have been isolated from some of the hardships and realities of the daily living of the lay people who have to support a family. And sometimes we have been sort of inconsistent in our philosophy. We are terribly shocked about any talk of birth control, but sometimes our employees are almost encouraged to practice birth control because of the cost of raising a family and the failure of the Catholic institutions to compensate them in a way to make it possible for them to raise a family in a Christian way. Again I say we never intended anything like that. But yet, when you look at these things from the point of view of the lay person and try to understand what it means—first of all, it would be very helpful for some of you to go down to the Cashier's Office and find out what is the actual take-home pay of some of the employees. What is taken out of the $300 salary for Social Security, for Blue Cross, for insurance, and for all of those things. And what is actually left goes to the grocer, and the landlord, and to buy clothing for children. We expect our employees, our Catholic employees, to be active members of their church, to contribute to the support of the Church, yet what do they use for money? They can't depend upon their salary. Now, I realize that when we face the problem of paying adequate salaries that are comparable to the salary in industry, we can't always do it, that we necessarily must think about higher costs, and it places upon us a burden of explaining to the public, of explaining to agencies what the cost of hospitals are, what the cost is to operate the hospital. When we go about a program taking care of the salary needs of our employees, then we must also take upon ourselves the responsibility for educating them, to explain to the people what it costs to operate a good hospital. And, Sisters, you could start very closely to home.[10]

John Flanagan also pointed to the need for improving working conditions, particularly the common occurrence of appointing a lay person to a position only to remove her or him when a qualified sister was available. He noted the general reluctance among leaders of Catholic hospitals to appoint lay persons to administrative positions. "They can go just so far. To take them into administration seems to be unheard of in some institutions, and they feel that if they are to advance in their profession . . . they perhaps should think of their future in terms of non-Catholic institutions." With remarkable insight into the tendency for administrators to treat the hospital personnel as religious superiors would treat young sisters Flanagan remarked "we are traditionally so secretive; there is so much 'hush, hush' and there's so much that reposes piously and carefully in administrator's files and is not shared with anybody." He admitted that there is a need for confidentiality but that the generally secretive character generates "suspicions in the minds of people that they think we are covering up and that is particularly true in the matter of financial reports." Hence, "nasty, ugly rumors" rooted in biases circulate in the hospital and among the public that patient fees and charitable bequests fill the treasuries of the motherhouse and the Vatican.[11]

John Flanagan's realistic assessment of the Catholic hospital of the 1950s took into consideration the fact that administration had become very complex. Indeed, the following statement has relevance in the 1990s: "It is not easy today in a modern hospital to be as efficient in a business way as one would like to be, and at the same time maintain the spirit of charity and kindness and personal attention that has been traditional in our Catholic institutions. To keep that balance in our Catholic institutions is a very definite, very difficult and very delicate responsibility. It is, however, a responsibility which, carried out, can make our institutions different from every other hospital."[12]

For Flanagan Catholic identity was not derived from separating the hospital from the putative dangers of the secular world but rather from a Christian apostolate that engages the public and is based on social-justice principles of the papal encyclicals blended with the doctrine of the Mystical Body of Christ. Contrary to the perceptions of Schwitalla, Flanagan viewed the public sphere not as a source of anti-Catholicism but as a vital center of the Catholic hospital's apostolate.

In the other address to the Franciscans Flanagan focused on professionalization within the context of Catholic identity and the tradition of Charles Moulinier. He stated that there was a general understanding of the "pure spiritual apostolate, the direct contact of the influence on souls," but that few consider the religious call "to influence people to illustrate the latter, through the quality of our professional services." He drew the analogy to the allegedly "good Catholic doctor" who is almost a daily communicant and very devotional in observing "the nine First Fridays" but who is not as dedicated to the utmost of professional competence. As if he were reacting to the Catholic idealism, the topic of chapter nine, Flanagan questioned whether or not "we have forgotten that . . . when we talk about the good Catholic doctor, about the good Catholic sister, about the good Catholic nurse" we have lost sight of the Catholic moral imperative "to be professionally as good as possible." He considered this an apostolate "because it is our means of bringing to the patients whom we say we love, in whom we say we see Christ, bringing to them the very best professional skill. That's an apostolate in itself. It's also an apostolate because it is a means of influencing those in the scientific world who do not believe that Catholics are interested in science for progress." By stressing the social-justice and professional dimensions of Catholic identity Flanagan was directing the sisters to balance their traditional idealism with practical realism as essential to an integrated hospital apostolate. He was not implying that the Glen Riddle Franciscans were particularly deviating from this balance but rather that in the contemporary hospital, traditional patterns of thought imbued with Catholic idealism were the only source of identity.[13]

II

As editor of *Hospital Progress* Flanagan's drive for social justice was manifested in the publication of several articles dealing with Catholic health care for African Americans. Because there is no comprehensive story of this ministry it is necessary to sketch several historical scenes in this neglected area of research.

In previous chapters we established the record of the Oblate Sisters of Providence during the cholera epidemics and the home for the aged run by the Holy Family Sisters, both communities of African-American women religious.[14] Another black community, The Handmaids of Mary, was established in Savannah, Georgia, in 1916. Founded by Ignatius Lissner, a French priest of the Society of African Missions responsible for missions to blacks in the diocese, the community was cofounded and led by Mother Theodore (Elizabeth) Williams, a former Franciscan sister. With Georgia's proposed legislation threatening to prohibit whites from teaching black children the community's ministry was originally intended to replace white sisters then teaching in the schools. Because the bill was never enacted into law the community was without a viable mission. Invited to Harlem by Cardinal Patrick Hayes in 1922, they established a day-care center and eventually became parochial school teachers. In 1929 they affiliated with the Third Order of St. Francis and adopted the title Franciscan Handmaids of the Most Pure Heart of Mary.[15]

In 1891 Katherine Drexel, a wealthy white heiress from Philadelphia, founded the Blessed Sacrament Sisters for Indians and Colored People, which staffed many missions, nine of which were in health care. No doubt many communities of women religious, particularly the three black communities, cared for African Americans in urban centers, but in the rural areas of the South there were few women religious available to respond to the desperate needs for health care. The inaccessibility of care persisted; the Surgeon General in 1993, an African-American woman from rural Arkansas, first visited a physician at age twenty-one.[16]

One community of women religious was established to nurse the urban poor, including many black patients. In New York, Mary Walsh, with the assistance of Peter J. O'Callaghan, C.S.P., Russell Nevins, C.S.P., and James T. McNicholas, O.P. (later archbishop of Cincinnati), formed a community to nurse the sick poor in their homes. Recognized as Tertiary Dominicans, the community officially entered the Dominican family in 1910, but since 1904 this small group of nurses called themselves the Dominican Sisters of the Sick Poor. Mother Mary Walsh remarked: "To be white and sick and poor is very hard but to be black and sick and poor is almost unbearable."[17] Sisters entered the tenements of New York, cleaned the rooms of sick, nursed the sick, fed and cared for the family, and counseled and prayed with the dying. Originally trained by nurses who had entered the community, the young sisters enrolled in Catholic nursing schools after World War I.

The Dominican Sisters of the Sick Poor spread to Ohio, Michigan, Colorado, Minnesota, and Massachusetts and in 1950 opened a new motherhouse in Ossining, New York. Though they specialized in social work as well as in nursing, the sisters still nurse the poor in their homes. The African-American poor are not central to their ministry, but their history as well as that of other home nursing orders such as the Bon Secours represents a personalist nondiscriminatory response to the poor. The Little Sisters of the Poor, though not trained nurses, cared for the elderly in their homes until they limited their ministry to nursing homes.[18]

The Black Catholic Congress of 1894 declared its opposition to racial discrimination in Catholic hospitals. The Committee of Grievances had surveyed dioceses on such discrimination and perhaps this survey was the reason why 1894 was the last congress in the nineteenth century.[19] Thomas Wyatt Turner, founder of the next movement of Black Catholics, formed the Committee for the Advancement of Colored Catholics. First organized in 1916 the committee's purpose was "the collection of data concerning colored Catholics, the protection of their interests, promotion of their welfare, and the propagation of faith among colored people." Cyprian Davis succinctly captured the committee's five-point focus: "(1) education (2) Catholic organization (3) Catholic University (4) black priests (5) racism in the Church."[20]

In 1924 the committee evolved into the Federated Colored Catholics, an attempt to organize local black activist groups into a national movement to achieve the goals of racial justice. Among the questions considered at their national meeting was the concern for health care, which was aimed at equal access to quality care and an end to racism in Catholic health care. A sense of unity prevailed among black laity and such white clerical leaders as John LaFarge, S.J., and William Markoe, S.J. However in 1932 a split occurred on the general direction of the movement; Turner was committed to black self-determination to achieve, among other goals, an end to racism in the church, while the Jesuits were in favor of promoting the cause of racial justice among white laity rather than direct action to end racism in the church. The split of 1932 resulted in Turner heading the East Coast Committee of Federated Catholics; Markoe's group in St. Louis was for a time known as the National Interracial Federation, and LaFarge founded the Catholic Interracial Council of New York. LaFarge, who had worked in the Jesuit Missions to African Americans in Ridge, Maryland, was in 1932 editor of *America*, the Jesuit weekly. He also edited the *Interracial Review*, a title that symbolized the goal of racial harmony rather than black Catholic advocacy. However, Turner, Markoe, and LaFarge considered health care among blacks to be a national disgrace.[21]

According to statistics gathered as a result of a 1928 survey of Catholic Mission Activity among the twelve million African Americans in the United States, there were 203,986 black Catholics, a figure that represented two percent of the entire black population. The vast majority lived in the South, where they encountered a Jim Crow Catholicism that reflected the area's institutionalized racism. In the North race relations were cold and distant at best. The American Medical Association reported the staggering failure of the nation's hospitals to respond equitably to the medical needs of the African-American community. In 1928 there were just 210 hospitals of all types; total beds available numbered 6,870 representing one bed for 1,941 people. Beds available for white people averaged one for every 139 persons.[22] John T. Gillard, S.S.J., whose book *The Catholic Church and the American Negro* was based on the 1928 Mission Survey, reflected on Catholic health care. "While no information is available as to how many of the 612 Catholic hospitals provide bed space for Negroes, it is definitely known that many of them refuse their ministrations to Negroes. While many Catholic hospitals receive Negroes in their wards, unofficial inquiries from a number of missioners [Gillard was a Josephite] brought to light knowledge of only one Catholic hospital with a total of two private rooms for Negroes." The latter resulted from an endowment. Gillard was appalled that black sisters "were forced to accept hospitalization in wards." The discrimination against "consecrated brides of Christ" reflected the general discrimination against blacks entering white communities of religious and the low number of vocations to the priesthood among blacks.[23] By 1928 there had only been twelve black men ordained priests, three of whom were then alive. Though there would be 120 African Americans ordained between 1933 and 1960, that was still a slim minority, considering the need for a black clergy.[24]

In contrast to Gillard's rather forceful criticism, Floyd Keeler, author of *Catholic Medical Missions,* published four years before Gillard's book, concluded that "everywhere the Catholic hospitals exist provision is made for admission of colored patients, and the contact with the Catholic sister nurse, priest or doctor is *all that could be given under the circumstances*"[25] (my italics).

The year Keeler's book was published, 1925, Anna Dengel, M.D., and three other women formed the Society of Catholic Medical Missionaries (later entitled Medical Missionary Sisters). As mentioned earlier, canon law prohibited sisters to practice medicine, surgery, and obstetrics, but in 1936 the ban was lifted for missionary sisters. Born in Steeg, Austria, in 1892 and educated to be a teacher, Anna Dengel was drawn into the study of medicine by a woman physician eager to respond to the needs of Muslim women for female physicians (Islamic law forbade them to be attended by a male doctor). After four years of service in India she sensed both a need for more women doctors and her own vocation to the religious life. During her leadership as superior general (1925–67) the society grew to seven hundred sisters, fifty health centers in thirty-three nations of the world.[26]

In her book *Mission for Samaritans,* Anna Dengel includes a section on the need for medical missions among the African-American community. She points out that while infant mortality among whites was thirty-two per ten thousand, that among blacks was seventy-eight; the average life expectancy among whites was twelve years longer than blacks. She quotes a Josephite priest, J. Schmutz, on hospital care for blacks in the diocese of Mobile, Alabama.

Of the ninety-one hospitals of Alabama and six in West Florida only sixty-five provide for Negro patients. Conditions in some of the hospitals are not the best. For example, in Morgan county the Negro beds are in a corridor of the basement. Several hospitals have no space for Negro patients, except beside a dusty coal bin, a hot boiler room, or near the steam exhaust of the laundry. A general observation shows that hospitalization of the Negro from all reports, plus a granted margin, may reach thirty thousand annually. This is part of the total of 127,496 hospitalizations reported in 1940, although by population the Alabama Negro has almost half of the total.

A fact worthy of note is that the seventh cause of death among whites is tuberculosis, while among Negroes it is the number two cause. For such cases there are 150 beds for Negroes.

Comparing Negro hospital facilities with white hospital facilities, one feels ashamed, since they are not much over twenty percent of the total, while the Negro population is almost fifty percent.[27]

According to Anna Dengel the conditions in Alabama were not untypical. In 1934 Mississippi, with blacks half of its population, only .7 beds per thousand were available to blacks. Massachusetts and New York, with their large public health-care facilities, had the most beds available for African Americans. She also listed the nine Catholic hospitals dedicated exclusively to blacks. In Austin, Texas, there was a twenty-one-bed hospital staffed by the Sisters of the Immaculate Conception of New Orleans; in Baltimore a small hospital for children and a training school for children's nursing; St. Mary's Infirmary Annex in East St. Louis, Illinois, was conducted by the Poor Handmaids of Jesus Christ, who still operate the only hospital in that impoverished city; in Ensley, Alabama, the Sisters of Charity of Nazareth, Kentucky, were planning to build a sixty-one-bed hospital that evolved from their clinic; the Daughters of Charity had a home for incurables in Perryville, Missouri; Bishop Thomas J. Toolan of Mobile sponsored a small maternity hospital in his see city; in Selma, Alabama, the Sisters of St. Joseph of Rochester, New York, conducted Good Samaritan Hospital with sixty-eight beds; the Franciscan Sisters of Peoria ran St. Philip's Annex hospital in Rock Hill, South Carolina; in St. Louis there was St. Mary's Infirmary conducted by the Sisters of St. Mary of the Third Order of St. Francis. Besides this very modest ministry there were fourteen Catholic clinics exclusively for African Americans, and the majority of free dispensaries sponsored by Catholic hospitals were open to blacks.[28]

St. Mary's Hospital in Cairo, Illinois, run by the Sisters of the Holy Cross, cared for its black patients in an annex. In its chronicle for 1931 it noted for May 15: "A colored man, Louis Randall, who had been a patient in the annex for nine weeks, expired this morning having been baptized by Father O'Flaherty at his request." On May 13, 1934, Clara Wagner died, a woman who had been cared for in the annex for eighteen years. Since St. Mary's had an arrangement with the county commission to care for indigent patients, Miss Wagner had been assigned to the hospital with a broken hip. When she recovered, "she had no place to go so we kept her, she made no trouble, and has been under Sister Brigdea's care since she came." The chronicler reported that Miss Wagner was a Lutheran "but did not want to see its minister so had Father O'Flaherty hear her confession after baptizing her conditionally and anointing her."[29] The official categories of patient admissions did not include race, but since the annex could provide extended care for eighteen years, this hospital had adequate space for black patients.

In an article soliciting funds and medical supplies in the *Linacre Quarterly*, Sister Alice Martha, S.C.N., reported on the development of Holy Family Hospital in Ensley, Alabama, in the diocese of Mobile. The Passionist priests staffed the mission there, which began as a chapel on the second floor of the rectory. A Trinitarian sister from the Cenacle was the catechist and three Felician sisters from Chicago staffed the school. Daughters of Charity of St. Vincent's Hospital in Birmingham sent a sister; two residents and two nurses set up a clinic in the school twice a week, but the need for a permanent facility was met by the Sisters of Charity of Nazareth, Kentucky, who arrived in 1941.[30] The war postponed the construction of a new hospital so they renovated three old houses previously occupied by black families to form Holy Family Hospital. The sisters lived in a duplex adjacent to the hospital. Sister Alice Martha described the housing and health conditions in Ensley: "[there were] overcrowded and miserable shacks, some have beds, others sleep on sacks or anything else they can find to put between themselves and the floor. Many of them are suffering from malnutrition, and the prevalence of tuberculosis is not surprising." She found the black people of Ensley "eager to hear about God and are much impressed with the beauties and splendor of the liturgical services. Just last Sunday fifty-five were confirmed. . . ." A strong missionary motivation was imbued into the sisters' ministry in Ensley. "Our work is to reach their souls through their broken bodies and to bring the knowledge of God to many of them who had scarcely heard of Him. Those who assist us in any way help us to realize this ideal."[31]

In 1946 Holy Family was a maternity hospital with five beds and ten bassinets with total of 167 patients treated that year. In Mobile three

Sisters of Mercy had opened Blessed Martin de Porres Hospital for the black population; in 1946 440 patients were treated in the hospital while 2,506 were outpatients in the clinic. In 1942 the Sisters of Mercy of the Baltimore Province took charge of the Martin de Porres "facility," which was actually a cottage that included a five-bed ward, a delivery room, nursery, kitchen, and a room for X-rays. At first two sisters commuted from a convent into the city while a lay nurse was responsible for the hospital at night.[32] In 1944 the sisters purchased an adjacent cottage. Father Vincent D. Warren, S.S.J., was responsible for initiating the hospital. He spent months arranging to purchase the property, meeting with politicians, black Protestant clergy and with six black and two white physicians.[33] Warren and Bishop Thomas J. Toolan were responsible for financing Martin de Porres; they initiated a fund-raising campaign for a new general-care hospital soon after the end of the war. Warren and Toolan successfully appealed to such national Catholic figures as Monsignor Fulton J. Sheen and Clare Booth Luce. The ground-breaking occurred as early as 1947. Three years later a thirty-five bed hospital opened with a staff of eight Sisters of Mercy and twenty-seven lay nurses. It was the only hospital in Mobile that had African-American physicians on the staff. Sister M. Romuald, R.S.M., wrote of her experience at Martin de Porres in 1951: "Class hatred, enmity, and bigotry are unknown. Patients are cared for in body and soul and sent home with memories of many acts of kindness and mercy."[34] The first Catholic hospital open to black physicians was in St. Louis, Missouri, a more southern than midwestern city in the 1930s and 40s.

St. Mary's Infirmary in St. Louis was the largest Catholic hospital for blacks in the United States. Operated by the Sisters of St. Mary of the Third Order of St. Francis (incorporated as simply the Sisters of St. Mary because their first community was in St. Mary's parish), the infirmary had 150 beds in 1945 and was staffed by six black physicians, thirty sisters, forty graduate nurses, and forty-five student nurses. Located near downtown St. Louis, St. Mary's Infirmary was affiliated with St. Louis University shortly after the opening of its medical school. In 1924 the community opened new St. Mary's in a western suburb and in 1933 took charge of the university's new hospital, Firmin Desloge. Though located in an area populated by many black families, the infirmary did not break the color barrier by accepting black patients. However, in preparation for their move to Firmin Desloge (which was not integrated), Mother Concordia Puppendahl , in consultation with Alphonse Schwitalla, S.J., and the president of St. Louis University, decided to continue ownership of the facility but one exclusively for black patients and physicians.[35] The Sisters of St. Mary ran the infirmary and the nursing school and continued to send sister-nurses to staff the institution. Because City Hospital Number Two, the black municipal hospital, was overcrowded, more than one hundred patients were transferred to St. Mary's Infirmary. Hence, within a year St. Mary's became a self-sustaining hospital.[36] The success of its staff physicians became a model for the city's decision to open the new black municipal hospital to black doctors. St. Mary's remained affiliated with St. Louis University (which was not integrated), and in time its physicians became faculty members at the university's medical school. It also remained as a member of the College of Physicians and the AMA. St. Mary's School of Nursing was the nation's first Catholic training school exclusively for black students.[37]

Despite the significance of St. Mary's Infirmary in the history of Catholic health care, the Episcopal Church had established hospitals and nursing schools in the later nineteenth century. There were black proprietary hospitals with private rooms for patients. Indeed by 1919 there were 118 black hospitals, seventy-five percent located in the South. There were also schools of nursing open to black students in the nineteenth century: Lincoln in New York, Freedman's in Washington, D.C., and Provident in Chicago. The National Medical Association (NMA) and the National Hospital Association (NHA), societies of black physicians and hospitals respectively, initiated reforms in accord with the standardization manual monitored by the College of Surgeons. Though the NMA and the NHA did not condone, in principle, the segregationist character of American health care, it strategically accommodated to predominant racial attitudes. During World War II there were a few integrated hospitals, but they were principally municipal facilities such as New York's Sydenham Hospital. According to historian Vanessa Northington Gamble, in 1923 there were 202 black hospitals; twenty-one years later that figure had dropped to 124 because many did not meet accreditation standards. Of these 202 hospitals the AMA approved nine and the American College of Surgeons approved twenty-three, and three were provisionally approved.[38] In this context, St. Mary's Infirmary and its nursing school were among the elite of black health-care institutions.

In the 1950s seven of the eleven nursing schools in St. Louis became integrated. The increasing breakdown of segregated education engendered the decision to close the segregated nursing school at St. Mary's Infirmary in 1958, twenty-five years after it was opened to blacks.[39] During that time 362 nurses had graduated. One of these students, Elizabeth

Louise (later Mary Antona) Ebo, was a convert to Catholicism from Bloomington, Illinois, who, after failing to break down the color barrier at a local Catholic nursing school, was admitted to St. Mary's in 1944 with tuition paid by the federal government in its cadet program. In 1946 she and two other young black women entered the segregated program of the sisters designed by Mother Puppendahl to form a separate community. The Sisters of the Good Shepherd had successfully developed such a segregated community. By the time Sister Ebo completed her undergraduate degree in 1962 the order was in the process of integrating. Active in the civil rights movement and in community governance she was the first black woman appointed administrator of a Catholic hospital, St. Clare Hospital in Barboo, Wisconsin.

The first black sister to teach at St. Mary's Infirmary was also a member of the first postulancy class of 1946.[40] Sister Hilda Rita Brickus, F.S.M., of Brooklyn, New York, who had a leg amputated at age two, at an early age "knew she wanted to enter a convent and become a nun ministering to the sick."[41] Eventually she wrote to Alphonse Schwitalla, who put her in touch with his associate and an officer of the CHA, Mother Puppendahl. Within five years she was in the postulancy program and, after completing an undergraduate degree in radiologic technology, was appointed to the staff of the hospital and nursing school. Over the years she taught in the Nursing School at St. Louis University, was a pastoral minister in a parish and hospitals, and was very active in the St. Louis community. Just as St. Mary's Infirmary and nursing school represent a first in Catholic health care Sisters Ebo and Brickus were setting the pace in integrating a religious community and dedication to health care.[42]

The foremost theologian of medical-moral issues during this period of the 1950s was Gerald Kelly, S.J. who wrote columns in *Hospital Progress* and the *Linacre Quarterly*. In his column for the latter, November 1953, Kelly included a section entitled "The Negro Physician," which opened with the news that black physicians had been admitted to the Medical Association of Charleston, South Carolina. After quoting the Associated Press article on the forthright rationale for the desegregation policy, Kelly stated: "Racial prejudice, with its external manifestation of segregation and discrimination, is a violation of justice and charity. It should have no place in any hospital or medical association, and least of all in a Catholic hospital or among Catholic members of the medical profession." To substantiate this theological reflection on racial prejudice Kelly cited Yves Congar, O.P., the prominent French theologian, who viewed such prejudice as a tacit rejection of the equality of all in God's creation and therefore an implicit "denial of God."[43]

In the same month Kelly's article appeared, there was an article in *Hospital Progress* on the first Catholic hospital founded specifically as a racially integrated facility. Bishop Edwin O'Hara, who as an activist priest had founded the Catholic Rural Life Bureau at the NCWC and the Confraternity of Christian Doctrine, was bishop of Great Falls, Montana (1930–1939), and of Kansas City (1939–1956). Influenced by the progressive social thought of John A. Ryan, O'Hara was instrumental in the passage of the nation's first minimum wage law in Oregon, supported the Jesuit Labor School at Rockhurst College, and joined the Urban League and NAACP in 1943.[44] When in 1947 a young black girl was enrolled at Loretto Academy with the approval of the sisters, O'Hara set the example for the entire diocese; she and the bishop drove to the academy, and he escorted her to class. That same year Archbishop Joseph E. Ritter desegregated the Catholic schools in the archdiocese of St. Louis; at O'Hara's suggestion St. Vincent's Maternity Hospital in Kansas City desegregated every phase of its operation, physicians, nurses, and patients. Though there had been an element of white backlash to the desegregation process a report of the Human Relations Department of the University of Kansas stated that the Daughters of Charity "would make everything work." It concluded that despite the fact the "entire gambit of racial emotions could be found" at St. Vincent's, integration was succeeding without overt rancor. Because maternity departments in general had been dominant for many years, most small specialty facilities for maternity cases were virtually obsolete. Hence, when the Daughters of Charity decided to close St. Vincent's in 1953, the decision was not caused by problems with integrating the facility. The November 1953 issue of *Hospital Progress* featured an article on the desegregation of St. Vincent's.[45] By this time O'Hara had decided that the diocese would purchase it to transform it into an integrated general hospital. At the annual Labor Day Mass in September 1953, Bishop O'Hara spoke on the need for racial justice in the community, particularly within the area of health care.

> In Kansas City, one tenth of our people are selfishly denied proper facilities for the adequate training of the physicians to whom they naturally look for medical advice and care. This is a disgrace. . . . I speak of the now well-known fact that there is not in the metropolitan area . . . an accredited and properly equipped general hospital to which a Negro doctor can take a patient for care. . . .
>
> This is my message to Kansas City on this Labor Day: no longer to deny intelligent Negro doctors the opportunity of employment in their skilled profession. . . . Kansas City must provide without delay accredited and

properly equipped hospital facilities in which competent Negro physicians may work side by side with white members of their profession in promoting the health of this community.[46]

Never one to speak in platitudes O'Hara immediately laid plans for a fully integrated general hospital with an emphasis on mission to the black community. O'Hara successfully appealed to the Maryknoll Sisters of St. Dominic to staff the hospital and received funds for renovation and a new addition to St. Vincent's from the Commission on Indian and Colored Missions and the American Board of Catholic Missions. According to the bishop's biographer, Timothy Michael Dolan, many people "were appalled by the thought of such an integrated institution. As O'Hara himself went from home to home, business to business, seeking help, he 'had many a door slammed in his face.'" The new facility, Queen of the World Hospital, was staffed by seventeen sisters and fifty-six lay nurses; it had a bed capacity of ninety-one. The hospital became a *de facto* black facility, but O'Hara "was delighted with the excellent new hospital offering first-class care to blacks. However, he was far more pleased that black physicians now had an accredited institution in which to treat their patients." With this experience as a basis, O'Hara strongly recommended that the administrators of all Catholic hospitals follow suit. "One of the most important matters is the unchristian status of colored doctors in the hospitals of Missouri. . . . The Consultors of our diocese have joined me in requesting the Catholic hospitals of the diocese to end this discrimination against competent Negro physicians during this Marian year."[47] As a result of the force of O'Hara's policy the hospitals became integrated.

In his doctoral dissertation, "The Catholic Church and the Washington Negro," Albert S. Foley, S.J., analyzed the historical patterns of segregation and the initial measures to break down the racist barriers in the late 1940s when Archbishop Patrick O'Boyle initiated integration of Catholic facilities. Segregation prevailed in both Georgetown and Providence hospitals until the late 1940s, when Georgetown allowed for integrated floors and an open admissions policy for private, semiprivate and four-bed wards. Hence, the annex system had been discarded, but segregated semiprivate and four-bed wards persisted. Providence continued the segregation practices until a new facility fostered change. The nursing school was desegregated, while Georgetown had an open enrollment but had not accepted a black student by 1949, the year Foley completed his research. However, without black students enrolled in the medical school the physicians' staff remained white enclaves.[48] Indeed, it would not be until several years after the passage of the Civil Rights Act of 1964 that all Catholic health-care facilities were desegregated. By that time the social activism of many lay and religious involved in health care was imbued with a determination to break down racial barriers in church and society.

III

In 1965 women religious were in the process of experimentation, renewal, and adaptation. Among communities designated as active or apostolic the rules governing the traditional enclosure had been revised. Because many sisters were becoming well versed in the trends in theology, spirituality, and in their areas of professional competence, a common refrain related to how well prepared they were for the changes emanating from Vatican Council II. Historians trace the source of this consciousness to the Sister Formation Conference.

In a seminal article in the *U.S. Catholic Historian* entitled "American Sisters and the Roots of Change: The 1950s," Mary L. Schneider, O.S.F., an authority on the conference, discusses three "key movements or developments" entailed in the initial stages of adaptation and renewal of religious life: "1) internal community [changes] . . . such as horarium and habit; 2) greater professionalization of sisters, especially those engaged in teaching, and [its] relationship of . . . professionalization to the overall formation program . . .; 3) the call to greater cooperation and collaboration among congregations."[49] Pius XII and the Congregation for Religious fostered "renovation and adaptation" particularly in accord with the spirit of the congregation's founder and with the demands of professional competency. Indeed the conference frequently cited Pius XII in encouraging adaptation. Professor Schneider points out that the simplifications of the habit occurred among relatively few congregations, and many of those were made to allow sisters to have lateral vision as drivers of automobiles. "If one call was to dress reasonably," said Schneider, "another was to pray reasonably," with the intention of balancing "prayer, work, and recreation," in order to strengthen the "apostolic effectiveness of the community."[50] The enclosures were restraints upon the professional nurse or teacher eager to attend meetings at night or on the weekends.

By 1942 there were 117 Catholic women's colleges in the United States, most of which were founded to provide higher education for sisters of the sponsoring congregation. However, by the late 1940s the demand for teaching and nursing sisters was so high that the young sisters' formation and education was often interrupted. Even when they were allowed to pursue an undergraduate degree there was a collision between religious formation and college education. Though adaptations were proceeding at a glacial pace in the late 1940s and early 50s there was still a conservative backlash that these changes represented capitulation to "worldliness." As Schneider points out, "the question of changes in the habit, horarium and life style . . . begged the very [question] . . . a *theology of the religious life* for active congregations"[51] (her italics).

The Sister Formation Conference originated in the National Catholic Educational Association (NCEA). Sister Madeleva Wolff, C.S.C., president of St. Mary's College, Notre Dame, well known for her academic leadership, was a force behind the 1948 establishment of the teacher education section of the NCEA. Four years later Sister Mary Emil Penet, I.H.M., initiated a survey of "pre-service" preparation among congregations, the results of which ultimately led to what was entitled in 1954 the Sister Formation Conference (SFC), chaired by Sister Penet. Originally aimed at improving "the pre-service and certification programs," Sister Emil later articulated its purpose as "not only for education of the sister in the formal and academic sense, but for all the influences, spiritual and intellectual, formal and informal, pre-service and in-service which go to make her a better religious and a better professional person."[52] The restructuring of formation included postponing ministry and incorporating a undergraduate degree program. For those who had such degrees, programs in theology, spirituality, and graduate studies were available. Though initially intended to provide for an integrated formation program for teaching sisters, the SFC soon applied to nursing sisters as well. The *Bulletin* for the conference represents the first publication by sisters and for sisters; the *Proceedings* published the papers of regional meetings. Located within the NCEA College and University Department, the SFC *Bulletin* listed the ten members of the National Consultation Committee, composed of nine priests and one brother active in the NCEA. However, the Governors Committee was entirely composed of sisters.[53]

The eighth issue of the *Sister Formation Bulletin* was devoted to hospital sisters. The lead article focused on the patterns of change occurring in medicine and nursing within the context of religious formation under the theme "From Bedside Nursing to Personnel Work," by Sister M. Agnita Claire Day, S.S.M., Director of the School of Nursing, Madison, Wisconsin. The article opened with a historical reflection of the evolution from the "tiny Catholic hospitals in which sisters, medical staff, and a few lay persons functioned together as a 'family unit.' . . . In their place in the space of a few short years have appeared multi-million dollar, highly organized institutions employing hundreds of professional, technical, and subsidiary personnel. . . ."[54] She related the "wonder drugs" and the enhanced communications of recent treatments to the increase in a "health conscious public" supported by "many types of health and hospital insurance." The result was "an almost insatiable demand for hospital services."[55] The rate of expansion of hospital beds to meet the demand was proportionally far greater than the rate of vocations to hospital sisterhoods and "has created unprecedented problems" particularly related to professional and religious formation of young sisters. Though she emphasized the spiritual, philosophical, psychological, and sociological understanding so necessary for balancing education and clinical service as well as profession and vocation, she made a strong case for preparing sisters to enter professional organizations and "civic health projects." Sister Day understood the benefits of such activism.

> The prudent, experienced, and tactful sister-nurse can do much good taking an active part in such work. If she will accept an office or a committee membership, she can exercise constructive leadership by helping to formulate sound organizational policies, point out errors of judgement, and stimulate the adoption of worthwhile programs. The sisters are welcomed and respected by other members of these organizations. Are they prepared to accept this role of active leadership on a local, state, or national level as a part of their apostolate? The well-educated, cultured, experienced religious has much to contribute to the welfare of the community in which she lives.[56]

Sister Olivia Gowan, O.S.B., dean of the School of Nursing at the Catholic University of America, had been articulating this professional activism since the early 1930s. Obviously, the customs of many religious congregations prohibited sisters from professional interaction within secular organizations or else this exhortation would not have been so strongly asserted. Catholic idealism with its defense of the feminine mystique against the professionalization of women, particularly sisters, was manifested in a triumphalistic separatism. Hence, the significance of the SFC is that structural changes in education, such as the pre-service requirement of an undergraduate degree, ultimately led to a new class of young sisters more professionally competent and religiously confident than their predecessors.

Another article in this edition of the *Sister Formation Bulletin* charted the developments in nursing that required changes in sister formation. Because the dominant trend was "to see that the patient is nursed rather than to do the nursing herself" sisters must be trained for these managerial responsibilities, that is, team leadership, supervision, and administration. Written by a Sister Mary Ruth, S.S.J., a Sister of St. Joseph of the Wheeling, West Virginia, congregation, this article is a remarkably realistic assessment of the need for religious and professional growth. "If sisters could adopt the rule of life that 'the need of the hour is the will of God' then they would find it less difficult to adjust to new tasks in nursing, new concepts in administration and new facts in the scientific and professional worlds. We are told that one may be 'old' psychologically at twenty-five if one refuses to accept new ideas and thereby acquires a closed mind."[57] Admitting that many Catholic lay nurses had received a theological background in their undergraduate program, Sister Ruth urged that formation include courses in theology "in order that . . . [a sister] may know the great truths of [her] religion, at least as well as some of the graduates of Catholic colleges with whom she will be associating." She also emphasized communications and human relations so that sisters "can spiritualize things as well as persons." Her list of topics in spirituality reveals an attempt to unify human and religious experiences: "(1) devotion to God's Holy Will; (2) the value of joy in God's service; (3) the cardinal virtues; (4) the positive aspects of the vows and the importance of Christ-like human relations." She said that since sisters will tend to be placed in supervisory positions with the imperative to "help staff personnel of all types realize their professional potentialities" they must have an abundance of human understanding. If the sister's own novitiate was dominated by a "climate of warmth and friendliness" and if "the young sister is accepted as a person and her basic needs are understood, she will develop feelings of relative adequacy and greater capacity for supervision. She will learn to be an interested listener and to accept persons as they are, with all their differences." Hence, she placed "skill in human relations" as the "one single quality needed by the sister-nurse today as compared with the past. . . . [The sister-nurse] is expected to deal with all types of persons as a cultured Christian woman. In essence good human relations are good Divine Relations."[58] A nascent feminist consciousness is implicit in the call for authority's recognition of the sisters' need for "feelings of relative adequacy."

The professional formation of the sister-nurse had been a principal motif of the Catholic Hospital Association. Charles B. Moulinier's Spring Bank experimentation in continuing education included religious as well as educational components. Under John J. Flanagan the

CHA cooperated with St. Louis University in organizing a graduate program in hospital administration in 1948. The association sponsored institutes for nurses, pharmacists, and others and formed a Council on Hospital Financial Management and regional conferences for provincial and general superiors on hospital operations on such topics as policies (1953 and 1954), on medical-moral issues, on the role of canon law and civil law in relation to Catholic hospitals and on many others.

At the 1956 CHA convention the Sister Formation Conference was represented by Sister Penet. She gave eloquent testimony to the conference's aim to help the young sister become "an informed, interesting, cultured person with a high degree of social ability."[59] In a paper presented to a CHA-sponsored symposium on the Formation of Hospital Religious in May of 1956 John J. Flanagan, S.J., listed the multifaceted character of hospital administration that calls for professional knowledge and skills, a refined religious perspective, and a personal sophistication. Hence, he enthusiastically endorsed the SFC and noted the CHA and SFC interests to "provide for future outstanding leaders able to carry on the work of Catholic hospitals."[60] In accord with the original thrust of the CHA, Flanagan referred to the significance of accreditation and the need for the sister-administrator to be a "diplomat to lead and guide highly professional men into an effectively organized staff which is conscious of responsibilities to the hospital, as well as to individual patients and to themselves. The psychology and art of human relations are most necessary tools of the administrator."[61] The SFC fostered a commitment among religious institutes to establish degree programs for their junior sisters, but St. Louis University and the CHA were committed to form department heads, hospital administrators capable of leading the Catholic hospital to accreditation and embodying a blend of professional expertise and the religious life. The significance of the SFC is clearly revealed in Marie Augusta Neal's sociological analysis of women religious included in her work *From Nuns to Sisters*: "Of those [sisters] living in 1966, only 5% had entered with a degree. Only 20% had fathers whose occupation was classified as professional, and only 6% of their fathers and 3% of their mothers had college degrees. Yet, in 1967, 68% of the sisters themselves had at least a college degree and by 1980 that number was 88%, with 68% having advanced degrees."[62]

Some of those junior sisters who received their degrees during this period were graduates of one of the two colleges established within the SFC movement: Marillac College in St. Louis was founded by the Daughters of Charity in 1955 exclusively for sisters and in the mid-sixties enrolled four hundred students representing thirty religious congregations; Providence Heights College (1957) sponsored by the Sisters of Charity of Providence in Seattle, with an enrollment of 240 sisters from four congregations. Each had nursing programs; Sister John Gabriel Ryan of the Sisters of Charity of Providence achieved national status as a nursing educator while Sister Bertrande Meyers, D.C., one of the founders of Marillac, had written a doctoral dissertation, "The Education of Sisters" (1941), that was a precursor to the speeches and documents fundamental to the SFC.[63] By the time these colleges were formed the SFC was under the Conference of the Major Superiors of Women. The latter encouraged attendance at the Institutes of Theology held at Notre Dame, introducing women religious to recent trends among European and American theologians.

Pius XII had not only encouraged religious to adapt to the demands of their professional requirements but he encouraged Catholic biblical scholars to adapt their studies to the methodologies of the general field of scripture scholarship. The Liturgical Press at St. John's in Collegeville, Minnsesota, published *Worship* and *Sponsa Regis*; the former reflected the advance in the liturgical movement and in theological and scripture studies; the latter was a publication for sisters that emphasized the spiritual basis of adaptation of structures and adoption of new academic programs. These developments represented a minority movement that prepared lay activists and religious for leadership roles in the 1960s.

IV

The election of Pope John XXIII, the social encyclicals *Mater et Magistra* (1961) and *Pacem in Terris* (1963) and conciliar documents issued during the years 1963–65 profoundly affected the religious self-understanding of a generation of Catholics, including those involved in health care. Of all the documents issued by the Second Vatican Council, those on the church, the missions, and the religious life had the most profound impact on religious communities. Joseph A. Komonchak, a theologian with a particular interest in ecclesiology, captures the significance of *Lumen Gentium*, the Dogmatic Constitution on the Church: "It begins with a view of the church as Mystery, as the community of men and women called together with participation in the triune God. This communion . . . makes them the people of God, the body of Christ, and the Temple of the Spirit." The church is sacrament, one of both unity and redemption; inspired by the Holy Spirit "each disciple of Christ has the obligation of spreading the faith to the best of his [or her] abilities."[64] Combined with the decree on the Apostolate on the Laity, *Lumen Gentium* is an official legitimation of the lay activism embodied in the Christian Family Movement, the Young Christian Workers, the Young Christian Students, and other forms of specialized Catholic Action. However the conciliar documents place the source of this call to action in the sacraments of initiation, baptism and confirmation.

The decree on the church's missionary activity, *Ad Gentes*, explored the process of bringing the gospel and the church to people unacquainted with Christianity but went beyond traditional notions as it emphasized the inherent relationship between mission and human development referred to as "inculturation." The Pastoral Constitution on the Church, *Gaudium et Spes*, states that the church grows in Catholicity when it enters "into communion with different forms of culture thereby enriching both itself and cultures themselves."[65] Based on an incarnational approach to all peoples, inculturation sounded the death knell to ecclesiastical triumphalism, the basis of Catholic separatism.

Lumen Gentium's chapter on the religious life is infused with "the universal call to holiness." Juliana Casey, I.H.M., notes the latter significance as a "call" to a new "understanding of religious life as part of the church's grace and mission, but not as one that is "higher," "more perfect." The choice of religious life is not a "better" choice than any other. *Lumen Gentium* describes religious life "as a gift of the Holy Spirit to the church, assisting it in carrying out its mission" as sacrament.[66]

The Decree on the Appropriate Renewal of the Religious Life, *Perfectae Caritatis,* builds on Pope Pius XII's 1950 exhortation that inspired the Sister Formation Conference. But the decree of Vatican II had a transformationist impact to the understanding of the principles of adaptation and renewal as they relate to the external and internal characters of renewing religious life: "(1) a continuous return to the sources of all Christian life and to the original inspiration behind any community; (2) an adjustment of the community to the changed conditions of the times."[67] The first principle fostered study of scripture, theology, and the history of the community changes which partially influenced the ways religious perceived the means to adapt to the times in terms of governance, ministry, the horaria, continuing education programs, religious garb, and meanings of community. As will be noted in the next chapter this entailed composition of new constitutions and rules of life that required several years to complete.

Because 13,618 women religious staffed about 803 hospitals in 1965 the Second Vatican Council is profoundly meaningful in the history of Catholic health care.[68] Even during the council a spirit of rising expectations was common among the young sisters and brothers influenced by the recent trends in theology, ecclesiology, scripture, and spirituality, and the wide-ranging coverage of the debates and movements for social and political change.

V

As noted in the beginning of this chapter the year 1965 marks the end of Vatican Council II as well as the massive civil rights demonstration in Selma, Alabama, the fiftieth anniversary of the Catholic Hospital Association, and the passage of Medicare and Medicaid legislation. The next chapter will deal with the new directions in church, society, and health care during the period 1965–1990. Though it will also consider the profound changes in the religious life of congregations of hospital sisters and brothers, the need for these changes is evident in the civil rights movement.

In his book *The History of Black Catholics in the United States,* Cyprian Davis, O.S.B., points out that by and large Catholics, both black and white, were not in the forefront of the civil rights movement or among the leadership of the protest organizations. The absence of Catholics in the movement derived from the paucity of black Catholic priests, sisters, and brothers and from the general "notion that it was unseemly" for priests and religious "to engage in public spectacles like demonstrations." There were Catholic laity, clergy, and religious at the interracial gathering at Lincoln Memorial (August 28, 1963), where the Reverend Martin Luther King, Jr., delivered his famous "I have a dream" speech, but it was the march at Selma, Alabama, to which the Reverend King invited clergy of all faiths that drew numerous priests, sisters, and brothers, a response that represented "a real change in Catholic attitudes."[69] Many orders of religious women and men were responding to the call for integration within their communities and an end to discrimination in society.

The Sisters of Mercy of the Union (formed in 1929 of thirty-nine of the sixty independent motherhouses) had evolved a policy on social equality by May of 1965. Based on a compilation of proposals from the provinces, Mother General M. Regina Cunningham's policies included immediate desegregation of the Mercy Sisters of the Union and all their schools, hospitals, and other institutions. Regina Werntz, R.S.M., summarized the policy. "Prayer, teaching, and example constituted three levels of involvement in promoting social equality."[70] Permission of the local bishop expressed through the sister provincial was required before sisters could engage in demonstrations for racial justice. Policy governing participation in protests had been operative in each province in February and March when some sisters marched in Selma. Nursing Sisters M. Aloysius Warnock and M. Charlene Curl were recruited by Archbishop John Dearden of Detroit for the demonstrations to implement the law guaranteeing the rights of all to register and vote. The two nursing sisters were dressed in their traditional habit with the white aprons, as they were "on duty" in the event violence erupted.[71] Thomas Joseph Toolen, bishop of Mobile-Birmingham, prohibited sisters from marching in his diocese; "he had little sympathy for the aspirations of the black community."[72] It is noteworthy that the 1958 statement "American Catholic Bishops and Racism" was not a pastoral letter but a simple letter published by the administrative board of the NCWC as representative of the bishops.[73] The pastoral letter was published in 1979. The strong Catholic presence in Selma illustrates the fact that the majority of bishops supported the demonstration.

Ten years later, after the passage of a new constitution, the Sisters of Mercy were no longer restrained by prior permission to exercise their First Amendment rights; policy statements were not derived from the views of provincials but from a committee structure based on a participatory rather than a hierarchical model, and there were developments of small communities and a proliferation of ministries. The Sisters of Mercy remained strongly committed to health care, but the changes in community life profoundly affected the way that commitment was realized.

In 1965 a revision of the bylaws of the CHA opened the association presidency to a woman religious for the first time. Two years later, Sister Mary Brigh Cassidy, O.S.F., administrator of St. Mary's Hospital, Rochester, Minnesota, became the first woman religious to serve as president of the board of trustees of the CHA.[74] Speeches at the 1966 convention reflected the council's initial influence upon the religious understanding of the association. One of the principal speakers, Mother Vincentia, of the Sisters of St. Francis, Maryville, Missouri, urged that religious institutes involved in health care learn to accept their interdependence with lay communities. "We are advocating a departure from the past not only in our thinking, but also in the actual workings of what we know as 'sisters' hospitals,'" she asserted. "I mean specifically the partnership of laymen [sic] and religious as opposed to a subservient role on the part of the layman."[75]

Another speaker, Robert G. Hoyt, editor of the *National Catholic Reporter*, noted that post-Vatican II laity were abandoning "formula religion" and seeking new structures and practices to narrow "the gap between principle and reality." Hoyt went on to assert that "among serious people of our time, personal intellectual integrity is perhaps the highest of all values."[76] John F. Cronin, S.S., assistant director of the NCWC's Department of Social Action, urged CHA members to recognize the benefits of working with organized labor and to acknowledge employees' rights to decent wages. "Canon Law," he noted, "makes no provision for vicarious vows of poverty." He also praised the stand on racial integration of Catholic schools taken by Cardinal Joseph Ritter in St. Louis, Cardinal Lawrence Shehan in Baltimore, and Cardinal Patrick O'Boyle in Washington, D.C. Father Cronin declared that Catholic health-care facilities should integrate all departments and end discriminatory personnel policies.[77]

Monsignor John A. Trese of Detroit, who became CHA president in June 1966, reminded the audience that one of the basic themes of Vatican II was that those in authority must serve. The church, Trese noted, must be committed to serving "the whole human family." To accept this obligation, he continued, is to participate "in a conversation with the community about man's problems" and to "engage in a cooperative effort with other community institutions . . . to lessen men's sufferings." Trese also stressed the importance of accepting "the role and responsibility of the laity in the family of God" and to "re-examine the traditional pattern of automatic assignment of religious to positions of administration and supervision."[78]

VI

The structural changes in the church were paralleled by transformation of health care. The growth of private hospital insurance plans between 1940-65 was phenomenal: from 9% of the population to 71.4%, figures that reflect the increasingly successful expansion of employee benefits packages either through union-management negotiations or through professional and administration's "rights" of employment. Total insurance benefits paid by Blue Cross and other types of health insurance increased from $772 million in 1948 to $8.7 billion in 1964. The increased demand in the medical marketplace engendered expenditures in facilities, medical technology in research, in additional personnel, and increases in physicians' fees. From 1945–64 personnel grew from 150 to 250 per 100 patients. Between 1945 and 1969 physicians' fees grew by 3.8% per year while the inflation rate was at 2.8%; annual income during those years went from $8,000 to $32,000.[79] Rather than collapse these latter figures into simplistic economic motivation, it is important to recall that altruism and the immersion in medical science were also significant motivational factors in the practice of medicine.

Rosemary Stevens captured the demand–supply dynamic: "The pot of gold held out by third-party payers encouraged hospitals to respond to the market incentives of increased demand by providing more expensive and better care, in areas that were most likely to be reimbursed." Without regional planning mechanisms there was an excessive utilization of hospital care which evolved from almost entirely acute care to include large outlays for rehabilitative and intensive care. By 1960 it was quite evident that the rise in hospital costs for quality care excluded millions of people without insurance, particularly the elderly. In response to a 1961 report of seven million elderly people without insurance and with an income of less that $3,000, the health-care spokesperson of the NCWC perceived this group as including "widows, orphans, disabled and dependent aged."[80] Since 1950 there was a federal program for the indigent—"vendor payments"—that is, grants to states which were directly allocated to pay hospitals and physicians' fees; but it was inadequate to meet the needs, was too dependent on the states, and the means test was a deterrence to anyone, even the poor, who had been absorbed into the ethos of social and economic independence. Certainly most of the elderly would not easily assert their indigent status, and because of savings and a small income they may not have qualified for state payments for hospital and physicians' fees.[81]

As mentioned in a previous chapter, in the 1930s and 40s there had been legislative proposals introduced that would impose a compulsory health insurance program financed through social security. In the 1950s liberals in government and the public and private sectors of insurance companies and hospital administrators were promoting compulsory insurance for only the poor and the elderly, but they could never muster congressional support until Lyndon Johnson's 1964 landslide victory brought a large Democratic majority in Congress under the banner of a War on Poverty. The result was the Kerr-Mills bill that provided Medicare coverage for hospitalization and physicians' fees for the elderly and Medicaid coverage for the poor. The emphasis was on acute care in hos-

pitals rather than treatment of chronic problems in a nonhospital setting. Funded and administrated by the Social Security Administration
private insurance companies acted as third parties or agents for the distribution of funds. Like private health insurance Medicare had its
deductible and limitations on days in hospital and in recovery nursing
homes.

The significant rise in insurance patients from twenty-four percent to
seventy-one percent led Rosemary Stevens to conclude: "Even in the
1950s relatively little care was actually given away deliberately by nonprofit hospitals. Charity by voluntary hospitals, where it did exist, was
often inadvertent."[82] Catholic hospitals, like most voluntary facilities,
almost entirely dependent on fees from patients, could not afford to
have a full open-door policy. The continuous increase in employees per
hundred patients would tend to decrease the visibility and influence of
the sisters and brothers, thereby supportive of Stevens's generalization.
However, the traditional charitable imperative, which Colin Jones refers
to as an aspect of hospital sisters' *raison d'être*, was viable in this era.[83]
Though I have not examined patient account records for the years 1945–
65, there were hundreds of Catholic hospitals located in small towns and
in heavily Catholic urban areas where physicians, priests, school sisters,
and laity could confidently refer uninsured patients and friends, where
portions of their bills would not be readily collectable. When the
Catholic hospital was the only facility in the town it frequently had a
contract with the city or county government to care for indigent patients
at a rate below the average. Also most outpatient facilities had originated
as free dispensaries and still maintained a charitable character. For
example, in 1965 thirty-one Adorers of the Blood of Christ of Ruma, Illinois, staffed St. Vincent Memorial Hospital, a 155-bed facility in Tay-
lorville, Illinois, an isolated area in the midwestern part of the state. Not
only did they care for 12,784 outpatients in 1964, but one may assume
that some of the 5,338 patients were charity cases, not inadvertently
admitted.[84] Though the sister-administrator was as fiscally responsible
as the typical hospital administrator, members of her religious community were on the board of directors; they represented countervailing factors influencing the fiscal equation. Many religious in hospital ministry
were members of communities with missions in Latin America, Africa,
and the Far East and were in solidarity with impoverished people of
developing nations. Characteristic of religious life in the 1960s was a
general response to the pleas for the preferential option for the poor and
the need for community action programs in the inner cities that fre-

quently included a health-care component. Influenced by liberation theology of the later 1960s many religious considered large health-care institutions to be almost impervious to a genuine response to the poor, thereby confirming Stevens's generalization. In 1965 the prevailing perspective was grounded in a strong sense of hope. Vatican II, the War on Poverty, the leadership of Martin Luther King, reforms of the CHA, and the establishment of the Medicare/Medicaid programs—all of these represented the culmination of developments originating in the late 1940s and early 50s. However, from the vantage point of 1965 the previous few years appeared almost revolutionary as the spirit and structure of religious and hospital life were in the process of a total transformation.

CHAPTER TWELVE

Religious Renewal, Lay Ministry, and the CHA

THE SOCIAL AND MEDICAL HISTORY of the voluntary hospital was profoundly affected by Medicare and Medicaid and by new technologies in several phases of diagnosis, treatment, and surgery. Designed to enhance the elderly's access to health care, Medicare also dramatically increased hospitals' operating margins. This was evident in the growth of the for-profit investor-owned hospital chains during the 1970s and the development of a new subspecialty, hospital financial management. The voluntary hospital departed from its traditional reliance on the community's philanthropy by generating capital-improvement funds, borrowing money, and issuing bonds. This breakdown in community voluntarism and the ascendancy of hospital administration along the lines of the corporate model with CEOs and "bottom line" rhetoric created a climate of doubt about the altruistic character of not-for-profit hospitals and eventually challenged their tax-exempt status.[1]

By increasing the hospital's operating margins, Medicare and new technologies also increased the cost of care. Since 1970 double-digit hospital inflation has become the norm, and by the 1980s the government's policy to hold down costs has been to designate in advance what it will pay for various services, the "prospective payment system." Beginning in the mid-1980s hospitals experienced losses from the Medicare program; patient-days were drastically reduced. To cut costs and increase patient services there has been a proliferation of out-patient facilities. The recent trends are toward satellite primary-care facilities, analogous to the old dispensaries, to expand access to medical care. Hence the 1980s began with the dominance of the marketplace and ended with the revival of the community consciousness of the mid-1960s.

Among Catholic care givers, these trends have challenged their sense of religious identity. As the hospitals were experiencing restructuring, the religious institutes sponsoring hospitals were also experiencing profound changes, many of which flowed out of the Second Vatican Council, while others stemmed from social factors relating to the rise of feminism and to the professional self-understanding of religious men and women as well as the religious self-understanding of lay nurses and administrators. Of course the quantitative decline of religious and the rise of lay ministry in general are especially significant factors in the recent history of Catholic health care. This chapter traces developments in religious life, pastoral care, moral theology, canon law, the Catholic Hospital (later Health) Association in the context of the post–Vatican II church.

I

The Sister Formation Conference, founded to prepare women religious to be well-educated, spiritually mature, cultured, professional teachers and nurses, was perceived in the 1950s as "change within stability; ferment within obedience."[2] In the post–Vatican II period stability tended to be viewed as tradition's inhibition of constructive change while obedience was transposed to consensus, collegiality, and subsidiarity, all new principles of governance in the ferment of renewal and reform.

Even before the end of Vatican II some religious had experienced a sense of frustrated expectations concerning traditional authority. Historian Patricia Byrne, C.S.J., cites Michele Bernstein's comments to illustrate the stresses and strains of professional women religious in the early 1960s. "Nuns were trying to do modern jobs under medieval systems." Women religious in responsible positions of authority in hospitals and schools lived according to traditions that stipulated such anachronisms as kneeling to ask for permission from a superior. "Every day life got smaller. Religious life had become a celebration of the trivial."[3] Theologian Patricia Smith, R.S.M., quoted a sister who noted her preposterous situation: "I am responsible for a $3 million budget but I can't drive to a meeting at night without special permission."[4]

Though in his 1966 motu proprio *Ecclesiae Sanctae* Paul VI referred to the need to call special chapters or assemblies for "renewal and adaptation," it would have been more accurate to designate these as "constitutional conventions." Patricia Byrne captures the significance of rewriting the constitutions and rules of life: "For many communities, chapters that were held during the 1960s were the first time there had been systematic community involvement in their preparation. Sisters undertook renewal from the ground up, in all that sisters were called to participate, through study, discussion groups, and recommendations to the chapter." Many delegates to these meetings found the process of redesigning governance, exploring spiritualities and new understandings of ministries exhilarating if not "transforming." However, many were alienated by the changes; most communities experienced polarization with its tendency to delegitimate the voices of moderation. Byrne remarks: "It was a time of excruciating pain for congregations when, for the first time in their remembered history, conflicting mentalities had to battle it out over new terrain, with no authoritative formulation ready at hand to settle disputes."[5]

From the vantage point of the traditionalists the changes appeared to signal the rise of individualism and the end of authority, the bonds of community. Amid the excitement of liturgical change, a full dialogue Mass in the vernacular with guitars and folk songs, conservatives reacted with a concern for loss of the sense of the sacred. The symbolic boundaries of the separate enclosures of the religious life, where devotionalism tended to thrive, was doubly drastic to those who identified meanings of religious life with symbols of distinction. The conciliar call to universal holiness among the people of God had been responsible for perceiving the cloister as "upperstory Christianity," a center of religious privilege, that had to be abandoned by sisters and brothers if they were to respond to the cries for social and racial justice with integrity.[6]

A recognition of pluralistic life-style gradually became the prevailing ethos of religious congregations. The drive toward professionalism that originated in the Sister Formation Conference would have eventually broken down traditional structures of the religious life. By the 1960s sister- and brother-nurses and administrators no longer perceived the hospital as their home but as a professional work place, with its perceived hectic pace of activity. The routine of traditional convent life could not have withstood the professional demands for continuing education, weekend conferences, and national organizations, all of which presupposed the need for personal autonomy. Vatican II fostered a personalist understanding of renewal of community that legitimated the needs for autonomy. By the early 1970s there were small communities of religious, many of whom were involved in "hands on" ministries ranging from parish soup kitchens to clinics in Appalachia. The religious activists were nurtured by various spiritualities, congregational charisms, and gospel readings but in the world of postconciliar renewal theirs was not the idealism of the early 1960s but rather one that was tempered by the declining expectations of the period of the late 1960s and early 70s.

In 1968 the dreams of the Great Society were foundering on the rocks of the war in Vietnam, the urban riots in the wake of Martin Luther King's assassination, and the violent confrontation at the Democratic National Convention. In Catholic life the year 1968 witnessed several areas of conflict: antiwar protests of the Catonsville Nine, led by Fathers Daniel and Philip Berrigan; the promulgation of *Humanae Vitae* reaffirming the ban on the use of artificial birth control, a teaching that elicited open dissent by many priest-theologians.[7] By 1975 Watergate, the end of the war in Vietnam, and Roe v. Wade were sources of social discontent. Between 1965 and 1975 the number of Catholic hospitals dropped from 803 to 671, and the number of sisters involved in health care fell from 13,618 to 8,980.[8] This loss in hospital sisters was not due to the proliferation of new ministries but rather to the growing numbers of women leaving the religious life.

The Conference of Major Superiors of Women (CMSW) sponsored a survey of women religious from 1966 to 1968, under the direction of Marie Augusta Neal, S.N.D.deN., of Emmanuel College in Boston. Lora Ann Quiñonez, C.D.P., and Mary David Turner, S.N.D.deN., summarized Neal's study. With an eighty-eight percent response rate, the survey "showed that 68.2 percent shared a strong preference for post-Vatican II ideals. That is, they tended to see God as acting among people in a world undergoing massive change (as opposed to God as transcendent other). They saw diverse projects directed toward social justice as places of ministry (as opposed to organized Catholic centers for the delivery of services)."[9]

In the early 1970s the CMSW initiated reforms based on a strong participatory model, particularly manifested in the committee structure and in the nomination and election processes. In 1972 the CMSW changed its name to the Leadership Conference of Women Religious (LCWR), which represented a shift from the old notion of "superior and subjects" to that of "Development of creative and responsive leadership" as well as to "those forms of service consistent with the evolving gospel mission of women religious in the world through the church." It aimed to effect "constructive attitudinal and structural change."[10] According to Mary Jo Weaver, who charted the expanding consciousness of "New Catholic Women," the title LCWR "allowed them to name themselves, to state their own identity as they experienced it. . . . The decade of the

1970s was devoted to world solidarity, liberation themes and women's issues."[11] Though not all religious institutes identified with solidarity and liberation themes of the feminist movement, most women religious were in accord with the movement, and those in hospital ministry, particularly in administration, tended to "own their own authority" as women, and were committed to integrate gospel values and health care. The visible identity of Catholic hospitals was no longer associated with the strong presence of sisters and brothers. Those religious and laity opting for a personalist health-care ministry outside the nursing structures of the hospital either went into pastoral care departments or in alternative nursing experiences among marginalized social groups remote from the traditional channels of access to health care.

II

The old chaplaincy model of pastoral care, based primarily on sacramental ministry, has given way to a pastoral-care team model based on participation of laity, sisters, brothers, Protestant ministers, and Catholic priests. Clinical pastoral education, with its strong counseling dimension that relies upon discerning the psychological/religious needs of the patient, had been present in Protestant chaplaincy since the 1930s and was just becoming incorporated in the Catholic hospitals in the late 1960s and 70s. To promote a team approach relies upon a commitment to post-Vatican II understanding of the role of the laity in the healing ministries. As the medical ethicist Kevin O'Rourke, O.P., stated, "the mystique of deathbed conversions or 'cheap grace' must be avoided [but] people should have adequate spiritual care . . . and this is not the prerogative of priests alone."[12]

Clinical Pastoral Education (CPE) was recommended by most advanced pastoral-care departments. The program was founded in Boston in the 1920s. Richard Cabot, founder of medical social work, professor of medicine at Harvard, and one of the many prominent Cabots of Boston, promoted the idea of a clinical year in the seminary curriculum in the mid-1920s as a means of introducing prospective ministers to the need for moral rigor in dealing with contemporary problems. Russell Dicks, a Protestant chaplain at Massachusetts General Hospital, ran a program in clinical education for ministers. Known for the method of verbatim transcriptions of conversations with patients, Dicks co-authored with Cabot The Art of Ministering to the Sick. E. Brooks Holifield captures the significance of the work: It "popularized the metaphor of the 'growing edge,' and it assigned to the minister the responsibility of finding and cultivating that growing edge, largely through good listening. Cabot and Dicks argued that the minister presented and represented the teachings of Jesus, especially his call for 'confidence in God.' . . . They defined God as 'that great power in ourselves that makes for health.' . . . By helping men and women discover the direction in which this immanent divinity was carrying them, helping them face and assimilate and obey the 'plan' of God in their lives, the minister helped them grow." By listening to and accepting patients "where they were" and then directing them "toward the point which the patient needs to reach" was at the core of clinical pastoral counseling.[13] Within two years the initial developments in Boston had become a movement with diverse ethical, psychological, and personal emphases. The advances in counseling courses in both Protestant and Catholic seminaries occurred during the 1950s when there were nearly 120 centers for CPE and about 500 full-time chaplains in general hospitals. By the mid-1970s there were many lay persons and priests involved in CPE training, some of whom were in programs sponsored by Catholic hospitals.

The traditional hospital chaplain, frequently retired priests or those on the brink of forced retirement because of inability to serve in a parish, received no specialized training. With developments in pastoral theology, fostered by the general ferment in theology during the early 1960s, there was a growing consensus among the clergy and hospital administrators that training beyond sacramental ministry was imperative. Hence, the National Association of Catholic Chaplains (NACC) was founded, and soon training programs were instituted that eventually led to certification as a Catholic chaplain. According to Sister Helen Hayes, O.S.F., executive director of the NACC in 1990, CPE "served as a model for the NACC training. The efforts . . . have resulted both in a certification process that assesses the personal, professional and theological competencies of chaplaincy candidates and in an accreditation process for CPE."[14]

The traditional "Last Rites" gave way to the Sacrament of Anointing administered individually to the sick or aged in various contexts: home, hospital, or chapel. Viaticum, the reception of communion, ideally within the eucharistic liturgy, represented the relatedness of the dying person and the people of God. In 1975 the NCCB published *Pastoral Care of the Sick: Rites of Anointing and Viaticum*, which represents a consensus on Catholic ritual and prayer for the sick and dying.[15] Traditional relics and prayers for the intervention of saints are still in use but sparingly.

At the 1974 Catholic Health Assembly a priest and a lay chaplain at St. Mary's Hospital in Minneapolis called for the expansion of "a sufficiently staffed and well-trained pastoral care department . . . [as an] effective means of developing Christian values among employees who render services to patients." To expand awareness of the need for "Christian witness" throughout the hospital the chaplains proposed pastoral-care programs for "staff attitudes related to the profession, patients and in the critical areas of coping with their own stress and the anxieties of patients."[16]

In December of 1974 the NACC opened its membership to women, who were required to have authorization of the ordinary of their dioceses. According to a 1977 publication of the NCCB only priests were designated as chaplains; others on the professional staff were called patient visitors. By the late 1970s the title chaplain was applied to lay persons. For example, in 1979 Sister M. Peggy Byrnes, R.S.M., of the Omaha Province of the Sisters of Mercy, wrote to Sister Fran Repka of Cincinnati: "I was certified by the National Association of Catholic Chaplains in December 1974—that was when the association finally permitted women to join. Now of course the organization can see the place of women in the organization."[17] To illustrate the prominence of CPE in institutions, Sister M. Carmelita Kellog, R.S.M., of Omaha wrote to Sister Cecile Sharkley of Cincinnati that because she and another sister did not have clinical pastoral training they were entitled "Pastoral Visitors—I say Howdy Doody sisters. We bring to our work fifty years of trying to imitate Catherine McAuley's concern for the People of God. There is only one other R.S.M. who has direct patient contact in the acute care hospital although there are about eight who work on the management level. So that is our job to try to bring the Mercy presence to every patient who comes to Bergan Mercy [Hospital]."[18]

In the late 1980s the College of Chaplains of the American Protestant Hospital Association and the NACC developed a common set of guidelines for certifying a pastoral-care department. Referred to as the Joint Commission on the Accreditation of Pastoral Services, it sent evaluation teams to hospitals in order to assess the pastoral care department's allocation of personnel and time according to its mission statement. This allowed the department to adapt national criteria to its own setting and informed the administration of standards that it should apply to the department, particularly specifying its fiscal relationship to include it in determining insurance reimbursements.[19]

Team ministries are making church happen; not only do lay chaplains pray with patients as the nurses were instructed to by Sister Berenice Beck in her book *The Handmaid of the Divine Physician,* but the chaplain today draws on training in psychology, familiarity with scripture, and experience in crisis intervention. Hospital ministry includes assisting those in grief and holding memorial services for departed patients and staff.

The evolution from the traditional priest-chaplain to the contemporary pastoral-care team has been uneven. At its best, the pastoral-care team experiences community in prayer, retreats, and continuing education; the team manifests its mission at the bedside with patients, in crisis with families and staff, and in sponsoring wellness programs based on an integrated approach of mind, body, and spirit. The most effective pastoral care department is recognized by the administration, physicians, nurses, and nonmedical staff as integral to the mission of the hospital. This missionary character is central to the meaning of contemporary health-care ministry.

III

The alternative nursing programs—that is, those outside the traditional nursing structures of the hospital—also possessed a mission identity. Medical missionaries in third-world nations increased during the early period of the Sister Formation Conference, particularly after the opening of the Second Vatican Council. Many of these programs continue today in urban and rural areas in Africa, Latin America, and Asia, staffed by professional volunteers among the laity and women and men religious. Many religious institutes sponsored home-medical missions in impoverished areas of the inner cities, the rural villages of Appalachia, and in the camps of migrant workers.

In the 1950s there were several institutes committed to home missionary work, some of which originated in frontier experiences of the nineteenth century. Those begun in the mid-twentieth century include the Hospital Sisters of the Third Order of St. Francis in Springfield, Illinois, who staffed a mission dispensary on the Navajo Reservation at Lukachuka, Arizona. For nearly thirty years the mission cared for over ten thousand patients annually.[20] The Glenmary Sisters, a home-missionary community founded by Father Howard Bishop, opened a home-nursing program and a clinic in Hayesville, North Carolina, in 1958. Located in an area populated by subsistence farmers, the clinic was the only health-care facility available for those mountain people. With a

Catholic population of .5% the sisters eventually became part of the community and in the early 1960s were given a mobile clinic. In the late 1980s the Glenmary Sisters sponsored a volunteer health-care effort in the area.[21]

Members of several religious institutes collaborate in health ministries in Appalachia; the Sisters of Mercy, in Virginia and North Carolina, while the Sisters of Divine Providence of Melbourne, Kentucky, and lay volunteers have been associated with a hospice program in Prestonberg, Kentucky.[22] The Sisters of Charity of Nazareth, Kentucky, initiated a home nursing program in two counties near their motherhouse in 1971. Led by Sister Dorothy Peterson, S.C.N., the program garnered support from various church and public agencies as it expanded into a modern mobile clinic with a student nursing program and a staff representing the various specialist areas from speech pathology to acute care nursing.[23] Always buttressed by a strong home-nursing component, the extended care service became a principal program, which by 1984 was providing "live-in companions, sitters, and nursing personnel for private party patients in their own homes." This expanded with several satellite offices and over fifty-five thousand annual home visitations.[24]

Traditional missionary efforts to migrant workers, most of whom have been Mexican Americans following the harvest seasons in the South and North in desperate need of health care and other services, have been ad hoc developments among some religious communities. Mercy Hospital in Bay City, Michigan, not only provided full care but sent physicians and nurses to the camps to establish temporary clinics.

IV

In the post–Vatican II period the CHA reflected changes in church, society, and health care. In 1968, on the retirement of Father Flanagan, Thomas F. Casey, S.J., became the CHA's executive director. He had served as assistant to the executive director since 1966. A native of Beverly, Massachusetts, Casey had been a practicing attorney before entering the Society of Jesus in 1952. Even before his ordination in 1962, the Jesuit provincial of the Missouri province had chosen him as Flanagan's successor. During his theological education Casey spent summers working at the CHA and at member hospitals. After his tertianship (a year of special ministry after ordination) he received a master's degree in hospital administration from the University of Chicago.[25]

In his 1969 report to the annual convention, Casey pointed out that the "changing culture" of the time was prompting a "reexamination of the purposes and structures of institutions and organizations, especially those committed to public service." He noted that the CHA had been helping many of its members reorganize and strengthen their management structures. He added that recent developments in health care and the church made it necessary for the CHA itself to rethink its purpose and reorganize.

Casey urged the membership to revise the CHA's articles and bylaws— which had been adopted only four years previously—to bring them more in line with the attitudes of the post–Vatican II Catholic community. His most significant proposal was that the association amend the bylaw stipulating that the presidency rotate between a religious and a bishop's representative. The nominating committee, Casey argued, should be free to propose the name of the best-qualified person. He also noted that, with the passage of Medicare, CHA members once again needed to develop a voice on public policy matters. In addition, he reported that the association had recently devoted much thought and energy to clarifying "the relationship between the religious congregation as the sponsoring group and the hospital as a community health facility."[26]

The most vexing problem during his administration was brokering a consensus in the theological review and revision of the 1954 *Code of Medical Ethics for Catholic Hospitals* and its companion document, *Ethical and Religious Directives for Catholic Health Facilities*. As mentioned in chapter eleven, Gerald Kelly, S.J., professor of theology at St. Mary's College, was head of the committee that compiled the code.[27] Through his column in *Hospital Progress* he provided a traditional natural-law rendering of medical-moral issues of the code. Prior to the publication of *Humanae Vitae*, July 25, 1968, there was a revolution of rising expectations because many considered the birth control pill would be left to the informed conscience of the married couple. On July 30, Charles E. Curran, a priest of the diocese of Rochester, New York, and an instructor in moral theology at Catholic University of America, and nine other professors at the university, held a press conference in which they issued in response to *Humanae Vitae* a six-hundred-word "Statement of Dissent," which was endorsed by seventy-two theologians throughout the country. Hence, within this polarized context the composition of a new moral-medical code was a severe challenge, particularly because it was to be promulgated within the teaching authority of the bishops.[28]

Casey and Monsignor Harrold Murray, director of the United States Catholic Conference's (USCC) Department of Health Affairs, frequently met with theologians who were engaged in the revision process, which, Casey reported to the CHA convention in 1970, entailed "critical questions confronting Catholic-sponsored hospitals, such as sterilization procedures and family planning services." Casey acknowledged that the absence of an updated code created frustration and difficulty for healthcare providers, who needed guidance in facing vexing ethical choices. Although a USCC leader in health issues, Bishop George H. Guilfoyle of Camden, New Jersey, strongly advised the hospitals to follow the existing code until the revised code was prepared; Casey urged that Catholic hospital administrators not "brush off medical staff's request for reconsideration of a hospital policy concerning application of the unrevised code." He pointed out that the *Directives* allowed physicians to be guided by "the principles of sound medicine" when facing issues "legitimately debated by theologians." Casey also called on CHA members to bring their problems to the attention of local episcopal authorities: "The grassroots must be heard from," he insisted. "The individual and the institution must speak up."[29]

In 1971 the National Conference of Catholic Bishops (NCCB) altered and approved a revised edition of the *Directives*. Within a year the CHA had distributed sixty thousand copies. The 1971 code included an eight-paragraph preamble and forty-three directives. There were several references to the need for Christian compassion, ecumenical sensitivity, and a respect for patients' rights, all of which achieved consensus. However, several moral theologians criticized the *Directives*, particularly its preamble, and in the process challenged the traditional identity of the Catholic hospital.

Richard A. McCormick, S.J., then professor of moral theology at the Bellarmine School of Theology in Chicago, viewed the *Directives* as too rigid, engendering more problems and ignoring advances in theological understanding of the complexities of moral decision-making. Principal among the problems cited by McCormick was the diversity of values among physicians and patients in Catholic hospitals. According to McCormick, this problem was compounded by the *Directives'* absolute prohibition of procedures that profoundly affected the hospital's ability to implement the code, such issues as family planning, tubal ligations, sperm donors for medical specimens and for artificial insemination, and artificial birth control. McCormick also noted that in a pluralistic setting the hospital administration must reevaluate the principle of material cooperation; the degree to which the administration perceives its moral responsibility in relation to a procedure deemed immoral by

Catholic teaching as specified by the code. Essential to McCormick's article were the role of conscience and the question of theological dissent in the church. In light of the widespread opposition to what was perceived as *Humanae Vitae's* negative treatment of the role of conscience in artificial birth control, and the fact that the Canadian bishops' directives were more affirmative, it appeared to McCormick and others that there was a geographical division among theologians in the church. McCormick's article on the *Directives* appeared in *America* and was reprinted in the *Linacre Quarterly*. The title "Not What Catholic Hospitals Ordered" highlighted McCormick's understanding of the Catholic administrator's dilemma in implementing the code within a pluralistic, community-based Catholic institution.[30]

Warren T. Reich, senior research scholar in medical ethics at the Kennedy Center for Bioethics at Georgetown University, agreed with McCormick. However, he opened his article with the remark that most informed theologians, chaplains, and health-care leaders were aware that the 1955 *Directives* desperately needed to be revised: "If one compares the recent revision with the *Directives* issued sixteen years ago there is little that is new and that is alarming." Reich listed six "factors [that] called for a profound re-thinking of the *Directives* and their purpose, and [that] should have had a much greater impact on the 1971 revision."[31] In many ways these factors paralleled McCormick's criticisms. However, Reich placed greater emphasis on the Second Vatican Council's document on religious liberty and its relationship to conscience and the role of pluralism in moral decision-making in a Catholic hospital. McCormick and Reich were in accord on the paradoxical problem facing the character of the Catholic hospital. McCormick stated:

> Finally, Catholic health facilities themselves have undergone subtle but discernible changes in their self-image. Increasingly they have become community hospitals, often with heavy non-Catholic staff and clienteles. They were frequently financed through public funds or by appeal to the whole community, and still often enough the only health facility reasonably available to a community. In this climate the concept itself of a "Catholic hospital" becomes problematic.[32]

In consultation with chaplains and ethicists, administrators of Catholic facilities have been responsible for evaluating the hospital's material cooperation or its moral role in a procedure that is prohibited by the church's teaching. Respect for the community character of the hospital and regard for pluralistic values within the ambiguous public/private identity of Catholic health care led McCormick to advise administrators to adopt a flexibility in determining the hospital's material cooperation in procedures contrary to the code.

In the next issue of the *Linacre Quarterly*, Vitale A. Paganelli, M.D., a leader of the National Federation of Catholic Physicians Guilds, and Richard McCormick exchanged views on the propriety of the *Directives*. It was a clear discussion of the issues couched in candor and civility. The conflict was partially one between the certitude of medical science and the variables that enter moral decision-making. It touched on conflicting understandings of the identity of the Catholic hospital; the divergent views on the implementation of the principle of material cooperation in a pluralistic setting expanded the conflict to irresolvable differences; the dialectic was intensified by their opposing views on ecclesiastical authority and dissent.[33]

Thomas J. O'Donnell, S.J., a medico-moral consultant of the *Linacre Quarterly*, responded to the critics of the *Directives* on specific points, but the thrust of his article was that the dissenters were undermining *the faith*:

> Let us be honest enough to acknowledge that the problem of the *Directives* is not so much of sexuality as of ecclesiology. The point of contention is not so much what the church teaches on sex—because that is perfectly clear— the point at issue is rather "Should Catholics go on believing it?"—and there precisely is the crisis of faith.
>
> In summary, then, the basic issue is faith in the Church, in its teaching with regard to contraception (and contraceptive pluralistic society today)— with abortion looming ever larger on the horizon.[34]

After affirming *Humanae Vitae* as the "authentic teaching of the Church" O'Donnell lamented that there were "more than a few" Catholics who rejected this teaching. "But the worse danger and damage is in priests and theological writers using their authority and prestige to say that this is not really the teaching of the Church, or if it is, that Catholics need not accept it. . . ."[35] O'Donnell's attack on the "contraceptive mentality" imbedded in pluralism was a tacit attack on McCormick's and Reich's understanding of the vital role of pluralism as a significant variable in moral reasoning on material cooperation. (One should recall that this dialogue occurred before Roe v. Wade of 1973.) O'Donnell's sincerity is quite apparent, and he seems to have greatly feared an unraveling of the fabric of faith once the theologians legitimated the broader notion of informed conscience and justified the hospital's material cooperation in procedures condemned by the code. O'Donnell's concept of the religious identity of Catholic hospitals reflects the views of Gerald Kelly and the certitude of the Catholic separatism of Alphonse Schwitalla. In general the controversy on the interpretation of the medico-moral *Directives* illustrates conflicts among moral theologians, the problem of legitimate dissent, the diversity of episcopal understanding of medico-moral issues, and the ambiguous identity of the Catholic hospital. The voices of medical ethics represent a broad range within the Catholic theological community making it enormously difficult to achieve a consensus on a revision of the 1971 *Directives*.[36]

Central to Richard McCormick's and Warren T. Reich's understanding of the Catholic hospital is their perception of its community character based on financial dependency on state and federal funding as well as moneys raised by appealing to the general public. Though the moral theologians did not substantiate their views with references to canon law, a work by Monsignor John J. McGrath of the canon law faculty at the Catholic University of America argued that Catholic hospitals and other institutions incorporated in civil law are not owned by the diocese or religious institute that sponsor them but rather are operated under their auspices. "Since the charitable corporations [were] created to serve the general public, the equitable title [a civil-law term] to charitable corporate property is vested in the general public."[37]

Professor Robert T. Kennedy, a canon law scholar writing in *The Jurist*, has noted that the "sole legal consequence of his [McGrath's] theory" concerns the distribution of assets when the hospital or college decided to close; "the assets of the corporation are to be distributed, on behalf of the public, to another non-profit corporation engaged in similar activity, and not to the religious community or other ecclesial entity under whose auspices the institution has been conducted."[38] The sponsoring religious order may be incorporated in civil law and recognized as a "moral person" in canon law, but the hospital "was solely a creature of civil law."[39]

In his introduction to his work *Catholic Institutions in the United States: Canonical and Civil Law Status*, McGrath referred to the presence of lay persons, both Catholic and non-Catholic, on the boards governing Catholic hospitals and colleges.[40] Because many religious orders perceived such changes in the lay–religious composition of governing boards as jeopardizing their ownership of these institutions it was necessary to clarify the civil and canonical status of the institutions. In his analysis of the issues McGrath specifically stated that "the real and personal property acquired by a corporation is owned by the corporation as such and not by its board of directors. . . . The general public, in the case of charitable corporations, [does] have an interest in the assets of the corporation, but *they do not own* the assets of the corporation" (emphasis in the original). McGrath reasoned that "since the charitable corporation is created to serve the general public, the equitable title to corporate property is vested in the general public."[41]

Kennedy, professor of Canon Law at Catholic University, points out that some of the proponents of the McGrath thesis found canonical justification for views on social and religious change while some viewed the thesis as facilitating government funding for Catholic hospitals free from the suspicion of church–state entanglements. Others found the thesis advantageous in seeking freedom from canon law restrictions on the administration and alienation of "church property," whereas McGrath had viewed virtually all civilly incorporated Catholic institutions as being creatures solely of the civil law.

In 1975 Adam J. Maida, a canon lawyer in the Pittsburgh diocese and in 1994 Cardinal Archbishop of Detroit, tacitly responded to McGrath in his work *Ownership, Control and Sponsorship of Catholic Institutions*. In a well-crafted scholarly analysis, Robert Kennedy nuances the Maida monograph. "The civilly incorporated institution remains, under canon law, simply an expression of the apostolate of its sponsor, and the assets of the civilly incorporated institution remain, canonically, the property of the sponsor."[42]

Maida offered two alternative theories in support of the proposition that such institutions were creations of the church and subject to canon law. The first theory viewed each Catholic institution as already sharing in the canonical statutes of its sponsoring diocese or religious order prior to the institution's civil-law incorporation. The opponents of the thesis greatly feared the secularization of Catholic institutions "with consequent erosion of episcopal authority over the mission and moral orientation of such institutions. . . ."[43]

Maida's second theory held that each Catholic institution, by the mere fact of its establishment, acquired juridic personality in the church in its own right and thereby became subject to canon law. With the Vatican, the Apostolic Delegate, and the NCCB calling for an in-depth study of the issue, Maida's work was distributed to all the bishops by the NCCB as a set of tentative directives. According to Kennedy, both McGrath and Maida oversimplified the issue canonically and as a result reached inaccurate conclusions. From the vantage point of the leadership of Catholic hospitals the controversy had exacerbated the problem of religious identity of their facilities and influenced the development of a number of diverse sponsorship arrangements, particularly the establishment of a system with the religious institute as a parent corporation of individual health-care facilities each separately incorporated in civil law and each enjoying juridic personality.[44]

Concurrent with the theological controversies of the *Directives* and the canon law conflicts on the juridic character of the Catholic hospital, the CHA sponsored a series of articles in *Hospital Progress* that were later compiled into a separate 1974 publication entitled *The Mission of Healing: Readings in Christian Values and Health Care.* Within the context of the controversies this publication appears to have been a conscious effort to elucidate the marks of religious identity that separate the Catholic hospital from all others. The authors did not reveal a triumphal separatism of the preconciliar period, but rather they manifested an indebtedness to the conciliar understanding of a "pilgrim people" making community.[45]

V

A controversy originating in the 1970s challenged the moral integrity of Catholic hospitals. Monsignor George G. Higgins, a nationally recognized labor priest and former director of the Social Action Department of the United States Catholic Conference, has been a consistent voice of criticism against the anti-union activity of Catholic hospitals. Though the National Labor Relations Act was amended in 1974 to protect the workers' right to organize in not-for-profit hospitals, Higgins referred to evidence that Catholic hospitals had contracted with consulting firms that specialized in discouraging union activity within the limits of the law.[46] Most hospital administrators have provided equitable wage and benefit plans, but they perceive unions as threats to the hospital's autonomy particularly by their threats to strike.

For over twenty years in his syndicated column and in his recently published autobiographical reflections, George G. Higgins has maintained that such anti-union policies run contrary to the social teaching of the church. Hospital executives counter that unions interfere with their pursuit of health-care ministry. Anecdotal evidence suggests that some hospital executives feel that Higgins is excessive in his criticism of Catholic hospitals in contrast to other institutions such as colleges and diocesan offices that have not been open to union organizing.

In a July 1975 issue of *Hospital Progress* Kevin O'Rourke, O.P., then director of the CHA's Department of Medical-Moral Affairs, contributed an article on "Christian Responsibility for Labor and Management."[47] Aimed at instructing hospital personnel on the church's social teaching from Leo XIII through John XXIII, O'Rourke's article specified principles of labor-management relations and the pro-labor history of the church in the United States. He recognized the role of unions in promoting the dignity of labor in the form of negotiated contracts for decent wages, conditions and benefits, frequently after justifiable strikes. However, O'Rourke also emphasized the church's teaching that "labor and management must have as their goal a greater good than simply realizing the interests of their own personal constituency. Whether the Christian represents labor or management, he should strive for justice and unity rather than domination and control."[48] Over the past twenty years labor-management relations in Catholic hospitals have seldom resulted in prolonged work stoppages. George Higgins does admonish unions to be sensitive to the religious character of the hospital, particularly in developing tactics such as strikes.[49] Some hospitals are unionized today, and many mission effectiveness directors, representing the praxis of their religious sponsors' charisms, have been advocates of workers' rights; but the controversy continues to affect the understanding of Catholic identity.

VI

Several controversies, particularly the conflict over the *Ethical and Religious Directives for Catholic Health Facilities*, took their toll upon Thomas Casey, S.J., and he resigned as executive director of the CHA. In July 1971, Mary Maurita Sengelaub, R.S.M., was appointed to the position. A native of Reed City, Michigan, Sengelaub had been a staff nurse, a head nurse, and an instructor at the Mercy Central School of Nursing in Bay City before she entered the Detroit Province of the Sisters of Mercy at the close of World War II. She went on to receive a master's degree in hospital administration from St. Louis University in 1954, became assistant provincial in 1961, and a member of the general council in 1965.

Sister Maurita Sengelaub's administration was particularly concerned with the relationship between the sponsoring religious institute and the hospital and the general reevaluation of the mission and structure of the CHA.[50] A major CHA initiative during Sengelaub's administration was the development of the Catholic Health Services Leadership Program (CHSLP). One of its primary goals was to help sponsoring groups and their health facilities establish systems. After several years of planning and consultation, CHA began publishing a series of nine models that sponsoring institutes could use when they were establishing a system.[51]

The first model was published in 1974. Focusing on corporate decision-making and information flow, this model proposed an organized system that sponsoring groups and their health-care facilities could follow to achieve their objectives and quality control. Other models focused on such areas as nursing care, pastoral care, and finance. Around 1970 the American Hospital Association and the CHA had proposed the formation of systems to help cope with the highly regulated and deeply competitive environment of health care. Sengelaub described a system as "a single corporate entity which owns, operates, and manages two or more hospitals or health-related institutions." It may be a local, regional, or national system. Rather than formal contracted relationships among hospitals, a system is direct ownership and, in the words of Sengelaub, "identity and commitment to and with one another are at the very core, and at the very being and within the spirit of a bona fide hospital system."[52]

The CHA promoted the development of systems to impel religious institutes to engage in long-range planning, to access their own commitment to their hospitals rather than be compelled to react to short-range market and public policy forces. As will be noted later, systems became even more important after the advent of the prospective payment system (PPS) in 1983. Sengelaub noted that the establishment of a system fostered continuity of the ministry in the post–Vatican II period when religious institutes experienced frequent changes in governance personnel; some councils were without members in hospital experience. The religious issues were paramount; the system created a "heightened sense of Catholic identity and sponsorship with a new sense of mission . . . [allowing the sponsor] to extend and to enhance . . . [the congregation's] unique gifts, charisms and spirit." It also encouraged sponsors "to bring about greater collaboration with the laity and other health professionals even to the point of involving them in partnership roles in governance and management structure. Corporate level officers could develop staff with expertise in various phases of health care including pastoral care, moral theology and eventually mission effectiveness."[53] To service the needs of sponsors and their systems, so vital to its members, entailed reforming the CHA.

Under Sengelaub's direction, many of the association's traditional departments (e.g., dietetics, X-ray, housekeeping) were dissolved. In their place the CHA established departments that focused exclusively on (1) preserving and promoting the Catholic identity of member institutions and (2) advocating member interests in the areas of health-care legislation and regulation. The association's office of government services, for example, was created in 1973 (it moved to Washington, D.C., in 1976).

By far the most significant development during Sengelaub's administration was the work of the CHA Study Committee. As early as 1973 the board of trustees had begun to address the association's long-term needs and established a committee to initiate future planning. The committee, assisted in early 1976 by the consulting firm of Arthur D. Little, Inc., which researched members' expectations in light of the CHA's goals,[54] recommended measures to deepen the CHA's commitment to public policy advocacy, to broaden its base of membership, and to continue the shift away from technically oriented education programs to a broader curriculum.[55]

Although illness forced Sister Sengelaub to resign from office in early 1977 before the study committee report was completed, she is generally recognized as being the prime force in bringing the project into being.

Sponsors, including religious congregations and dioceses that own hospitals, incorporated in the mid-1970s the system approach to operations. In the early 1980s, the prospective payment system that designated reimbursement according to the categories of illness (Diagnosis Related Groups) rather than according to the days of treatment in the hospital made a system an even more viable way for Catholic hospitals to deal with the demands of a competitive marketplace. Between 1979 and 1988 the number of Catholic health-care systems grew from twenty-nine to sixty. Sponsorship has evolved and effected substantive changes in the direction of their systems. The religious mission is of paramount significance and is still at the core of the ownership-governance models.[56]

During Sister Sengelaub's administration of the CHA the title of her office was changed twice—from executive director to executive vice-president (in 1972), and then from executive vice-president to president (in 1974). The title of the chief elected official of the CHA, formerly known as the "president," became the "Chairperson of the Board of Trustees."

In January 1977, Sister Helen Kelley, D.C., administrator of Our Lady of Lourdes Hospital in Binghamton, New York, succeeded Sengelaub as CHA president. A 1957 graduate of St. Louis University's graduate program in hospital administration, Kelley had served as an administrator in several hospitals in the Northeast Province of the Daughters of Charity from 1958 to 1976. She had become CHA executive vice-president on July 1, 1976.

When Kelley assumed the presidency, she also became chairperson of the study committee. During her tenure she was so thoroughly committed to this dual role that, when the committee had completed its task, she announced her retirement as CHA president. "Since I served as both chairman of the Study Committee and CHA chief executive officer," she explained in June 1978, "it is time for the association to undergo a change in leadership."[57]

In May 1979, John E. Curley, Jr., was appointed CHA president. A native of San Francisco, Curley left his position as executive director of the California Association of Catholic Hospitals in Sacramento to become the CHA's first lay chief executive officer. Curley had been active in the CHA since 1975. His experience with the medical profession in California and in the insurance business, as well as his background in Catholic health-care mission, advocacy, and public-policy efforts, made him a strong candidate for the CHA presidency. Curley's appointment illustrates the ascendancy of the laity in leadership positions in Catholic hospitals.[58]

Since the mid-1950s, when concern for the lay apostolate was widely articulated, the role of the laity in the hospitals was limited to nurses involved in diocesan councils of Catholic nurses. The precipitous decline of specialized lay Catholic Action, such as the Young Christian Workers, and other Catholic organizations that promoted many of the changes associated with the Second Vatican Council, had achieved many of their goals and lost their raison d'être. For example, the diocesan councils of Catholic nurses no longer had an appeal. By 1969 so many councils had dissolved that the national council decided to terminate its journal, *The Catholic Nurse*. According to its last editor, Dorothy N. Kelly, the journal was a casualty of the postconciliar climate that drastically reduced interest in traditional lay activism.[59]

The proliferation of lay ministries in the post–Vatican II period derived from several streams of change within church and society. Many of the social-activist projects of the 1960s and 1970s became institutionalized in diocesan and parish programs staffed by lay women and men. The new models of ecclesiology, such as the pilgrim-people-of-God and the suffering-servant models, combined with liturgical changes promoting lay participation, fostered an expanding consciousness of the laity's responsibility to engage in a variety of roles in the life of the church that included religious education, social outreach projects, and pastoral care programs in parishes, dioceses, and hospitals. The positive chracter of lay ministries filled an increasing void created by the decreasing numbers of sisters, brothers, and priests. Hence, the many hospital administrators, members of boards of trustees, nurses, and some physicians understood their commitments in terms of lay ministry. With more than fifty percent of hospital administrators lay women and men in 1979, the election of John E. Curley, Jr., symbolizes the recognition of the vitality of lay ministry in Catholic health care. Because the fifteen-year Curley administration parallels a new era in the contemporary life of the health-care ministry as it moves toward the twenty-first century, the book concludes with an epilogue on missionary adaptability, a central theme of this history.

CHAPTER THIRTEEN

Epilogue:
Crisis, Reform, and Mission

—————— ✤ ——————

THE CRISIS IN HEALTH CARE, a highly charged element in the political climate in 1993-94, is related to historical developments in the not-for-profit hospital's mission, its symbolic role, and its structure, particularly as the hospital has interacted with public policy, the market, local constituents, and trends in medical science and technology. Throughout the twentieth century few institutions so clearly reflect the impact of myriad cultural factors as the hospital: struggles against racism, sexism, nativism, poverty, and conflicts on religious and moral issues have been manifested in the life of the hospital. (Perhaps this is a major reason why "General Hospital" is such a popular and long-running soap opera.) Hence, the American hospital defies a clear definition. Rosemary Stevens refers to this dominant historical theme as "constructive ambiguity." The modern hospital's strength has been its indeterminate character. Because it has adapted and changed in response to the "dominant communities of interest as they in turn have shifted and changed in the twentieth century it has survived and prospered under one label—that of 'hospital'—throughout great transformations of function and role."[1]

Driven by economic, social, class, race, gender, and medical forces, the modern hospital is, according to Stevens, "defined by change, under the umbrella of apparent semantic consistency. The ambiguity inherent in [the hospital's] role has allowed for constant transformation."[2] From the historian's perspective the contemporary changes are, in the words of Stevens, "dramatic" but "not revolutionary." She also notes that among the strong threads of continuity "physicians, administrators and boards of trustees continue to be major communities of interest. Their various agendas affect the type of services offered, location, architectural design, roles and prestige of its various occupations."[3]

Since its origin, the CHA has provided continuing education to sisters, brothers, and lay professionals, some of whom have been administrators and trustees, those communities of interest that Stevens refers to, who direct the flow of continuous change within the channels of Catholic tradition. The leadership of the CHA from Moulinier to Curley has articulated gospel imperatives and the mission of hospitals as a response to a religious call to provide compassionate curing, caring, and healing.

To transpose "constructive ambiguity" to the religious character of the Catholic hospital the designation "missionary" is appropriate; from its origins American Catholic health care has manifested adaptability to religious pluralism, to the cholera and yellow-fever crises, to the demands of war, of immigration and of the modernization and professionalization processes. But Catholic health care's adaptability occurred in the mission context of religious witness to those on the existential boundary situation of sickness and death.

I

Creative adaptability characterizes the ministry and the CHA during the fifteen years of the Curley administration, when the issues of leadership, sponsorship, advocacy, reform, ecclesial affiliation, and Catholic identity have been paramount concerns. Curley's first presidential report to the House of Delegates illustrated these concerns as he specified the three pillars on which a reorganized staff would build its programs: mission services, member services, and government relations. Mission services, Curley explained, would "enhance institutional relationships with the Church . . . strengthen the pastoral dimensions of care, and . . . define and address medical-moral dilemmas." He said member services would complement this work by emphasizing "network building with regional and state CHA meetings." He promised the delegates that the CHA would be "creative, assertive, practical, and results oriented," adding that members would "receive a CHA product of value for their dues dollar."[4]

Curley noted that the pledge to improve government services was a vital manifestation of the CHA's commitment to fulfilling its mission and serving its members. In tandem with the NCCB and the USCC, the association would attempt to influence public policy on medical-moral issues and legislation dealing with Medicare, Medicaid, and the voluntary sector of the United States health-care system.[5]

In 1979 the CHA implemented a study-committee recommendation and officially changed its name to the Catholic Health Association of the United States. The new name also better indicates the range of health-care organizations the CHA was serving and intended to serve, which included not only hospitals but also long-term care facilites, special-care facilites, hospices, and clinics. In accord with its growth and its need to be more accessible to its members, the association moved from its old offices near the St. Louis University Medical School to a site near the St. Louis airport in 1981. The move also illustrates the association's increasing reliance on member participation, as well as its independence from St. Louis University's graduate program in hospital administration.

Lay sponsorship also became a key issue in the 1980s. Since the majority of Catholic hospitals had been managed by lay CEOs since 1981, questions arose about the potential for greater lay sponsorship. Beginning in 1986, when the CHA launched a pilot program to test lay sponsorship, the association has been concerned with helping the ministry study the status and options of lay sponsorship under canon law; to help establish proper relationships among the local bishop, the sponsoring group, and health-care facility; and to set up a process for the annual review of the sponsor's stewardship.[6]

In the area of public policy the National Conference of Catholic Bishops issued a 1981 pastoral letter on health and health care. The letter listed five principles that were the products of a dialogue among the CHA, the NCCB, and the USCC: that health care was a basic right; that public policy should respect the private, voluntary, not-for-profit sector of the health-care system, as well as the rights of individual conscience; that there should be widespread community participation in health-care maintenance and delivery decisions; that efforts to make health care more efficient and inexpensive should be promoted; and—most significantly—that a national health insurance (NHI) program should be established.

The bishops' call for an NHI program did not, however, come at a propitious time. A major topic on the legislative agenda throughout most of the Carter administration, NHI had become a dead issue by the time Ronald Reagan took office in 1981. Moreover, the CHA never endorsed a specific NHI program, although it had agreed in principle to explore such federal reform programs.[7]

Although the CHA had declined to endorse a specific NHI proposal, the association's Stewardship Task Force (established in the early 1980s) conducted a number of studies that made Catholic health-care leaders acutely aware of the growing seriousness and complexity of the situation of the nation's "health-care poor." At the task force's recommendation, the CHA board established the Task Force on Health Care of the Poor in 1984. In 1986 the task force released its report, *No Room in the Marketplace: The Health Care of the Poor*, which recommended ways for the Catholic health-care ministry, the church as a whole, and the federal government to help address the problems of the nation's poor. The task force favored a long-term strategy that included federally mandated universal health insurance.[8]

As a direct outgrowth of this report, in 1986 the CHA board established the Task Force on Long Term Care Policy. In 1988 the task force published its report, *A Time to Be Old, A Time to Flourish: The Special Needs of the Elderly-at-Risk*. The report described the state of the long-term care system in the United States, outlined the health-care needs of the elderly, discussed the responsibilities of the Catholic long-term care providers, and recommended federal programs to help finance health care for the elderly.[9]

In response to the continuing crisis in health care the association sponsored the Catholic Leadership Symposium on Systemic Reform of the National Healthcare System, held at Georgetown University in November 1989. Participants at the symposium worked out a set of principles to form the basis of any systemic reform. In April 1990, the CHA board of trustees officially endorsed these principles. By 1992 the CHA had been a principal player in health-care reform based on universal access.

The CHA principles were generally in accord with the Clinton administration's reform package. The CHA insisted, however, that coverage for abortion services be removed from the basic benefit package. John E. Curley, Jr. stated in late September 1993: "The president has set the terms of the debate and demonstrated the bold presidential leadership that is required to elevate health-care reform to a national priority." Sister Maryanna Coyle, S.C., president of the Sisters of Charity of Cincinnati and 1993–94 chairperson of the CHA board of trustees, remarked, "CHA applauds President Clinton for his courage in taking the first step on what will be, no doubt, an ardous journey of a thousand miles." Auxiliary Bishop John H. Ricard of Baltimore also endorsed the president's "commitment to universal access" but regretted the "tragic step backward in the [Clinton proposal's] inclusion of abortion coverage as an integral part of national health-care reform."[10] Phillip Keane's book, *Health Care Reform: A Catholic View*, which is a theological, moral, and social reflection on contemporary health-care issues, provides a perspective for the above responses to President Clinton's proposals.[11]

A national health-care-reform program, aimed at severely reducing costs, could lead to rigid enforcement of balanced distribution of expensive medical technologies. Controls and consolidation could strongly threaten the Catholic presence in health care. However, the development of sponsorship, the rise of systems, and the CHA's myriad programs to foster leadership to respond to these challenges within a missionary commitment to adaptability in representing the gospel message means that the ministry has a deep sense of hope in the continuity of its vital role in the twenty-first century.

In 1990, of the 592 CHA-member hospitals, 428 were members of a system. Over the past several years some freestanding Catholic facilities with few sisters have become affiliated members of systems. The advantages of such affiliation include a wide range of services: management expertise; shared services, such as investment, insurance, and purchasing programs; mission effectiveness; pastoral services; and access to the ethics committee. Local autonomy of administration and the cultivation of the affiliate's individual charism are strongly appealing characteristics obviating the fear of being totally absorbed into the system.

The CHA, during Curley's administration, reflected the prevailing sentiment among those in the ministry. The association had been committed to the permeation of the Catholic presence in the contemporary facilities. The mission and identity of Catholic health care were clearly articulated during Pope John Paul's visit at a special CHA assembly in Phoenix, Arizona, on September 14, 1987. Sister Mary Eileen Wilhelm, R.S.M., presented the official welcome. With a sense of the historical significance of the ministry she said:

> Ours is a ministry of bringing life, of healing brokenness, of confronting death—one in which people care for one another, comfort and touch one another, and often journey with one another into the very mystery of God's love—the hope of resurrection. This ministry is a concrete manifestation of the power of the risen Christ, here and now.[12]

John Curley's remarks represent a candid report on the four challenges confronting Catholic health care. He cited the following challenges: (1) fidelity to stewardship and ministry responsibilities as laypersons, women religious, and dioceses to explore together "alternatives to traditional forms of sponsorship"; (2) commitment to organizational structures that respond to environmental complexities, ensure Catholic identity, and protect "the personhood of patients" despite an impersonal "medical and management maze"; (3) continuation of a ministry of service, especially to those "least able to care for themselves," in a "potentially ruinous economic climate"; and (4) renewed vigor in responding to contemporary moral dilemmas as "a countersign" that penetrates our pluralistic society "rather than merely paralleling" it.[13]

In his address, Pope John Paul II focused on the four challenges Curley articulated and emphasized Catholic identity, particularly in the commitments to the poor and needy that "witness to moral truth in the formation of society's moral vision" and how that identity "is essential for your ecclesial mission." He commended those in the health-care ministry for "their zeal and efficiency when, despite formidable costs, you still succeed in preventing the economic factor from being the determinate factor in human and Christian service." The Pope lauded the presence of women and men religious who ensured the religious mission of the past and present. He reminded the assembly that "new forms of ownership and management should not lead to a loss of spiritual atmosphere. . . . This is an area in which the Catholic laity, at all levels of healthcare, have an opportunity . . . to play their own specific part in the Church's mission of evangelization and service."[14]

The visit of Pope John Paul II appears to have energized the drive to continue refining the message of Catholic identity. For example, at Fordham University's April 1991 conference on that topic John Curley spoke on "Catholic Identity: Catholic Integrity." Curley's speech was a tripartite discussion of the who, why and what "we do" in Catholic health-care ministry.

In response to "who are we?" he referred to the healing ministry of Jesus, the Vatican II understanding of the people of God "called to holiness and ministry," and to a "faith tradition that includes rather than excludes."[15] Noting that most of the patients, physicians, nurses, and general employees and sources of funding are not Catholic, Curley emphasized that the inclusive character means "all who are gathered within the Catholic healing ministry are an essential witness to the name we bear."

"Why do we do what we do?" focused on the ministry's motivation to be sacrament. The CHA's leadership-formation manual, Healthcare Leadership: Shaping a Tomorrow, explained that "wherever life is being created, saved and sanctified, God is present as the ultimate author of

that activity." This motivation to sacrament "by intention and extension
. . . makes the communities we form Catholic."[16]

"What is it we are doing?" required an explanation of the inseparabil-
ity of identity and integrity. It entailed responses to three ecclesial challenges to Catholic identity—namely, formation of leadership in lay
ministry, promotion of the "sanctity of life and human dignity," and
management of the "tensions of change most often arising from the
intersection of principle and practice." Leadership formation during a
period when seventy percent of the administrators of Catholic facilities
are lay men and women must be recognized by the church as vital to its
ministry, while the leaders must be accountable to church reality. To
respond to the need for clear moral guidelines, complex clinical issues
demand that leaders of the health-care ministry must "penetrate, rather
than merely parallel our society." Management of these tensions of
change and obvious ecclesial polarization requires a spirit of inclusion,
honest respect for opposing views, and the commitment to "fashion
acceptable and accessible forums within our Church to enable and
encourage dialogue, understanding and trust."[17]

The general direction of Curley's address coincided with the Commission on Catholic Health Care Ministry (initiated by superiors of religious congregations sponsoring health-care facilities), which in 1988
issued its report, *Catholic Health Ministry: A New Vision for a New Century*. Concurrent with the commission's recommendations, a series of
CHA efforts culminated in the creation of the CHA's Center for Leadership Excellence. This center initiated a study to determine "what kind of
leader is best able to preserve the Catholic healing tradition in a period
of alliances, mergers and integrated delivery networks. What does that
leadership look like and how can we develop its underlying characteristics."[18]

The result was a CHA-sponsored study conducted by the Center for
Applied Social Research of DePaul University in Chicago and the Boston-
based firm, Hay McBer. The study was entitled "Transformational Leadership for the Healing Ministry: Competencies for the Future."[©] It found
that the executives in Catholic health care not only compared favorably
to their counterparts in business and industry, but also displayed unique
competencies that never or rarely have been found in other leadership
groups. These competencies, which drive superior performance among
executives in Catholic health care, are rooted in a personally defined
spirituality.[19]

To delve into a detailed description of this study is beyond the scope of this history. However, much of Curley's Fordham address presaged the general contours of the study, despite the fact that it preceded the initiation of the leadership study by three years. Both the study and the address emphasize the motives of the ministry's mission—to manage change with a missionary's transformationist vision and a preservationist understanding of the continuities derived from two centuries of Catholic health care in the United States.

II

The contemporary concern for a Catholic presence brings this history full circle. The need for a Catholic presence prompted Bishop Joseph Rosati, C.M., to ask the Sisters of Charity to staff Mullanphy Hospital in St. Louis in 1828. The drive for Catholic benevolence in health care led several bishops to seek religious for their hospitals in the burgeoning immigrant church. The Catholic response to the cholera epidemic has its contemporary analogue in the several Catholic hospices for persons with AIDS.[20] For example, the Alexian Brothers, who first gathered together in community to care for those struck by epidemics in the fourteenth century, have established Bonaventure House in Chicago for men and women with AIDS. The frontier experiences of Mother Joseph Pariseau, S.P., in Seattle, Mother Baptist Russell, R.S.M., in San Fransisco, the Incarnate Word Sisters in San Antonio and Houston, the Sisters of Charity of Leavenworth in Helena, Montana, have contemporary parallels in the lay and religious volunteer nurses in the clinics of Appalachia today. There are no Latino or Asian religious communities dedicated to nursing, like the Polish Felician sisters, but many Catholic hospitals have established satellite out-patient facilites in immigrant Latino and Asian neighborhoods in Florida, Texas, and California, while institutes have organized volunteers to serve migrant workers in various sections of the country.

The CHA's founder, Charles B. Moulinier, S.J., conceived modern health care in terms of the transcendent; religious dedication and the determination to achieve high standards of medical care were understood as providential for the church in America. Moulinier's legacy is manifested in the persistence to identify medical care with religious motivation. Alphonse Schwitalla, S.J., vigorously pursued Catholic influence in public policy, a style of advocacy that is embodied in the CHA's commitment to affecting the direction of health-care reform in the last decade of the twentieth century. The charisms of Sisters Mary Xavier

Clark, D.C., and Matilda Coskery, D.C., appear to animate, even today, many nurses, physicians, and pastoral ministers who attempt to balance professional and personal vocations to be both care givers and healers.

As mentioned earlier, Catholic identity is a protean term dependent on ethnicity, regional variations, struggles between modernity and tradition, and the structural ambiguities intrinsic to the private/public role of the general hospital. To maintain a religious ethos in the pluralistic spheres of a modern health-care facility demands several kinds of expertise among leaders in the ministry. Though it is not uncommon for large corporations to devise their own mission statements, Catholic health-care facilities strive to *be missionary*, committed to making religion come to life. Such a "missionary" understands that to inculturate the gospel in medical contexts it is necessary to engage in the personalist dynamic of health care. Perhaps Vincent de Paul's directive to the Daughters of Charity captures the myriad religious meanings of health-care ministry within pluralistic society. "When you leave your prayers for the bedside of a patient, you are leaving God for God. Looking after the sick is praying."[21]

Notes

Notes to the Introduction
EXPLORING THE BOUNDARIES

1. David Tracy, *Blessed Rage for Order: The New Pluralism in Theology* (New York, 1975), 105.

2. Victor Turner, *Dramas, Fields, and Metaphors: Symbolic Action in Human Society* (Ithaca, 1974).

3. Peter Berger, *The Sacred Canopy, Elements of a Sociological Theory of Religion* (Garden City, NY, 1967); Robert Wuthnow, *Rediscovering the Sacred* (Grand Rapids, MI, 1992).

4. Martin E. Marty, *The Irony of It All, 1893-1919: Modern American Religion*, Vol. 2 (Chicago, 1986).

5. Martin E. Marty, "Religion: A Private Affair, in Public Affairs," *Religion in American Culture: A Journal of Interpretation* 3 (Summer 1993): 126.

6. Quoted by Jean Delumeau, *Catholicism Between Luther and Voltaire: A New View of the Counter-Reformation* (Philadelphia, 1977), 59.

7. Charles E. Rosenberg, *The Care of Strangers: The Rise of America's Hospital System* (New York, 1987); and "Community and Communities: The Evolution of the American Hospital," in *The American General Hospital, Communities and Social Contexts*, ed. Diana Elizabeth Long and Janet Golden (Ithaca, NY, 1989); Rosemary A. Stevens, *In Sickness and in Wealth: American Hospitals in the Twentieth Century* (New York, 1989); and "Times Past, Times Present," in *The American General Hospital*, ed. Long and Golden.

8. David O'Brien, *Public Catholicism* (New York, 1989).

9. For an excellent analysis of pluralism, see Martin E. Marty, *Religion and Republic: The American Circumstance* (Boston, 1989).

10. For this idea I am indebted to Joseph P. Chinnici, O.F.M., *Living Stones: The History and Structure of Catholic Spirituality in America* (New York, 1989).

11. Elizabeth Johnson, *She Who Is: The Mystery of God in Feminist Theological Discourse* (New York, 1993), 28.

12. Margaret Susan Thompson, "Women, Feminism and New Religious History," in *Belief and Behavior: Essays in New Religious History*, ed. Philip R. Vandermeer and Robert P. Swierenga (New Brunswick, NJ, 1991), 137. For an excellent treatment of the public role of women religious, see Maureen Fitzgerald, "Irish-Catholic Nuns and the Development of New York City's Welfare System 1840–1900" (Ph.D. diss., University of Wisconsin, Madison, 1992).

13. Stevens, *In Sickness and in Wealth*, 3–16.

14. H. Stuart Hughes, *History as Art and as Science* (New York, 1964).

Notes to Chapter One
PROLOGUE: THE EUROPEAN TRADITIONS

1. Elliot N. Dorff, "The Jewish Tradition," in *Caring and Curing: Health and Medicine in the Western Religious Traditions,* ed. Ronald Numbers and Darrell W. Amundsen (New York, 1986), 15. Also see Patricia Maloof, "Sickness and Health in Societies," in *The Pastoral Care of the Sick,* ed. Mary C. Collins and David N. Power (Concilium 2; Philadelphia, 1991). There are many histories of medicine. For an overview, see A. Ackerknect, *A Short History of Medicine* (Baltimore, 1982). For a brief summary on Catholic attitudes, see Andrea Richardson, "Compassion and Cures, A Historical Look at Catholicism and Medicine," *The Journal of the American Medical Association* (December 1991): 3063.

2. Darrell W. Amundsen and Gary B. Ferngren, "The Early Christian Era," in *Curing and Caring*, 58.

3. Ibid. Also see Francis X. Cleary, S.J., "Suffering in Biblical Perspective," *The Mission of Healing: Readings in Christian Values and Health Care*, ed. Kevin O'Rourke (St. Louis, 1974), 1–10.

4. "The Early Christian Era," in *Curing and Caring*, p. 49.

5. Ibid.

6. Quoted by Charles W. Gusmer, "Anointing of the Sick," in *New Dictionary of Theology*, ed. Joseph Komonchak, Mary Collins, and Dermot Lane (Wilmington, DE, 1987), 23. Also see Dionisio Borobio, "An Inquiry into Healing Anointing in the Early Church," in *Pastoral Care of the Sick*, 37–49.

7. Mary Collins, O.S.B., "The Roman Ritual: Pastoral Care and Anointing of the Sick," in *The Pastoral Care of the Sick*, 3–18.

8. Bernard Poschmann, *Penance and Christian Anointing* (New York, 1964) 243–44.

9. Ibid.

10. "The Early Christian Era," in *Curing and Caring*, 49.

11. C. M. Frank, "History of Nursing," in *The New Catholic Encyclopedia* (New York, 1967), 10: 582.

12. Natalie Boynel Kampden, "Before Florence Nightingale: A Pre-history of Nursing in Painting and Sculpture," in *Images of Nurses: Perspectives from History, Art and Literature*, ed. Anne Hudson Jones (Philadelphia, 1988), 23.

13. Ibid., 29.

14. Muriel Joy Hughes, *Women Healers in Medieval Life and Literature* (New York, 1943), 120–23.

15. Ibid., 132.

16. Ibid., 138.

17. Albert Huyskens, "Die Anfänge der Aachener im Zusammenhang der Ordens-und Ortsgeschichte," *Zeitschrift des Aachener Geschichtsvereins*, 1928 (English translation in Alexian Brothers Archives, Elk Grove, IL), 2.

18. M. D. Chenu, O.P., *Nature, Man and Society in the Twelfth Century*, ed. and trans. Jerome Taylor and Lester K. Little (Chicago, 1957); Ernest W. McDonnell, "The Vita Apostolica: Diversity or Dissent," *Church History* 24 (March 1955); and Jean Delumeau, *Sin and Fear* (New York, 1990).

19. Bruder Bernard Giergen, *Das Alexianer Kloster in Köln-Lindenthal in seiner geschichtlichen Entwicklung* (from the manuscript of the deceased Thomas Paas) (Cologne-Lindenthal, 1934).

20. Floris Prims, *Geschiedenis van Antwerpen* (Antwerp, 1929), 2: 264.

21. Henry Charles Lea, *A History of the Inquisition of the Middle Ages* (New York, 1955), 2: 355.

22. For a general statement of the etymology, see Ernst W. McDonnell, *The Beguines and Beghards in Medieval Culture* (New Brunswick, 1954), 432.

23. *Oxford English Dictionary* (Oxford, 1961), 6: 202.

24. Dietrich von Kurze, "Die festländischen Lollarden," *Archiv für Kulturgeschichte* 47 (1965): 76.

25. McDonnell, *Beguines and Beghards*, 266 n. 5.

26. Prims, *Geschiedenis*, 2: 264.

27. Heinrich Goos, *Geschichte der rheinischen Stadtkultur* (Berlin, 1897), 3: 208.

28. "Die letzten mittalterlichen Laienbrüder," *Alexiana* 12 (Aachen, 1950): 89.

29. McDonnell, *Beguines and Beghards*, 267.

30. Walter John Marx, "The Development of Charity in Medieval Louvain" (Ph.D. diss., Columbia University, 1936), 9.

31. "Bull of Pope Eugene IV," 1431, English translation in the Alexian Brothers Archives, Elk Grove, IL.

32. A. F. C. Van Schevensteen, *Documents pour L'Etude des Maladies pestélentielles dans le marquisot d'Anvers jusque La Chute de L'Ancien Regime*, ed. Lamertin (Brussels: Commission Royale d'Histoire, 1931), 1: 48.

33. Ibid., 2: 12.

34. Ibid., 2: 26.

35. Giergen, *Das Alexianer Kloster*, 68.

36. H. D. J. van Schevichaven, *Oud-Nijmegens Kerken, Klooster, Gasthuizen, Stichtingen en Opengare Gebouwen* (Nijmegen: Firma H. Ten Hoet, 1909), 60.

37. Quoted in "An Enthusiastic Eulogy of the Old Cellites or Alexian Brothers," *St. Alexius Almanac* (Aachen, 1934), 7: 9.

38. Quoted by Elizabeth Rapley, *The Devôtes, Women and Church in Seventeenth Century France* (Montreal, 1990), 19.

39. Jean Delumeau, *Catholicism Between Luther and Voltaire: A New View of the Counter-Reformation* (Philadelphia, 1977).

40. Ibid., 36–37.

41. Ibid., 37.

42. Rapley, *The Devôtes*, 21.

43. Ibid., 7.

44. Ibid., 7–8.

45. Ibid., 8.

46. Delumeau, *Catholicism*, 37–38. Vincent's quote is found in Delumeau but I used a preferred translation in M. M. Considine, "Daughters of Charity of St. Vincent de Paul" in *The New Catholic Encyclopedia* (New York, 1967), 3: 470.

47. Colin Jones, *The Charitable Imperative: Hospitals and Nursing in Ancient Regime and Revolutionary France* (London, 1989), 37–38.

48. Ibid., 39.

49. Ibid., 40–43.

50. Ibid., 95–96.

51. Ibid., 101.

52. Quoted by Jones, *The Charitable Imperative*, 104.

53. Ibid., 105. Also see Colin Jones, "Sisters of Charity and the Ailing Poor," *Social History of Medicine* (1989).

54. Cf. M. B. Bauman, *A Way of Mercy: Catherine McAuley's Contribution to Nursing* (New York, 1958); M. B. Degnan, *Mercy Unto Thousands: Life of Mother Mary Catherine McAuley* (Westminster, MD, 1957); M. J. Gately, *The Sisters of Mercy: Historical Sketches, 1831–1931* (New York, 1931); M. B. Herron, *The Sisters of Mercy in the United States, 1843–1928* (New York, 1929); M. I. Lennon, *Mother Catherine McAuley* (St. Louis, 1958); R. Savage, *Catherine McAuley: The First Sister of Mercy* (Dublin, 1949).

55. *The Rule and Constitutions of the Religious Called Sisters of Mercy* (Dublin, 1863), 5. This is an English translation of the documents approved by Pope Gregory XVI in June 1841.

56. Ibid., 7.

57. Ibid., 8.

58. Ibid., 10.

59. Ibid., 11.

60. Ibid., 12.

61. Quoted by M. B. Bauman, *A Way of Mercy*, 108–9.

62. Sister Mary Cecilia O'Sullivan, *The Sisters of Bon Secours in the United States, 1881–1981: A Century of Caring* (York, PA, 1982).

Notes to Chapter Two
THE MARYLAND EXPERIENCE, 1634–1850

1. Marvin O'Connell, "The Roman Catholic Tradition" in *Curing and Caring: Health and Medicine in the Western Religious Traditions,* ed. Ronald Numbers and Darrell W. Amundsen (New York, 1986), 119.

2. Ibid., 120.

3. Robert Emmett Curran, S.J., *American Jesuit Spirituality, The Maryland Tradition* (Mahwah, NJ, 1988), 64–65.

4. Ibid., 65.

5. O'Connell, "The Roman Catholic Tradition," 112–17.

6. Ibid., 121.

7. Ibid., 130–31.

8. Paul Starr, *The Social Transformation of American Medicine* (New York, 1982), 35.

9. Jon Butler, *Awash in the Sea of Faith* (New Haven, 1990), 67–97.

10. Thomas O'Brien Hanley, "Pastoral on Epidemic," in *The John Carroll Papers* (Notre Dame, IN, 1976), 2: 314–16. On Carroll's spirituality, see Joseph P. Chinnici, O.F.M., *Living Stones: The History and Structures of the Catholic Spiritual Life in the United States* (New York, 1989). For works on Carroll, see: John Tracy Ellis, *American Catholicism* (Chicago, 1969); James Hennesey, S.J., "An Eighteenth Century Bishop: John Carroll of Baltimore," in *Patterns of Episcopal Leadership,* ed. Gerald P. Fogarty, S.J. (New York, 1989), 5–34; and "The Vision of John Carroll," *Thought* 54 (1979): 322–33; Annabelle Melville, *John Carroll* (New York, 1955); David O'Brien, *Public Catholicism* (New York, 1989), 8–34; and Margaret M. Reher, *Catholic Intellectual Life in America* (New York, 1989), 1–28; Thomas Spalding, C.F.X., *The Premier See: A History of the Archdiocese of Baltimore* (Baltimore, 1989).

11. Hanley, "Pastoral on Epidemic," 316.

12. Ibid.

13. *Souvenir Book, Sesquicentennial of St. Patrick's 1792–1942* (Baltimore, 1942), 49–51.

14. Ibid., 52–53.

15. Ibid., 53–57.

16. Bernard U. Campbell, "Memoir of the Reverend John Francis Moranville," *Religious Cabinet* 1 (1842): 629–35.

17. Charles E. Rosenberg, *The Care of Strangers: The Rise of America's Hospital System* (New York, 1987), 18–20.

18. Ibid., 15.

19. Ibid., 18–30.

20. Sister Bernadette Armiger, "The Work of the Daughters of Charity of St. Vincent de Paul in the Eastern Province of the United States, 1823–1860" (M.A. thesis, Catholic University of America, 1947).

21. Armiger, "The Work of the Daughters of Charity," 2. Also see Carlan Kraman, O.S.F., "Women Religious in Health Care, The Early Years," in *Pioneer Healers: The History of Women Religious in American Healthcare,* ed. Ursula Step-

sis, C.S.A., and Dolores Liptak, R.S.M. (New York, 1989), 15-38. For a comprehensive history of women religious, see George C. Stewart, Jr., *Marvels of Charity: History of American Sisters and Nuns* (Huntington, IN, 1994). For
bibliography on this topic, see Elizabeth Kolmer, A.S.C., *Religious Women in the
United States: A Survey of Influential Literature from 1950 to 1983* (Wilmington,
DE, 1984).

22. Barbara Misner, S.C.S.C., "Highly Respected and Accomplished Ladies,"
Catholic Women Religious in America (New York, 1988), 57. Also see Ann Doyle,
"Nursing by Religious in the United States, part 1, 1809-1840," *American Journal of Nursing* 29 (July 1929): 775- 85. For a study of the history of Baltimore
hospitals, see Jon Mikingsdale, *The Growth of Hospitals 1850-1939* (New York,
1989).

23. Armiger, "The Work of the Daughters of Charity," 3.

24. Ibid., 4.

25. Ibid., 8.

26. Ibid., 8-9.

27. "Reference work," part one, anonymous. Part two was composed by
Mother Mary Xavier Clark, S.C. I am grateful to Sister Daniel Hannefin, D.C., for
providing me with a copy of this valuable document. Since there is no pagination I will footnote with ibid. at appropriate places in the text and will use Sister
Clark's title "Instructions on the Care of the Sick." Hereafter cited as "Instructions."

28. Sister Daniel Hannefin, D.C., *Daughters of the Church: A Popular History of
the Daughters of Charity in the United States 1809- 1987* (Brooklyn, 1987), 34, 67.

29. "Instructions."

30. Ibid.

31. Ibid.

32. Ibid.

33. Ibid.

34. Joseph Menard, "Maternity of the Spirit, Nuns and Domesticity in
Ante-bellum America," *U.S. Catholic Historian* 5 (1986): 310-25.

35. Starr, *Social Transformation,* 32.

36. Ibid., 33.

37. John R. Guinan, *Medical Annals of Baltimore* (Baltimore, 1844), 34.

38. Ibid.

39. On Deluol, see Christopher J. Kauffman, *Tradition and Transformation in
Catholic Culture: The Priests of St. Sulpice in the United States, 1791 to the Present*
(New York, 1988).

40. Quoted by Misner, *"Highly Respected and Accomplished Ladies,"* 221.

41. Quoted by Hannefin, *Daughters of the Church,* 56.

42. Ibid., 57.

43. Ibid.

44. Wm. H. Stokes, M.D., "Mount Hope; An Institution Belonging to and Conducted by the Sisters of Charity of St. Joseph and attended by William H. Stokes,
M.D.," *The Catholic Magazine* 6 (September 1847): 487.

45. Ibid., 489.

46. For an identity of this manuscript, see Hannefin, *Daughters of the Church,* 58.

47. "A Manual for the Care of the Sick," 11.

48. Ibid., 12.

49. Ibid., 13.

50. Ibid., 16.

51. Ibid., 18.

52. Ibid.

53. See Gerda Lerner, *The Creation of Feminist Consciousness from the Middle Ages to Eighteen Seventy* (New York, 1993), 3–20.

Notes to Chapter Three
EPIDEMICS: RESPONSES TO THE CHOLERA 1832–1852

1. William B. Faherty, *Dream by the River: Two Centuries of St. Louis Catholicism* (St. Louis, 1973).

2. Annabelle Melville, *Louis William DuBourg* (Chicago, 1987). Also see Frederick J. Easterly, C.M., *The Life of Rt. Rev. Joseph Rosati, First Bishop of St. Louis, 1789–1843* (Washington, DC, 1942).

3. Quoted by Sister M. Lillian Quinn, *The St. Louis Hospital* (St. Louis, 1915), 18.

4. Ibid.

5. Charles E. Rosenberg, *The Cholera Years: The United States in 1832, 1849, and 1866* (Chicago, 1962), 3.

6. Ibid., 3–5.

7. Ibid., 40.

8. Ibid., 40.

9. Ibid., 48–49.

10. Whitfield's Pastoral Letters, June 29, 1832, RG 26, Box 8, Sulpician Archives Baltimore (hereafter cited as SAB).

11. Ibid.

12. Joubert Diary, 29 September 1832, 18, Archives of the Oblate Sisters of Providence, copy SAB. For historical works on the Oblate Sisters, see Sister M. Reginald Gerdes, O.S. P., "To Educate and Evangelize: Black Catholic Schools of the Oblate Sisters of Providence (1828–1880)," *U.S. Catholic Historian* 7 (Spring–Summer 1988): 183–200; Thaddeus Posey, "An Unwanted Commitment: The Spirituality of the Early Oblates, Sisters of Providence, 1829–1890" (Ph.D. diss., St. Louis University, 1993); Margaret Susan Thompson, "Philemon's Dilemma: Nuns and the Black Community: Some Findings," *Records of the American Catholic Historical Society of Philadelphia* 96 (March–December 1986): 3–8.

13. Joubert Diary, 26 August 1832, 16.

14. Armiger, "The Work of the Daughters of Charity," 30–31.

15. Joubert Diary, 26 September 1832, 17.

16. Quoted by Armiger, "The Work of the Daughters of Charity," 35.

17. Ibid., 39.

18. Ibid., 43.

19. Rosenberg, *The Cholera Years*, 95.

20. Cyprian Davis, *The History of Black Catholics in the United States* (New York, 1990), 92.

21. Ibid., 93.

22. Quinn, *The St. Louis Hospital*, 20-21.

23. Ibid., 23.

24. Faherty, *Dream by the River*, 44-45.

25. Quinn, *The St. Louis Hospital*, 23.

26. Quoted by Leslie Woodcock Tentler, *Seasons of Grace: The History of the Archdiocese of Detroit* (Detroit, 1990), 17.

27. George Paré, *The Catholic Church in Detroit 1701-1888* (Detroit, 1951), 659.

28. Ibid., 663.

29. Tentler, *Seasons of Grace,* 78.

30. Quoted by Quinn, *The St. Louis Hospital*, 28-30.

31. Rosenberg, *The Cholera Years*, 115.

32. Misner, *"Highly Respected and Accomplished Ladies,"* 224-33.

33. Sister Doloreta Marie Dougherty, C.S.J., et al., *Sisters of St. Joseph of Carondelet* (St. Louis, 1961), 61.

34. *The Metropolitan Catholic Almanac* (Baltimore, 1849), 78-84. For the foundation of the Sisters of Mercy in Pittsburgh, see Sister M. Jerome McHale, R.S.M., *On The Wing: The Story of the Pittsburgh Sisters of Mercy 1843-1868* (New York, 1980).

35. Charles I. White, "Reflections on the Time of Cholera," *United States Catholic Magazine* 8 (June 16, 1849), 378-79.

36. M. Edmund Hussey, "John Baptist Purcell, First Archbishop of Cincinnati" in *Patterns of Episcopal Leadership*, ed. Gerald P. Fogarty (New York, 1989), 92.

37. Ibid., 90.

38. John Baptist Purcell, "Pastoral Letter," *United States Catholic Magazine* 8 (1849): 475.

39. Ibid.

40. Rosenberg, *The Cholera Years*, 135.

41. Ibid., 137.

42. Purcell, "Pastoral Letter," 475.

43. Ibid., 476.

44. "The Pastoral Letter of the Third Provincial Council of Baltimore 1837," in *The National Pastorals of the American Hierarchy*, ed. Peter Guilday (Washington, DC, 1923), 116.

45. *The Metropolitan Catholic Almanac* (Baltimore, 1850), 125-26.

Notes to Chapter Four
CATHOLIC BENEVOLENCE

1. Charles E. Rosenberg, *The Care of Strangers: The Rise of America's Hospital System* (New York, 1989), 102. The literature on immigration is vast; for general treatment of Catholic immigration, see Jay P. Dolan, *The American Catholic*

Catholic Church in Nebraska (Milwaukee, 1960-66); Carlos E. Castañeda, *Our Catholic Heritage in Texas,* 6 vols. (Austin, 1936-50); Robert J. Dwyer, *The Gentile Comes to Utah* (Washington, DC, 1941); Michael E. Engh, S.J., *Frontier Faiths: Church, Temple, and Synagogue in Los Angeles, 1846-1888* (Albuquerque, 1993); Gilbert J. Garraghan, S.J., *The Jesuits of the Middle United States,* 3 vols. (New York, 1938); William Howlett, *Life of the Right Reverend Joseph Machebeuf* (Pueblo, 1908); Thomas A. Kinsella, *A Century of Catholicity in Kansas, 1822-1922* (Kansas City, 1921); John Bernard McGloin, S.J., *California's First Archbishop: The Life of Joseph Sadoc Alemany, O.P., 1848-1888* (New York, 1966); Francis J. Weber, *California's Reluctant Prelate: The Life and Times of Right Reverend Thaddeus Amat, 1811-1878* (Los Angeles, 1964).

2. Quoted by Martin E. Marty, *Pilgrims in Their Own Land* (Chicago, 1984), 1.

3. Spalding, "Frontier Catholicism," 4.

4. Thomas V. McAvoy, "Americanism and Frontier Catholicism," *Review of Politics* 5 (1943): 275-301.

5. *The Metropolitan Catholic Almanac and Laity Directory* (Baltimore, 1855), 243.

6. Quoted by James M. Moynihan, *John Ireland: A Definitive Biography* (New York, 1953), 33-34.

7. Helen Angela Hurley, C.S.J., "The St. Paul Province," in *Sisters of St. Joseph of Carondelet* (St. Louis, 1966), 194. Also see *Sadliers' Directory and Ordo* (New York, 1885), 306-13.

8. Hurley, "The St. Paul Province," 197. Ann Thomasina Sampson, C.S.J., *Care with Prayer: The History of St. Mary's Hospital and Rehabilitation Center Minneapolis, Minnesota 1887-1897* (Minneapolis, 1987), 2-3.

9. Kathleen O'Brien, *Journeys: A Pre-Amalgamation History of the Sisters of Mercy Omaha Province* (Omaha, 1987), 399.

10. Letitia M. Lyons, *Francis Norbert Blanchet and the Founding of the Oregon Missions, 1838-1848* (Washington, DC, 1940).

11. Wilfred Schoenberg, S.J., *A History of the Catholic Church in the Northwest* (Washington, DC, 1987), 137-38.

12. Quoted by Schoenberg, *A History of the Catholic Church,* 154.

13. Ibid., 159.

14. From the sisters of Vancouver to the sisters of the motherhouse, January 14, 1861, Sisters of Providence Archives Seattle (SPAS) 3/1-3/2.

15. Ibid.

16. Ibid.

17. Mother Joseph to Bishop Bourget, February 28, 1860, or December 18, 1858, SPAS 6/1 to 6/6.

18. Mother Joseph to Bishop Laroque, March, 1859, SPAS 4/1 to 4/4.

19. Schoenberg, *A History of the Catholic Church,* 258.

20. Each of these quotes is cited by Gerald McKevitt, S.J., "The Art of Conversion: Jesuits and Flatheads in Nineteenth-Century Montana," *The U.S. Catholic Historian* 21 (Fall 1994): 60

21. *Sadlier's Catholic Almanac and Ordo* (New York, 1865), 202.

22. Mother Joseph to B. Brouillet, December 13, 1862, SPAS #13.

23. "Our Hospitals," *The Catholic Northwest Progress*, October 22, 1965, 24.

24. Mother Joseph to B. Brouillet, December 13, 1862, SPAS, #13.

25. *Sadlier's Catholic Almanac and Ordo* (New York, 1875), 275–58.

26. "Providence Hospital," newspaper cutting undated, SPAS #15.

27. Ibid.

28. *Catholic Directory Almanac and City List Quarterly* (New York, 1902): 122, 426–27.

29. Quoted by Alice St. Hilare, S.P., "Charisms of the Sisters of Providence," 9, copy SPAS.

30. Ibid., 10.

31. Schoenberg, *A History of the Catholic Church*, 37–39.

32. For the foundation story of the Sisters of Charity of Leavenworth, see Sister Mary Buckner, S.C.L., *History of the Sisters of Charity of Leavenworth, Kansas* (Kansas City, MO, 1898, reprinted 1985), 22–23. See also Clyde Crews, *An American Holy Land: A History of the Archdiocese of Louisville* (Wilmington, DE, 1987), 87–88; and Ann Blanche McGill, *The Sisters of Charity of Nazareth, Kentucky* (New York, 1917), 3: 55; Thomas Stritch, *The Catholic Church in Tennessee: The Sesquicentennial Story* (Nashville, 1987), 107–10.

33. Buckner, 34–43.

34. Ibid., 44–55.

35. Julia Gilmore, S.C.L., *We Came North* (Leavenworth, 1969), 16–17.

36. *Catholic Directory* (New York, 1884), 496. Also see Cornelia M. Flaherty, *A History of the Diocese of Helena* (Helena, 1984).

37. L. B. Palladino, "The Sisters of Charity of Leavenworth, Kansas, in Montana," in Buckner, 471.

38. Gilmore, *We Came North*, 79.

39. Buckner, 260.

40. Gilmore, *We Came North*, 49.

41. Quoted by Thomas Noel, *Colorado Catholicism and the Archdiocese of Denver 1852–1859* (Denver, 1989), 25.

42. Ibid., 30.

43. "A Hospital for Georgetown, August 14, 1880," *The Colorado Miner*, newspaper cutting, Georgetown files, Sisters of St. Joseph Archives, Carondelet, Missouri.

44. "The Holy Cross Hospital: The Early Years" (Salt Lake City, 1976), 11–12, Sisters of the Holy Cross Archives, Notre Dame, Indiana (hereafter cited as SHCA).

45. Ibid., 13–14.

46. Francis J. Weber, ed., "The Church in Utah, 1882. A Contemporary Account," *Records* 81 (December 1970): 203.

47. Ibid., 204.

48. Mary Ewens, O.P., *The Role of the Nun in Nineteenth-Century America* (New York, 1978).

49. Ibid., 92–105.

50. Brother Franklin Cullin, C.S.C., "Holy Cross in the Black Hills: The

Dakota Apostolates, 1878-1897," 1-4. A privately circulated article; copy in SHCA.

51. Ibid., 5.

52. Ibid., 7.

53. "Holy Cross Sisters in Deadwood," a one page summary, SHCA.

54. "Holy Cross Sisters in Lead City," a one page summary, SHCA.

55. Sister M. Magdeline Callahan, O.S.B., "The Beginnings of the Benedictine Convent of St. Martin, SD, 1889-1915" (M.A. thesis, St. Benedict's College, 1963), 9; copy SHCA.

56. *The Catholic Directory, Almanac and Clergy List Quarterly* (Milwaukee, 1900), 503.

57. James Talmadge Moore, *Through Fire and Flood, The Catholic Church in Frontier Texas, 1836-1900* (Lubbock, TX, 1992).

58. Quoted in Sister Mary Helena Fink, *The Congregation of the Incarnate Word of San Antonio Texas* (Washington, DC, 1925), 34.

59. Ibid., 35-36.

60. Ibid., 43-44.

61. Ibid., 88.

62. Maria Luisa Valez, "The Pilgrimage of Hispanics in the Sisters of Charity of the Incarnate Word," *The U.S. Catholic Historian* 9 (Winter/Spring 1990), 181-94.

63. *Catholic Almanac and Yearbook* (New York, 1929).

64. Paul Horgan, *Lamy of Sante Fe* (New York, 1963), 321-23.

65. Quoted in Horgan, *Lamy,* 321.

66. A. Chaves, *The Old Faith and the Old Glory: Story of the Church in New Mexico Since the American Occupation 1846-1946* (Santa Fe, 1946).

67. Summary histories of these foundations are located in the Archives of the Sisters of Mercy, Burlingame, CA. (hereafter cited as ASMB).

68. Michael E. Engh, S.J., *Frontier Faiths,* 139-63.

69. Sister Mary Athanasius Sheridan, R.S.M., . . . *and Some Fell on Good Ground, A History of the Sisters of Mercy of California and Arizona* (New York, 1975), 76.

70. Catherine Ann Curry, P.B.V.M., "Three Irish Women and Social Action in San Francisco: Mother Teresa Comerford, Mother Baptist Russell and Kate Kennedy," *Journal of the West* 31 (April 1992): 66-71.

71. Quoted by Sheridan, . . . *and Some Fell,* 76.

72. Ibid., 77.

73. Ibid.

74. Quoted in manuscript "Annals of the Sisters of Mercy, Burlingame, 1868-69," ASMB.

75. Ibid.

76. Matthew Russell, *The Life of Baptist Russell* (New York, 1902), 117. Also see Sister Aurelia (Rose) McArdle, R.S.M., *California's Pioneer Sister of Mercy, Mother Mary Baptist Russell 1829-1898* (Fresno, 1954).

77. Ibid., 120.

78. Quoted by Sheridan, . . . *and Some Fell,* 94-96.

79. Ibid., 98.

80. Copy of this letter is in the "Annals of the Sisters of Mercy, Burlingame 1855-1898," ASMB.

81. San Francisco *Call,* August 10, 1898. Copy ASMB.

Part Two
MODERNIZATION AND THE PERSISTENCE OF TRADITION: 1890-1948

1. Mary Ewens, "Removing the Veil: The Liberated Nun in the 19th Century," Working Paper No. 3 (Spring 1978) CUSHWA Center, University of Notre Dame: 23.

Notes to Chapter Seven
THE CONVERGENCE OF SUBCULTURES: MEDICAL,
RELIGIOUS, AND ETHNIC, 1890-1915

1. Charles E. Rosenberg, *The Care of Strangers: The Rise of America's Hospital System* (New York, 1986), 121.

2. Ibid., 160.

3. Ibid., 130.

4. Charles E. Rosenberg, "Florence Nightingale on Contagion: The Hospital as a Moral Universe" in *Healing and History,* ed. Charles E. Rosenberg (New York, 1979), 124.

5. Rosenberg, *Care of Strangers,* 158-62.

6. Paul Starr, *The Social Transformation of American Medicine* (New York, 1982), 156.

7. Mary Ewens, O.P., *The Nun in Nineteenth-Century America* (New York, 1978), 252.

8. John O'Grady, *Catholic Charities in the United States* (Washington, DC, 1930), 195-201. For works on immigration and ethnicity, see Colman J. Barry, *The Catholic Church and German Americans* (Milwaukee, 1953); John Bodnar, *The Transplanted: A History of Immigrants in Early America* (Bloomington, IN, 1985); Hasia R. Diner, *Erin's Daughters in America: Irish Immigrant Women in the Nineteenth Century* (Baltimore, 1982); Jay P. Dolan, *The American Catholic Experience: A History from the Colonial Times to the Present* (New York, 1986); Dolores Liptak, R.S.M., *Immigrants and Their Church* (New York, 1989); Margaret Susan Thompson, "Cultural Conundrum: Sisters, Ethnicity and the Adaptation of American Catholicism," *Mid-America, An Historical Review* 74 (October 1992): 205-30.

9. Starr, *Social Transformation,* 169.

10. Carlan Kraman, O.S.F., *Odyssey of Faith: The Story of Mother Alfred Moes* (Rochester, 1990), 1-6.

11. Ibid., 179.

12. Ibid., 177–83.

13. "Mayo, Charles Horace," and "Mayo, William James," *The Encyclopedia Britannica* (Chicago, 1962), 45: 124-28.

14. Minutes of the Medical Staff, Alexian Brothers' Hospital, Chicago, February 6, 1894. Archives of the Alexian Brothers of America (hereafter cited as AAB-EG) Elk Grove, Illinois.

15. Ibid., February 1893.

16. Report of Alexian Brothers' Hospital (Chicago, 1899), 11. AAB-EG.

17. See Christopher Kauffman, *Ministry of Healing: The History of the Alexian Brothers, 1789 to the Present* (New York, 1978), 174.

18. "Act of Incorporation," C-2, Box 1, Folder 1, AAB-EG.

19. Alfred Theodore Andreas, *History of Chicago* (New York: Arno Press reprint of the 1884-86 edition, 1975), 2: 357.

20. Ibid.

21. Nineteenth Annual Report of the Alexian Brothers' Hospital, Chicago, Illinois (Chicago, 1886), 27. Copy AAB-EG.

22. Andreas, *History of Chicago,* 2: 352.

23. See Kauffman, *Ministry of Healing,* 86-87.

24. Report of the Alexian Brothers' Hospital (1898), 11-12. AAB-EG.

25. Ibid., 12-13.

26. "History of the Nursing School," unpublished manuscript, AAB-EG.

27. "Brief Diary of the Establishment of the St. Louis House, September 24, 1869." Document 13 Pro-11, Box 3, Folder 1, AAB-EG.

28. Peter Clement Walrath to the American Province, June 12, 1869. Pro-1 Document 9, Box 1, Folder 1, AAB-EG.

29. *Golden Jubilee Alexian Brothers Hospital, St. Louis, Missouri.* AAB-EG.

30. Kauffman, *Ministry of Healing,* 104-5.

31. Ibid., 106-8.

32. Newspaper cuttings, C-10, AAB-EG.

33. Kauffman, *Ministry of Healing,* 112.

34. *Golden Jubilee,* 45.

35. Rosemary Stevens, *In Sickness and in Wealth: American Hospitals in the Twentieth Century* (New York, 1989), 29.

36. *Catholic Directory and Almanac* (Baltimore, 1903), 51.

37. Quoted by Joy Clough, R.S.M., *Mercy Hospital* (Chicago, 1979), 47.

38. Charles Shanabruch, *Chicago's Catholics* (Notre Dame, IN, 1981), 39.

39. Berenice Beck, "Manuscript History of the Wheaton Franciscans," 11. Archives of the Wheaton Franciscans, Wheaton, Illinois.

40. Ibid., 24.

41. O'Grady, *Catholic Charities,* 399.

42. Beck, "Manuscript History," 105.

43. Ibid.

44. *The Official Catholic Directory* (New York, 1915), 209.

45. "History of St. Joseph's German Hospital from its Commencement,"

unpublished manuscript located in the archives St. Joseph's Hospital, Towson, Maryland.

46. Ibid.

47. Ibid., 3.

48. Ibid., 36.

49. Minutes of the Medical Board.

50. "History of the Nursing School," unpublished manuscript.

51. *Rules and Constitutions of the Franciscan Sisters of Philadelphia* (Glen Riddle, PA, 1900), 70. For a history of the Tertiaries and health care, see William A. Ellert, T.O.R., "The Franciscan Ministry of Healing," *Review for Religious* 47 (Sept./Oct. 1988): 718-29.

52. *Rules and Constitutions of the Franciscan Sisters of Philadelphia*, 99.

53. Ibid., 102.

54. *The Catholic Directory and Almanac* (Baltimore, 1901), 17-18.

55. O'Grady, *Catholic Charities*, 397-403.

56. Quoted by Silvano M. Tomasi, C.S., "Scalabrinians and the Pastoral Care of the Immigrants, 1887-1987," *The U.S. Catholic Historian* 6 (Fall 1987): 258. Also see Marco Caliaro and Mario Francesconi, *John Baptist Scalabrini: Apostle to Emigrants* (New York, 1977). For Frances Cabrini, see Mary Louise Sullivan M.S.C., "Mother Cabrini: 'Italian Immigrant of the Century,'" (Ph.D. diss., Bryn Mawr College, 1984), and her recent book of the same title (New York, 1992), and her article "Mother Cabrini: Missionary to Italian Immigrants," *The U.S. Catholic Historian* 6 (Fall 1987): 265-79. Also see, Robert Anthony Orsi, *The Madonna of 115th Street: Faith and Community in Italian Harlem 1880-1950* (New Haven, 1985).

57. Stephen Michael DiGiovanni, "Mother Cabrini's Early Years in New York," *Catholic Historical Review* 77 (January 1991): 139-59.

58. Mary Louis Sullivan, *Mother Cabrini: "Italian Immigrant of the Century"* (New York, 1990), 192-97.

59. Ibid., 278.

60. Ibid., 269.

61. Ibid., 270.

62. Quoted in "Early History of St. Joseph's Infirmary," *St. Joseph's Nurse* I (July 1939): 1-14. Archives of St. Joseph's Hospital, Atlanta (hereafter cited as ASJH), RG 6-1, Folder 14.

63. Michael McNally, "A Peculiar Institution: History of the Catholic Parish in the Southeast," in *The American Catholic Parish*, ed. Jay Dolan (Mahwah, NJ, 1987), 1: 131.

64. *History of St. Joseph's Hospital, Savannah, Georgia* (Savannah, 1945), 3. I am grateful to Sister Felicitas Powers, R.S.M., for providing me with a copy of this work.

65. Ibid., 7-13.

66. Ibid., 23.

67. Paul Starr, *The Social Transformation of American Medicine* (New York, 1982), 144.

68. John Higham, *Strangers in the Land: Patterns of American Nativism 1860-1925* (New York, 1963).

69. *Annual Report of Carney Hospital for the Year 1908*, 11, Archives of the Daughters of Charity, Eastern Province (hereafter cited as ADCEP), 11-35, 1-12 #8.

70. Ibid., 12. For an excellent study of Boston hospitals, see J. Morris Vogel, *The Invention of the Modern Hospital Boston: 1870-1931* (Chicago, 1980).

71. Joan E. Lynaugh, "From Respectable Domesticity to Medical Efficiency: The Changing Kansas City Hospital" in *The American General Hospital,* ed. Diana Elizabeth Long and Janet Golden (Ithaca, NY, 1989), 28.

72. *Fifth Report of the Medical Staff,* St. John's Hospital, Lowell. ADCEP, 11-40, 1-1, #11a.

73. Lynaugh, "From Respectable Domesticity," 32-39.

74. *Annual Report of Carney Hospital 1908 . . .* , see note 69.

75. Diana Culbertson, O.P., *Rose Hawthorne Lathrop: Selected Writings* (Mahwah, NJ, 1994), Introduction, 3-96.

76. Ibid., 51.

77. Ibid., 181-83.

78. Ibid., 183-84.

79. On her domesticity, see James Kenneally, *The History of American Catholic Women: A Historical Exploration* (New York, 1990), 53.

80. Vern L. Bullough, Bonnie Bullough, *Care of the Sick: The Emergence of Modern Nursing* (New York, 1978), 85.

81. Ibid., 85-92.

82. Charles E. Rosenberg, *Care of Strangers,* 217-18.

83. Quoted by Rosenberg, *Care of Strangers,* 94.

84. Ibid., 218; also see Susan M. Reverby, "A Legitimate Relationship: Nursing, Hospitals and Science in the Twentieth Century," *The American General Hospital,* ed. Diane Elizabeth Long and Janet Gordon (Ithaca and London, 1989), 135-56.

85. Quoted by Sister Olivia Gowan, O.S.B., "System of Nursing Under Catholic Auspices," unpublished manuscript, 8, Catholic University Library of the School of Nursing, Catholic University of America.

86. Ibid., 10.

87. Dorothy Alice Sheahen, "The Social Origins of American Nursing and Its Movement into the University: A Microscopic Approach" (Ph.D. diss., New York University, 1979), 180-203.

88. Quoted by Lillian Peglow Waring, "American Nursing and the Concept of the Calling: Selected Periods, 1846-1945. An Historical Consideration" (D.Ed. diss., Columbia University Teachers College, 1983), 156.

89. Quoted by JoAnn G. Widerquist, "Florence Nightingale's Calling," *Second Opinion* 17 (January 1992): 117.

90. Ibid., 119.

91. Ibid.

92. Sister M. Francis Cooke, O.S.F., Ph.D., *His Love Heals: History of the Hos-*

pital *Sisters of the Third Order of St. Francis of Springfield, 1875-1975* (Chicago, 1977), 10.

93. Ibid.

94. Sister Mary Irene Watson, "The Historical Development of Nursing by the Various Catholic Communities in the United States During the Years 1873-1893 Inclusive" (M.A. thesis, Nursing Education, The Catholic University of America, 1939), 7. Also see Ann Doyle, "Nursing by Religious in the United States, Parts I-VI," *American Journal of Nursing* 29 (July–December 1929).

95. Reverend Louis Hinssen, *The Nursing Sister* (Springfield, 1899), iv. Archives of St. John's Hospital, Springfield, IL.

96. Ibid., 3.

97. Ibid., 5.

98. Ibid., 12.

99. Ibid., 14.

100. Cooke, *His Love Heals,* 10.

101. Sister Agnes McDougal, O.S.J., *Duty: The History of St. John's Hospital School of Nursing, Springfield, Illinois* (Springfield, 1986), 5-9.

102. Quoted by Watson, "Historical Development," 1.

103. Ibid., 4.

104. Sister Marie LeGras Byrne, S.C., "A History of St. Vincent's School of Nursing" (M.A. thesis, Nursing Education, The Catholic University of America, 1940), 1-51.

105. Sister Mary Magdeline Wirmel, O.S.F., "Sisterhoods in the Spanish American War, " *Historical Records and Studies* 32 (1941): 13-15.

106. Ibid., 60.

107. Ibid., 15.

108. Quoted by Mary Ewens, O.P., *The Nun in Nineteenth-Century America* (New York, 1978), 272.

109. Ibid., 273.

110. Ibid. Also see Judith Metz, S.C., "In Times of War," in *Pioneer Healers: The History of Women Religious in American Health Care*, ed. Ursula Stepsis, C.S.A., and Dolores Liptak, R.S.M. (New York, 1989), 57-65, 110.

111. Copy in the Archives of the Sisters of the Holy Cross, Notre Dame, Indiana.

112. Letters of Sister Mariana, October, 1898, Carney Hospital, ADCNE 11-35.

113. Ibid.

114. Sister Mary Giles Philips, *The History of St. Joseph's School of Nursing of Kansas City, Missouri* (Kansas City, 1929), unpaginated. Archives of the Sisters of St. Joseph, Carondelet, Missouri.

115. Watson, "Historical Development," 6.

116. Sister Rita Voss, "The History of Providence Hospital School of Nursing Washington, D.C." (M.A. thesis, Nursing Education, The Catholic University of America, 1940), 9.

117. Ibid., 2-8. For an excellent summary of nursing education, see Sister Rita Marie Bergeron, O.S.B., R.N., "The Development of Professional Nursing at

the Catholic University of America 1921–1958, Relationships to National Scene" (privately printed manuscript, The College of St. Scholastica, Department of Nursing, Duluth, Minnesota); copy in the library of the Nursing School, Catholic University of America. The first nurse anesthetist was a sister. For an excellent study of this field, see Marianne Bankert, *A History of America's Nurse Anesthetists* (New York: Continuum, 1989).

118. Philip A. Caulfield, M.D., "History of Providence Hospital, 1861–1961," *Records of the Columbian Historical Society of Washington, D.C.* (1960–62): 242.

119. Voss, "History of Providence Nursing School," 31.

120. Philips, *History of St. Joseph's School of Nursing*, n.p.

121. Sister Aloysia Ames, C.S.J., *The St. Mary's I Knew* (Tucson, 1970), 101. Archives of the Sisters of St. Joseph, Carondelet, Missouri.

122. Clough, *Mercy Hospital*, 39–40.

123. Quoted by Clough, *Mercy Hospital*, 50.

Notes to Chapter Eight
NATIONAL STRUCTURES AND HOSPITAL STANDARDIZATION

1. Robert J. Shanahan, S.J., *The History of the Catholic Hospital Association* (St. Louis, 1965). Also see Christopher J. Kauffman, *A Commitment to Healthcare: Celebrating 95 Years of the Catholic Health Association of the United States* (St. Louis, 1990).

2. Rosemary Stevens, *In Sickness and in Wealth: American Hospitals in the Twentieth Century* (New York, 1989), 57.

3. Ibid., 57–58.

4. Ibid., 69.

5. *Transactions of the Catholic Hospital Association, 1915*.

6. *Transactions of the Catholic Hospital Association, 1915*, 135–55, Article II, The Constitution of The Catholic Hospital Association, CHA.

7. Charles B. Moulinier, S.J., File, Archives of the Society of Jesus, Missouri Province, St. Louis, Missouri (hereafter cited as ASJMP).

8. Charles B. Moulinier, S.J., "President's Address," *Transactions of the Catholic Hospital Association, 1918*, 1.

9. Ibid.

10. Brother Roy Godwin File, AAB-EG.

11. Sebastian Messmer, "The Catholic Hospital Association," *The Ecclesiastical Review* IV (LIV) (June 1916): 393.

12. Ibid., Sixth Series IV (LIV) (April 1916): 385–87.

13. Ibid., 386.

14. Ibid., 387.

15. Sebastian Messmer to Right Rev. John J. Lawler, Lead, North Dakota, April 11, 1916. Messmer papers, Archdiocese of Milwaukee Archives.

16. *Transactions of the Catholic Hospital Association, 1916*.

17. Ibid.

18. Stanislaus Waywood, O.F.M., "The Moral and Juridical Aspect of Certain

Hospital Work," *The Ecclesiastical Review,* Sixth Series VI (LVI) (February 1916): 186–88.

19. Mary Ewens, O.P., *The Nun in Nineteenth-Century America* (New York, 1978).

20. Waywood, "Moral and Juridical Aspect," 189–90.

21. Sebastian Messmer, "The Catholic Hospital Association: Objections Answered," *The Ecclesiastical Review* IV (LVI) (June 1916): 711.

22. Ibid., 712.

23. Ibid., 713–714.

24. Ibid., 711.

25. Ibid., 715.

26. Ibid.

27. Quoted by Shanahan, *History of the Catholic Hospital Association,* 25–26.

28. Ibid., 26.

29. Ibid., 27. For material on Gibbons, see John Tracy Ellis, *The Life of James Cardinal Gibbons, Archbishop of Baltimore 1834–1921* (Milwaukee, 1952), 2 vols.

30. Quoted by Shanahan, *History,* 34.

31. *Transactions of the Catholic Hospital Association, 1918,* 6.

32. Quoted by Shanahan, *History,* 36.

33. Ibid., 31.

34. Minutes of the Medical Board, St. Joseph's Hospital, Baltimore, January 14, 1919, 1. Archives of St. Joseph's Hospital, Baltimore (hereafter cited as ASJHB).

35. Ibid., May 7, 1924, 109, ASJHB.

36. Ibid., June 23, 1920, 39, ASJHB.

37. Ibid., June 4, 1924, 112, ASJHB.

38. Sister Ann Thomasine Sampson, C.S.J., *History of St. Mary's Hospital and Rehabilitation Center* (St. Paul, MN 1987), 17.

39. Mother M. Esperance Finn, C.S.J., "What the Sisters Should Contribute To The Team-Work," *Transactions of the Catholic Hospital Association,* 65–72.

40. Ibid.

41. Ibid., *Transactions of the Catholic Hospital Association, 1918,* 137.

42. *Transactions of the Catholic Hospital Association, 1919,* 199.

43. Ibid.

44. Charles B. Moulinier, "The President's Address," *Hospital Progress* 1 (August 1920): 145.

45. Ibid.

46. John Bonzano to Charles B. Moulinier, August 21, 1918, Moulinier File, ASJMP.

47. Charles B. Moulinier to John Bonzano, August 24, 1918, Moulinier File, ASJMP.

48. "Remarks Concerning: Diocesan Superintendents and Wearing Washable Habits While on Duty," no pagination, CHA Archives, St. Louis, MO.

49. Ibid.

50. Ibid.

51. Ibid.

52. Ibid.

53. Ibid.

54. Ibid.

55. Ibid.

56. Ibid.

57. Charles B. Moulinier, S.J., "The Understanding Heart of the Hospital," *Hospital Progress* 2 (August 1921): 383.

58. Pietro Fumasoni-Biondi to Charles B. Moulinier, December 16, 1923, Moulinier File, ASJMP.

59. Charles B. Moulinier to Pietro Fumasoni-Biondi, January 1924. ASJMP.

60. Ibid.

61. For an excellent analysis of the challenges to Moulinier's leadership, see Shanahan, *History,* 36–41.

62. For the standards, see *Hospital Progress* 3 (September 1923): 362–63.

63. Shanahan, *History,* 41–51.

64. Ibid., 47–48.

65. Ibid., 51.

66. Moulinier File, ASJMP.

67. Charles B. Moulinier, S.J., "Hospital Normal School," *Hospital Progress* 3 (November 1922): 449. Also see Shanahan, *History,* 55–60.

68. Moulinier-Fox correspondence in the formers' file. ASJMP.

69. Ibid.

70. See convention sections of *Hospital Progress* (1927, Folder 28).

71. Charles B. Moulinier, S.J., "Standardization," *Hospital Progress* 3 (September 1922): 300.

72. Ibid.

73. Ibid.

74. Charles B. Moulinier, "Standardization."

75. Ibid.

76. Ibid.

77. Moulinier File, ASJMP.

78. Ibid.

79. Ibid.

80. Shanahan, *History,* 77–91.

81. Moulinier file, ASJMP.

Notes to Chapter Nine
ILLNESS AND POPULAR DEVOTION

1. Robert A. Orsi, "'He Keeps Me Going,' Women's Devotion to St. Jude and the Dialectics of Gender in American Catholicism," in *Belief in History, Innovative Approaches to European and American Religion,* ed. Thomas Kselman (Notre Dame, IN, 1991), 137–69.

2. Two excellent works on spirituality and devotionalism in the United States are: Joseph P. Chinnici, O.F.M., *Living Stones: The History and Structure of Catholic Spiritual Life in the United States* (New York, 1989); and Ann Taves, *The Household of Faith: Roman Catholic Devotionalism in Mid-Nineteenth Century America* (Notre Dame, IN, 1986).

3. For an excellent analysis of the meanings of suffering, see Robert A. Orsi, "'Mildred, is it fun to be a cripple?' The Culture of Suffering in Mid-Twentieth Century American Catholicism," *South Atlantic Quarterly* 93 (Summer 1994): 547–91.

4. Quoted by Robert Emmett Curran, S.J., "The Finger of God is Here . . . ," *The Catholic Historical Review* 72 (January 1987), 49.

5. William W. Warner, *At Peace with All Their Neighbors: Catholics and Catholicism in the Nation's Capital, 1787-1860* (Washington, DC, 1994) 194–99.

6. Hugh L. McElrone, *The Choice Works of the Rt. Rev. John England* (New York, 1894), 221–23.

7. Sister Daniel Hannefin, D.C., *Daughters of the Church: A Popular History of the Daughters of Charity in the United States, 1807-1987* (Brooklyn, 1989), 59–60. On Chanche, see Christopher J. Kauffman, *Tradition and Transformation in Catholic Culture: The Priests of St. Sulpice in the United States From 1791 to the Present* (New York, 1988).

8. For a fascinating iconographical study of the Immaculate Conception, see Quentin Quesnell, "The Search for Sophia" *Continuum* 2 (1993): 6–26. The dogma of the Immaculate Conception was promulgated on December 8, 1854, and Catherine was declared a saint by Pius XII in 1947. The promulgation was not preceded by a General Council of the church, an omission that prefigured the opening of Vatican Council I, on December 8, the Council which proclaimed the dogma of infallibility. See James Hennesey, S.J., "Prelude to Vatican I: American Bishops and the Definition of the Immaculate Conception," *Theological Studies* 25 (1964): 409–19; and idem, *The First Council of the Vatican: The American Experience* (New York, 1963).

9. The holy card with the prayer is in the collection in the Provincial Archives of the Sisters of Providence, Seattle, Washington (hereafter cited as ASPS).

10. Taves, *The Household of Faith,* 47. On the devotional revolution, see Emmet Larkin, "The Devotional Revolution in Ireland 1850-1875," *American Historical Review* 77 (June 1972): 625–52.

11. Quoted by Taves, *The Household of Faith,* 47.

12. Ibid., 63. Quoted by Taves, 49.

13. Ibid., 61.

14. Jay P. Dolan, *Catholic Revivalism, The American Catholic Experience* (Notre Dame, IN, 1978), 145.

15. Quoted by Dolan, *Catholic Revivalism,* 145. Also see Taves, *The Household of Faith,* 12, 60.

16. Ibid., 146.

17. Thomas Kselman, *The Miraculous in Nineteenth Century France* (Brunswick, NJ, 1983).

18. Frances Beauchesne Thornton, *Catholic Shrines in the United States and Canada* (New York, 1954), 41–42.

19. Ibid., 69–72.

20. Ibid., 211–19.

21. Ibid., 247–52.

22. Ibid., 251.

23. Ralph Gibson, *A Social History of French Catholicism, 1789-1914* (New York, 1989).

24. Raymond Cunningham, "From Holiness to Healing: The Faith Cure in America 1872-1892," in *Modern American Protestantism and its World,* ed. Martin E. Marty (New York, 1993), 3.

25. Ibid., 3–5.

26. Ibid., 16.

27. Ibid., 16–17.

28. Ibid., 17.

29. See chapters two and six.

30. Chronicle of the Troy Hospital, 11–23, 1–2, Document #28. ADCSEP.

31. Ibid.

32. B. Randolf, "Holy Agony," *The Catholic Encyclopedia* (New York, 1910), 7: 397–98.

33. Unsigned letter, 11–50, 15–3, #8. ADCSEP.

34. James Cardinal Gibbons, *Discourses and Sermons on Various Subjects* (Baltimore, 1908), 181–82.

35. Bernard O'Reilly, *The Mirror of True Womanhood: A Book of Instructions for Woman in the World* (New York, 1876), 484.

36. Ibid., 484-85.

37. Gibbons, *Discourses,* 182.

38. L. Siger and L. A. Leite, "Jesus Christ, Iconography of," *The New Catholic Encyclopedia* (New York, 1967) 7: 968.

39. C. Francis Werts, M.D., "Saints Cosmas and Damian," *Linacre Quarterly* 18 (August 1951): 61–63. The Walters Art Gallery's medieval collection includes statues of Cosmas and Damian which originated in a hospital. I am grateful to Mary Ellen Bur, docent at the gallery in Baltimore.

40. Quoted by Herbert Ratner, "October 18, Feast of St. Luke, Patron of Physicians," *Linacre Quarterly* 18 (October 1951): 73.

41. Ibid., 73.

42. Ibid.

43. Berenice Beck, O.S.F., *Handmaid of the Divine Physician* (Milwaukee, 1952), iv.

44. Ibid., 243.

45. Ibid., 170.

46. Ibid., 173.

47. Ibid., 229–32.

48. William Stang, *Pastoral Theology* (New York, 1907), 204.

49. Ibid.

50. Alexander E. Sanford, *Pastoral Medicine: A Handbook for the Catholic Clergy* (Milwaukee, 1905), 3–4.

51. Ibid., 163.

52. "St. Peregrine, The Cancer Saint," A Servite publication, Holy Card Collection, ASPP.

53. "St. Dymphna Patroness of Those Afflicted With Nervous and Emotional Diseases," Francis Mission publication, Mount Vernon, NY, Holy Card Collection, ASPP.

54. "Apostolate of the Suffering," Holy Card Collection, ASPP.

55. "Prayer for Those in Suffering," Holy Card Collection, ASPP.

56. Orsi, "The Culture of Suffering," 570.

57. "Dear _____ and All Sisters, from a Sister pupil," Sept. 12, 1928. Archives of the Wheaton Franciscans, Wheaton, IL.

58. Robert A. Orsi, *The Madonna of 115th Street* (New Haven, 1988), 132.

59. Ibid., 193–95.

60. Ibid.

61. Peter W. Williams, *Popular Religion In America: Symbolic Change and the Modernization Process in Historical Perspective* (Urbana and Chicago, 1989), 79, 147.

62. Coleen McDannell, "Catholic Domesticity" in *American Catholic Women: A Historical Exploration*, ed. Karen Kennelly, C.S.J. (New York, 1989), 69.

Notes to Chapter Ten
CATHOLIC IDEALISM: HOSPITALS, PHYSICIANS, NURSES

1. Quoted by William M. Halsey, *The Survival of American Innocence: Catholicism in an Era of Disillusionment* (Notre Dame, IN, 1980), 45. Halsey's themes elucidate the idealism in Catholic health care.

2. Ibid., 46.

3. Ibid., 47.

4. Ibid., 56–57.

5. Charles B. Moulinier, S.J., "Fundamentals of Medical Activities," *Hospital Progress* 2 (October 1922): 384–85.

6. Halsey, *Survival of American Innocence,* 118.

7. William B. Faherty, S.J., "A Half-Century With *The Queen's Work*," *Woodstock Letters* 92 (1963): 99–101. Also see E. R. Volmar, S.J., "Edward F. Garesché," *The New Catholic Encyclopedia* (New York, 1967), 6: 289–90.

8. Edward F. Garesché, S.J., *The Soul of the Hospital* (Philadelphia, 1928), 45.

9. Ibid., 46–47.

10. Ibid., 48.

11. Ibid., 49.

12. Robert J. Shanahan, S.J., *The History of the Catholic Hospital Association 1915–1965* (St. Louis, 1965), 191–92; William B. Faherty, S.J., *Better the Dream: St. Louis University and Community, 1818–1968* (St. Louis, 1968), 353. Also see the Schwitalla file in AMPSJ.

13. Shanahan, *History of the Catholic Hospital Association*, 92–99.

14. For information on CHA's organization, structure, and composition of the board of directors during the Schwitalla years, see introductory pages of *Hospital Progress* vols. 9–10

15. Rosemary Stevens, *In Sickness and in Wealth: American Hospitals in the Twentieth Century* (New York, 1989), 140–41.

16. Ibid., 140.

17. Shanahan, *History,* 113–21 and Stevens, *In Sickness,* 162–70.

18. Stevens, *In Sickness,* 112.

19. Alphonse Schwitalla, S.J., "Presidential Address," *Hospital Progress* 14 (July 1933): 266.

20. Ibid.

21. Ibid.

22. Alphonse Schwitalla, S.J., "The Charity of Christ in the Eucharist," copy NCWC Department of Legal Affairs, 1935–40. ACUA.

23. Ibid.

24. Ibid. Joseph P. Chinnici, O.F.M., *Living Stones: The History and Structure of the Spiritual Life in the United States* (New York, 1989), 135–37.

25. Alphonse Schwitalla, S.J., "President's Report," Silver Jubilee Convention, *Hospital Progress* (October 1940): 203.

26. Ibid.

27. Ibid., 204.

28. Ibid.

29. Alphonse Schwitalla, S.J., an untitled reprint of an article in *Hospital Progress* in NCWC Department of Legal Affairs, 1935–40. ACUA.

30. Ibid.

31. Ibid.

32. Stevens, *In Sickness,* 147.

33. Alphonse Schwitalla, S.J., "The President's Address," *Hospital Progress* 22 (June 1941): 198.

34. Quoted by Phil Rheinecker, "Crisis and Reconstruction," in Christopher J. Kauffman, *A Commitment to Healthcare . . . Celebrating 75 Years of The Catholic Health Association of the United States* (St. Louis, 1990), 32.

35. Alphonse Schwitalla, S.J., "Transcript of Testimony by The Reverend Alphonse M. Schwitalla, S.J.," *Hospital Progress* 25 (March 1945): 81.

36. Rheinecker, "Crisis," 35.

37. Shanahan, *History,* 77–81.

38. For a detailed account of this conflict and its resolution, see Shanahan, *History,* 92–112.

39. Ibid., 96.

40. The Schwitalla-O'Grady correspondence is in the Social Action Files NCWC, ACUA. Also see Thomas W. Tifft, "Toward a More Humane Social Policy: The Work and Influence of Monsignor John O'Grady," (Ph.D. diss., The Catholic University of America, 1979), 276–99; and Donald Gavin, *The National Conference of Catholic Charities 1910-1960* (Milwaukee, 1962).

41. Edward O'Brien to Joseph M. Nelligan, Friday, no date, 1939. Papers on

Catholic Hospitals in the Nelligan Papers, AAB.

42. Shanahan, *History,* 110-12.

43. Alphonse Schwitalla to Michael J. Ready, November 4, 1938. General Secretary's Papers NCWC, ACUA.

44. Edward A. Fitzpatrick, "Grading Schools of Nursing," *Hospital Progress* 7 (September 1926): 356. Also see Shanahan, *History,* 66-76.

45. Shanahan has devoted a chapter to nursing education, which includes the conflict, *History,* 139-74.

46. M. Emmanuel Hanley, O.S.B., "Olivia Gowan, O.S.B.," in *Pioneer Healers,* ed. Ursula Stepsis, C.S.A., and Dolores Liptak, R.S.M. (New York, 1989), 224-29.

47. For this correspondence, see the papers of the Department of Legal Affairs, 1935-39. NCWC, ACUA.

48. Alphonse Schwitalla, S.J., to Michael J. Ready, November 1932. NCWC, General Secretary's Papers, S652, ACUA.

49. Michael J. Ready to Alphonse Schwitalla, S.J., December 6, 1932. General Secretary's Papers S653 NCWC, ACUA.

50. Schwitalla to Ready, January 6, 1938. General Secretary's Papers S654, NCWC, ACUA.

51. Sister Mary Laurentine to James Ready, January 8, 1938. General Secretary's Papers 437A, NCWC, ACUA.

52. Sister Conchessa, C.S.J., to Sister Olivia Gowan, November 30, 1937. Copy General Secretary's Papers 473A, NCWC, ACUA.

53. Hanley, "Olivia Gowan," 227.

54. Alphonse Schwitalla, S.J., "Present Problems of Catholic Schools of Nursing and Hospitals," *Hospital Progress* 18 (September 1938): 301.

55. Shanahan, *History,* 169-73.

56. Ibid., 234-45.

57. Alphonse Schwitalla, S.J., "With Reference to A National Health Program—Wagner-Murray Bill," *Linacre Quarterly* 12 (January 1944): 48-56.

58. James Gilroy, "Who is Thomas Linacre?," *Linacre Quarterly* 22 (August 1955): 86-89.

59. "Guild News," *Linacre Quarterly* 7 (October 1939): 81.

60. For an excellent biography of O'Connell, see James O'Toole, *Militant and Triumphant, William Henry O'Connell and the Catholic Church in Boston, 1859-1944* (Notre Dame, IN, 1992).

61. "Minutes of the St. Luke's Guild," June 20, 1919. St. Luke's Guild Papers, Archives of the Archdiocese of Boston (hereafter cited as AABo). I am grateful to Ron Patkus, archivist of the archdiocese, for his assistance.

62. "Minutes of the St. Luke's Guild," October 18, 1910. AABo.

63. Edward McLaughlin, M.D., "A History of the Guild Movement," *Linacre Quarterly* 8 (October 1940): 96-98.

64. Ibid., 98.

65. Henry W. Kirwin, "James J. Walsh, Medical Historian and Pathfinder," *Catholic Historical Review* 45 (January 1960): 424-25.

66. Francis Gerrity, "Flick, Lawrence," *The New Catholic Encyclopedia* (New York, 1967) 5: 965-66.

67. Joseph A. Dillon, M.D., "The Catholic Physician and His Sphere of Influence," *Linacre Quarterly* 10 (October 1942): 86.

68. Ibid., 87–88.

69. Ibid., 90–91.

70. John J. Masterson, M.D., "Letter from the President of the Federation to Members of the Executive Board September 13, 1944," *Linacre Quarterly* 12 (October 1947): 7.

71. Dillon, "The Catholic Physician," 90–91.

72. Shanahan, *History,* 216–19.

73. Edward F. Garesché, S.J., "The International Catholic Guild of Nurses," *The Catholic Yearbook and Directory* (New York, 1928), 517.

74. Ibid., 520.

75. Sister Mary Victory Lewis, C.C.V.I., R.N., "A Critical Survey of the Professional Relationship of Sister Nurses Conducting Schools of Nursing" (Ph.D. diss., The Catholic University of America, 1935), 12–13.

76. "Mercy Hospital's School of Nursing, 1927–28" (Baltimore, 1927), 27–28. I am grateful to Sister Anella Martin, R.S.M., for providing me with copies of these catalogues.

77. Ibid., 32–37.

78. Ibid., 23.

79. Alphonse Schwitalla, S.J., "To the Bishops of the Administrative Committee," General Secretary's Papers NCWC, ACUA.

80. "Mercy Hospital's School of Nursing, 1941–42" (Baltimore, 1941), 8–9.

81. Ibid., 17.

82. For an excellent overview of Catholic action, see Debra Campbell, "The Struggle to Survive," in *Transforming Parish Ministry: The Changing Role of Catholic Clergy, Laity and Women Religious,* ed. Jay P. Dolan (New York, 1989), 222–52.

83. "Mercy Hospital's School of Nursing, 1941–42," 17.

84. Ibid., 19.

85. "Mercy Hospital's School of Nursing, 1948" (Baltimore, 1948).

86. Ann Zerheusen to Dear Fellow Members, December 9, 1939. Catholic Nurses' Guilds, Nelligan Papers. AAB.

87. Most Reverend Michael J. Curley, D.D., "Archbishop Wishes Organization of Catholic Nurses," manuscript copy of this letter that later appeared in the *Catholic Review.* Catholic Nurses' Guilds, Nelligan Papers, AAB.

88. Mary Alice Suburt to Joseph Nelligan, November 11, 1942. In the file, Catholic Nurses' Guilds, Nelligan Papers, AAB.

89. "NCCN News Items," *The Catholic Nurse* 1 (September 1952): 51.

90. "Holy Father Speaking to Nurses," *The Catholic Nurse* 1 (September 1952): 11–13.

91. Sister Mary Ranson, S.C.N., *The Catholic Nurse* 1 (September 1952): 29.

92. Ellen C. Stark, "The Spiritual Care of the Patient," *The Catholic Nurse* 1 (September 1952): 48.

93. "Sermon, Most Reverend Richard J. Cushing, D.D., Archbishop of Boston, Union Baccalaureate Exercises for Five Catholic Hospitals, Cathedral, Sunday,

June 29, 1947," Cushing Papers, AABo.

94. "NCCN Convention," *The Catholic Nurse* (September 1952): 2.

Notes to Chapter Eleven
TRANSITIONS IN CHURCH, SOCIETY, AND HEALTH CARE, 1948–1965

1. For the trends of the 1950s, see James Hennesey, S.J., *American Catholics: A History of the Roman Catholic Community in the United States* (New York, 1981); Jay P. Dolan, *The American Catholic Experience: A History From Colonial Times to the Present* (New York, 1985); David O'Brien, *Public Catholicism* (New York, 1989); "Transitions in Catholic Culture: The Fifties" *The U.S. Catholic Historian* 7 (Winter 1988); Philip Gleason, *Keeping the Faith: American Catholicism Past and Present* (Notre Dame, IN, 1987), 58–81.

2. William Barnaby Faherty, S.J., *Dream by the River: Two Centuries of St. Louis Catholicism* (St. Louis, 1973), 186–96; Timothy M. Dolan, "*Some Seed Fell on Good Ground*": *The Life of Edwin O'Hara* (Washington, DC, 1992), 230–33.

3. *Pioneer Healers: The History of Women Religious in American Health Care*, ed. Ursula Stepsis, C.S.A., and Dolores Liptak, R.S.M. (New York, 1989), Appendix 2: Statistics, Table 2, 285, compiled by Ursula Stepsis, C.S.A.

4. Robert Shanahan, S.J., *The History of the Catholic Hospital Association* (St. Louis, 1965), 188–93.

5. Ibid., 201.

6. Ibid., 202–5.

7. Ibid., 211–16.

8. Ibid., 246–53. Also see Marvin O'Connell, "The Roman Catholic Tradition Since 1945" in *Curing and Caring: Health and Medicine in the Western Religious Traditions*, ed. Ronald L. Numbers and Darrell W. Amundsen (New York, 1986), 139–41.

9. John J. Flanagan, S.J., "Spiritual Aspects of Personnel Relations," Institute, Glen Riddle Franciscans, December 1959. Copy, Archives of St. Joseph's Hospital, Baltimore, MD.

10. Ibid.

11. Ibid.

12. Ibid.

13. Ibid.

14. See chapter three, "The Responses to the Cholera"; and chapter four, "Catholic Benevolence."

15. Cyprian Davis, *The History of Black Catholics in the United States* (New York, 1990), 109, 240–42.

16. Ibid., 135–36.

17. "Some of the Sayings of Mother Mary," Archives of the Dominican Sisters of the Sick Poor, Ossining, New York.

18. E. M. Blumenhauer, "Dominican Sisters of the Sick Poor," *The New Catholic Encyclopedia* (New York, 1967), 4: 991–92.

19. Davis, *History of Black Catholics,* 163-81.

20. Ibid., 218. Also see Marilyn Nickels, *Black Catholic Protest and the Federated Colored Catholics* (New York, 1988).

21. Ibid., 214-29.

22. John Gillard, S.S.J., *The Catholic Church and the American Negro* (Baltimore, 1930), 201.

23. Ibid., 207.

24. Stephen J. Ochs, *Desegregating the Altar: The Josephites and the Struggle for Black Priests* (Baton Rouge, LA, 1990), 456-60.

25. Floyd Keeler, *Catholic Medical Missions* (New York, 1925), 191-92.

26. M. M. McGinley, "Dengel, Anna," *The New Catholic Encyclopedia* (New York, 1989), 18: 118-19.

27. Quoted by Anna Dengel, *Mission for Samaritans* (Milwaukee, 1945), 105-6.

28. Ibid., 106-8.

29. Archives notes, St. Mary's Hospital, Cairo, IL. Archives of the Sisters of the Holy Cross, Notre Dame, IN. It is interesting to note that the record shows from July 1, 1924, to July 1, 1925, there were 1,327 admitted, 85 died and 60 were baptized. The religious breakdown was: 140 Catholics, 12 Greek Orthodox, 305 Protestants, 30 Jews, and 840 of no religious affiliation.

30. Sister Alice Martha, S.C.N., "Catholic Hospitals and Catholic Doctors, Here is Your Chance," *Linacre Quarterly* 11 (January 1943): 15. Also see Clarence J. Howard, S.V.D., "Another Catholic Hospital for Negroes," *St. Augustine's Messenger* 21 (September 1943): 19. Copy, Josephite Archives.

31. Sister Alice Martha, "Catholic Hospitals," 16.

32. Mary Regina Werntz, R.S.M., *Our Beloved Union: A History of the Sisters of Mercy of the Union* (Westminster, MD, 1989), 180.

33. The Josephite archivist, Peter E. Hogan, S.S.J., interviewed Vincent D. Warren, founder of Martin de Porres Hospital in Mobile. Transcriptions of the interview dealing with the hospital and the life of Black Catholics in the diocese takes up forty pages. See Mobile File, Josephite Archives, Baltimore. Also see Elmer S. Powell, S.V.D., "Martin de Porres Hospital," *St. Augustine's Messenger* 29 (October 1951): 1. Copy Josephite Archives.

34. Sister M. Romuald, R.S.M., "Dream Come True," *St. Augustine's Messenger* 29 (October 1951): 214, 221. Copy Josephite Archives.

35. Dengel, *Mission for Samaritans,* 108.

36. Ann Katherine Webster, "Catholic Hospitals in St. Louis" (Ph.D. diss., St. Louis University, 1968), Appendix.

37. Clemmie Jean Smith, "A History of St. Mary's Infirmary" (M.S. thesis, Nursing Education, St. Louis University, 1958), 13-24.

38. Vanessa Northington Gamble, "The Negro Hospital Renaissance," in *The American General Hospital: Communities and Contexts,* ed. Diana Elizabeth Long and Janet Golden (Ithaca and London, 1989), 82-100.

39. Smith, "St. Mary's Infirmary," 48.

40. Carol Bales, F.S.M., "Sister Mary Antona Ebo, F.S.M." in Profiles, *Pioneer Healers,* 209-11.

41. Carol Bales, F.S.M., "Sister Hilda Rita Brickus" in Profiles, *Pioneer Healers*, 206.

42. Ibid., 206-8.

43. Gerald Kelly, S.J., "The Negro Physician," *Linacre Quarterly* 20 (November 1953): 110.

44. Timothy Michael Dolan, *"Some Seed Fell on Good Ground": The Life of Edwin V. O'Hara* (Washington, DC, 1992), 230.

45. "Non-Segregation Works at St. Vincent's, Kansas City," *Hospital Progress* 34 (November 1953): 47-49.

46. Dolan, *The Life of Edwin V. O'Hara*, 231-32.

47. Ibid., 233.

48. Albert Sydney Foley, S.J., "The Catholic Church and the Washington Negro" (Ph.D. diss., The University of North Carolina, Chapel Hill, NC, 1950), 237-45. Copy ACUA.

49. Mary L. Schneider, O.S.F., "American Sisters and the Roots of Change," *The U.S. Catholic Historian* 7 (Winter 1988): 56. For a recent study of the conference see Marjorie Notterman Beane, *From Framework to Freedom, A History of the Sister Formation Conference* (Lanham, MD, 1993). Also see Angelyn Dries, O.S.F., "Living in Ambiguity: A Paradigm Shift Experienced by the Sister Formation Movement," *The Catholic Historical Review* 79 (July 1993): 478-87.

50. Schneider, "American Sister," 58.

51. Ibid., 61.

52. Quoted by Schneider, "American Sisters," 63.

53. *Sister Formation Bulletin* 2 (hereafter cited as *SFB*) (Summer 1956), Title Page. Copy, Sisters of Providence Archives, Seattle, Washington.

54. Sister M. Agnita Claire Day, S.S.M., "Formation Implications in the Change From Bedside Nursing to Personnel Work," *SFB* 2 (Summer 1956): 1.

55. Ibid., 2.

56. Ibid., 3.

57. Sister Mary Ruth, S.S.J., "The Changing Role of the Nurse: Implications for the Sister Formation Program," *SFB* 2 (Summer 1956): 6.

58. Ibid.

59. Quoted by Beane, *From Framework to Freedom*, 71.

60. John J. Flanagan, "Sister Formation and Accreditation and Administration Problems," *SFB* 2 (Summer 1956): 13.

61. Ibid.

62. Sister Marie Augusta Neal, S.N.D.deN., *From Nuns to Sisters: An Expanding Vocation* (Mystic, CT, 1990), 32.

63. Sister Daniel Hannefin, D.C., *Daughters of the Church: A Popular History of the Daughters of Charity in the United States* (New York, 1989), 241.

64. Joseph A. Komonchak, "Vatican Council II," *The New Dictionary of Theology* (Wilmington, DE, 1987), 1074.

65. Juliana Casey, I.H.M., "Religious Life," *The New Dictionary of Theology*, 872.

66. Ibid., 871.

67. Ibid., 871–72.

68. Stepsis and Liptak, *Pioneer Healers*, Appendix 2: statistics, compiled by Ursula Stepsis, C.S.A., 285.

69. Davis, *History of Black Catholics*, 256.

70. Werntz, *Our Beloved Union*, 202.

71. Ibid.

72. Davis, *History of Black Catholics*, 321, n. 56.

73. Ibid., 321, n. 51.

74. "66 CHA Convention," *Hospital Progress* 47 (August 1966): 59.

75. Mother Vincentia, in ibid., 61.

76. Robert G. Hoyt, in ibid., 62.

77. John F. Cronin, S.S., in ibid., 62.

78. John A. Trese, "Presidential Inaugural Address," *Hospital Progress* 47 (August 1966): 82.

79. Rosemary Stevens, *In Sickness and in Wealth: American Hospitals in the Twentieth Century* (New York, 1989), 258–59.

80. Ibid., 263.

81. Paul Starr, *The Transformation of American Medicine* (New York, 1982), 134.

82. Stevens, *In Sickness*, 269.

83. See chapter one, "The European Traditions."

84. Sister Pauline Grady, *Ruma: Home and Heritage. The Story of a Convent in Rural Southern Illinois 1987–1984* (St. Louis, 1984), 237.

Notes to Chapter Twelve
RELIGIOUS RENEWAL, LAY MINISTRY, AND THE CHA

1. Rosemary Stevens, *In Sickness and in Wealth: American Hospitals in the Twentieth Century* (New York, 1989), 284–86. For information on the prospective payment system and the diagnosis-related groups (DRGs) see pp. 323–27.

2. Mary L. Schneider, O.S.F., "American Sisters and the Roots of Change: The 1950s," *The U.S. Catholic Historian* 7 (Winter 1988): 70.

3. Quoted by Patricia Byrne, C.S.J., "In the Parish But Not of It: Sisters," in *Transforming Parish Ministry,* ed. Jay P. Dolan (New York, 1989), 155.

4. Interview, Patricia Smith, R.S.M., on July 19, 1993.

5. Byrne, "In the Parish," 159.

6. Ibid., 159–60.

7. For the 1960s, see David O'Brien, *Public Catholicism* (New York, 1989); Philip Gleason, *Keeping the Faith: American Catholicism Past and Present* (Notre Dame, IN, 1987); Robert Wuthnow, *The Restructuring of American Religion* (Princeton, NJ, 1988), 142–72.

8. *Pioneer Healers: The History of Women Religious in American Health Care,* ed. Ursula Stepsis, C.S.A., and Dolores Liptak, R.S.M. (New York, 1989), Appendix 2: statistics compiled by Stepsis, 285.

9. Lora Ann Quiñonez, C.D.P., and Mary Daniel Turner, S.N.D.deN., *The Transformation of American Sisters* (Philadelphia, 1992), 47.

10. Ibid., 21, 97.

11. Mary Jo Weaver, *New American Women* (San Francisco, 1985), 85. For an excellent treatment of the women's movement in the Catholic context, see Rosemary Rader, O.S.B., "Catholic Feminism: Its Impact on United States Women," in *American Catholic Women: A Historical Exploration,* ed. Karen Kennelly, C.S.J. (New York, 1989), 182–88. For general background, see James K. Kenneally, *The History of American Catholic Women* (New York, 1990).

12. Kevin O'Rourke, O.P., "Is Your Health Facility Catholic?" in *The Mission of Healing: Readings in Christian Values and Health Care* (St. Louis, 1974), 60.

13. E. Brooks Holifield, *The History of Pastoral Care* (Nashville, 1983), 237.

14. Helen Hayes, O.S.F., "The Professional Chaplain," *Health Progress* 70 (March 1990): 62.

15. *Pastoral Care of the Sick: Rites of Anointing and Viaticum* (Washington, DC, 1975).

16. William J. Kenney and Charles P. Ceronsky, *Hospital Progress* 55 (October 1974): 32, 36–37.

17. Quoted by Mary Regina Werntz, *Our Beloved Union: The History of the Sisters of Mercy of the Union* (Westminster, MD, 1988), 207.

18. Ibid.

19. Helen Hayes, O.S.F., 62–63.

20. Edna Marie Leroux, R.S.M., "In Times of Social and Economic Crisis," in *Pioneer Healers*, 127. Also see Christopher J. Kauffman, *Mission to Rural America: The Life of William Howard Bishop, Founder of Glenmary* (Mahwah, NJ, 1991).

21. Ibid., 132.

22. Leroux, "In Times," 133.

23. Ann Murphy, S.C.N., "Sister Dorothy Peterson, S.C.N.," in Profiles, *Pioneer Healers*, 243–47.

24. Ibid., 242.

25. "Father Casey Named CHA Executive Director," *Hospital Progress* 48 (May 1968): 107.

26. Thomas F. Casey, "Executive Director's Report," *Hospital Progress* 49 (August 1969): 74.

27. See chapter eleven, "Transitions in Church, Society and Health Care."

28. Christopher J. Kauffman, *Tradition and Transformation in Catholic Culture: The Priests of St. Sulpice in the United States, 1791–1991* (New York, 1988).

29. Thomas F. Casey, "Executive Director's Report," *Hospital Progress* 50 (August 1970): 36.

30. Richard A. McCormick, S.J., "Not What Catholic Hospitals Ordered," *Linacre Quarterly* 39 (February 1972): 21–25.

31. Warren T. Reich, "Policy vs Ethics," *Linacre Quarterly* 39 (February 1972): 23–24.

32. McCormick, "Not What Catholic Hospitals Ordered," 16–17.

33. "'Not What the Catholic Hospital Ordered?' A Reply to Father McCormick,"

by Vitale H. Paganelli, MD, and "Reply to Dr. Paganelli," *Linacre Quarterly* 39 (May 1972): 115-22.

34. Thomas J. O'Donnell, S.J., "The Directives, A Crisis of Faith," *Linacre Quarterly* 39 (August 1972): 146.

35. Ibid.

36. The debates continue but they are less acrimonious. See Richard A. McCormick, S.J., *Health and Medicine in the Catholic Tradition* (New York, 1984); Allan Verhey and Stephen E. Lammers, eds., *Theological Voices in Medical Ethics* (Grand Rapids, MI, 1993).

37. Quoted by Robert T. Kennedy, "McGrath, Maida, Michiels: Introduction to a Study of the Canonical and Civil-Law Status of Church-Related Institutions in the United States." *The Jurist* 50 (1990): 360.

38. Ibid., 361.

39. Ibid., 354.

40. John J. McGrath, *Catholic Institutions in the United States: Canonical and Civil Law Status* (Washington, DC, 1968), 1.

41. Ibid., 8-9.

42. Kennedy, "McGrath, Maida, Michiels," 370.

43. Ibid., 363.

44. Ibid.

45. Kevin O'Rourke, O.P. ed., *The Mission of Healing: Readings in Christian Values and Healthcare* (St. Louis, 1974).

46. Monsignor George G. Higgins with William Bole, *Organized Labor and the Church: Reflections of a "Labor Priest"* (New York and Mahwah, NJ, 1993), 109-24.

47. Kevin D. O'Rourke, O.P., "Christian Responsibility for Labor and Management," *Hospital Progress* 55 (July 1975).

48. Ibid.

49. Higgins., *Organized Labor,* 128.

50. Edna Marie Leroux, R.S.M., "Maurita Singelaub, R.S.M.," Profiles in *Pioneer Healers,* 239-42.

51. M. Maurita Sengelaub, R.S.M., "Strengths and Weaknesses of the Catholic Health Care System," *Hospital Progress* 53 (April 1973): 58.

52. M. Maurita Sengelaub, R.S.M., "Why a System?" One Approach to a Religious-Sponsored Health Corporation, Proceedings of a Conference on the Sisters of Mercy Health Corporation, May 12-13, 1978, Farmington Hills, MI (CHA, St. Louis, 1978) 11.

53. Ibid., 18-19.

54. Christopher J. Kauffman, *A Commitment to Health Care. Celebrating 75 Years of the Catholic Health Association of the United States* (St. Louis, 1990), 52.

55. Ibid.

56. Kauffman, *Commitment to Health Care,* 52.

57. Ibid., 53.

58. Ibid., 53-54.

59. Telephone interview with Dorothy Kelly, the last editor of *The Catholic Nurse*, September 29, 1993.

Notes to Chapter Thirteen
EPILOGUE: CRISIS, REFORM, AND MISSION

1. Rosemary A. Stevens, "Times Past, Times Present," *The American General Hospital: Communities and Social Contexts*, ed. Diana Elizabeth Long and Janet Golden (Ithaca, 1989), 199.

2. Ibid., 200.

3. Ibid.

4. John E. Curley, Jr., "President's Report," Meeting of the House of Delegates, *Hospital Progress* 59 (July 1979): 41.

5. Ibid.

6. Christopher J. Kauffman, *Commitment to Health Care* (St. Louis, 1990), 56.

7. Ibid., 56.

8. *No Room in the Marketplace: The Health Care of the Poor* (St. Louis: Catholic Health Association, 1986).

9. *A Time to Be Old, A Time to Flourish: The Special Needs of the Elderly-at-Risk* (St. Louis: Catholic Health Association, 1988).

10. Nancy Frazier O'Brien, "Abortion May Fuel Health Care Debate," *The Progress* (Seattle) 96 (September 30, 1993): 4.

11. Philip Keane, S.S., *Health Care Reform: A Catholic View* (New York and Mahwah, NJ, 1993). Also see Richard A. McCormick, S.J., *Health and Medicine in the Catholic Tradition* (New York, 1984).

12. Sr. Mary Eileen Wilhelm, R.S.M., "Welcome" in a special reprint of *Health Progress* entitled "Pope Affirms Catholic Healthcare Ministry" (St. Louis, 1987): 3.

13. John E. Curley, Jr., "General Remarks," in ibid., 5–8.

14. Pope John Paul II, "The Pope Responds," in ibid., 17.

15. John E. Curley, Jr., "Catholic Identity, Catholic Integrity," *Health Progress* 72 (October 1991): 56.

16. Ibid., 57.

17. Ibid., 58–59.

18. John Larrere and David McClelland, Ph.D., "Leadership for the Catholic Healing Ministry," *Health Progress* 74 (June 1994): 28.

19. Ibid., 29.

20. Felix Bettendorf, C.F.A., "Contemporizing a Charism: The Alexians Opt for AIDS Ministry," CMSM (Conference of Major Superiors of Men) *Forum* 56 (Spring/Summer 1990): 8–9.

21. Quoted by Jean Delumeau, *Catholicism Between Luther and Voltaire: A New View of the Counter Reformation* (Philadelphia, 1977), 59.

Index